International Business and the Dilemmas of Development

International Business and the Dilemmas of Development

Case Studies in South Africa, Madagascar, Pakistan, South Korea, Mexico and Colombia

Edited by

Frederick Bird, Emmanuel Raufflet and Joseph Smucker

First published 2004 by
PALGRAVE MACMILLAN
Houndmills, Basingstoke, Hampshire RG21 6XS and
175 Fifth Avenue, New York, N.Y. 10010
Companies and representatives throughout the world.

PALGRAVE MACMILLAN is the global academic imprint of the Palgrave
Macmillan division of St. Martin's Press, LLC and of Palgrave Macmillan Ltd.
Macmillan® is a registered trademark in the United States, United Kingdom
and other countries. Palgrave is a registered trademark in the European
Union and other countries.

ISBN 1–4039–2129–6 hardback

This book is printed on paper suitable for recycling and made from fully
managed and sustained forest sources.

A catalogue record for this book is available from the British Library.

Library of Congress Cataloging-in-Publication Data
    International business and the dilemmas of development : case studies in
South Africa, Madagascar, Pakistan, South Korea, Mexico and Columbia /
edited by Frederick Bird, Emmanuel Raufflet and Joseph Smucker.
        p. cm.
    Includes bibliographical references and index.
    ISBN 1–4039–2129–6
        1. International business enterprises. 2. Developing countries – Economic
conditions. I. Bird, Frederick B. (Frederick Bruce), 1938– II. Raufflet, Emmanuel,
1967– III. Smucker, Joseph, 1934–

HD2755.5.I5358 2004
338.8′881724—dc22   2004052104

10 9 8 7 6 5 4 3 2 1
13 12 11 10 09 08 07 06 05 04

Printed and bound in Great Britain by
Antony Rowe Ltd, Chippenham and Eastbourne.

Contents

Preface

We have written this book because we are interested in exploring what international businesses can do (or have done already) to reduce poverty and enhance the well-being of the developing world. As in our previous volume, we have prepared case studies of specific businesses and countries. We have reviewed their various management strategies and examined the ways in which these firms have identified and responded to the dilemmas and difficulties they encountered in developing countries. We have argued that it is important to respect the diverse cultures, economies and environments of the developing world – diversity with which international business must increasingly come to terms as developing countries achieve something approaching economic parity. Nonetheless, in a world where more than 1.3 billion people live in abject poverty, with incomes of less than one dollar a day, and another 1 billion live on less than two dollars a day, we believe there is an imperative and urgent need to suggest, as carefully as possible, how international businesses can best apply their strengths in a socially and economically responsible manner so as to create growth *for* as well as *within* the countries in which they operate.

To be sure, international businesses are not the only agents for remedying widespread destitution. National and international governments bear major responsibilities; local business initiatives especially matter. Still, through trade and investment, international businesses have played and can play a decisive role.

With these assumptions in mind, we began in 1999 to build a research team, which now includes 33 scholars from 15 countries, to prepare a series of three volumes of case studies and essays, of which this is the second to be published by Palgrave Macmillan. During the past five years our research group has met annually as a whole at workshops and seminars, commenting on each other's work and developing our respective studies in light of what our colleagues were writing.

An initial volume, entitled *International Businesses and the Challenges of Poverty in the Developing World*, includes case studies of particular international businesses operating in Nigeria, Ghana, Uganda, Vietnam, Guyana and northern Canada, as well as a study of the Body Shop's international community trade initiative.

In this volume, we explore what can be learned about managing the dilemmas of development by reviewing the experiences of internationally connected firms in South Africa, Madagascar, Pakistan, South Korea, Mexico and Colombia.

A subsequent volume, provisionally titled *Just Business Practices in a Diverse and Developing World* ..., will present a series of reflective essays on a number of topics that have emerged from our case studies: the quest for common ethical standards in a world of moral diversity; models of corporate social responsibility from the perspective of the developing world; causes and remedies for global poverty; and reflections on business–government relations in the developing world.

We have also undertaken extensive research on international businesses in Sudan, Fiji, Malaysia, Indonesia, Guatemala and China.

I would like to thank all those who have conducted research, prepared research reports or helped to draft the studies that appear in this book and its companion volumes. These include Sylvie Babarik, Concordia University, Montreal (Canada); Dr Thomas Beschorner, Centre de recherche en éthique de l'Université de Montréal (Canada) and Carl von Ossietzky Universität (Germany); Dr Ding Bocheng, Beijing Administrative College (China); Dr Hevina Dashwood, Brock University, Ontario (Canada); Dr Russell Daye, Pacific Theological College (Fiji); Dr William Flanagan, Queens University (Ontario); Dr Titus Fossgard-Moser, Shell International (United Kingdom); Dr Margaret Griesse, Universite Methodista de Piracicaba (Brazil); Rifai Hasan, Concordia University; Dr Stewart Herman, Concordia College, Moorehead, Minnesota (United States); Dr William Holder (United States); Dr Jan Jorgensen, McGill University, Montreal (Canada); Kathrine Jorgensen, Roskilde University (Denmark); Farzad R. Khan, McGill University and Lahore University of Management Sciences (Pakistan); Dr Elize Kotze, University of Stellenbosch (South Africa); Dr Kobus Kotze, University of Stellenbosch; Dr David Krueger, Baldwin-Wallace College, Ohio (United States); Dr Terri Lituchy, Concordia University; Dr Alhaji Marong, Institute of Comparative Law, McGill University; Jacqui MacDonald, Prince of Wales International Business Leaders Forum (IBLF, United Kingdom); Marco Mingarelli, Concordia University; Anders Riel Müller, Institute for Food and Development Policy, Oakland, California (United States); Ida Mutoigo, Christian Reform World Relief Committee (Uganda); Rabia Naguib, Université de Montréal; Dr Robert Nixon, Universalia Management Group, Montreal (Canada); Dr Nelson Phillips, Cambridge University (United Kingdom); Dr Bill Buenar Puplampu, University of Ghana (Ghana); Dr Emmanuel Raufflet, Université de Montréal; Samuel Sejjaaka, Makerere University (Uganda); Dr Joseph Smucker, Concordia University; Dr Manuel Velasquez, Santa Clara University, California (United States); Dr William Westley, McGill University; and Dr Gail Whiteman, Erasmus University, Rotterdam (Netherlands).

I would like to thank the people who have helped prepare this manuscript for publication: Audrey Bean and Fred Louder for copyreading and editing; Munit Merid, Jackie Desjardin and Martine Montandon, secretaries for the Department of Religion at Concordia University, for their help with budgets, correspondence, logistics, data gathering and facilitating comfortable and pleasant working conditions. I am especially grateful to my co-editors, Joseph Smucker and Emmanuel Raufflet, for their many stimulating contributions to the preparation of this book.

The research on which the essays in this book is based was made possible by a research grant from the Social Sciences and Humanities Research Council of Canada, augmented by additional research grants from Concordia University, Santa Clara University, Concordia College (Minnesota), McGill University, Direction de La Recherche, HEC Montréal and the Resource Centre for the Social Dimensions of Business in London.

Frederick Bird
Montreal, April 2004

Foreword

by Henry Mintzberg

In an area now so dominated by a particular ideology, this book presents an important and refreshingly eclectic set of 'on the ground' essays. The contrast is stark: the general promotion of 'globalization' that we so often read about, with the specific experiences throughout the developing world presented here.

Globalization has not been the first ideology of development. State intervention was. But belief in that collapsed with the fall of communism, and globalization emerged as not only the favoured but in a sense the only view of how countries must develop.

Yet consideration of countries that have developed – the United States, United Kingdom, Japan, and South Korea (as discussed in this book) – tell another story. For one thing, the state has played a major role in most success stories, far more significant, in fact, than the role of globalization, or its equivalent, namely the opening up of an economy to foreign capital, foreign experts, foreign firms, and so on. For another, a third factor has played a key role in development, probably far more significantly so than the two mentioned above, namely indigenous development: people in the country in question exercising initiatives in their own ways with a thorough understanding of their country's issues and needs.

Happily this book brings this factor out, with rich stories and experiences. In a sense, it pits localized nuance against globalized theory. But just as happily, as a consequence of this, it does not come out on the side of any particular dogma. Several essays in fact focus on the useful roles that multinational companies can play in local economies, just so long as they recognize and adapt to the local culture and conditions. The clear message: get on the ground, as these researchers have done, and respond to what you see before your eyes.

The richness and variety of local conditions are well discussed in this book – not just across regions and countries of the world, but across industries, across dilemmas, and across possible solutions. The need for nuance comes out loud and clear, and international executives would do well to read it here.

One last point. The introduction states: 'All the studies in this book appear to converge on this point,' namely that 'socially responsible managers are again and again called upon to use their imaginations and to exercise responsible judgment.' How true. And how sad. For 'Shareholder Value,' which I believe stands for corporate social irresponsibility (acting in favour of the shareholders and everyone else be damned), is dominant these days, at least in the executive suites of the Anglo-Saxon countries, and that makes it difficult to heed the robust lessons of this book.

Hopefully that will change soon.

List of Contributors

Frederick Bird holds the Concordia University (Montreal) Research Chair in Comparative Ethics. He is the co-editor of *International Businesses and the Challenges of Poverty in the Developing World* (2004), the author of *The Muted Conscience: Moral Silence and the Practice of Ethics in Business* (1996) and co-author of *Good Management: Business Ethics in Practice* (1990). He is the author of many articles, including 'How Do Religions Affect Moralities?' (1989), 'Empowerment and Justice' (1999), 'Good Governance' (2001), 'Early Christianity as an Ecumenical Movement' (2002), and 'The Valued-Added Approach to Business Ethics' (2003). He is a graduate of Harvard College, Harvard Divinity School and the Graduate Theological Union.

Russell Daye is a lecturer in ethics at the Pacific Theological College, Suva, Fiji. A graduate of Concordia University, McGill University (Montréal), and St. Francis Xavier University (Antigonish, Nova Scotia), he is the author of *Political Forgiveness: Lessons from South Africa* (2004). A minister of the United Church of Canada, he has worked with a number of NGOs, including the Ecumenical Centre for Research Education and Advocacy in Fiji and the Social Justice Committees of Montréal and the Eastern Townships (Quebec).

Titus Fossgard-Moser is a senior advisor within Shell International's Social Performance Management Unit, a central unit charged with developing policy and guiding practice across the Shell Group in relation to improved social performance. He holds a PhD from the University of Cambridge (United Kingdom), an MBA from McGill University and a mechanical engineering degree from the University of Warwick (United Kingdom). He has published a number of articles related to multinational corporations and sustainable development in journals including *World Development* and *Greener Management International*.

Farzad Rafi Khan holds an MPhil (Economics of Developing Countries) from the University of Cambridge and a PhD (Organization Theory) from McGill University. He is currently an Assistant Professor in the Graduate School of Business, Lahore University of Management Sciences (LUMS), Pakistan.

Elize Kotze is Professor in Industrial Psychology in the Faculty of Military Science, Stellenbosch University, South Africa (SA Military Academy), where she teaches Research Methodology and Career Psychology. She obtained a PhD in Industrial Psychology in 1998 from Stellenbosch University and is registered as a Counselling Psychologist with the Health Professions Council

of South Africa. She has published in the areas of military career development, military management, psychometrics and work values.

Henry Mintzberg is Cleghorn Professor of Management Studies at McGill
University in Montreal Canada. He recently completed the book *Managers
not MBAs*, and is working on an electronic pamphlet entitled Getting Past
Smith and Marx towards a Balanced Society. He is also promoting the development of a family of masters programs for practicing managers. He is the
author of a number of books on the practice of management including The
Structuring of Organizations, Mintzberg on Management, and *The Rise and Fall
of Strategic Planning*.

Anders Riel Müller is working with the Institute for Food and Development
Policy (FoodFirst) in Oakland, California, where he is currently researching
the impact of economic liberalization on the rural poor in South Africa and
India. He holds a joint MA in Business Studies and Environmental Planning
from Roskilde University, Denmark.

Emmanuel Raufflet holds a PhD in Management from McGill University.
He is Assistant Professor in Management at the École des Hautes Études
Commerciales (HEC) in Montréal. His research concerns the changing relations between organizations and their social and natural environment. He
has conducted research on forest management in Mexico, and is the author
of *Cambio Institucional en el Manejo de los Bosques de Tlalmanalco, México*
(Plaza y Valdes-UAM Editores: Mexico, 2004). A French and Canadian
national, he has lived in Spain, Brazil and Mexico. He is currently involved
in social innovation projects for Canadian non-governmental organizations
active in international development.

Joseph Smucker holds a PhD from Michigan State University. He is Adjunct
Professor in the Department of Sociology and Anthropology, Concordia
University (Montréal). His research has been in the areas of industrialization,
labour markets, international comparisons of labour market policies and
their effects and, more recently, models of economic development. He is the
author of *Industrialization in Canada* (1980) and editor (with Axel van den
Berg) of *The Sociology of Labour Markets* (1997). He has also contributed
numerous articles in professional journals. In 1956–59 he was engaged in
relief and rehabilitation work with the Mennonite Central Committee in
South Korea.

Introduction

Frederick Bird, Emmanuel Raufflet and Joseph Smucker

Challenges and complexities

We live in a world in which diverse economies are increasingly interconnected while great disparities in wealth remain and significant differences in defining civil rights continue. Through trade, investments and communications, international businesses have played a major role in linking together people of diverse economic circumstances and varied cultures. They have generated wealth and reduced poverty. In various settings, however, international businesses have also aggravated conflicts, depleted natural resources, depressed local economies, encouraged corruption and fostered social disruption. The authors of the essays and case studies found in this volume are fully aware that international businesses face countless challenges and dilemmas associated with, among other things, cultural differences, conflicting views of workplace equity, security problems and community relations.[1] Few, if any, of these can be automatically resolved, and it is obvious that international businesses have sometimes played their cards wrong. But it must also be appreciated that they can, and do, play a major role in promoting economic development and social justice, as our studies show.

This book offers a perspective that is different from most books on globalization, international business and economic development. It is written neither to praise nor to condemn the role of international businesses in development. Rather it examines a series of case and country studies in detail on the assumptions, one, that internationally inter-connected businesses can make a difference and, two, that we can best understand how they can make a difference by reviewing both the value-adding practices and missed opportunities of particular businesses in particular settings.

The processes of economic development are multi-dimensional and diverse. They involve increased trade and commerce, industrialization, urbanization and other dramatic changes in the patterns of social life. These processes unfold through varied phases and stages, and in ways that have

1

differed markedly around the world. By definition economic development implies that individuals have found ways to utilize human and natural resources more effectively. But increasingly the concept of economic development has come to imply that human and social life can be enriched and made more just. In these chapters we are especially interested in the role that internationally connected businesses can play in initiating and strengthening the institutional arrangements that foster and support these developments.

The studies in this book are set in South Africa, Madagascar, Pakistan, South Korea, Mexico and Colombia. They are part of a larger project that has examined the practices of international businesses and their contributions to economic development in a number of other developing countries including Uganda, Ghana, Nigeria, Guyana, Vietnam, Malaysia, China, Guatemala, Brazil, Sudan and Fiji. In the previous volume we were especially interested in learning about the ways businesses have acted, or might have acted, to augment their own assets as well as those of their constituents including their host communities. We defined assets broadly so as to include not only financial and productive assets but also human, social and ecological assets (Bird and Herman, 2004). In this book, we review the experiences of businesses from a related but different perspective. We are especially interested in the ways firms *respond* to a range of complexities and dilemmas in different institutional settings and diverse economic circumstances – their exemplary initiatives as well as their mistakes and shortfalls.[2]

Many studies of international businesses in developing areas examine the conditions necessary for business success. They focus upon the factors that maximize earnings and contribute to a firm's competitive advantage in specific markets. We recognize the importance of this interest; after all these are major objectives – some would say, the only true objectives – of the business enterprise. Successful businesses do of course create 'spin-offs' such as opportunities for employment and skills development, increased sales of goods and services by related businesses, tax revenues and improved infrastructures. Nonetheless, in this book we adopt a different perspective. We review the difficulties these firms face, not only in pursuing their economic objectives, but also in dealing with difficult social and political environments. These are not insignificant problems. They often entail moral hazards. Failure to respond in ethically fitting ways may have, directly or indirectly, a number of adverse moral and economic consequences.

These chapters argue that social responsibilities that are implicit in the operations of international businesses in developing areas cannot be understood merely as 'good things to do'. They are not simply extra social and environmental duties that have often been described as the second and third 'bottom lines'. We argue instead that social and environmental responsibilities are embedded in each strategic objective a firm may pursue. Hence they are integral to basic business operations.

Responsible businesses *respond* to the contingencies of their particular social and economic environments. Their managers are sensitive to historical legacies, cultural traditions and networks of power and influence. The contingencies faced by Rio Tinto in South-eastern Madagascar, discussed in Chapter 6, differ appreciably from those faced by Toyota South Africa, discussed in Chapter 3; the basic challenges of the coffee cooperative in southern Mexico, discussed in Chapter 12, differ markedly from those of a Colombian petroleum firm discussed in Chapter 13.

Because these contingent circumstances matter so much, we have deliberately prefaced our case studies with narratives that describe the historical legacies of their host countries. In the cases of South Africa, South Korea and Mexico we have utilized these historical essays as a means to consider critically the ways public policies and national patterns of industrialization have directly impeded or facilitated overall economic development.

In many cases no simple, morally straightforward options are available in choosing a course of action. As they seek to act responsibly, managers must often compromise. They must seek viable ways to balance contrasting moral expectations that are grounded in quite different local cultures. These essays consider a number of perplexing situations, dealing, for example, with environmental issues, labour problems, contractual relations, security problems, community involvement, ethnic and national identity and government relations.

Review of chapters

In Chapter 1, Frederick Bird reviews a number of challenges and dilemmas which businesses in developing countries often encounter. These include the following: respecting cultural differences while developing common cross-cultural guidelines for business practices; finding ways of respecting the special needs of workers while developing their work skills; finding ways to achieve equity among a workforce that includes individuals of diverse ethnicity as well as expatriate employees accustomed to higher wages; finding acceptable solutions to the employment of under age children; and finding morally acceptable ways to deal with the problem of questionable payments and bribes. He examines a number of problems businesses encounter as they attempt to develop viable relations with local communities and with host governments, especially when the latter are weak or autocratic. Bird also considers the consequences of 'fractured' versus 'interconnected' economic development.

Bird adopts a modified issues management perspective. He argues that executives are expected to manage their risks effectively and to take account of relevant legal, cultural and ethical standards. However, they are also expected to exercise judgement in relation to local exigencies and possibilities, and integrate the views and interests of their relevant stakeholders in ways that add value to constituents and their firms.

Chapters 2 through 5 consider the experiences of international businesses in South Africa, especially in the years since the end of apartheid. In Chapter 2 Emmanuel Raufflet provides a brief historical over-view of business practices in South Africa during the past century. The chapter begins by examining the creation of a segregationist state (1875–1948) and notes the influential role played by the gold mining lobby, with its links to other international businesses. Raufflet reviews the apartheid regime between 1948 and 1990, as well as the internal and external protests that arose in response, and the remarkable transition from apartheid to the new democratic South Africa. Finally he describes the new roles for businesses in the current period of reconstruction (1990–2003), when overcoming the legacies of apartheid has proven to be very difficult, while rates of unemployment and crime have also risen. The chapters that follow provide accounts of three firms in their attempts to resolve these problems in their local settings.

In Chapter 3 Russell Daye examines how Toyota South Africa (TSA) has responded to the challenges of the post-apartheid era. In the past this firm, initiated by local Afrikaners, supported the apartheid government and provided few advancement opportunities for its black workers. During the last decade TSA has made remarkable changes. It has greatly expanded its social investment and affirmative action initiatives, worked to improve supplier relations, and developed a workplace forum. It has overtly sought to become a responsible corporate citizen in the new South Africa. These social initiatives have developed at the same time as the firm has expanded its business objectives to sell several car models not only in South Africa but internationally. TSA management was forced to respond to rapidly changing social, political and economic realities. Its attempt to integrate initiatives on these fronts provides an interesting example of how corporate responsibility and business strategy can interface.

In Chapter 4 Kotze analyses the social practices of Saldanha Steel, a state-of-the-art steel plant in South Africa's Western Cape province. Operating with a flat organizational structure, leanly staffed with highly qualified, multi-skilled and flexible personnel Saldanha is an export-driven corporation and manufactures a high quality product. The production process is technologically complex. Launched in 1996 by the South African government, the steel giant Iscor Ltd and the state-owned development corporation, Saldanha has been faced with a number of challenges, such as dealing with opposition from environmentalists, managing its young and heterogeneous workforce, addressing technical problems in the plant, adjusting to a drop of prices in global steel markets and higher-than-expected interest rates and coping with international protectionist policies. Kotze also examines the efforts of Saldanha Steel to increase the number of blacks and coloured in its labour force.

Elize Kotze examines the evolution of Ko-operatiewe Wynbouersvereniging (KWV or Co-operative Wine Growers Association), which throughout its history has sought to support the policies of the established governments. In Chapter 5 Kotze reviews the firm's largely paternalistic social programmes during the latter years of the apartheid era. Since 1994 the firm has taken several initiatives to change its employment policies, curb the notorious 'tot' system of paying farm labourers in wine and develop a policy forum for plant workers. The firm has also taken a few small steps toward developing opportunities and skill training for blacks to become wine growers. Although these gestures are somewhat minimal, they represent a growing commitment by a traditional Afrikaner-dominated industry to address and overcome past injustices.

In Chapter 6 Frederick Bird examines how Rio Tinto (RT), one of the world's largest mining companies, has responded to multiple environmental, social and economic challenges in exploring the possibility of launching a major mining venture in Madagascar. In 1986, RT discovered rich black sand deposits of iron-titanium ore along several beaches in south-eastern Madagascar. Once this mine becomes operational, RT estimates that it could supply up to one tenth of the world market for this mineral for about 60 years. As of March 2004 RT had not yet made a decision to proceed, though it has spent over US$45 million in exploratory studies, including social and environmental impact studies and consultations, as well as prospecting and test work. Recognizing that Madagascar had both an exceptionally vulnerable environment and a socially and economically vulnerable population, RT already in 1994 had begun forest conservation and tree-planting projects. It had decided to collaborate with the government to investigate building a major port. It had begun working with national and regional governments to foresee and develop a number of additional infrastructure projects.

In Chapter 7 Farzad R. Khan explores the origins and consequences of initiatives undertaken by the soccer industry to phase out child labour from soccer ball production processes in Sialkot, Pakistan. In the mid-1990s the international media revealed that children, along with their parents, were stitching soccer balls in their village homes. In reaction to adverse publicity campaigns the industry put together an initiative to remove children from soccer ball production. This initiative came to be known as the 'Sialkot Child Labour Elimination Project'. Khan argues that this project was largely generated to placate Western consumers and to preserve the reputations of the leading brands in the sports goods industry; it paid little attention to the local context and the needs of the child soccer ball stitchers and their families. He observes that child labour was intricately enmeshed in the social fabric of the local community, particularly the household economy of the poor. By focusing solely on child labour without seeing the deep interconnections between it and other parts of the local economy and culture (e.g. women's home-based employment) the interventions weakened the fabric of community life and caused severe social and economic disruptions.

In Chapter 8, Joseph Smucker describes the unique history of economic development in South Korea where development has been both faster and more successful than in most other developing countries. Smucker draws attention to the importance of South Korea's geopolitical position, the strong role played by successive governments, the decisive importance of the 'chaebol' conglomerates that have dominated the Korean economy, and the importance of Confucian values in motivating and legitimating these developments. Focusing on an export-oriented model, the South Koreans developed their economy largely on their own terms. They worked diligently to develop their capabilities as individuals, organizations and conglomerates. They worked extraordinarily long hours; they saved and re-invested. They successfully marketed their goods internationally and, more recently, have extended their production operations into various industrialized and developing nations.

But while South Korean firms have been successful in creating wealth and have maintained impressive economic growth rates, some sectors of the population have sacrificed more than others to achieve these results. Smucker notes that labour has become increasingly restive. Many middle class families have become less willing to continue the old patterns of discipline and sacrifice for future benefits. It is almost as if the values and institutional arrangements that fostered the initial stages of development in South Korea so successfully now need to be re-examined and modified to respond to new sets of challenges and dilemmas that economic development itself has created. In addition to these challenges, South Korea has had to deal with the effects of massive corporate restructuring and foreign direct investment following the conditions imposed on its economy by the International Monetary Fund. These conditions were part of a huge loan granted by the IMF South Korea following the financial crisis that struck the Far East in 1997–98.

In Chapter 9, Smucker focuses on the first American takeover of a South Korean bank. This event represents one example of the structural changes imposed on the Korean financial sector. Smucker begins by describing the events leading up to the take-over. The new CEO introduced major changes in banking practices. These were assessed quite differently by the international (largely American) press and the Korean media. At the same time the CEO attempted to support tacit expectations of the Korean government in ways that conflicted with standard operating procedures held by the American firm. Smucker examines some of the alleged reasons for the CEO's sudden resignation and then describes subsequent developments under the second American administration of the bank. This chapter raises a number of issues regarding the social responsibilities of managers of foreign firms. On the one hand, they are responsible to their investors in their home country; on the other hand, they must also consider the vested interests and cultural practices in the host country. It is not always easy to know what set of standards to employ or how priorities should be established.

Chapters 10 through 12 examine a number of dilemmas facing the managers of businesses in Mexico. The presence of international businesses in Mexico has gone through a long and conflicted history. In Chapter 10 Emmanuel Raufflet reviews the alternating praise and criticism regarding the effects of foreign direct investment on national development. Many have welcomed international businesses as engines of national economic growth and vital technology transfers. Others have vilified the presence of foreign corporations, portraying them as intruders, exploiters of Mexico's workers and natural resources and the authors of Mexico's misfortunes in economic development. Without attempting to settle the debate, Raufflet reviews the processes and outcomes of international businesses in Mexico, observing that while foreign investments have helped to raise overall national levels of productivity, the fact remains that international firms have often operated in fortunate enclaves while other areas of the society have languished. In Chapter 11 Raufflet examines the experiences of a large paper mill, located in central Mexico. The San Rafael company, a multinational firm that dominated the pulp and paper industry in Mexico for most of the twentieth century, while operating for much of its history with a style of paternalistic management that reproduced the hierarchy of the older rural society in which the mill originated. By mid-century the firm had become wholly Mexican; but after three decades of seeming prosperity, during which the local area developed materially and socially, San Rafael was suddenly sold to the banks in 1970 because it had become overly indebted. Raufflet suggests that this failure was due in part to the company's paternalistic relationship with its labour force (which remained only moderately productive) and an associated want of responsiveness to changes in national and international business management, technologies and markets. The San Rafael mill was closed in 1991; but a hundred years of paternalism had created dependencies from which the local community has not been able to extricate itself. In 1996 the mill reopened as a branch of a foreign-owned multinational pulp and paper company.

In Chapter 12 Anders Müller reports on the efforts of Green Mountain Coffee Roasters (GMCR) to develop 'fair trade' supplier relationships with two coffee producer cooperatives in southern Mexico. The Vermont-based company has in recent years gained widespread recognition for the integration of profitability with environmental and social responsibility. This chapter analyses how GMCR's social and environmental commitments have been carried out in two of the Mexican coffee cooperatives' quite different social contexts. After examining the current worldwide coffee crisis, Muller looks more closely at recent changes in these two cooperatives and GMCR's responses to them. While GMCR has gained reliable sources for high quality coffee, both cooperatives have gained from higher prices for their beans. GMCR's collaborative links have also encouraged investments in the local communities and supported the cultivation of other marketable products. Nonetheless, the problematic local histories of the two cooperatives have limited the benefits from these socially sustainable business partnerships.

The final case study examines the creative ways a small, independent oil community responded to security challenges in Colombia. Titus Fossgard-Moser and Frederick Bird examine how this company, operating in a country that has endured a long history of civil strife successfully managed its security problems not by hiring guards, nor by divesting, but by engaging in programmes of community relations. Fossgard-Moser and Bird contrast this firm's strategy with that of a large multinational corporation, which hired a force of security guards to protect its operations in the same region. The smaller firm could not really afford this cost for its widely dispersed operations. Instead it collaborated with local communities in a number of social and business activities. As a result, the firm gained extensive legitimacy in the eyes of the conflicting forces in the local area. In contrast to other oil companies in Colombia, this firm experienced no acts of sabotage for more than a decade.

Observations and insights

These case studies provide the basis for a number of useful observations and insights.

First, they demonstrate the importance of being sensitive to historical legacies, cultural differences and structural variations. Economic development has followed very different trajectories among different countries. Managers of international businesses need to be aware of these differences if they are to pursue their objectives in a socially responsible manner. The cases in this book examine how these kinds of contingencies – whether local traditions, unstable political circumstances, or underdeveloped infrastructures – set limits for firms, challenge their ingenuity, but also at times provide unexpected opportunities What especially matters is how firms respond to these contingencies. A good example is the independent oil company that dealt with its security problems in Colombia by devising a variety of community projects.

Second, these case studies demonstrate how changes in global markets measurably influence what local businesses can accomplish. Despite exemplary, concerted efforts to realize particular social objectives – whether employment equity for South African steelworkers or fair trade with coffee cooperatives in Mexico – changes in world markets may at least temporarily frustrate or complicate international firms' local initiatives. After nearly 20 years in which the Rio Tinto mining concern, while exploring the technical prospects for mining in Madagascar, has worked actively to promote conservation and collaborated with local groups on regional community development, its final decision to launch mining operations must ultimately depend upon the state of the global market for titanium dioxide. The initiatives of local soccer ball manufacturers in Pakistan to abolish child labour were directly mandated by the large retailers in Europe and North America, who wanted to eliminate child labour with little regard for how these changes might affect households involved. On the other hand, Toyota South Africa recently turned more of its attention to affirmative hiring and social investment initiatives as soon as its economic prospects improved with sales to wider markets beyond South Africa.

Third, these case studies indicate that conditions are not always stable and that mistakes will be made. Managers must be sensitive to the need to devise correctives. Paternalistic management of the San Rafael pulp and paper mill in Mexico probably served a useful purpose when there were few other opportunities for local residents; but when more competitive conditions developed, this type of relationship with the local community proved to be inadequate. Korean businesses likewise grew dramatically for nearly four decades through regimented work patterns, which by the late 1990s were becoming much less widely and willingly accepted.

Fourth, in a number of the case studies, we can discern the ways in which effective public policies often play a decisive role in fostering responsible business practices. Toyota South Africa, KWV wineries and Saldanha Steel all have initiated affirmative employment practices in part because the South African government enacted legislation that requires firms to work steadily so that the composition of their labour forces correlates more closely with the composition of the population as a whole. Petroleum firms operating in Colombia, unlike their neighbours in Peru, have adopted rigorous environmental practices because Colombian policies are simply more fully developed and more stringent (Fossgard-Moser, 2001).

Last, as all these case studies demonstrate, the situations that businesses in developing countries face are often complex. Businesses operate in diverse and changing circumstances. They are challenged to find ways of resolving conflicting imperatives, not only between economic, political, cultural and moral interests and demands, but often between highly regarded moral imperatives. Many of the firms studied in this book face or have faced dilemmas like these. Should a Mexican firm maintain its traditional paternalism, even with its workers' acquiescence, when such practices may doom it to economic extinction? Should a North American retailer, committed to fostering cooperative enterprises, intervene to alter the autocratic patterns of leadership in a local cooperative from which it is buying? With increasingly high rates of unemployment, businesses in South Africa face a daunting challenge in creating more employment opportunities for unskilled blacks, because many of the available jobs require skilled workers. What initiatives seem most feasible? These varied studies repeatedly indicate that it is impossible to foster responsible and sustainable business practices simply by complying with laws and following preconceived codes of behaviour. The challenges are diverse, complex and changing. It is not enough to comply with existing standards. More thought and more attention to exigencies in context are required. In dialogue with local constituencies, socially responsible managers are again and again called upon to use their imaginations and to exercise responsible judgement. All of the studies in this book appear to converge on this point.

Notes

1. The expression 'international business' as used by the contributors to this series refers to any business firm or corporation that is linked with businesses in other countries, whether as subsidiaries, or joint ventures, sources for commodity chains or trading partners. In this sense, 'multinational enterprises' (MNEs) represent just one form of international business. The expression also refers equally to firms legally or economically based in the industrialized 'north' or in developing 'south'. For the purposes of these studies, what matters is that such firms are internationally linked in ways that can (but do not always do) add economic value to the developing countries.

2. These dilemmas are not, to be sure, restricted to developing countries. Businesses in industrialized settings confront comparable challenges. However, we discuss these dilemmas especially as they have been experienced by businesses in developing areas.

References

Bird, F. and Herman, S. (eds) (2004) *International Businesses and the Challenges of Poverty in the Developing World* (London: Palgrave Macmillan).

Fossgard-Moser, T. (2001) 'MNC and Sustainable Business Practices: The Case of Colombian and Peruvian Petroleum Industries', *World Development*, vol. 29(2), pp. 291–309.

1
Dilemmas of Development: Managing Socially Responsible International Businesses in Developing Areas

Frederick Bird

Introduction

As the twenty-first century begins, increasingly large numbers of international firms are conducting business in developing areas. Whether they are purchasing goods or resources, mining natural resources, manufacturing or refining products, dealing in retail trade or services, more and more businesses have established international connections with countries in the developing world. These firms face a variety of not easily resolved challenges and dilemmas: they must learn to deal with diverse cultural traditions, social unrest, volatile political regimes, well-organized social protest groups and heightened expectations that their operations will bring about improved living conditions. International businesses possess 'the capacity to foster economic well-being and development', in the words of the recently adopted UN *Norms on the Responsibilities of Transnational Corporations*, 'as well as the capacity to cause harmful impacts' (Sub-Commission, 2003).[1]

Operating businesses in the developing world is challenging in part because economic development itself involves dramatic changes and social disruptions. Characteristically, as societies industrialize, workplaces become separated from households, isolated villages become linked and increasing numbers of workers seek their fortunes in urban areas. As a result of increased productivity and commerce, some people gain great wealth even as many others remain as impoverished as before. Those workers who enter industrial labour forces face economic insecurities if their ability to work and their corresponding incomes are cut short by accidents, unemployment and retirement for which they have been unable to adequately prepare themselves. Workforces become more mobile and more restive in regions that experience high rates of unemployment. Because economic development increases productivity and creates added wealth, these changes give rise to expectations for enhanced living conditions as well as to anger and resentment when these expectations are disappointed.[2]

If they are to maintain and grow their businesses, international firms operating in developing areas must find ways of responding effectively to these kinds of changes, which they are in part helping to bring about. They must find ways of operating in terms of diverse cultural and legal conventions. They must also find ways of addressing heightened expectations that they should operate in ways that are socially responsible (Reed, 2002). International businesses are expected at once to be profitable, socially and environmentally responsible, humane employers and globally good citizens (Queiroz and Wood, 2003).

Many businesses adopt one or both of two typical approaches to putting these ideas about social responsibility into practice. I will review and critique these approaches and then propose and argue for a third approach.

One approach is to view all of these environmental, social and political challenges in relation to a 'risk management' business model – to consider them strategically in terms of the firm's own competitive advantage. Addressing these challenges constructively may reduce the risks of being accused of violating community values or exposed for harming vulnerable ecosystems. Getting involved in these extra-business community concerns may also enhance the company's reputation and develop potentially useful links with national and local political elites. In other words, international firms may be led to reduce pollution, conserve resources and work with local businesses as suppliers and partners because they see that these initiatives will in fact further their own interests in ways that advance their competitive advantage (Porter, 1980, 1990; Smutniak, 2004).

The dilemmas international businesses face are viewed as a potential source of additional risk in developing areas. Managers are cautioned to be aware of these risks and to manage them effectively. Since every situation is unique in some respects, managers are well advised to become as informed as possible about local contingencies as well as the various resources available to deal with them. From this perspective, managers may do well to view many risks, apart from obviously unnecessary ones, as opportunities in disguise. They should consider their own unique strengths and weaknesses as well as options and threats of particular situations. In particular, they should obey laws of both host and home countries, develop effective collaborative relations with local power brokers and strengthen and build on their own unique competencies.

International firms are well advised, from this perspective, to conduct effective and thorough environmental and social impact assessments with respect not only to new but ongoing operations. These assessments provide useful information about risks a firm might otherwise overlook or discount. It makes sense to continue to monitor their operations in order to be alert and responsive to new threats – and unanticipated opportunities as well.

Many retailers and brand name manufacturers in the apparel, sporting goods and toys businesses buy their stock of goods from producers in developing areas. These are increasingly competitive markets, and since the early 1990s, much of the production has moved to developing areas where labour costs are much lower. While it is in the interest of these international firms to maintain or expand their market share, they also have an interest in avoiding reputational risks, which might adversely affect them if their eventual customers perceive them as conducting their affairs in objectionable or even unconscionable ways. Nike faced a significant boycott in the late 1990s because it was claimed that its suppliers in Pakistan employed children in the production of soccer balls (see Chapter 7). In order to avoid this kind of negative exposure, it is in the interest of these firms to act in ways that comply with basic standards. When Levi Strauss & Co. temporarily decided to stop contracting with Chinese suppliers, they were no doubt concerned to avoid the reputational risk of seeming to condone perceived human rights abuses (Schoenberger, 2000, chs 6, 7).

A risk management perspective provides a comparatively robust way of approaching dilemmas associated with running a business in developing areas. In so far as they adopt this approach, managers have a motive to stay alert, to keep well informed, to seek out chances to enhance their positive recognition and to avoid practices that make their firms especially vulnerable to legal action or popular protest. This is an open-ended, problem-solving approach. This approach uses the language of responsibility, but adopts a loosely utilitarian approach towards ethical issues. Since managers must of course assume a degree of fiduciary responsibility for the material and human resources entrusted to them, they must keep promises, speak honestly and act legally, if only because reducing avoidable risks is also a fiduciary responsibility. But they in no way think of their firms in relation to any larger social responsibilities. They take for granted the right to incorporate and do business, mandated through legislation and court rulings. Their responsibility, as Milton Friedman classically argued, is to make profits, while avoiding illegal acts and fraud (Friedman, 1970). As a result, the exigencies of any particular situation tend to be viewed unidimensionally, not on their own terms in relation to specific issues such as security, questionable payments, fractured development or effective workmanship, but rather abstractly as instances either for managing risk or maximizing competitive advantage.

A second approach for international firms in developing areas is to consider their situation and interests in much more explicitly ethical terms. This ethical approach complements and corrects the risk management approach. Efforts have been made, for example, to define and prohibit corrupt practices, to delineate appropriate uses of security forces, to forbid forced labour and to identify and censure all forms of discrimination and child labour. In keeping with this perspective, the New York – based Interfaith Center on

Corporate Responsibility and its partners have developed benchmarks for measuring business performance. These are spelled out in considerable detail with respect to ecosystems and national, local or indigenous communities, as well employees, suppliers, customers, shareholders and partners (ICCR, 1998). EthicScan Canada has developed an even more elaborate and detailed set of scoring indices for measuring and assigning grades for business practices. These indices are in fact used not only to criticize businesses, to diagnose their shortfalls and wrongs, but also to rank businesses for the purposes of attracting people who want to invest in, or purchase from, ethically responsible businesses (Pellizarri, 2002). Individual firms as well as industries have developed codes of conduct for responsible business practices. Beginning in Canada, the petrochemical industry in more than 30 countries has 'Responsible Care' codes, which establish standards for health, environment, safety and community relations. Several other standardized codes have been constructed, such as the SA 8000. These codes have in turn been adopted by hundreds of firms.

These varied codes function essentially to establish basic limits on business practices. They identify guiding frameworks, often constructed with regard to particular sets of stakeholders, and then draw specific guidelines within which businesses are expected to operate. In order to ensure compliance with these standards, businesses arrange to monitor their own practices as well as those of their immediate suppliers, both through internal review processes and through external auditors. In a number of developing countries, non-government organizations, such as Verité or Coverco have been hired by large firms to monitor the practices of their suppliers (Stern, 2002; Wick, 2003).

Much effort has been devoted over the past decade to develop, refine, publish and gain corporate endorsement of a number of codes embodying international standards for business practice. Social investment funds use these standards to recommend which firms investors should support. Social and political activists invoke these standards to single out abuses. Academics and ethical reformers work on elaborating these standards because they hope thereby to make a difference in practice as well as in theory. Businesses themselves adopt and circulate standard codes in order to police their own workforces and to gain fuller cooperation with corporate goals.

This high-minded approach to the dilemmas faced by international businesses in developing countries is driven both by outrage against widespread abuses by international firms and by an idealism that assumes it is possible to transform these businesses into responsible corporate citizens (McIntosh *et al.*, 1998). Many who argue for an ethical approach seem to assume that complexities and moral conundrums faced by international firms in developing areas will become more manageable if managers simply adopt standardized guidelines to rule out unacceptable practices and establish basic ethical frames of reference. In a way these guidelines establish parameters within which managers can exercise discretion as they see fit to advance the interests of their firms. As in the risk management approach, however, typical dilemmas of development are not primarily viewed on their own terms. Rather, they are regarded as arenas of turmoil and temptation, in relation to which businesses need to be guided and restrained.

There are advantages but also serious limitations to the utilization of codes of conduct as the primary points of reference for responsibly addressing the exigencies and challenges experienced by international firms in developing areas. Detailed codes invite firms and their critics to become distracted by violations that may at first seem blatant but are not necessarily significant in the long run. In many cases the codes themselves do not recognize and clearly distinguish the classical and decisive difference between minimal obligations that absolutely must be met (e.g. the obligation to conduct regular fiscal audits) and standards of excellence to which business people may aspire but only partially realize (e.g. imaginative human resources policies) (Fuller, 1964). The excessive reliance upon codes often leads businesses to overlook the extent to which particular exigencies call for special responses. For example, as traditional businesses in South Africa adjust to their new post-apartheid society, they must seek ways to create more job and advancement opportunities for blacks; but their solutions must also be feasible and effective in their particular locales. They may not be able initially to comply with more universal standards. Most seriously, these codes sometimes lead businesses (or their critics) to direct moral attention solely towards correcting instances of improper conduct rather than the realization of other positive contributions. For example, the international outcry against child labour in rural Pakistan households that had earned their living by stitching soccer balls, dramatically changed the way these balls were manufactured. Reformers identified an example of a questionable practice, and took action to outlaw this practice with almost no concern that the solution they imposed would reduce the incomes of the affected families and give rise to new, equally unacceptable social problems (see Chapter 7).

In what follows I argue that businesses should indeed employ risk management and should use codes of conduct as points of reference for their operations. I argue, however, that they should regard both as relative and approximate guides. For a number of reasons, which I will explore further in this chapter, neither approach is wholly adequate as a guide for managing responsibly and effectively the dilemmas and challenges facing businesses in the developing world. Nor are they adequate in combination. I shall argue that what is most important is that those managing international businesses in developing areas should exercise responsible judgements. This may sound obvious; but what does it really mean? Exercising judgement responsibly entails a number of things besides sizing up risks and taking account of ideal moral standards. It also requires that we make efforts to identify, and work to realize, particular valued objectives – often referred to as ethical 'goods' – such as the goal of increasing local employment or local industry; to acknowledge, honour, evaluate and critique social conventions, and to explore imaginatively historical contingencies and possibilities. Exercising judgement calls for us to undertake several moral activities in a related manner. Thus, when we exercise ethical judgement we are called upon both (1) to take account of varied and sometimes conflicting moral considerations that arise in relation to particular moral issues, and (2) to weigh and assign priority to these considerations in relation to the exigencies we are facing. It is important to add that exercising moral judgement is inherently a *timely* activity. We make judgements, not out of time nor in relation to issues defined in general terms, but at particular moments in relation to current contingencies.

Pre-eminently the social responsibility of businesses in developing areas is exhibited by the manner and the degree they are able to develop effective and historically appropriate responses to a wide variety of complex moral dilemmas. In the next section of this paper I will briefly review a number of these dilemmas. I will then conclude this essay by arguing that ethics, understood as the practice of exercising responsible judgement, provides a way of addressing these situations that is both effective and morally compelling.

Dilemmas of development

International businesses operating in developing areas face a number of morally perplexing situations. At the outset they must find ways of dealing with diverse and at times conflicting cultural expectations. In Korea, Pakistan, South Africa and Mexico, for example, attitudes towards the pace of work and the relation of work to family life have, for example, been shaped respectively by Confucian, Muslim, Afrikaner and Iberian Catholic traditions. Businesses face quite different expectations in countries with little industrialization than those where industrialization is much further advanced. Businesses face quite different prospects in countries with strong, independent governments that function professionally according to impersonal standards of due process than in countries where doing business with the authorities traditionally depends upon the exercise of personal influence. How businesses negotiate contracts, pay taxes, schedule work, reward achievements and arrange work settings for women with respect to men will certainly differ in important ways from culture to culture. Clearly, whatever other challenges international business in developing areas face, they must find ways of adjusting to these kinds of cultural differences.

In this section we shall consider several of the more prominent of these challenges that international businesses face in developing areas:[3]

1. Labour productivity
2. Workplace equity

3. Interconnected versus fractured development
4. Questionable payments
5. Aggravated security problems
6. Good corporate citizenship in the local community
7. Autocratic, corrupt or weak political regimes

Enhancing labour productivity

One set of dilemmas revolves around the challenge of enhancing labour productivity – fostering productive work patterns among employees at a reasonable cost in terms of wages, benefits, working conditions, job supervision and other human-resources expenses. Many of the primary producers for clothing, shoes and toys as well as many assembly plants for automobiles and electronic equipment have moved their operations to developing countries precisely in the hope of reducing overall employment costs. Whether employees work in primary production, at assembly plants, in extraction industries, or in other kinds of settings, whether they work in developing or developed areas, managers seek ways at once to render employees' work as efficient as possible and their costs as minimal as possible.

The cost of production increases if workers are absent from work or arrive late, because more work hours will be required to accomplish the same production objectives. Similar results occur whenever there are large turnover rates: as efforts are diverted to recruiting and orienting new workers, the overall level of productivity falls. Productivity also falls to the extent that employees pursue their assigned tasks intermittently or with noticeable resistance. In contrast, when employees feel committed to performing the work their employers require of them, they will present fewer cases of absence, late arrival, turnover and resistance, and will work with more regularity. Such commitment usually rises with skill levels and work experience; however, it is often hard to generate this kind of commitment among low-skilled employees not used to working in modern industrial settings (Mowday *et al.*, 1982).

Many employees recruited to work at newly established international business sites in developing areas exhibit varying signs of low work commitment. In northern Quebec, for example, although the Raglan Mine undertook special efforts to welcome Inuit employees as part of their workforce, turnover was very high, as the Inuits had been used to varying their pace and times of work with the seasons (Bird and Nixon, 2004). Likewise, many of the employees working in maquiladoras in Mexico or Guatemala or in factories in South Africa have not been used to working as part of large, impersonally organized workforces in production-oriented plants. They are not accustomed to work tasks organized and administered in this impersonal deadline-disciplined manner.

Many international businesses operating in developing areas take it for granted that their employees will show little commitment to their jobs.

Except perhaps in countries such as Korea, where workers are influenced by a Confucian work ethic (see Chapter 8), they assume that most employees will hold typical Western attitudes toward work, viewing it as no more than the means (for the most part, unpleasant) of getting income to be spent satisfying their individual desires above and beyond the necessities of life (Weber, 1958). Workers, in this view, will demonstrate little identification with their impersonally designated tasks; they will show a marked preference for leisure over work, a disposition to be absent or late when it is convenient and a preference for casually paced work. To the extent that employees hold such attitudes towards work, there are several possible strategies that managers can pursue.

One widely adopted strategy is simply to take for granted higher turnover rates, absenteeism, late arrivals and casually paced and inefficiently performed work – and pay employees as little as possible. For the most part, this is a short-term strategy in any area. It becomes less realizable as workers become more restive and demand higher wages, as production deadlines and quality standards become more pressing and as alternative locales for this kind of low cost labour beckon.

An alternative strategy is to adopt a personal and paternalistic approach. Managers can make an effort to show special interest in their workers, especially those with seniority, by staging occasional corporate festivities, dispensing small bonus payments on holidays and sending personal notes when children graduate or family members die. Managers may also offer workers various fringe benefits, such as childcare services or free transportation to worksites. The basic assumption is that although workers' traditional attitudes cannot be easily changed, executives can make the workplace seem more welcoming and thereby elicit a somewhat greater sense of loyalty to the workplace. While this approach may reduce turnover, it does not guarantee more productive work patterns (see Chapter 11).

A third strategy is to regiment the workplace as strictly as possible: to supervise workers closely and penalize them when they break the rules. To emphasize the importance of being on time, managers sometimes lock out workers who are late; to get as much work out of employees as possible, long hours are imposed. Various penalties are imposed for absences, carelessness or poor-quality work. Here, managers assume that workers will naturally hold traditional work attitudes, and then seek by forceful means to prevent workers from acting on these attitudes. This approach may temporarily raise output, in so far as workers can be regimented; but in the long run they will become resentful of abrasive treatment, and at that point productivity will fall even further.

In a fourth strategy, employers can seek to foster greater work commitment by investing more directly in their workers. They can provide adequate wages, benefits and working conditions. Where workers feel that their actual workmanship is valued and where they are not subjected to close surveillance, they tend to exhibit greater work commitment. They are less likely under these conditions to be absent, arrive late, look for other employment or work intermittently (Glisson and Durrick, 1988). To foster productive labour, workplaces must be organized so that employees will feel more empowered and more directly valued for their job performance. This can be realized under various circumstances, for example, in cooperatives where workers hold each other accountable to for achieving collective production or performance goals, in settings where workers are treated as professionals. This approach works better where employees have sufficient knowledge and experience to direct their own work efforts.

In practice, managers of international businesses may seek to address the challenge of effective workmanship by using several approaches at once. It is tempting, especially when operating in developing areas, to adopt some combination of paternalism and regimentation. External disciplinary measures proliferate. These measures often reinforce patterns of work that are neither particularly productive nor humane. The challenge of finding contextually fitting ways of enhancing the productivity of labour is considered in a number of the cases in this book, especially the studies of San Rafael paper mill in Mexico, labour issues in Korea and the wine industry in South Africa.

Fostering workplace equity

A second set of problems revolves around the difficulties in addressing conflicting claims with respect to hiring policies and remuneration. These dilemmas appear in several typical forms and include (for example) setting expatriate salaries, preferential hiring from population groups that have been discriminated against in the past and employing children for work in traditional family settings alongside their parents or older siblings. Contrasting and competing claims arise in each of these cases, yet each of these situations is unique, and managers must determine what is fair by taking account of different viewpoints and determining how their responses will affect the morale of other workers and the life chances of the affected workers and their families. These are not simple matters.

With respect to expatriate workers, firms must determine how much to pay these employees, who have been accustomed to receiving much higher wages in their home countries than workers at the same levels receive in the host country. To be sure, lower wages in host countries may reflect much lower consumer prices. However, for the most part expatriate workers expect to return to their home countries with enough savings to pay for pensions, school expenses for their children and mortgages on property. Many expatriate workers expect additional compensation for being willing to leave home and work in unfamiliar settings. However, when expatriate workers are paid markedly higher wages host country employees often feel resentful. They feel their contributions are being under-valued; they often feel that excessive sums are being paid to foreign workers while home country workers are underpaid. A morale problem arises, and the workforce ceases to work collaboratively and effectively in the firm's best interest. To resolve this dilemma, the international firm's management must balance these competing claims in ways that seem fair to all those involved – not only in the size of the overall compensations but also as to how these compensations are administered.

Turning to another issue, what steps should an international firm take in hiring so that its workforce reasonably reflects not only the overall population of the host country but also the demographics of the areas where the firm is located? Firms typically face several intermixed demands. Residents from local communities expect to be well represented as employees, even though they may in general have less education and possess fewer of the expected skills. At the same time if locals are disproportionately favoured, then job applicants from other parts of the country may feel unjustly treated, especially if they have higher levels of educational attainment and are more skilled. If particular population groups have suffered from social or economic discrimination in the past, is the international firm now obligated to take special measures to hire and promote workers from these groups, even if other job applicants may be more qualified? These issues are not easily resolved. Currently in South Africa, firms are expected by law to hire and promote so that the composition of their workforces reflects the population of the country as a whole. Even though populations may vary from region to region, firms are expected to make every effort to comply with national averages. Problems emerge when less qualified workers seem to be picked for jobs or promotions over more qualified competitors on the basis of their race, gender or ethnicity. This practice may or may not represent overt discrimination. If certain tasks can be adequately performed by workers with moderate capacities, then particular applicants do not necessarily become more qualified by possessing extra skills. Other factors may appropriately come into play. Nonetheless, executives face the challenge of managing these situations in ways that seem fair to all parties. Otherwise, they will have to deal with a disgruntled and demoralized workforce.

Consider another situation where managers face conflicting claims about who should work and for how much. What steps should an international business take when their adult employees bring to work their children or younger siblings that are less than 15 years old? Should they simply and absolutely ban all children from working? What if they are working in comparative security at home? Many parents appear to want their children to work with them. In the late 1990s it was estimated that worldwide more than 350 million children under 14 were labourers (Basu, 1999). Many of these children were working in rural agricultural settings as part of family farming operations (Akabayashi and Psacharopoulos, 1999). In many cases, these children either lacked opportunities to attend school regularly because the school systems were themselves inadequately staffed; or they might attend school regularly but achieve only at the lowest levels, thereby becoming socially marginalized. In some cases, children banned from employment in particular workplaces sought employment in even more hazardous work settings (Basu, 1999; Bessell, 1999; Kenny, 1999).

Any retailer purchasing clothes, toys, sporting goods or other merchandise from primary manufacturers in developing areas may well discover that some of its suppliers allow children to work in their workshops from time to time. What steps should the buyer take? If firms fire the parents and older siblings who bring children with them to work, they will drastically reduce the income of these families, and thus inadvertently put the children at greater risk. In many settings parents want these children to work alongside them. But can international businesses continue to allow such children to work in clear violation of their own codes of good practice and their consumers' avowed values (Klein, 2000)? Rather than simply banning the employment of these children, should they instead find ways of instituting classes for them at their worksites? It is not easy to answer these questions. To be sure, these kinds of issues in part arise especially during early phases of industrialization as the primary locale of production moves from households and cottages to factories and manufacturing sites. In later phases of industrialization, as wage levels rise and as more public funds become available for education, these problems decline. Nonetheless, today the dilemma is widely experienced.

Work place equity dilemmas are considered in the case studies of businesses operating in South Africa and Pakistan that appear in this book (Chapters 2–5 and 7). The parties involved in these cases often champion quite different beliefs about what policies would be just – often taking strong, uncompromising positions. Viable solutions not only need to be just towards those who thereby benefit, but they must also seem to be just, even to those who may initially oppose them.

Encouraging interconnected development

One of the most troubling problems is the way in which international business operations give rise to what I call *fractured development*: the creation of new or added forms of wealth in developing areas that benefit local elites or power brokers without fostering overall economic growth, industrial and technical advancement or viable local commercial markets. Typically, fractured development occurs when international businesses intensively exploit particular resource areas – such as oil, minerals, coffee, cotton, sugar or tourism – almost exclusively for the benefit of foreign consumers and elite stakeholders without corresponding efforts to develop the wider networks of local commerce and industry (Auty, 1993). While local magnates may enrich themselves on the international business presence, governments may fracture development further by rent seeking through royalties, partnerships and special agreements designed to appropriate a substantial share of the new wealth. Government rent seeking typically adds little or nothing to local commercial networks and infrastructure. Fractured development seems to be the new economic regime in certain developing areas today. This is particularly obvious in countries where international agreements have created free import–export zones that allow international businesses to operate assembly plants, pay little or no taxes, create low-paying jobs for the workers who migrate to these areas and considerable wealth for a few local entrepreneurs. The maquiladora system in Mexico is the most notorious example. Independent local industry in these areas is weakened, while many local suppliers of goods and services, unable or unwilling to enter the long international supply chain at its least remunerative end, lose their markets altogether. At the same time, the added social costs associated with population change are not balanced by investments in social, commercial and physical infrastructures. In a number of counties intense investment in export-focused industries such as garments, electronic parts, mining operations and coffee plantations, has weakened local agriculture drawing local investment away from farm production and distribution (Evans, 1979; Broad, 1988).

Of course there has never been anything easy, obvious or automatic about economic development, particularly along the laissez-faire lines extolled by international business. Historically, though offering the prospect of general prosperity, development has also occasioned periods of social disruption and economic misery. In today's global context even the best-intentioned investments by international businesses may inadvertently become fractured, blocked, derailed or reversed.

Modern-day international businesses often recognize that they must necessarily take into account the policies of national governments and local economic interests. They do not intentionally plan to aggravate social strife. They have little to gain and much to lose by intensifying inequalities or frustrating non-competing forms of economic development. Certainly they have no desire to be held hostage by governments or ruling interests in any country or region. Yet it is not always easy to envision alternative ways of operating so as to integrate international business operations more fully into the local economy. In any case the process begins by avoiding fractured development – an exercise that cannot rely upon simplistic or automatic assumptions.

Managing issues related to questionable payments

Another set of issues for international businesses concerns questionable payments. How do international businesses respond to various explicit and implicit requests for off-budget gifts, facilitation fees, and/or agent payments that may seem questionable? How can they distinguish between culturally acceptable and unacceptable payments, especially in cultures where the practice of giving gifts seems widespread? We can, I think, get a sense of the complexities of these matters by considering several examples.[4] In one case a European international firm had contracted to construct a natural gas pipeline in a southern hemisphere country. Local police informed the firm that a protection ring had been threatening residents in a middle-class neighbourhood where the firm had housing for its expatriate managers, engineers and other professional staff. The police, however, then demanded to be paid for the 'extra hours' they would require to control the protection gang. The firm in question wondered if the police might be in league with the protection gang. Off-budget demands also arose at the docks. The firm was informed by the warehouse staff that they would require extra payments to arrange the release of the equipment the firm had shipped to the port – purportedly to hire extra workers. Again, managers of the firm feared they might be giving in to a mild form of extortion.

Another international firm selling high-tech equipment to governments in developing countries decided to employ local agents, who knew their markets and had developed contacts with appropriate government officials. It used a standardized contract for these agents, in which they promised to obey local laws and provide a written account of their transactions. These agents charged for their offices, time and any fees levied by government. Agent charges were sometimes as high as 25 per cent of the total cost to the buyer. The firm was clearly acting in keeping with its own country's laws; but did not know if contracted agents were offering government officials extra payments to secure sales.

When another international firm adopted strict company-wide guidelines with respect to gifts and off-budget payments, officials of its long-standing East Asia branch successfully asked for an exception. They explained that executives of local firms with whom they did business expected to receive lavish gifts for the weddings and funerals of family members; it would be simply impossible to arrange business transaction with local firms unless they were prepared to offer these unsolicited gifts.

Another international firm put in a bid to help construct a power grid in a South Asian country. The government official that had the responsibility to select which bids would be finally considered for the assignment demanded an extra payment from all applicants. The bids were indeed complicated. This public official and his staff had to screen these bids carefully. Other firms competing for this project offered the official even more than he requested. They explained that all of these officials were underpaid. The firm in question worried whether such payments violated their own company code, which prohibited all forms of bribery.

It is clear that corruption is a huge problem. As a result of bribes and extortion, some firms win contracts even though their products or services are inferior. As a result, consumers, whether governments, firms or retail customers, pay decidedly more for purchases; in effect, they pay an illegal hidden tax that benefits a private individual rather than the public. The cost of corruption for developing countries has been enormous; wealth that might have been invested in government programmes or local business ventures instead is captured by small groups of people inside and outside governments.

There are, to be sure, those who excuse off-budget payments as sometimes providing helpful personal connections that serve to get around typical bureaucratic roadblocks, or even allow officials to exercise personal discretion so as to facilitate effective public action (Banfield and Wilson, 1963). Others note that personal relationships, cemented by exchanges of gifts and favours, have been honoured ways of transacting business in many traditional societies. These observers compare ostensibly irregular payments in developing countries to accepted Western practices of lobbying, tipping and partnering with privileged suppliers. Still, in spite of these voices of dissent, for the most part corrupt practices are almost universally condemned (Gillespie, 1987; Klitgaard, 1988; Thomas *et al.*, 2000, ch. 6; Hodess *et al.*, 2001; *The Economist*, 2002).

Nonetheless the universal denunciation of corruption does not always help managers sort out how to respond to the kinds of ambiguous demands illustrated by the previous examples. In a sense, the word 'corruption' is an oversimplification. In given settings it may not be always easy to distinguish corrupt payments from payments that may be justifiable on discretionary grounds. What is culturally acceptable differs from country to country: quietly offering gifts and favours may well be regarded as acceptable practice when viewed as part of a larger, traditional system of reciprocity – what is known, for example, in China as *quanxi*. The more businesses offer these kinds of payments as they negotiate and re-negotiate transactions, the harder it becomes to know where to draw the line; and therefore it is not enough simply to invoke notions of cultural relativity. In recent years, for example, the Chinese government has initiated a campaign to eliminate corruption, that is, acts of offering gifts and favours that in some ways exceed the assumed limits set by traditional notions of *quanxi* (Kwong, 1997; *The Economist*, 2000). Some kinds of off-line payments may well be respected and honoured while others are regarded with suspicion if not outright censure.

Managers of international businesses in developing areas are likely to find themselves in settings where they must make case-by-case judgements among a range of essentially off-line payments. These may include ostensibly legal agent fees that are in fact padded, as well as sizeable gifts for officials and contractual partners. They may take the form of tips and or payments of facilitation fees that other international businesses are also paying. Or they may well be asked to offer kickbacks for volume sales or timely deliveries. They may be asked to second skilled employees to enable local or national governments develop the technical and legal infrastructures to facilitate the development of their own operations. They may be asked to donate to particular local charities, closely associated with interest or policies of their transactional partners. International business executives who attempt to avoid all ostensibly ambiguous payments may put their firms at financial risk from lost business activity, or cause offence by flouting what appear to be generally tolerated practices. However, if they do not exercise vigilance, they are likely to support practices that may be generally tolerated but in fact really amount to corruption. In addition, their own attempts to sort out these situations may be further clouded both by the fragmentary and partial information they received from associates (who may be pursuing their own private agendas, as well as their own personal career and corporate interests).

Aggravated security problems

Many international businesses may face an additional set of challenges that revolve around security issues especially in areas characterized by social unrest, violent civil conflict or high rates of vandalism. There are ongoing civil conflicts, which often have become violent, in Russia, Indonesia, the Philippines, India, Pakistan, central Asia, the Middle East, Colombia, Guatemala, Uganda, the Republic of Congo, Angola, Sudan, Uganda and Sierra Leone. There are high rates of vandalism in many of these countries as well as in South Africa. In many other countries there have been outbreaks of violence fuelled by ethnic conflicts, economic disparities and political disenfranchisement. The high crime rates of South Africa are certainly correlated with excessively high rates of unemployment. Insurgencies in many rural areas are supported by many low-income groups who possess little real title to lands on which they work and live; in other regions, such insurgencies are simply popular responses to oppressive regimes. Many governments, for example, those in The Philippines or Colombia, do not seem to possess the means to suppress ongoing violent conflicts; in some countries, such as Sudan and Angola, national governments have acted as parties in these conflicts.

What action should international businesses take to protect their own plants, offices and facilities as well as the people working for them? How should they most effectively manage their own security arrangements? Can they realistically establish security for their own operations without addressing to some extent the security problems faced by the larger region in which they are conducting their business? Is it enough simply to build security perimeters around their facilities? On the other hand, do they have the means or the mandate to address these larger, more complex security issues and the underlying causes that give rise to them?

Consider the situation facing the Shell Petroleum Development Corporation in Nigeria in the early 1990s. Royal Dutch/Shell, with a 30 per cent share, managed this firm, in which the Nigeria government held a 55 per cent share. The national government at the time had arbitrarily voided recent elections, jailed opposition political leaders, used its military power to attack dissidents and ignored the calls for greater self-government voiced by the Ijaw, Ogoni and other indigenous peoples of the Niger Delta region. In response to mounting ethnic conflicts, the government used excessive force, resulting in several very violent encounters. At this time there were a growing number of attacks, which assumed the form of vandalism against Shell facilities – in particular, sabotaging its pipelines. For the most part Shell followed standard procedures, and hired security guards; yet overall security issues became more aggravated through out the 1990s (Bird, 2004). In these circumstances, what kinds of realistic alternatives might Shell have pursued to make the security problem more manageable?

Some critics have called upon international businesses to limit abusive practices of their own and exercise greater diligence in protecting the human rights both of their own employees and the populations living in areas where their sites are located (Gagnon *et al.*, 2003). They have called for stricter corporate codes and more rigorous monitoring of actual practices by outside auditors. These suggestions do not, however, provide much practical guidance for managing complex ambiguities associated with sorting out and addressing security issues. Many dilemmas remain. To what degree, for example, should firms like Shell in Nigeria, Talisman in Sudan, British Petroleum in Colombia, or Barama in Guyana provide protection primarily if not exclusively for their own sites and personnel? In contrast, to what extent and in what ways do they also possess implicit obligations to help address and resolve the roots of these conflicts, which their operations may in fact aggravate?

Becoming good citizens in local communities

International businesses in developing areas face an additional series of interrelated dilemmas with regard to the kind and quality of the relationships they establish with neighbouring communities. Their operations often markedly affect the economies and social relationships within these communities, both directly by the jobs they offer and the natural resources they utilize, and indirectly by their impact on local consumer and housing markets and their interactions with varied community groups. Many international firms have built company towns in which the firm dominates local economic, social and political life. They have built housing for employees, operated retail stores, helped to build and administer schools and constructed recreational and cultural facilities. They have helped as well to build roads, railways and port facilities that link these communities to the larger society. Other firms have invested in local community projects, supported local charities and offered scholarships and training programmes. In the process, the firms in question typically cooperate with interested groups and work with local leaders. In contrast, many other international businesses have adopted more distant and restricted relationships with local communities.

What kinds of relationships should international businesses foster with these communities? If they establish company towns, these firms may be accused wielding excessive power. However, if they make no benevolent contributions, they may be accused of exploiting these communities for their own narrow business interests. Is it appropriate for firms to offer various social welfare services? Or is it more fitting to treat community relations strictly as a business exchange?

Consider the case of Rio Tinto's prospective mine in Madagascar (discussed at greater length in Chapter 6). In order to ship the extracted minerals, the firm will need to develop modernized port facilities, which will also be useable by other business enterprises. With other businesses potentially moving to the area, the new mine's presence will attract large numbers of job seekers. This anticipated surge in population will require new roads, water systems, housing, markets, schools and jobs. How should Rio Tinto respond to these and other possible developments occasioned by the construction of its proposed mine? To what degree are these concerns legally the responsibility of municipal, regional and national governments? If Rio Tinto assumes direct responsibility for these developments, is it then using its own power and wealth to dominate local politics? Compare the situation of the maquiladoras, the international export manufacturing concerns which have similarly attracted large numbers of job seekers in Mexico and Central America. Rarely have the maquiladoras or their parent firms assumed direct or indirect responsibility for social and infrastructural developments. The costs of dislocation have been borne by the households involved and the costs for infrastructures have been financed by governments.

As international businesses interact with their contiguous communities, they may confront one or more of a number of conundrums. If they seek to collaborate with the local community leaders, with which should they establish contact? Royal Dutch/Shell found itself in several cases in a difficult position in Nigeria, for example, because when they sought to work with the elders of several indigenous peoples, leaders of younger, more radical groups protested. Many firms have faced unanticipated resentment as a result of their decision to invest in community projects in particular villages – drilling wells for water, assistance with school constructions or the opening of small health clinics – from other villages that do not receive as extensive assistance.

The contrast between the perceived wealth of international businesses and the poverty of local communities often aggravates feelings of resentment. Communities begin to hope for more jobs, higher incomes for those offered, more side-investments in roads and services and more opportunities for local businesses than can be feasibly provided. How do firms handle these rising expectations, especially when the wealth invested in their own productive systems and salaries are so evident?

Interactions with weak and/or autocratic governments

A large number of international businesses face dilemmas occasioned by the fact that they are operating in countries governed by autocratic, weak or corrupt regimes. Many governments of developing countries have gained or maintained power through military force and by cancelling or manipulating democratic processes. Some of these governments are dominated by powerful and wealthy elites who exploit or effectively commandeer government offices to serve their own interests (Evans, 1979). At times international firms have directly faced the prospect of being expropriated or charged excessively high taxes by such governments. Assuming, however, for the purpose of the present discussion, that such danger is not immediate the fact remains that these firms face dangers of several sorts. Merely by continuing their operations, they may become complicit as these governments use the taxes and royalties from international firms to oppress their own people or attack minorities, fight wars against internal regions seeking greater representation or spend lavishly on monuments and white-elephant projects celebrating their own power. Simply by continuing to do business with these regimes, international firms may reinforce the seeming legitimacy of administrations that have violated their own national laws, or are widely opposed by popular movements. What are the viable options for international businesses in countries with autocratic or oppressive regimes?

Some international businesses have responded to these situations by divesting. For many critics of autocratic or oppressive regimes, divestment is a morally appealing response (Gagnon *et al.*, 2003). Certainly it supplies an immediate solution for firms caught in the position of seeming to be morally complicit in the abuses of the governments they de facto help to finance. But divestment's positive results are not always clean-cut.

A number of American firms withdrew from South Africa in the 1980s in response to organized international protest against the apartheid system (Sethi and Williamson, 2001). Many of these firms made the decision to withdraw from South Africa as a result of protests by consumers, shareholders and the public groups in North America. Divestment has, however, not been without ambiguities. As a strategy, it may well have strengthened the political hand of the African National Congress as it sought both to overturn the apartheid system and gain political power; but it also reduced foreign investments in ways that aggravated unemployment problems. The present ANC government has not succeeded in persuading many of the divested American firms to re-invest in South Africa.

The ambiguity of divestment is well illustrated by an example concerning the operations of Talisman, a Canadian independent oil company, which invested in Sudan in 1998. Protesters and critics in North America argued that Talisman was de facto supporting the Sudanese government, both through royalty payments and by allowing the government occasionally to use its private airport facilities. They pointed to the government's excessive human rights violations and its continuing war against insurgents in the country's southern regions, whose legitimate rights had long been ignored by Sudanese governments. As a result of these protests, Talisman's share prices fell dramatically and the company decided to sell off its operations and withdraw from Sudan. Only after Talisman withdrew from Sudan did the protesters realize that they no longer had a corporate vehicle through which they might put pressure on the Sudanese government.

Strong arguments have been made for maintaining operations in spite of these difficulties. International business operations provide means of transferring technologies to and fostering skill development in developing areas. They serve as means, however imperfectly, for augmenting economic development and increasing local wealth. They often occasion at least some accompanying infrastructural developments. They provide jobs. While these arguments may indeed be valid, they still sidestep the central issue of how these firms should act towards the autocratic and oppressive governments. These arguments provide a rational for continued investment. Yet the dilemma of *how* to interact with these governments remains to be addressed.

One typical but not entirely satisfactory response is to adopt a politically neutral but legally correct position. At a minimum many firms take the position that they will in no way condone or cooperate in illegal or corrupt practices, even when pressured by government officials. They will engage in no partisan political activities. They will politely and publicly note human rights abuses but not directly lobby the governments involved. They will seek to be sure that their own practices honour human rights. Even though they may be involved in joint ventures with the governments in question, such as Shell was in Nigeria or Talisman in Sudan, they will seek to act as independent from these governments as possible. When the governments in question act to violate legal codes, they will overtly but civilly voice their objections. The problem with this stance is that the firms still maintain what their critics view as a complicit relationship with the governments in question.

The real dilemma is how actively to oppose autocratic and oppressive government actions while still managing to secure these governments' cooperation for legitimate business purposes. No doubt the situation in each developing country governed by such a regime calls for different responses. Nonetheless, the response of the US firms that adopted the Sullivan Principles in South Africa in the decade or so after 1976 provides an instructive example. While continuing to operate in South Africa, these firms actively sought to put into practice policies that directly ignored a number of apartheid laws. They committed themselves to end segregation in the workplace, provide equal pay for equal work, initiate training to advance blacks to supervisory and management positions and improve all employees' living conditions and schooling (Sethi and Williamson, 2001, p. 4). This was a modestly successful effort at dissent, reform and polite protest. The conditions of black and non-white employees moderately improved in these firms, while these firms' initiatives reinforced the argument that apartheid was becoming increasingly unworkable in a modern industrialized society.

Exercising responsible judgement

As they operate their businesses in developing areas, managers of international firms face a variety of dilemmas such as those I have briefly reviewed. The approach they take will affect how well they prosper. It will have an impact on their reputation and the morale of their workforce. It will either add or diminish economic value to areas in which they operate. It will facilitate or frustrate their overall development.

What is especially striking about these kinds of dilemmas is how different they are and how differently they are experienced by particular firms in distinct developing areas. Issues arising out of questionable payment often bear few similarities to problems associated with enhancing the productivity of labour. The challenges businesses face with respect to security issues call for quite different sorts of responses than the dilemmas connected with achieving workplace equity. Even though the patterns by which firms interact with local communities may be connected with the de facto ways they act to foster fractured or integrated economic development, these interconnections differ markedly from country to country and from firm to firm. Referring to the chapters that follow, we can observe that the workplace issues faced by the soccer ball merchants in Pakistan differ appreciably from those of the paper mill owners and maquiladoras in Mexico. Both Rio Tinto in Madagascar and KWV wineries in South Africa have been actively exploring ways to develop more collaborative relations with local villagers; but the two firms face quite different constraints and possibilities. The economic issues facing firms in South Korea currently contrast considerably not only from issues experienced by businesses in Madagascar but also from those experienced by Korean firms 30 years ago. Their national economies are passing through disparate stages of development.

If businesses, whether international or not, are to operate in socially responsible ways, they must at a minimum be responsive to specific social issues and the exigencies that arise from those issues. To be responsible means to be able to respond – to be aware and attentive – to contingencies they face not only in relation to differences in cultural expectations and changing historical conditions but also in relation to the evolving character of the dilemmas they are seeking to manage.

At the outset I identified two characteristic ways of addressing these kinds of challenges. On the one hand, many firms address these situations as instances of risk, which they in turn seek to manage effectively to their own advantage. On the other hand, many firms additionally define what is at stake in these situations in relation to basic ethical codes and principles especially designed to guide socially responsible business practices. Both of these approaches provide useful frames of reference, provided that they are treated as practical but not absolute guides. However, each approach, or even both approaches taken together, will present problems when adhered to slavishly.

But much more is involved. All of these dilemmas also call for firms to recognize and sort out basic ethical claims. They raise issues about productive labour, humane and challenging work relations, honest transactions, fiduciary responsibilities, reciprocal obligations and much more. In each case firms are challenged not only to avoid certain wrongs and limit unnecessary harms but also to realize particular valued objectives. Accordingly firms are well advised to study the various codes developed for international business practices. Some codes, like the *Benchmarks* of the Interfaith Center for Corporate Responsibility, alert firms to minimal moral and legal obligations they should respect; other codes, like the Global Compact, remind businesses of basic aspirations. In general, however, these codes define moral issues with little or no reference to changing historical circumstances; as well, they typically fail to take cultural differences and local contingencies seriously. More importantly, most codes fail to acknowledge the extent to which the kinds of moral challenges that I have just reviewed constitute genuine and often complex dilemmas, for which there are no simple and unambiguous answers. It is possible to mount compelling moral arguments for a range of diverse responses to most of these dilemmas. As practical ways for helping international firms manage their operations responsibly, the practices of risk management and code compliance help to set the parameters for their practices, the outer limits for morally appropriate action.

In the meantime, between these limits firms are called upon to exercise responsible judgement. What does that mean?[5] There are diverse models of responsible decision-making. Basically, exercising responsible judgement involves six steps:

1. Personally assuming responsibility;
2. Taking account of and responding to current contingencies;
3. Broadly considering all relevant claims and interests;
4. Consulting with relevant stakeholders;
5. Weighing and assigning priority to these contingencies, claims and interests in relation to the good or value that can thereby be realized; and
6. Continuously monitoring actions in order to learn from ongoing experiences.

First and foremost, it is important to emphasize that responsibility is exercised by human agents, that is, by individuals or groups who assume the task of responding, deliberating and initiating action. Responsibility is not really put into practice by codes or principles or theories; rather it is enacted as particular humans respond, think, consult and act. Individuals or groups, who take the initiative, who assume the responsibility for acting, make the difference. Productive and socially responsible changes occurred in Toyota South Africa and the coffee cooperatives in Mexico in large part because particular individuals and groups initiated these developments. Likewise, particular managers played key roles in developing the effective, insecurity-reducing community relations programme at the petroleum company in Colombia examined in Chapter 13. Similarly, several executives were instrumental in developing the affirmative action programmes at KWV wineries in South Africa. It is individuals, alone and/or together, who are faced with dilemmas and are in position, thereby, to judge and act in ways that make a difference. Firms act in socially responsible ways because individuals connected with these businesses, whether they are senior managers, board members, employees, members of community association, choose to act on these matters.

Second, to act responsibly entails acting during specific times in response to the possibilities and constraints of particular situations. The opportunities, burdens, resources and limitations of each situation are unique. Each of the dilemmas reviewed above has its own character and dimensions. To view them broadly either in terms of managing risks or complying with standardized codes is to impose abstractions upon them instead of thinking about them on their own terms; in so doing we run the risk of missing what is really important or decisive.

Third, to exercise judgement responsibly, we must take account of all relevant considerations; multiple factors are always involved, and these may give rise to contradictory claims. This process can either be deliberate, open, inquiring and interactive or it can take place in ways that are restrictive, closed-minded or unreceptive. However, if individuals and groups are to make genuinely responsible choices, they will not be bound by customs and conventions or current economic wisdom; they will consult widely, consider extensively the possibilities and constraints of their situations and explore ways to realize as fully as possible whatever value or interest seems good to them. They would be unwise not to think rationally about their risks. On this basis alone, they are well advised to consult and comply with minimal moral and legal obligations as well as cultural conventions. Therefore, all of these factors must be taken note of, weighed and assigned some kind of priority.

Fourth, to exercise judgement responsibly businesses must pay attention to and converse with their internal and external stakeholders. For a number of reasons, the basic ethical activity of deliberating and acting are appropriately regarded as interactive, conversation-like practices. In order to know what is really going on, we need to engage others and solicit their views and accounts. In order to gain their support and/or active collaboration, we need to respond to their voiced concerns. Only through reciprocating conversations can we arrive at shared understandings of the challenges we face and shared commitments to act.

Fifth, there are good reasons for assigning special importance to the possible good or value that can be realized as a result of our actions. Broadly understood, what firms are expected to do as a result of their business activities, whatever else they do, is to add economic value. They receive or purchase natural and human resources, assets including goodwill, and then utilizing productive processes, they transform these resources and assets so as to add value to goods or services they then sell to others. As they face any dilemma, firms can then appropriately ask whether and how they can act in response to current and long-term exigencies in order to add value in balanced ways to the firms and their constituencies and to the larger society in which they are embedded.

Sixth, if businesses are to act responsibly, and therefore responsively, they must continuously monitor their own practices – not primarily to rate and score themselves but rather as an active commitment to an ongoing review process that invites feedback, learns from successes and shortfalls and fosters renewed commitment to realize both organizational goals and personal objectives.

The chapters in this book were written to provide occasions for learning. They were written neither to celebrate so-called 'best practices' nor to point accusing fingers at particular abuses. Rather, they were written as exercises in monitoring the practices of selected international businesses as they face specific sets of dilemmas in hopes that others – whether managers, policy-makers, NGOs, or students – may draw instructive lessons as they review these cases.

Notes

1. For a discussion of the meaning of 'international businesses', see Introduction, note 1.
2. For various accounts of these developments, see especially Braudel (1981, 1982, 1984), Landes (1998, ch. 13–18), Polanyi (1944) and Weber (1961, parts 3 and 4).
3. To be sure, all businesses and not just those in developing areas face the dilemmas described here. However, for the purpose of this essay I analyse these dilemmas as they are especially experienced by firms in developing areas.
4. The following examples are based on real events. These accounts are based upon confidential interviews, so that the firms involved cannot be identified.
5. The model of responsibility spelled out briefly here in varying degrees reflects the models for an ethics of responsibility developed by H. Richard Niebuhr (1963) and Max Weber (Weber, 1946) as well as models of deliberation developed by Jonsen and Toulmin (1988) and Nussbaum (1986).

References

Akabayashi, H. and Psacharopoulos, G. (1999) 'The Trade Off Between Child Labour and Human Capital Formation: A Tanzanian Case Study', *Journal of Development Studies*, vol. 35, pp. 120–40.

Auty, R. M. (1993) *Sustaining Development in Mineral Economies: The Resource Curse Thesis* (London: Routledge).

Banfield, E. and Wilson, J. Q. (1963) *City Politics* (New York: Vintage).

Basu, K. (1999) 'Child Labour: Causes, Consequences and Cure: with Remarks on International Labour Standards', *Journal of Economic Literature*, vol. xxxvi, pp. 1083–119.

Bessell, S. (1999) 'The Politics of Child Labor in Indonesia; Global Trends and Domestic Policy', *Pacific Affairs*, pp. 353–371.

Bird, F. and Nixon, R. (2004) 'The Raglan Mine and Nunavit Inuit' in F. Bird and S. Herman (eds), *International Businesses and the Challenges of Poverty in the Developing World* (London: Palgrave Macmillan).

Bird, F. (2004) 'Wealth and Poverty in the Niger Delta' in F. Bird and S. Herman (eds), *International Businesses and the Challenges of Poverty in the Developing World* (London: Palgrave Macmillan).

Braudel, F. (1981) *The Structures of Everyday Life: Civilization and Capitalism 15th–18th Century*, vol. 1 (New York: Harper and Row).

Braudel, F. (1982) *The Wheels of Commerce: Civilization and Capitalism, 15th–18th Century*, vol. 2 (New York: Harper and Row).

Braudel, F. (1984) *The Perspective of the World: Civilization and Capitalism 15th–18th Century*, vol. 3 (New York: Harper and Row).

Broad, R. (1988) *Unequal Alliance: The World Bank, the International Monetary Fund and the Philippines* (Berkeley CA: University of California Press).

The Economist (2000) 'China – Another War on Corruption', 22 April, pp. 65–71.

The Economist (2002) 'The Short Arm of the Law: Special Report: Bribery and Business', 2 March, pp. 63–5.

Evans, P. (1979) *Dependent Development: The Alliance of Multinational, State and Local Capital in Brazil* (Princeton, NJ: Princeton University Press).

Friedman, M. (1970) 'The Social Responsibility of Business is to Increase its Profit', *New York Times Magazine*, 13 September, pp. 32–3.

Fuller, L. L. (1964) *The Morality of Law* (New Haven: Yale University Press).

Gagnon, G., Macklin, A. and Simons, P. (2003) *Deconstructing Engagement: Corporate Self-Regulation in Conflicts Zones: Implications for Human Rights and Canadian Public Policy.* A Strategic Joint Initiative of the Social Science and Humanities Research Council and the Law Commission of Canada.

Gillespie, K. (1987) 'Middle East Responses to the U.S. Foreign Corrupt Practices Act', *California Management Review*, vol. xxix(4), pp. 9–30.

Glisson, C. and Durrick, M. (1988) 'Prediction of Job Satisfaction and Organizational Commitment in Human Service Organizations', *Administrative Science Quarterly*, vol. 37, pp. 161–81.

Hodess, R., Banfield, J. and Wolfe, T. (eds) (2001) *Global Corruption Report 2001* (Berlin: Transparency International).

ICCR (1998): The Interfaith Center on Corporate Responsibility, *Principles for Global Corporate Responsibility: Benchmarks for Measuring Business Performance.* In cooperation with the Ecumenical Council for Corporate Responsibility in the United Kingdom and the Taskforce on the Churches and Corporate Responsibility in Canada (New York: ICCR).

Jonsen, A. and Toulmin, S. (1988) *The Abuse of Casuistry: A History of Moral Reasoning* (Berkeley CA: University of California Press).

Kenny, M. L. (1999) 'No Visible Means of Support: Child Labour in Urban Northeast Brazil', *Human Organization*, vol. 5(4), pp. 375–86.

Klein, N. (2000) *No Logo* (London: Flamingo).

Klitgaard, R. (1988) *Controlling Corruption* (Berkeley CA: University of California Press).

Kwong, J. (1997) *The Political Economy of Corruption in China* (New York: M. E. Sharpe).

Landes, D. S. (1998) *The Wealth and Poverty of Nations* (New York: W. W. Norton and Company).

McIntosh, M., Leipziger, D., Jones, K. and Coleman, G. (1998) *Corporate Citizenship: Successful Strategies for Responsible Companies* (London: The Financial Times).

Mowday, R. W., Parker, R. W. and Steers, R. (1982) *Employee – Organizational Linkages: The Psychology of Commitment, Absenteeism and Turnover* (New York: Academic Press).

Niebuhr, H. R. (1963) *The Responsible Self* (New York: Harper and Row).

Nussbaum, M. C. (1986) *The Fragility of Goodness* (Cambridge University Press).

Pellizari, P. (2002) *Conscious Consumption: Corporate Responsibility and Canadian Grocery Giants* (Toronto: EthicScan Canada).

Polanyi, K. (1944) *The Great Transformation: the Political and Economic Origins of Our Times* (Boston: Beacon Press).

Porter, M. E. (1980) *Competitive Strategy* (New York: The Free Press).

Porter, M. E. (1990) *The Competitive Advantage of Nations* (New York: The Free Press).

Queiruz, A. S. and Wood, D. (2003) 'In Search of Theory: Global Standards of Business Conduct,' 2003 Proceedings of the Annual Conference of the international Association of Business and Society.

Reed, D. (2002) 'Employing Normative Stakeholder Theory in Developing Countries: A Critical Theory Perspective', *Business and Society*, vol. 41(2), June, pp. 166–207.

Schoenberger, K. (2000) *Levi's Children: Coming to Terms with Human Rights in the Global Marketplace* (New York: Atlantic Monthly Press).

Sethi, S. P. and Williams, O. F. (2001) *Economic Imperatives and Ethical Values in Global Business: The South African Experience and International Codes Today* (Notre Dame, IN: University of Notre Dame Press).

Smutniak, J. (2004) 'Living Dangerously: A Survey of Risk', *The Economist*, 24 January.

Stern, K. (2002) *Techniques of Independent Monitoring in Guatemala and El Salvador* (New York: Public Report for the Workers Rights Programme of the Lawyers' Committee for Human Rights).

Sub-Commission (2003): Sub-Commission on Promotion and Protection of Human Rights, *Norms on the Responsibilities of Transnational Corporations and Other Business Enterprises with Respect to Human Rights*, United Nations Commission on Human Rights, adopted on 13 August.

Thomas, V., Dailami, M., Dhareshwar, A., Kaufmann, D., Kishor, N. and Wang, Y. (2000) *The Quality of Growth* (The World Bank and Oxford University Press).

Weber, M. (1946) *Essays in Sociology* (New York: Oxford University Press).

Weber, M. (1958) *The Protestant Ethic and the Spirit Of Capitalism* (New York: Charles Scribner's Sons).

Weber, M. (1961) *General Economic History* (New York: Collier-Macmillan).

Wick, I. (2003) *Workers' Tool or PR Ploy: A Guide to International Labour Practices*. (Siueberg, Germany: SUDWIN Institut für Ökonomie und Ökumene).

2
International Businesses in the Political Economy of South Africa

Emmanuel Raufflet

Economic and social challenges in South Africa at the turn of the millennium

In 2003, South Africa ranked twenty-sixth in size among the world's national economies. Its economy is the largest in Africa, with the third-largest gross domestic product per capita; only Mauritius and Botswana, smaller countries, have larger per capita income. At the same time, the distribution of wealth among its population of 45.5 million makes South Africa the second most *unequal* society in the world, ranking only behind Brazil. Almost two-thirds of its labour force earns less than US$250 per month. Unemployment rates stand at about 29 per cent of the labour force. Half of the population lives below the poverty line. These inequalities in turn are key factors associated with indices of social and political instability, including the country's crime rate – one of the highest in the world. While South Africa has the best physical infrastructure in Africa, with its network of roads, ports and airports, these features are not properly distributed. Thirty-five per cent of the economic activity is centred in Gauteng Province, (the region around Johannesburg-Pretoria), where one-fourth of the total population of South Africa lives. Areas that were previously homelands have poor primary and secondary roads, deficient housing and an inadequate physical infrastructure. These inequities are further exacerbated by the fact that South Africa is also one of the world's epicentres for the AIDS pandemic crisis.

Despite its problems, South Africa has become one of the darlings of the international community for its model process of peace and reconciliation in the 1990s following the abolition of institutionalized racial segregation after four and a half decades under the apartheid system (1948–94). The current democratic institutional structure has transformed South Africa from a banned country with an economy under siege into a country of hopes and realization open to international businesses.

South Africa has a dynamic, diverse and internationally connected economy. It hosts large corporations that expand all over Africa and it is a major pole of international investments in Africa. Johannesburg, its main economic and financial centre, qualifies as 'the major economic pole and the only world-level mega-city' in Africa (Bernstein and McCarthy, 2002, p. 9). However, extremely wealthy enclaves coexist with areas characterized by appalling living conditions for large segments of the African population.

In the new South Africa, companies have actively responded to these social, educational, health and economic challenges over the last decade. They are gradually changing their human resources management practices so as to empower black workers and they have been involved in a vast array of corporate social investment programmes. Much can be learned from the creativity of the emerging forms of social investment of national and international businesses in South Africa (Corporate Social Investment Handbook, 2002). In addition, unlike their US counterparts that have favoured voluntary forms of social engagement over state regulated ones, South African and other international businesses have in general accepted the need for a progressive legislative framework for transforming the country into a better and less unequal one. Most businesses recognize that reducing the inequalities and tensions is a central condition for social and economic sustained growth and they have actively engaged in several forms of social investments (Bernstein and McCarthy, 2002).

However, this has not been always so. The social, economic and political record of business – and more particularly multinational enterprises (MNEs) – in South Africa before 1994 is controversial. A central policy document by the African National Congress (ANC) stated that MNEs had played a central role in maintaining the apartheid:

[U]nder the Apartheid system the state co-operated with a handful of conglomerates to shape the economy to benefit a minority of whites at the expense of black people. Economic policy and the main economic actors in industry systematically excluded and hindered black people. (ANC, 1994, p. 75)

To understand how corporations and MNEs got actively involved in addressing South Africa's social injustices since 1994, we must examine the history of their relations with the rest of the country. This chapter examines how businesses – and especially international businesses – have contributed to shaping South African society over the last century. I will first present the formative period, from the discovery of the diamond and gold mines in the interior toward the end of the nineteenth century until after the Second World War (1875–1948). During this period, a segregationist state was created, in which the gold mining lobby, tightly linked with other international businesses, was the most powerful pressure group (Davenport, 1987). Second I will examine how the segregationist regime became more radical and sophisticated, finally evolving into the apartheid system (1948–76). These three decades were an era of sustained economic growth in which large international investments took place simultaneously with the use of sophisticated mechanisms of social and economic exclusion. The third section (1976–94) examines the gradual erosion of the apartheid regime and the increasing challenges faced by South African businesses and MNEs operating in a country under siege. The last section concerns the remarkable transition from apartheid to the new democratic South Africa. I describe the new roles for businesses in this context of reconstruction (1994–2003). For each of the above periods, I examine the social, political and economic conditions and identify the roles of businesses in South African society within that context.

Resource-based corporations and segregation (1875–1948)

The discovery of diamonds at Kimberley in 1875 and huge gold reserves in Gauteng Province in 1886 created a major demand for capital, equipment and consumer products from international sources. While the diamond and gold rush was initially racially mixed and composed of individual entrepreneurs, the influx of major international (mainly British) investments led to the establishment of a few corporations that dominated their respective industries and eliminated small-scale competitors (Davenport, 1987). Cecil Rhodes established the DeBeers Consolidated Mines in 1888, which was funded by a London-based price-fixing syndicate, through which the uncut diamonds had to be marketed (Litvin, 2002; *Ecologist*, 2003). The Anglo Company, established in 1896, controlled the gold industry.

Manufacturing segregation: land and labour monopolies

In 1910, following the two Anglo-Boer Wars (1899–1902) between British settlers in the Cape Colony and Natal province, and the Dutch-speaking Boers or 'Afrikaners' in the independent Transvaal and Orange Free State, the Union of South Africa was established as an independent state with dominion status within the British Empire. The 1910 constitution denied civil rights to native Africans and other non-whites, except for a limited franchise in the Cape Colony (Davenport, 1987; Terreblanche, 2003).

The Native Land Act of 1913 allocated only 7 per cent of national land to Africans, to be extended to 13 per cent in 1936 (*Reader's Digest*, 1989). The remaining 87 per cent was allocated to whites. The Land Act prohibited the purchase or lease of land by Africans except in specified reserves, most often far removed from commercial centres of agriculture. This had two effects. It provided white farmers with large tracts of the most fertile lands. As well, it contributed to making large segments of the black African population landless and deprived of livelihood opportunities. To support their families, large numbers of African men were then forced to join the ranks of the migrant labourers who toiled in mines, often under brutal conditions. Others were forced to move their families onto white-owned farms, where they would become indentured workers. Millions of African women served as domestic workers in white households. While the Land Act forced Africans from their traditional lands into urban areas in search of livelihood opportunities, the Labour Act (1913) centralized the control of corporations, such as large international mining companies, over African labour supply. Aimed at avoiding competition between corporations for human labour, the Act limited the possibility for black workers to work in different mining companies. Reducing the mobility of black labour from one company to another limited labour costs for business (Hull, 1990, p. 67). Last, in the 1920s and 1930s, a number of laws further restricted the rights and mobility of Africans (Worden, 1994). Africans were assigned rights to land and some measure of self-government within the ten homelands, which covered seven per cent of the most often poorest and most remote land areas of South Africa. Different reserves were generally assigned to distinct African peoples like the Zulu, Xhosa, Pedi and others (Davenport, 1987, p. 256).

During this period the economy of South Africa greatly expanded, based on wealth created by manufacturing, agriculture and, above all, the mining industry (especially gold, diamonds, platinum, manganese, chrome, etc.). While capital came from Britain, mining expertise and technology was often imported from the US. Firms such as General Electric, Ingersoll and Westinghouse, already leading players on the US market, created subsidiaries in South Africa at the end of the nineteenth century. Cash registers, cameras, sewing machines and many other 'high tech' consumer goods of the time were also imported from the US (Hull, 1990, p. 70).

Reactions inside and outside

Various groups within South Africa attempted to oppose or reform the overall system of segregation. The African National Congress (ANC) was first formed in 1912 and adopted a non-violent orientation. After the 1913 Natives Land Act was passed, ANC leaders went to Britain to ask the government to intervene. Britain responded that the matter was internal to South Africa, as it was an independent country – even though the largest corporations that dominated the South African landscape were British and gold was maintained at a stable price on the London Stock Exchange (Davenport, 1987).

However, some tensions between the need for steady labour in urban areas and the policy of segregation arose. While companies expected a steady supply of African labour, several white groups were reluctant to accept permanent settlements of the African population in the white-only urban areas. The initial scheme was to have African workers migrate for a period of 6 to 18 months to mining areas, while maintaining their families in the rural areas, in order to prevent Africans from settling permanently in the cities, and to keep urban areas predominantly white. By the 1930s this was evolving into more permanent African urban settlements such as Alexandria and Orlando. The population living in the area near to the mining areas of Johannesburg was estimated to be around 400 000 in 1939. One of the aims of The Urban Land Act in the 1930s was to keep urban areas in the hands of the whites – and to allow blacks into these areas only for purposes of accommodating white needs.[1]

This policy was translated into the Natives Urban Act legislated in 1923 and amended in 1930, 1937, 1944, 1952, 1957, 1964 and 1971. This Act aimed to clear out Africans from mixed residential areas located in the outskirts of large towns, and re-house them further out of the towns (Davenport, 1987, p. 548).

Beginning in late nineteenth century, international corporations contributed to building long lasting mechanisms of oppression of the African population that ensured them a steady labour supply. They also produced inequalities between white and black workers in income and in access to training and management positions (Davenport, 1987; ANC, 1994; Litvin, 2002; Terreblanche, 2003). Many years later, Cole (1967) highlights the differences in salaries between African and white workers:

> [An African worker] would work nine or ten hours a day, six days a week and his starting pay would be forty-six American cents a day (in 1967). The most he could look forward to, after many years in the mines in the highest grade he could attain, was $38, one-sixth of the beginning pay for novice white miners. (p. 24)

Apartheid and the Nationalist Era (1948–76)

Economy and society

In 1948, after a brief post-war recession, the Nationalist Party formed the government, and set about transforming the segregation system into the more complete system of apartheid – a complex mechanism of exclusion and segregation enacted through more than 150 pieces of legislation. H. F. Verwoerd, the National Party leader, minister of Native Affairs (1950–58) and prime minister (1958–66), justified these acts with the rationale that:

> There is no place for the African man in the European community above the level of certain forms of labour. For that reason it is of no avail for him to receive a training which has as its aim the absorption in the European community. (Cole, 1967, p. 96)

These mechanisms for apartheid included restrictions to mobility in professions, restrictions to labour and civil rights and the creation of the Bantustans or 'homelands'. Transkei, the first of the Bantustans, was established by the South African government in 1962. None of these reserves, made up of broken, poor-quality land, were economically viable (Davenport, 1987). In addition, the policies such as the Native Urban Land Act continued to restrict settlements in urban areas. Separate education systems were created for whites and Africans. Africans and non-whites were restricted to certain types of jobs; Africans were prevented from occupying managerial and professional positions. Black trade unions were outlawed. Restrictions to mobility for blacks increased dramatically. Blacks were moved away from white urban areas, or authorized to enter 'white-only' urban areas only with identity passes and at specific hours. The status of Bantustans as black-only areas was strengthened, which later, in 1970, through the Bantu Homelands Citizenship Act, culminated in declaring four of the homelands – Transkei, Cicsei, Venda and Bophthatswana – nominally independent states. This act was viewed by most blacks as a move to deprive 8 million people of South African citizenship.

Separate education systems were established in order to create an African population 'groomed to serve as hewers of wood and drawers of water' (Terreblanche, 2003) through the imposition of an ideology that sought to impose an internalized relationship of domination and subordination upon African students, inducing them to thus accept restrictions to professional training and exclusion from the private white universities. State investment per student was four times larger for whites than for Africans (Terreblanche, 2003).

In response to the Afrikaner government's radicalization of the system, the ANC itself became more radical. In its Freedom Charter in 1955, it called for an end to all forms of segregation and discrimination, a democratic vote and an active role for the state in overcoming inequalities. The Pan-African Congress (PAC), an even more militant organization, was formed and in 1960 staged a demonstration in Sharpesville against the pass laws; a riot ensued and 70 people were killed, mainly children and women. The government then moved to ban the ANC, PAC and the Communist Party. In response, these organizations pursued their goals either from outside South Africa or through underground organizations, which were committed to meeting the threat of violence with violence. In 1963 a number of ANC leaders, including Nelson Mandela, were arrested and later imprisoned. Even Verwoerd's assassination in 1966 caused no major discontinuity in the policies of apartheid (Davenport, 1987, p. 407).

While these political developments were taking place, the South African economy was greatly expanding in all of its major business sectors: state-owned corporations, South African private-sector firms and MNEs. New state-owned South African corporations such as ESKOM, ISCOR, IDC emerged as important players in the nation. In the 1960s, economic growth increased from an average of 4 per cent in the 1950s to 5.9 per cent, rivalling that of Japan. This economic expansion attracted foreign investments, which increased five-fold between 1958 and 1963. Hundreds of British,

European and American firms invested in South Africa's manufacturing and service sectors. This marked economic expansion had several consequences. It raised the standard of living of the country, but on grossly unequal terms between whites and blacks. In 1960, the average African miner earned US$196, while the white miner earned US$3214 – 16 times more than the black worker (Lipton, 1985).

These economic and social changes also modified the demographic profile of the country. While South Africa attracted a number of North Atlantic immigrants to the urban areas where industries were expanding, an ever-larger number of blacks had moved to areas around the large cities to live permanently in shantytowns – some larger than the white-only cities themselves.

Life in the mines, meanwhile, had remained virtually unchanged since the turn of the twentieth century. Ernest Cole's *The House of Bondage* (1967) describes the working conditions of life of miners employed by international companies in the 1960s (p. 22):

> The [South African] mines produce about seventy per cent of the world's supply of gold. ... The work of mining the gold – and three tons of earth from shafts two miles deep must be sifted to yield one ounce – falls entirely to Africans. Twenty-four hours a day, six days a week, half a million Africans are at work in the earth. Of course, the mining companies also employ many whites, but all in supervisory capacities. Even those working underground and designated as miners, never touch picks or shovels or drilling machines. ... Recruits from all points are brought to the tremendous Witwatersrand Native Labour Association main depot in Johannesburg. Here they are processed and assigned to the mines where they will work for the duration of their contract.

Above ground, the migrant workers' living conditions were scarcely better (p. 23):

> The miners are quartered in long, brick-walled structures with corrugated iron roofs. They live twenty to a room that measures eighteen by twenty-five feet. Each man has a concrete cubicle, the slab floor of which is his bed. What little furniture the common room contains – a few rough wooden tables and benches – is made by the occupants. Threadbare tunics and trousers hang about; it is a jungle of clothes. The most privacy a man can get is to hang a blanket in front of his bunk.

Cole highlights the links between poverty in the homelands and work in the mines of the Gauteng as well as the cost in health and human lives (p. 24):

> The majority of miners re-enlist when their contracts are up. Poor as mine living is, for these men, it is even poorer at home. One will tell you: 'I'll

be going home when the drought ends.' But it never does and life in the mine goes on. Finally, there are the men who never reach their contracts' end. They are the unlucky victims of mine accidents or phthisis, a deadly and so far incurable disease of the lungs, which is prevalent among South African miners.

Volatile times: the erosion of apartheid (1976–94)

The year 1976 was a turning point in the apartheid era. Students in Soweto (South Western Township), a black shantytown near Johannesburg, rebelled against a decree requiring black youth to learn Afrikaans. As a result several hundred were killed in brutal police repression. The picture of Lulu Peterson, age 14, holding his younger brother Hector who had just been killed by the police travelled the world. After the first student protest, between 1976 and 1977, more than 700 blacks – including 85 youth and children – were killed by the military and police forces in the Soweto uprising (Beinart, 2001). The subsequent banning of many black organizations and the murder of the charismatic leader Steve Biko while in detention in 1977 increased the pressure of international public opinion against the regime increasingly perceived as brutal and morally unjustifiable. Massive demonstrations on university campuses and in front of South African diplomatic missions worldwide pressured international governments to react (Beinart, 2001).

However, the events of 1976 were only the tip of the iceberg – symptoms of a far deeper social and economic crisis. After almost 30 years of interrupted growth, South Africa in the mid-1970s entered a period of structural crisis, characterized by stagnant output, high inflation, weak exports, a weakened currency, low reserves, low savings and increasingly high unemployment. Growth fell from an average of 5.9 per cent in the 1960s to 3.3 per cent in the 1970s (*The Economist*, 1989). According to Iliffe (1999), the causes of this economic crisis stemmed from the contradictions the model of 'racial Fordism' was going through:

> [M]ass production of consumer goods for an internal market [was] so limited by the unequal racial distribution of income that production and unemployment could only expand further by drawing in imports for which South Africa's small, protected and uncompetitive manufacturing sector could not pay. (p. 98)

A volatile era

The era following the Soweto uprising in 1976–77 was characterized by cycles of repression and relaxation between the government and the opposition groups (Lipton, 1985). During the 1980s the political, economic and social situation in South Africa became more volatile. The government sent signals that it was moving towards a gradual political opening. A new constitution introduced in 1983 increased political powers for the 'coloured' and Asian population, an attempt to co-opt non-African groups. Already in 1979 it had removed restrictions against black businesses and recognized black unions as negotiating bodies. It also abolished reservations of specific jobs for whites. By 1986 it was evident that, in the words of Van den Berg (undated, p. 10) '... countervailing power of the black trade unions has set limits to the power of both the state and large conglomerates'. As for individual rights, blacks were allowed more freedom of movement. After decades of non-official activities, the Congress of South African Trade Unions (COSATU) was recognized as negotiating body in 1979 at a time when the ANC, as a political party, was still banned. The unions led a general strike in 1989 in which more than 3 million workers participated. This labour unrest began to threaten the stability of the entire socio-economic system (Davenport, 1987, p. 538).

What made these gradual changes more challenging was the poor economic performance of the country. From 1975 to 1990, the South African GDP per capita fell by 15 per cent. The labour force grew by 3.9 million (1975–88), while official employment figures rose by only 900 000. The economic decline resulted in a drop in living standards, particularly for the most deprived. Amid increasing unemployment and poverty, the government was faced with growing restraints on its resources (Van der Berg, p. 4). As a consequence of this tense political, economic and social situation, in the late 1980s both sides became more militant. In July 1985 the government passed emergency legislation, proclaimed in 36 magisterial districts, and subsequently extended to Cape Town in October 1985 (Beinart, 2001).

Divestment strategies and the Sullivan Principles

The 1976 riots and their aftermath put the situation of South Africa at the centre stage of world media attention. Pressures started to be exerted on international firms with investments in South Africa. In the 1970s, international organizations such as the United Nations General Assembly, the International Labour Organization, the Organization of African Unity and the World Council of Churches condemned the apartheid regime and called upon countries with economic interests in South Africa to withdraw (Schmidt, 1989, p. 4). Under these pressures, various countries, such as the UK in 1977, followed by the other eight countries from the European Common Market and Canada in 1978, adopted principles and rules of conduct for their companies operating under the apartheid regime (Schmidt, 1989, p. 90).

In response to this pressure, some international businesses in South Africa opted for divestment strategies, that is the withdrawal of capital or the selling-off of shares for ethical rather than for 'purely' economic reasons (Schmidt, 1989, p. 215).[2] Others withdrew by ceasing operations. Advocates of divestment (including universities and pension fund organizations, as well as private investors) argued that it was wrong to maintain economic relations with a country whose economy was built upon state-enforced exploitation of black labour: withdrawal of funds from companies exploiting this labour would lead to the economic collapse of South Africa, thus creating the conditions for rapid social and political change. MNEs based in the United States came under particular criticism as major supporters of the apartheid regime, which they provided with capital and technology that it could not supply on its own. At the same time, however, their effects on black empowerment were relatively limited, since US companies directly employed only 1 to 2 per cent of the total black labour force (p. 211). Divestment, it was argued, would therefore have a major impact on the South African regime but a relatively minor impact on employment opportunities for the black population.

A second strategy for international firms consisted of adopting principles and rules of conduct for South African operations. It was hoped that this strategy would gradually introduce necessary changes. Beginning in 1977, a group of companies led by GM, Union Carbide and Mobile Oil sought to introduce a set of reforms to limit and to overcome the impact of apartheid within their businesses. They were guided by a set of principles, which were developed by the Rev. Leon Sullivan, a member of the GM Board of Directors. By 1980 more than 140 US companies had agreed to abide by the Sullivan Principles:

- Equal and fair employment practices for all employees;
- Equal pay for all employees doing equal or comparable work for the same period of time;
- Initiation and development of training programmes that will prepare, in substantial numbers, black and other non-whites for supervisory, administrative, clerical and technical jobs;
- Increasing the number of blacks and nonwhites in supervisory positions;
- Improving the quality of employees' lives outside the work environment in such areas as housing, transportation, schooling, recreation and health facilities (Leape *et al.*, 1989, pp. 217–18).

The programme was dissolved in 1994. After 1994, many major financial supporters and funding sources decided to fund South African government-led projects rather than NGO initiatives or the Sullivan project (Sethi and Williams, 2001, p. 399).

Rev. Sullivan considered these principles as a living document that would evolve as companies gradually expanded their efforts toward reform. His approach had two features. First, it proposed a gradual strategy for transforming corporations into agents of social change in South Africa. Corporations would contribute to shaping a society in which 'all South Africans would not only vote, but also have jobs' (Sethi and Williams, 2001, p. 384) and would use their economic influence with the South African government to accelerate political reforms, while increasing livelihood opportunities for black communities (p. 390). He thus expected the actions based on these principles to expand in scope as all participating signatories gained experience, ultimately shifting their actions from the economic to the political arena. The second feature of the Principles was to propose an assessment of corporate efforts through an independent and external monitoring scheme. The Arthur D. Little consulting firm did take on the task of monitoring. This monitoring was essentially qualitative and group-oriented. More than 150 companies were grouped into three broad categories, without being publicly disclosed on an individual basis, and no companies were identified individually in terms of their efforts to comply (Sethi and Williams, 2001, p. 397). Over 17 years, between 1977 and 1993, more than 150 US signatories spent US$300 million in South Africa to comply with the Sullivan Principles in a system free of scandals (Sethi and Williams, 2001, p. 383).

Two opposite views on the Sullivan Principles

Critics contended that the Sullivan Principles represented a 'corporate camouflage that gilds the prison' (Schmidt, 1989, p. 95). They argued that the Sullivan Principles assumed a trickle-down effect by which the need to maintain conditions for the creation of economic wealth would gradually benefit the least favoured segments of the population. They noted that the economic abundance that the South African economy had created so far had not been accompanied by redistribution; while South Africa's GNP had grown over the previous decades, inequalities between whites and blacks had actually increased. They further argued that as US firms were mainly present in capital-intensive sectors and brought capital, technical innovation and expertise to the regime, these benefits had been instrumental in the past to the regime's maintenance and expansion (p. 12). Lastly, they argued that the Sullivan principles aimed to create a black middle class that would be closer to the white minority and would have interests different from those held by the excluded black majority of the population (pp. 83–4):

> The Sullivan reforms and similar government initiatives measures serve to strengthen, rather than minimize, the divisions within the non-white population. They are helping to create a mass of non-whites with a vested interest in the reformed system, a stake of society that will make its members 'natural' allies of the white-controlled political and economic structures.

Advocates of the Sullivan Principles identified some benefits. Although Sullivan expected a shift in the role of corporations from economic agents to social change agents, they did retain an economic agenda. According to Sethi and Williams (2001, p. 383), 'they saw compliance with the Principles as a means of limiting external pressures on the companies to withdraw from South Africa'. But corporations remained reluctant to be assessed by non-economic criteria, particularly ethical ones. That said, one of the concrete side-benefits of the Sullivan Principles was to raise the issue of black labour and to increase shareholders' information on the topic. It also provided a monitored and measurable benchmark for affirmative actions enacted in the 1995 Employment Act (p. 221). Furthermore, the application of the Sullivan Principles has gradually increased the legitimacy of the demands for increased social justice embodied in the codes. As Williams writes (p. xv) 'the fact remains that the legitimacy of these demands is now accepted by all sides. Debate has accordingly shifted to the content and implementation of these codes'. Although the programme of the Sullivan Principles was dissolved in South Africa in 1994 many companies carried on reporting their investment and performance on employee and workplace practices.

While many US corporations signed the Sullivan Principles, many others divested. National pressures on the apartheid regime gradually changed the origin of the investments; over these years of intense international pressures and debates, the share of US investments increased vis-à-vis the share of European ones. European firms seem to have retrenched more than US firms. Investments from the then nine members of the EEC declined from 66 per cent of the overall international investments in South Africa in 1973 to 56 per cent in 1981, while US investments rose from 17 to 23 per cent of the total, according to the South Africa Reserve Bank (Sethi and Williams, 2001, p. 400). Altogether, several hundred firms from North Atlantic countries withdrew their investments, most leaving in the years after 1986 (Mutambirwa, 1989).

Building the new South Africa: post-apartheid (1994–2003)

A new government formed by F. W. De Klerk in 1989 began a series of moves to end apartheid and institute democratic reforms. The government legalized the ANC and other opposition groups in February 1990 and freed political prisoners, including Nelson Mandela, who had been in detention for 27 years. In 1992, De Klerk, with a firm mandate for change obtained in a white-only election, began to dismantle the apartheid laws and eventually worked with the ANC to create a transitional government. A new constitution was prepared and adopted. This constitution abolished the homelands, divided the country into nine provinces and established democratic elections.

A rapprochement occurred between moderate ANC leaders and progressive business leaders. It set the parameters of the new post-apartheid economic model. On the one hand, the ANC softened its left wing political position and its plans for the economic future of South Africa. At its 1992 Congress, the party officially renounced the creation of a state-planned economy and the implementation a socialist state it had formerly professed.[3] Two factors explain this radical change from a socialist to a market economic model. First, the ANC leadership received strong opposition to their economic ideas from domestic and international business. Nationalization, businesses argued, would be accomplished only at a prohibitive cost: there would be high opportunity costs for the government, problems in retaining skilled and experienced personnel and inhibition of foreign investment. Furthermore, the collapse of state-led and centrally planned economies in Eastern Europe and the failures of most state-led economic experiments elsewhere in Africa had dampened enthusiasm for a strong state-planned economy. On the other hand, the business community recognized that social justice was a precondition for economic stability; even hard line supporters of the free enterprise model came to agree that racial inequality and poverty were detrimental to economic progress in South Africa. The threat of renewed labour unrest finally persuaded political and business leaders alike to reach consensus. The debate, initially framed in ideological terms – state-planned versus market economy – gradually shifted towards what Draper (1991, p. 23) called a debate over strategies of economic growth: increasing the gross national product first, followed by policies of redistribution, versus redistributing wealth as a means to achieve growth.

At the political level, this transition period faced some moments of tension before the 1994 election. The main challenge to this rapprochement between ANC and De Klerk's National Party came from the extremist parties on both sides of the political spectrum. On the one hand was the Inkatha Freedom Party (IKP), the right-wing ruling party in KwaZulu Homeland, which had been engaged in an unofficial war with the left-wing ANC since the mid-1980s. This party fuelled violence in the KwaZulu region as well as in townships around Johannesburg and Pretoria, which led to some hundreds of deaths in 1994–95. On the other side, the Afrikaner-only 'Weerstandbeweging' resistance movement led by Eugène Terreblanche, marginalized in the 1994 elections, attempted to create an Afrikaner-only, separate state. Terreblanche was eventually convicted of crime and jailed in 2000.

The elections of April 1994 were a success for the reconciliation process. First, both Mandela's ANC and De Klerk's National Party (NP) received large support: 60 per cent for the ANC and 23 per cent for the NP. Nor did the election bring the violence that some had feared. A new government was elected in April 1994. The ANC, led by the newly elected president Nelson Mandela, had become the dominant party. In February 1997, the new Constitution came into force. The 1999 general election again supported the ANC, and Thabo Mbeki replaced Nelson Mandela as president.

New country, old challenges

The new South Africa faced the problem of seeking to reduce inequalities and promote economic growth at the same time. It also faced strongly held and differing views about how these objectives ought best to be pursued. One constraint was that South Africa is an internationally connected economy; the new government therefore had to maintain a fine balance between enhancing its capacity to attract investments while decreasing inequalities and increasing access to education, employment and health services among the least favoured sections of the population. This challenge was aggravated by high levels of violence and the HIV/AIDS pandemics that erupted in the mid-1990s.

Access to employment, professional positions and wages particularly affected black youth. In 1993, only 4.5 per cent of the economically active white population were unemployed compared to 38 per cent of Africans. While one out of two white workers had a highly skilled job such as manager, professional or technician, only 7 per cent of Africans had reached such a professional level. Lacking skills and access to professional positions, African male workers earned about 20 per cent of a white male worker's average wage (Rosbape, 2002, p. 203).

Levels of violence were especially acute in the urban Gauteng Province (which includes the Johannesburg and Pretoria regions) and in Cape Town. A World Health Organization study in 1995 showed that SA had the highest rate of violent crime in the world. Fortunately, this figure has been recently declining (*The Economist*, 2003a, p. 17).[4]

The problem of HIV/AIDS continues. It is estimated that between 2.5 million (Ministry of Health) and 4.5 million (UN-AIDS) South Africans are HIV-positive (*The Economist*, 2001, p. 8). One out of seven workers in South Africa is HIV positive (*The Economist*, 2003b). It is estimated that some companies will lose between 40 and 50 per cent of their workforce in the next 10 years. In the mining sector, one of four workers is HIV positive. While the problem affects South African families, communities and businesses on a widespread level, governments have long not addressed the problem. After years of slowly mounting pressure, the cabinet eventually decided to publish a national HIV/AIDS plan by the end of September 2003 outlining how the government is to provide anti-retroviral drugs to the general population through the public health system (*The Economist*, 2003b).

In mid-November 2003, the cabinet finally approved an outline of its plan to provide anti-retroviral drugs for those infected by HIV/AIDS. The key aims of the government plan are to provide a comprehensive HIV and AIDS care and treatment point in each of the country's health districts before the end of the first year of the plan. All South Africans and permanent residents will have equal access to comprehensive care and treatment of HIV/AIDS within five years. In particular, all individuals requiring treatment for AIDS (1.4 million people) will have comprehensive care by 2009. Finally, the plan proposes a major upgrade of the health care system, including the recruitment of substantial numbers of new healthcare professionals. About 50 per cent of the new expenditures will be in this area.

Meanwhile, added to the problems of adjustments in the 1990s was the emigration of large segments of the skilled labour force, especially among whites, Indians and the coloured population. Most of these emigrants migrated to Australia, New Zealand, the US, Canada and the UK. This out-migration further sharpened South Africa's shortage of skilled labour (*The Economist*, 2003a, p. 20).

South Africa continues to be faced by the problems caused by the apartheid policies and conflicts between national groups. The Truth and Reconciliation Commission (TRC), inspired and led by Bishop Desmond Tutu, heard many stories of the brutality of the Apartheid Regime and offered some catharsis to communities and individuals shattered by their past. The TRC operated by allowing victims to tell their stories and perpetrators to confess their guilt; amnesty was proposed for full and truthful revelation of information about the relevant human rights violations (Daye, 2004).[5]

Economic and social policies

The new government adopted a strategy of embracing an open free-market economy while bringing about change in the workplace. In pursuing these changes it has relied on forums and consensus-building mechanisms (Daye, 2004, p. 8). Its economic policies were enacted shortly after the elections of 1994. They followed the Reconstruction and Development Programme. The programme aimed (1) to create a strong, dynamic and balanced economy in order to eliminate poverty and meet the basic needs of every South African; (2) to develop the human-resource capacities of all South Africans by ensuring that no one suffers racial or gender discrimination in hiring, promotion or training situations, while (3) developing a prosperous and balanced regional economy in Southern Africa and (4) integrating the South African economy into the global arena. The RDP was replaced by the macro-economic Growth, Employment and Redistribution strategy, based on the International Monetary Fund's austerity measures. This programme aimed to create 400 000 jobs annually between 1995 and 2000 so as to alleviate unemployment (Calitz, 2002).

The social policies launched by the ANC-led government have rarely been radical or dramatic. Efforts have been made to alleviate poverty, including broad initiatives in housing, education, health care, water services and other social-service areas. However, these programmes suffer from a lack of funding, as the government has been reluctant to increase corporate income taxes or private taxes. A number of legislative initiatives have been made to deal with inequality in the workplace.[6]

1. The Labour Relations Act of 1995 facilitates worker participation and decision-making in the workplace. It entrenches the right to strike, encourages sectoral and enterprise collective bargaining and clarifies the

law on unfair dismissals and information disclosure, as well as introducing workplace forums and new mechanisms for dispute resolution.

2. The Basic Conditions of Employment Act of 1997 provides for a 45-hour working week, with 40 hours as a long-term goal, four months maternity leave with full pay, maximum overtime of three hours a day and 10 hours a week and Sunday work to be paid at double the normal rate.

3. The Competition Act of 1998 provides for the establishment of a competition commission, tribunal and appeal court, which would regulate mergers and investigate restrictive practices and the abuse of dominant market positions by companies.

4. The Employment Equity Act of 1998 aims to accelerate the hiring, training and promotion of people from disadvantaged groups. Designated employers (employing 50 people or more, or with a turnover above a specified level) must implement plans to achieve equitable representation of the demographics of South Africa. Such affirmative-action programmes focus on achieving representation, redressing disadvantages and developing a more diverse management culture. Furthermore, business is to follow the lead of the public service in increasing the numbers of black managers, of women in middle and senior management and of disabled people in their employment. Instead of compulsory affirmative-action quotas, a system of incentives was introduced for private sector companies to promote employment equity.

5. The National Empowerment Fund Act of 1998 provides for the establishment of a national empowerment fund to assist historically disadvantaged persons by supporting business ventures, facilitating share ownership in privatised state assets and private enterprises and encouraging investment, savings and meaningful economic participation. Supplementing these objectives was the Promotion of Equality and Prevention of Unfair Discrimination Bill, tabled in Parliament in October 1999.

6. The Mineral and Petroleum Resource Development Bill (June 2002). This legislation backed by the government and supported by black empowerment groups, CONASU and various left-wing political parties, aims to pass 'good quality ore currently in the hands of the big mining corporations into black hands' (*The Economist*, 2003b, p. 6). This bill will include specific percentage black empowerment targets on the ownership of the national ore reserves.

New roles and responses of international businesses

The efforts of corporations to contribute toward addressing these challenges have been manifold. They include philanthropic activities including grant-making and investments; addressing organizational level issues, such as employee and workplace practices; market-based approaches, such as procurement and outsourcing opportunities to least-favoured segments of the population; and leadership and policy advocacy, such as the advancement of the inter-firm actions to fight poverty beyond actions pertaining to the internal dimensions of the firm's activities, such as human resources policies – as distinct from external actions, such as community investments. Examples of these actions include the publication of the *Corporate Social Investment Handbook* (2002), which reviews projects led and organized by corporations in order to address the challenges that South African society is facing. Corporate social investments range from creating universities for Africans to aiding projects for communities stricken by HIV/AIDS. Many of these corporate efforts are conducted through employee involvement.

A specific example of market-based approaches to resolving inequities is illustrated by a programme adopted by ESKOM, the national energy utility company. It has been attempting to improve black access to the utility's procurement programme. Between 1997 and 2001, the level of procurement of coal from mainly black-owned Small Medium and Micro-Enterprises (SMMEs) was raised from R 200 million to R 1.8 billion, representing about 20 per cent of the total procurement in coal for the whole company (Mangaliso and Nkomo, 2001). The City Centre University, Community Individual Development Association (CIDA), is another example of innovation in the South African corporate social investment landscape. Established in 1999, CIDA provides professional training for black youth deprived of access to higher education, by channelling corporate support in various forms such as donations in kind (computers, equipment, food, books, clothing and materials); participation in building infrastructure both for academic facilities such as office space and residential buildings; providing financial support for teachers and lecturers, tutors and mentors. While it costs about US$100 000 to train a student in the US, it only costs US$1000 to sponsor a student for a full 4-year degree, including books and materials, on the CIDA campus. In 4 years, CIDA has trained 1400 students, fully supported by several international and South African corporations (KPMG, 2002).

Unlike the North American context, there is a strong consensus about South African corporate social efforts and affirmative-action programmes. Rossow (1997) asserts: 'It is accepted by government and business that affirmative action should be implemented as a means of addressing the imbalances that the apartheid regime produced' (p. 1541). According to the *Corporate Social Investment Handbook* (2003), 'Businesses should be proactive in these affirmtive-action campaigns both with their own initiatives and by supporting the government in positive actions' (p. 131). In all, there is a sense of need to 'give back' in the business community to the South African society.

Two unresolved issues

Two issues concerning international businesses remain unresolved in post-apartheid South Africa. The first concerns the proper way to address the past. If there is consensus that businesses were instrumental in creating and sustaining the apartheid system, some argue that the legacies left by corporations in the current South Africa remain an open issue and should be settled in the form of reparations. The second issue concerns the pace and the course of national social and economic policies. There is a growing awareness that the post-apartheid government policies and corporate efforts are important, but not sufficient to reduce significantly, let alone eliminate, poverty.

While the Truth and Reconciliation Commission process has been praised by many as a remarkable achievement for the construction of New South Africa, some argue that the TRC dealt almost entirely with the apartheid regime, while sparing international businesses from claims for reparations. These critics note that MNEs played a pivotal role in the creation and the maintenance of the regime for decades; yet in 3 years of TRC hearings, only four days were devoted to the role played by these businesses. In all, the reparation programme of the TRC regarding businesses has not achieved its goals (Daye, 2004).

The Khulumani Support Group, a national organization of about 30 000 members with headquarters in Johannesburg, which assists victims of apartheid violence, has led a court action seeking reparations for the various acts of violence (including murder and sexual assault) inflicted on its members by the South African police and paramilitary groups supported by the regime during the apartheid years. In September 2002 two lawsuits in the US against corporations that worked with apartheid were initiated: one against financial institutions and one against multinationals at large. A lawsuit was filed in 2002 'on behalf of victims of state-sanctioned torture, murder, rape, arbitrary detention and inhumane treatment', by the Khulumani support group.[7] 'These firms knowingly propped up the apartheid state and made huge profits by doing so', according to Jubilee spokesman Neville Gabriel. These lawsuits are currently being heard in South Africa and in US courts (*The Economist*, 2004).

The second issue concerns the pace and content of social, economic policies since 1994. An important question remains unresolved: will the current policy options – a diminished role for the state, support a free-market economy, integration with international markets and encouragement of corporate social investments – be sufficient to address the blatant inequalities that still affect the country?

On the one hand, much has been achieved. The new legislation has been generally well accepted by different constituencies. Within 6 years, non-whites have come to dominate the legislative and administrative branches of government at all levels and progress is being made at making the bureaucracy representative of the population at all levels of seniority. However, the accession of coloured persons, Indians and especially Africans to senior positions in the private sector is happening at a much slower pace. For a total population of 75 per cent African, 9 per cent coloured, 2.5 per cent Indian and 10 per cent white, about 85 per cent of the country's senior managers are still white[8] in 2001. The government has also allocated resources to supply the basic needs of the most deprived segments of the population. Since 1994, more than 9 million people have gained access to clean water and 1.5 millions households have gained access to electricity (*The Economist*, 2001, p. 4). Redistribution of land has been initiated. The objective is to redistribute 30 per cent of South Africa's farmland by 2014. However, between 1994 and the end of 2000, only 0.81 per cent had been transferred to blacks (*The Economist*, 2001, p. 5). At this pace, the targets of land redistribution for 2030 might be achieved by 2080 at the earliest.

Other critics argue that political transformation, though remarkable and necessary, is not of itself sufficient condition for fighting poverty. According to Terreblanche (2003), the share of the poorest 40 per cent of households in the national income dropped from 5.2 per cent in 1975 to 3.8 per cent in 1991 and from 3.4 per cent in 1996 to 3.3 per cent in 2001 (p. 33).[9] Terreblanche flatly states (p. 39):

> The notion that the benefits of market-driven economic growth will 'trickle down' to the poor is a fiction. Without aggressive redistributive intervention by the government on their behalf, the poorest will remain trapped in a situation of pauperization.

As for corporate efforts, despite being numerous and innovative, they are not sufficient to eradicate poverty. A study conducted by the Centre for Development and Enterprise, in 1998, noted that for 100 Rand of after-tax profit, the major corporate sector generated R 280 in wages, salaries and benefits, R118 in export earnings, R118 in investments of all types and R69 in taxes, Corporate Social Investment (CSI) funding represented a mere R1.30 (Corporate Social Investment Handbook, 2003). Such figures cast serious doubts on the ability of corporate social investment to address the continuing social inequality issues in South Africa.

Acknowledgement

I am grateful to Frederick Bird, Russell Daye, Elize Kotze and Kobus Kotze for preparing research notes that I used in writing this chapter.

Notes

1. R. F. A. Herlé, professor of philosophy at University of Wiwatersrand, Johannesburg in the 1930s and 1940s, a pivotal figure in the development of South African thought, distinguished between 'segregation' and 'separation' in the following way: 'Segregation … is most perfectly realised in a multi-racial caste society. Separation, falsely called "segregation", is most perfectly realised when the

different racial groups are sorted out into their own territorially distinct societies' (Davenport, 1987, p. 542).

2. Divestment, the withdrawal of capital as a matter of principle, is not to be confused with disinvestment – the reduction of capital investment based on a decision either to realize invested assets or else not replace depleted capital goods. Effects of the anti-apartheid divestment campaign were often measured in terms of the funds withdrawn from foreign companies operating in South Africa.

3. I am grateful to Professor Kobus Kotze of the University of Stellenbosch for the information necessary for these paragraphs.

4. There were fewer murders in 1999 than in 1994, and most are economically motivated; the political violence that erupted in the early 1990s has been reduced. Of the three non-political forms of crime – violent crime, social-fabric crime and property crime – most crimes are in the first two categories; property crimes have decreased.

5. For a complete evaluation of the TRC, see Daye (2004). I am especially thankful to Russell Daye for his comments on a previous version of this chapter.

6. I am grateful to Professor Elize Kotze of the University of Stellenbsoch for the information provided here on new legislation.

7. Financial institutions listed in the suit include the Swiss banks Credit Suisse and UBS; Deutsche Bank and Dresdner Bank (Germany); Barclays Bank (UK); and Citigroup and JP Morgan Chase (US). The suit also names the oil firms Exxon Mobil; Shell, Total, Caltex and BP; the car makers DaimlerChrysler, Ford and General Motors; the computer giant IBM; the electronics firms ICL and Fujitsu; and the Rio Tinto mining group.

8. Terreblanche (2003) identifies the dynamics of disrupted social structures and poverty as '(1) high and rising levels of unemployment in a sluggish economy; (2) deeply institutionalized inequalities in the distribution of power, property and opportunities between whites and the black elite and the poorest half of the pop-ulation; (3) disrupted and fragmented social structures and the syndrome of chronic community poverty among the poorest 50 per cent of the population; and (4) the mutually reinforcing dynamics of violence, criminality and ill-health on the one hand and the process of pauperization on the other'(pp. 30–1).

9. South African Department of Labour Figures, March 2000. They are selected from larger tables with more categories.

References

ANC (1994): African National Congress *Reconstruction and Development Programme* (Johannesburg: Umanyano Publications).

Beinart, W. (2001) *Twentieth Century South Africa* (Oxford University Press).

Bernstein, A. and McCarthy, J. (2002) *Johannesburg: Africa's World City – A Challenge to Action* (Johannesburg: CDE).

Calitz, E. (2002) 'Structural Economic Reform in South Africa', *The South African Journal of Economics*, vol. 70(2), pp. 218–62.

Cole, E. (1967) *House of Bondage* (New York: Random House).

Corporate Social Investment Handbook (2002) 5th edn (Cape Town: Trialogue).

Davenport, T. R. H. (1987) *South Africa, A Modern History*, 3rd edn (South Africa: Macmillan).

Daye, R. (2004) *Political Forgiveness: Lessons from South Africa* (Maryknoll, NY: Orbis Books).

Draper, P. (1991) 'Foreign Direct Investment in a Post-Apartheid Economy', *Perspectives*, vol. 1(1), pp. 23–7.

The Ecologist (2003) 'Dying for DeBeers', vol. 33(7), September, pp. 27–43.

The Economist (1989) vol. 313 (7624), 14 October, pp. 45–50.

The Economist (2001) Country Report, South Africa (Economist Intelligence Unit).

The Economist (2003a) Country Profile, South Africa (Economist Intelligence Unit).

The Economist (2003b) 'Mining in South Africa, Heavy Pressure', 17 May, pp. 58–9.

The Economist (2004) 'Facing Up to the Past, Again', 21 February, pp. 44–5.

Hull, R. W. (1990) *American Enterprise in South Africa: Historical Dimensions of Engagement and Disengagement* (New York University Press).

Iliffe, J. (1999) 'Essays in Bibliography and Criticism, The South African Economy, 1652–1997', *Economic History Review*, vol. lii, pp. 87–103.

KMPG (2002) 'CIDA City Centre University: The First Ubuntu University' (Johannesburg: KPMG).

Leape, J., Baskin, B. and Underhill, S. (1989) *Business in the Shadow of Apartheid: U.S. Firms in South Africa* (Lexington, MA: Lexington Books).

Lipton, M. (1985) *Capitalism and Apartheid* (Aldershot, Great Britain: Gower Publishing Company).

Litvin, D. (2002) *Empires of Profit, Commerce, Conquest and Corporate Responsibility* (New York, London: Texere).

Mangaliso, M. P. and Nkomo, S. M. (2001) 'Eskom's Chairman Reuel Khoza on The Transformation of South African Business', in *The Academy of Management Executive*, vol. 15(3), pp. 8–15.

Mutambirwa, J. (1989) *South Africa: The Sanctions Mission, Report of the Eminent Church Persons Group* (London: Zed Books).

Reader's Digest (1989) *Illustrated History of South Africa* (Cape Town).

Rosbape, S. (2002) 'How Did Labour Market Racial Discrimination Evolve After the End of Apartheid?', *The South African Journal of Economics*, vol. 70(1), pp. 185–217.

Rossouw, G. J. (1997) 'Business Ethics in South Africa', *Journal of Business Ethics*, vol. 16, pp. 1539–47.

Schmidt, E. (1989) *Decoding Corporate Camouflage, U.S. Business Support for Apartheid*, (Washington DC: Institute for Policy Studies).

Sethi, S. P. and Williams, O. F. (2001) *Economic Imperatives and Ethical Values in Global Busines: The South African Experience and International Codes Today* (Notre Dame, IN: University of Notre Dame Press).

Terreblanche, S. (2003) *A History of Inequality in South Africa, 1652–2002* (Pietermaritzburg: University of Natal Press).

Van der Berg, S. 'The Post-Apartheid Economy: An Agenda for the Debate', Economic Papers, Centre for Contextual Hermeneutics, No. 2, pp. 1–28 (University of Stellenbosch, n.d.).

Worden, N. (1994) *The Making of Modern South Africa: Conquest, Segregation and Apartheid* (Oxford: Blackwell Publishers).

3

Responsible Change in the Wake of Apartheid: The Case of Toyota South Africa

Russell Daye

Introduction

During the final years of the apartheid era, many of the transnational companies operating in South Africa made attempts to be socially responsible. Some of these acted on their own initiative; others had their hands forced by public pressure. Signatory companies to the Sullivan Principles were perhaps the most visible among the international businesses trying to live up to (or be seen to live up to) moral standards appropriate to the context. By the 1980s international scrutiny of overseas businesses in South Africa and pressure from organizations such as the Interfaith Center on Corporate Responsibility in the US had become so intense that no sizeable company could dodge the issue of appropriate corporate behaviour in circumstances of such glaring injustice.

Toyota South Africa (TSA) was scarcely remarkable in this context, whether for its visibility or its achievements. Certainly no objective observer would have held it up as a progressive example. The view among unionists and liberation-oriented workers was that TSA management was 'on the side' of the apartheid government. This view was understandable, considering the lamentable wages, working conditions and advancement opportunities of black workers at TSA, and in view of the close relationship between the ruling National Party leaders and the company's founder, Albert Wessels. Leaping ahead to the present, then, it is a surprise to find TSA winning awards for corporate social responsibility.[1] Of course prizes are not always given to the most deserving; but a cursory look at TSA's social investment and affirmative-action initiatives seems to show that its growing reputation for enlightenment in these areas is warranted.

The investigations reported in this chapter move in two directions. We will try to dig below the surface to see if TSA's image as a responsible company matches reality. We will also try to uncover factors that encouraged and impeded positive change within the company. Special attention will be given to a period of time that was particularly important for the transformation at TSA: the late 1990s, when the country was experiencing its democratic spring and both the ANC-led government and businesses were struggling to draw interpretive maps for the new socio-political terrain.

The first part of the chapter discusses the evolution of TSA: its origins, its business approach and treatment of workers, its experiences with politically oriented industrial action and the ways it sought to reform itself in the new reality after the free elections of 1994. The second section will offer some interpretation and evaluation of the changes at TSA in the light of issues identified in corporate social responsibility literature.

Toyota South Africa: origins and evolution

Origins: the Albert Wessels years

Toyota South Africa was not a creation of Toyota Motor Corporation, Japan, but rather a product of the initiative of an Afrikaner businessman named Albert Wessels. After some success in the clothing industry, in 1960 Wessels approached Toyota Motor Corporation and contracted with it to import and sell light commercial trucks in South Africa. Because of import restrictions, he was not able to sell passenger vehicles at first. Within a handful of years, however, TSA was assembling and marketing both trucks and cars. The assembly plant was located in Durban, using parts manufactured in both Japan and South Africa. TSA's products rapidly gained market share. By the 1970s it was (and still is) South Africa's leading retailer of light trucks and passenger cars. Its manufacturing and assembly division is located in facilities near Durban and a large parts distribution plant has been added in Johannesburg, next to its corporate headquarters.

The fact that Wessels was an Afrikaner is significant because English-speaking South Africans dominated the commercial sector in South Africa at that time. TSA's development into a major company made Wessels one of the few Afrikaner 'captains of industry'. It is also significant in this context that the National Party government (and to a certain extent its civil service), which held uninterrupted power during the first three decades of TSA's life, was Afrikaner dominated. While Wessels hired a number of 'English speakers' for key management and engineering positions, TSA was until very recently controlled by the Wessels family (Wesco Investments Limited, the family's holding company) and Afrikaners dominated senior management.

From the beginning, the ranks of TSA's labour force in Durban have largely been made up of Africans and Indians. Most of the labourers at the parts distribution centre are Africans. In both locations, a high percentage of workers live in townships that were created under the apartheid-era policy of separation of the races. The dynamics of poverty, unemployment and inadequate education mentioned in the previous chapter are true of these communities, especially the African ones.

Through the 1960s and 1970s TSA's workers were paid the typically low wages of non-whites. In the 1980s, as the era of international sanctions began and US and European auto companies operating in South Africa came under scrutiny, wages across the auto sector rose significantly. By First World standards they were still low, but for black labourers in South Africa they were among the highest. Even during this time, however, blacks made very little progress in terms of advancing to (and within) the white-collar strata at TSA.

Interestingly, Albert Wessels' autobiography allots very little space to race issues, but its final paragraph is devoted to the fate of Africans:

> And for the blacks, it is that they shall only win political equality with the whites when they too have become intellectually and economically equal. Earlier in my story I had much to say about the struggle of the Afrikaner to gain full equality with his English-speaking fellow country-men and that it was only possible by means of education and training. The Afrikaners' road to equality wended its way through primary and high school, through colleges and universities. And hard work. For my black fellow citizens there is no other way. (Wessels, 1987, p. 214)

This paragraph reflects the paternalistic attitude of the man whose personality gave TSA its ethos. It also foreshadows an impressive commitment on the part of TSA to improve the quality of education in the black townships from which Toyota draws its workforce – a commitment that would be manifest starting in the early 1990s.

When Wessels visited Toyota plants in Japan during the 1960s, he was impressed by the low wages, the small number of holidays and the orderly workplace. His own wish was for a pliant workforce; and outside of indus-trial action connected with political liberation movements, he was able to maintain ironclad control into the 1980s. Under the surface, however, all of the tensions of the apartheid era festered at TSA. From the time the company began manufacturing motor vehicles in the early 1960s, it had embodied (and benefited from) the inequalities of South African society.

The challenges of the 1990s

In the 1990s these tensions burst through. In 1991 Albert Wessels' son Bert became executive chairman and had to see TSA through a decade marked by repeated industrial action. Labour leaders decried the 'racist attitudes' of white managers at Toyota. Long-standing resentment by black workers of their white bosses was given expression on the shop floor. A good example of the industrial action was the 'Toyota Incentive strikes' of 1996. In 1995 TSA introduced an incentive programme that offered bonuses if production and profit targets were met. Twice production bonuses were offered to work-ers and accepted by them. In March 1996 TSA decided to pay out a 10 per cent bonus across the board to blue- and white-collar workers because profit targets were met. The bonuses were awarded as a percentage of wages or salaries. As a result, instead of celebrating their gain, low-wage workers resented the fact that white-collar workers, who worked under far more appealing conditions, would benefit much more than themselves. Six thousand workers participated in a three-week strike. Two factors seemed to be central: first, strong antipathy toward the white managers by black workers – an antipathy rooted in society-wide resentments that blacks were now free to express; second, the fact that TSA management had unilaterally implemented the incentive plan, bypassing consultation processes that workers and union leaders were hoping would be part of the new dispensation in South Africa (Desai and Bohmke, 1996, pp. 52–6).

Another labour relations event of the late 1990s bears mentioning. This is the retrenchment of 400 workers in 1999. When the workers appealed this action, the case was sent to a dispute resolution body and eventually to arbitration. The arbitrator decided that the workers were to be reinstated with full retroactive pay and benefits for the year during which their case was under appeal – a result that cost TSA both a sizeable amount of money and a significant loss of face.

These two episodes illustrate a couple of important factors for TSA and the South African auto sector that were in flux during the late 1990s (and which remain so today to a certain extent). The perceived need by TSA to retrench hundreds of workers reflects the generally difficult situation of the auto industry at that time. As apartheid-era tariffs came down, the auto companies began to lose market share to imports. This was especially true of TSA, which was not as well integrated into its international parent company as some of the other manufacturers were, especially the German ones.[2]

The domestic market in South Africa is very small. Toyota South Africa, the sales leader, reached a peak in 1997 with just over 100 000 units sold: 60 000 passenger vehicles and 40 000 commercial vehicles. With sales at this level, an auto company is not able to invest large amounts in the regular development of new or upgraded models – unless it has access to foreign markets such that sales are pushed to significantly higher levels. Because TSA was a franchise not controlled by the parent company, Toyota Motor Corporation was giving TSA access only to very small markets in sub-Saharan Africa. It had not been able to invest in major upgrades and was left to market passenger vehicles that were versions of the same cars they had been selling in the 1980s. In 1999 TSA's passenger car sales fell to just over 40 000 – a one-third drop in 2 years. That same year TSA lost more than US$7 million.[3]

Another factor highlighted by the two episodes was the situation created by the new Labour Relations Act, which expanded the rights of workers and embraced the principles of co-determination and tripartism (see Chapter 2). With legislated workplace forums, clearer rules of collective bargaining, dispute resolution bodies and a broader right to strike, labour relations moved to a new playing field. The strike and reversal of TSA's retrenchments are signs that management was struggling to come to terms with the new socio-political reality of South Africa and to break free of a national labour management paradigm in which paternalism, arrogance and even racism were the norms.

It is difficult to know if senior management at Toyota South Africa was concerned with the issue of corporate responsibility in the late 1990s. During my interviews, it was not a term that was brought up except by me. What seems clearer is that the company learned from its struggles that it would have to find a new way of doing business in South Africa and that this new way would involve paying much more attention to the needs and concerns of the majority population, whose membership dominated both the TSA workforce and the national government. Perhaps attention to these needs and concerns was a better way to cultivate just and constructive change than adherence to a formalized corporate responsibility agenda would have been.

In any case, by the late 1990s there is clear evidence of a will, at least among TSA senior management, to move beyond old corporate conventions. Business cultures take time to evolve, however, and people who have operated for decades under one set of assumptions do not easily make the transition to another. As the turn of the century approached, there seems to have been an inner wrestling at TSA. Old attitudes and entrenched interests kept alive the apartheid era paradigm to some extent; but a new paradigm was emerging, as initiatives in a number of areas would show.

One of these areas was affirmative action, or 'employment equity' as it is called in South Africa. Here again, TSA had to grapple with, and overcome, its own legacy. Even into the late 1990s TSA had little representation by blacks in management and no African directors – this despite the fact that government and labour leaders had been calling for voluntary affirmative action since the mid-1990s. The National Union of Metalworkers (NUMSA), which represents TSA employees, had been demanding an affirmative-action policy since 1996 but TSA did not provide one until 1999. A manager was appointed to develop this policy in 1996, but appears to have encountered resistance within the TSA corporate culture. Labour publications and the views of union representatives of the time bear witness to this culture. In labour circles, TSA was considered to be the auto manufacturer with the most rigid colour bar and greater managerial resistance to opening a place for blacks.[4]

Despite this legacy, TSA did as much as any other auto manufacturer to prepare itself to meet the goals of the Employment Equity Act of 1998. In fact, Toyota quickly came to be seen nationally as a model for developing the kind of human resource and policy infrastructure that would advance employment equity. A key shift seems to have come about in 1999, when an

African senior manager was hired from outside the company. He was put in charge of launching employment equity forums, finalizing the employment equity policy for submission to the government, educating the various departments and stakeholders and initiating the first steps towards new hiring, training and advancement practices that would lead to more members of designated groups being placed in managerial, supervisory, technical and other white-collar positions. The plan was impressively comprehensive: it included four employment equity forums (based on geographical and administrative divisions, each of which had representation from a wide range of employees and outside experts), an internal programme designed to train supervisor-level workers for managerial positions, a bursary programme for employees who would prefer to be trained at a college or university and an auditing system to survey appointments, budget allocations and turnover.

Short-term goals were not lavish. Targets for black representation by the end of 2000 (Toyota, 1999) were:

- Administration and supervisory: 70 per cent
- Junior managers: 50 per cent
- Managers: 20 per cent
- General managers: 15 per cent
- Executive directors: 10 per cent

Stakeholders appear to have been impressed with the system put in place by the new manager, who seems to have been supported by the most senior levels of management. Even union leaders that I interviewed, who were not quick to offer praise for TSA, seemed optimistic about the prospects for Toyota's affirmative-action programme. They reluctantly admitted that TSA had moved from being the 'worst to the best' in the auto-sector on this issue.

Laying the groundwork and setting goals is one thing; obtaining results is another. Despite the solid preparations, TSA's employment equity initiative met with difficulties. The union was not totally satisfied with the policy and called for a review by the end of 2000. There was concern that some managers who were responsible for the hiring and promotion of other managers and white-collar workers were specifying job qualifications that served as barriers to blacks or favoured the hiring of white protégés. Shop stewards were showing a reluctance to be involved in employment equity forums. As more blacks entered management there were some culture clashes between them and white managers.

Some headway has been made in dealing with these difficulties. Now that the employment equity programme has been seeking to meet annual goals for several years, its strengths and weaknesses are somewhat clearer. Each year since 2000 the bar has been set a little higher, and in each year targets have been met at every level except the two most senior ones – at least in terms of the number of positions to be filled by blacks. Progress has been less satisfactory when it comes to the hiring of women and people with disabilities.

Another 1990s initiative that showed a change of approach was TSA's social investment programme. This programme got under way in the early years of the decade – before the democratic elections. In 1999, about US$550 000 was spent on social investments.[5] Most of this funding came from the Toyota South Africa Foundation, which received funds from TSA as well as Toyota Motor Corporation. There were also voluntary contributions by employees to a social development fund. At the time, 70 per cent of social investments went into education and the largest commitment in this area was the Toyota Teach Primary School Project, which involved 36 schools in KwaZulu Natal (the state containing Durban).

TSA became involved with support for education in the community first at the technical college and secondary school level; but efforts at these levels were frustrated by the students' poor math and science skills coming out of primary school. In response, TSA cooperated with a number of colleges and educational organizations to develop a Further Diploma of Education (FDE) for primary school teachers.[6] Participating teachers improved their teaching methods and skills, especially in mathematics, science, environmental education, classroom management and cognitive development.

Besides the FDE programme, TSA's ongoing educational expenditures included grants and assistance for colleges and vocational schools. In 1999 about US$115 000 was devoted to the TSA High School Financial Assistance Programme. These expenditures meshed well with Toyota's employment equity plans. In order for the company to hire more blacks to senior positions, especially in technical fields, it would need to have a larger pool of potential employees with quality education. By focusing on support for existing schools in the communities from which they drew most of their blue-collar workers, they were helping to make this a future reality.

The 30 per cent of social expenditures that were not devoted to education went to a variety of other projects: as a women's food garden, an old age home, the government's 'Adopt a Police Station' programme, a soccer referee development programme, the Youth Transformational Leadership Project and some employment resource centres. Some of these commitments were long-standing and others came in the form of one-time grants. Again, priority was given to projects in the townships from which TSA drew its labour.

TSA also showed willingness to help members of the majority population through its relations with suppliers, even if progress here was less impressive. It chose to focus on what it called 'affirmative procurements'. In the mid-1990s, a Small Business Development Office was established at the manufacturing centre in Durban, and at the end of the decade a policy was developed to cover operations in Johannesburg, where managers had been trying to support black businesses through targeted procurements, but without the guidance of formal policy. Affirmative procurements largely focused on types of business activity in which there were no significant barriers to entry, such as quality control standards. Mostly, businesses such as cleaning service companies or manufacturers of simple goods like household paper products were contracted. There appears to have been little transfer of technology, except in the area of security, where a black-owned company was engaged and operated in close contact with Toyota officials responsible for security. By the late 1990s TSA affirmative procurements were in the range of US$1.4 million per year (compared to a total of US$689 million paid to suppliers for materials and services in 1999).

This figure could have been much higher if TSA had used its leverage to help black entrepreneurs get started in the auto parts sector and then integrated their products into TSA's supply chain. After all, TSA assembly operations in Durban were essential to the auto component industry in KwaZulu-Natal, purchasing over half of the parts manufactured in the region. But this kind of assistance would have been difficult for several reasons. First of all, parts manufacturers must meet the auto industry's high quality accreditation standards: this requires a level of upfront investment and technical expertise that precludes the participation of small enterprises. Second, the position of TSA in the industry was weakened by its diminishing domestic market share and lack of access to foreign markets, as mentioned above. The company was running annual losses and was not well placed to make supply-chain changes based on altruism.

Managers interviewed in 2000 acknowledged that the size of their affirmative procurements was not very large, but pointed out that the company's Small Business Development Purchasing Policy called for a periodic review of all goods and services purchased by TSA, so it was possible that other, more technically advanced businesses would be contracted as the sphere of black business operations expanded. The policy also stated a willingness to use Toyota personnel to assist suppliers with administration, technical matters, training, transportation and the obtaining of credit, even though there had been little of that kind of assistance upto that time.

A number of other developments and programmes at TSA reinforce the notion that the company has been treating its workers and their communities with more respect and care. These include a housing assistance scheme that ran for about 5 years, the bursary programme for employees, insertion of workplace forums into many areas of operation, a free medical clinic for employees and HIV/AIDS awareness programmes. The company does not get full credit, however, since some of these programmes were developed under the Motor Industry Development Programme (a government-sponsored programme with which the auto manufacturers cooperate); of these, TSA was supportive, but not innovative.

Still, a certain fresh breeze was renewing the company at the turn of the millennium. One reason for this may have been that, as auto industry observers were saying with increasing frequency, TSA would have to fundamentally alter its relationship with Toyota Motor Corporation (TMC) in order to survive. There was much speculation that TSA would have to sell a majority share to TMC in order to gain access to larger markets through greater integration into the global supply chain.[7] A couple of years later these predictions were proved right.

Further changes in the new millennium

In July 2002 Toyota Motor Corporation increased its holding in TSA from 35 per cent to 75 per cent by purchasing shares from Wesco, the Wessels family's holding company. At the same time it announced that TSA would begin building the new Corolla model for the Australian market and that it would more than double production at the Prospecton plant near Durban (to 150 000 units) over the following 5 years. The Hilux, a light truck, has been earmarked for export along with the Corolla; in addition to Australia, the European market was identified as a likely target.

In order to rise to these opportunities, TSA must face some challenges. One is to achieve global accreditation standards. Another is to retool to reduce the number of product lines and then to produce the remaining models in much greater numbers; this will involve closing lines and either shifting workers and managers to other tasks or letting them go. To manage the education and training needs engendered by this shift, TMC has opened one, comprehensive training academy for Africa, which will be managed in South Africa. Interestingly, supplier, dealer and community development also come under the purview of this academy – in other words, a large measure of responsibility for social investments and affirmative procurements. Since it oversees staff development, it is also responsible for the employment equity programme. The African manager who was appointed to run the employment equity programme in 1999 has been made an executive director of TSA and placed in charge of the academy.

Given the change in ownership and new structures at TSA, another shift of direction in the areas of community relations and corporate responsibility might have been expected; but the change, such as it is, might best be described as a redoubling of efforts rather than the setting of a new course. Toyota Motor Corporation has articulated its '2010 Vision' and empowerment of society has an important place. TSA and its parent company are well placed to aid each other in this area. Help is being made available from Japan for the new academy's efforts. The expertise gained by TSA during its struggle to adapt to a dramatically changing and conflicted social reality will also be a significant value to Toyota Motor Corporation as it seeks to implement its new vision.

There is evidence of a desire to improve in areas where TSA has fallen short. For example, the academy is taking seriously the possibility of including black empowerment enterprises among its core component suppliers. It is trying to identify black empowerment enterprises to work with in related manufacturing areas. There is also a renewed commitment to bring blacks into the most senior levels of management and to do better on the affirmative-action front for women and the disabled. Social investments are structured much the same way as they were in 1999, but the number of schools and communities engaged have increased.

These are early days for the academy and it will be a couple of years before its effectiveness can be assessed. Despite certain shortcomings in the broader area of corporate social responsibility, there is reason to be optimistic. TSA has a reputation in South Africa for being a well-managed company, and there is a perception that it has been involved in employment equity and community empowerment long enough to have a good handle on what it is doing.

Lessons to be learned and future directions

In this section we review the developments at Toyota South Africa in order to learn from the company's choices, achievements and shortcomings, particularly with reference to some of the major issues raised in the growing body of literature on corporate responsibility.[8] As TSA continues to change its way of doing business, what is the shape of things today?

One key issue in the field of corporate social responsibility is *relations with stakeholders*. Employees are the most obvious group of stakeholders, and the most obvious responsibility is to pay a fair wage and benefits package. Here TSA is removed from full, direct responsibility: wage levels, benefits and other aspects of collective bargaining are set at the industry-wide level, with government participation in negotiations. But this does not mean that motor companies have no opportunities to make a significant contribution in matters where they might have less obvious responsibility – for instance, by providing aid in areas of weak human capacity.[9] Workers in South Africa, especially members of the black majority population, have major needs in areas such as the prevention and treatment of HIV/AIDS, reliable health care in general, access to better education and training and decent housing. A move to respond to these needs could be understood as a general commitment to improve employees' human capacity.

One area of human capacity has particular importance for South Africa because of its history of race relations; this is the capacity to live with self-respect and the esteem of others. TSA's employment equity initiatives have special relevance here, not only because blacks who gain highly sought after positions will have their self-esteem (and those of their families and communities) bolstered, but also because greater racial balance at all levels of staffing will erode the 'white *manager* versus black *worker*' dynamic that is so injurious to mutual respect. In general, the equity programme at TSA looks impressive, but the failure to meet its goals in the two most senior levels of management is troublesome. One wonders why these echelons have been resistant. Is it because they contain fewer managers and therefore fewer opportunities for new hiring? Is there a shortage of qualified candidates in the majority population? Certainly one hears of fierce competition among companies in South Africa for blacks with the experience and training for senior management. The appointment of an African to head the new training academy (and his being made an executive director) is welcome news. It can be hoped that this appointment is the thin edge of the wedge.

Another type of capacity that is highly relevant for TSA's black employees is the ability to participate in decisions that affect their quality of life. There is evidence that improvements were made at TSA in the 1990s – due in part to industry-wide developments, though the company's role in creating those developments and its willingness to embrace them should not be forgotten; TSA seems to have been one of the companies, along with the German firms like BMW and Daimler-Benz (now Daimler-Chrysler), that displayed progressive thinking. Industry-wide implementation of workplace forums gave workers a voice in many aspects of their daily working life. This development is compatible with Toyota Motor Corporation's way of doing business and has received encouragement from senior management at TSA. Despite a certain amount of worker cynicism initially, and resistance from shop stewards who feared their own roles might be undercut,[10] the forums do seem generally to be a positive development.

Another positive development is the expansion of worker choice in healthcare benefits. Besides receiving free primary care on site, workers can opt into any of a half-dozen healthcare plans for which TSA pays half of the cost. Some of these offer family benefits. The variety of education and training options available also reflects freedom of choice.

The issue of inclusion in decision-making (that affects the larger community) remains relevant as we shift our focus to relations with another set of stakeholders: the local population. It is difficult to know how much this actually happens. Certainly, TSA consults with colleges and universities regarding its community education programmes and works with local organizations for its other social investments. The manager who oversees these investments is a member of the majority population, and she appears to consult well with affected communities. In the late 1990s, however, the final decisions about social investments were still being made by the trustees of the Toyota South Africa Foundation, who were mostly white senior managers. Perhaps this will change as the new training academy's role becomes clearer.

One way a profitable international business can positively impact on local communities is to share its surplus in a fashion that augments physical and human infrastructures. The impressive nature of TSA's social investments makes a strong statement here. The expenditures in the late 1990s were not enormous, but they were significant at a time when the company was losing money. With the change of ownership, commitment to such investments seems to be more secure than ever.

It is of course critical to implement social investments in a way that is sensitive, as TSA appears to do. In fact such sensitivity is vital wherever a multinational distributes wealth; it should be done in a manner that does not destabilize society. Avoidance of wildly divergent salaries is perhaps of greatest importance here. The auto industry offers very good remuneration and benefits for labourers by South African manufacturing standards, which helps fight inequality by pushing up bottom end earnings, but auto sector executives still receive very high salaries compared to the lowest-paid workers. Moving more blacks into senior positions will not solve this problem. Inequality would continue to be fostered, if now within racial groupings as much as between them. This places companies like TSA in a dilemma: auto companies are not in a position to raise suddenly bottom-level salaries, which are already high by national standards and the companies are struggling to remain profitable; but neither are they in a position to bring down (even in relative terms) salaries of executives – not if they want to compete for able black managers.

Perhaps more progress can be made by bolstering economic power among marginalized groups. Empowering black-owned enterprises through targeted supplier relations would be one way to do this. In this arena, TSA comes up short by its own standards, but part of the reason for this is that its standards have been lifted. In the late 1990s there was no clear intention to move beyond affirmative procurements that were 'low tech' and involved enterprises of limited size. Today such an ambition exists, perhaps spurred by the example of other auto companies. Some of the German companies seem to have made more headway working with black empowerment enterprises and investment groups, rather than on the manufacturing front, but with dealer networks.

True to its nature, TSA is not rushing to open its core (auto parts manufacturing) sector to black-owned businesses. Its approach is to build the necessary foundations by identifying potential suppliers, training them and building their credibility. This will be the job of the new academy. As with employment equity, this careful and methodical approach can seem frustratingly slow, but as an overall way of doing business it serves TSA well.

Another way of fostering positive change within society is to advance democratic values and respect for human rights. TSA's improvement on this front since the time of Albert Wessels' close relationship with the National Party has been considerable. This was a shift not only in TSA's external relations, but was also achieved internally through the workplace forums and other measures. Much has already been said in favour of this transformation; but it should be pointed out that from the point of view of union representatives it is still not complete. Racism, antagonism between managers and workers and the compromising of equal opportunity still exist. A key issue here is the general culture or ethos of the workplace. I was not given the kind of access that would allow me to witness this at first hand.

My impression from interviews with managers and union representatives was that things were in flux at the turn of the millennium. Changes were taking place and mid-to-senior level managers were voicing a new philosophy; but this change of approach had apparently not filtered down to everyone working and supervising on the shop floor. An interesting question is what constructive steps can now be taken by management to alter workplace culture.

In the Introduction to Volume I of this series, Frederick Bird (2004) has raised the issue of an international company's fundamental business strategy. At issue is whether a transnational corporation sees itself integrating into a society and becoming a part of a web of mutually beneficial relationships and exchanges or, conversely, whether it sees itself in that society but remote from it, entering into relations with it that are mainly contractual and of limited depth. Bird is critical of transnationals that follow a cost minimization strategy and restrict engagement, even when they operate within the law and attempt to maintain international standards. Instead, he supports an asset development approach, in which businesses invest in developing areas in ways that add to their long-term value.

TSA shows a fundamental approach very much in line with the asset development strategy praised by Bird. All of the activities he highlights – spending to install quality technology, cultivating the skills of workers and organizing them in a productive fashion, working with local supply chains and marketing products locally – are activities in which TSA is deeply engaged. This is even truer today than it was at the end of the 1990s. It was and is a company very much imbedded in the fabric of society.

An obvious question is, 'Why has TSA come to embrace this approach?' There appear to be several partial answers. First, it was until very recently a South African owned and operated company; it was founded by a man deeply committed to his country; and it had nowhere else to go. Second, TSA has been a well-run company from the beginning, and its managers were insightful enough in the 1990s to see that the new political reality would call for a deep paradigm shift within the company. It was not a matter of altruism but rather good contextual analysis: senior managers understood that without help from the corporate sector the government would not be able to keep the country from deteriorating to an extent that would make doing business very difficult. A third partial answer is that some of the Toyota's competitors in the auto sector were themselves developing new business paradigms and good relations with the ANC. TSA would have been influenced by their modelling and threatened by the prospect of being left behind. Finally, the new approach at TSA is compatible with the way Toyota Motor Corporation has come to do business. To the extent that TSA managers knew that closer relations with the parent company would be a necessity, they may have been motivated to emulate its approach. Of course, there is also the 'X factor' – the unknown ingredient in any complex situation of human behaviour. Key actors may have been motivated by a social vision or the desire to simply 'do the right thing'.

Looking at Toyota South Africa's history, we can say that it has changed, and not changed. It has embraced a new philosophy of race relations and a new vision of development for South Africa, but in doing so it has done what it did during the time of Albert Wessels: accept the paradigm of the government of the day. It has embarked upon new ventures – large-scale production for overseas markets, employment equity, affirmative procurements, the new training academy – but it has employed its long-standing methods in these ventures: study the terrain, build foundations, move systematically. Some might find this methodical approach frustratingly slow; but there is something reassuring about the fact that the company views social investments and community relations in the same manner that it views other aspects of its operations. This shows that it perceives these to be integral activities not simply philanthropic add-ons.

In conclusion, our examination shows TSA's reputation for enlightenment in the areas of employment equity, community relations and social investments is not unwarranted. Even by its own standards, it sometimes falls short and it is still subject to criticism from labour and other sources; but it must be said that the company has shown sincere commitment and strong progress. All signs indicate that this progress will not be reversed. The mid-to-late 1990s were an important time for turning things around, but the achievements of that era were partially based on concerns and commitments articulated earlier. The turnaround, while only partly explainable, seems to have been facilitated by a happy convergence of changing attitudes and changing pressures in the social, political and business spheres. Much can be learned from the way TSA managers responded to those pressures.

Notes

Research for this case study was conducted during two periods of time. In April 2000 I interviewed several managers – ranging from those with junior positions to an executive director – at TSA's Johannesburg headquarters. During the same period of time, I interviewed representatives and executives of the National Union of Metal Workers of South Africa (NUMSA). I also interviewed a number of academics and NGO staff involved in the auto sector. In the months before this, while researching for my book *Political Forgiveness: Lessons from South Africa* (Maryknoll: Orbis Books, 2004), I conducted several dozen interviews with South Africans from a wide variety of backgrounds. Though not concerned with corporate social responsibility as such, these interviews have provided additional insight into the changes in South African society during the post-apartheid reconciliation period. In November 2003 several follow-up interviews were conducted by telephone with a TSA executive as well as academics, journalists and NGO staff.

1. In November 2003 for example, TSA received an award from the Professional Management Review for its progress in the areas of black economic empowerment, employment equity and corporate social responsibility.

2. For a comprehensive discussion of developments within South Africa's auto sector during this time of tariff lifting and global integration, see Barnes (1999).
3. Most of the dollar figures I provide in this essay were actually reported in rand. I have converted all figures at a 7–1 rate, which is roughly accurate for the early months of 2004.
4. Remarks cited here and on p. 62 are based on interviews with NUMSA officials conducted in April 2000.
5. This can be compared to approximately US$189 000 000 total value created by TSA according to the Value Added Statement of its 1999 annual report.
6. The cooperating organizations were the Centre for Cognitive Development at Vista University, RADMASTE at the University of Witswatersrand, the Natal College of Education, the Umlazi College for Further Education, the READ Organisation and the Primary Science Programme of Natal. The initial course intake consisted of 36 primary teachers in 1996, followed by 32 in 1997 and 13 in 1998.
7. Based on interviews with academics at the University of Natal in Durban, in April 2000.
8. I have relied primarily on two sources to shape my discussion. The first is the work of S. Prakash Sethi and Oliver F. Williams in *Economic Imperatives and Ethical Values in Global Business: The South African Experience and International Codes Today* (2001). Sethi and Williams carefully examine how the Sullivan Principles were applied and operated at a time when many of South Africa's critics were calling for divestment and withdrawal. I also rely upon an earlier article by Sethi (1993), in which he offers a 'code of affirmative action'. My other source is the introductory essay to the first volume of this series, *International Businesses and the Challenges of Poverty in the Developing World* (2004). In the chapter 'Ethical Reflections on the Challenges Facing International Businesses in Developing Areas', Frederick Bird shares many of the same concerns and embraces many of the same imperatives as Sethi and Williams, but outlines a different approach.
9. Following the United Nations Development Programme, Bird (2004) identifies the following areas of human capacity: the capacity to nourish, shelter and clothe people; the capacity to avoid high rates of morbidity and mortality; the capacity to provide educational opportunities; the capacity to participate in community life; the capacity to live with self-respect and the esteem of others. (This area of human capacity deserves special attention because of the marginalization and attempted dehumanization of South Africa's majority population under apartheid.)
10. See Klerck (1999) for an extensive discussion of the dangers of workplace forums and the challenges of their implementation in South Africa.

References

Barnes, J. (1999) 'Changing Lanes: The Political Economy of the South African Automotive Value Chain', *Centre for Social and Development Studies, Working Paper 22*.

Bird, F. (2004) 'Ethical Reflections on the Challenges Facing International Businesses in Developing Areas', in F. Bird and S. Herman (eds), *International Businesses and the Challenges of Poverty in the Developing World* (London: Palgrave Macmillan).

Desai, A. and Bohmke, H. (1996) 'Everything Keeps Going Wrong ... Toyota', *South African Labour Bulletin*, vol. 20.

Klerck, G. (1999) 'Adversarial Participation and Antagonistic Cooperation? Workplace Forums, Employee Participation and Lean Production', *Transformation: Critical Perspectives on Southern Africa*, vol. 40.

Sethi, S. P. (1993) 'Operational Modes for Multinational Corporations in Post-Apartheid South Africa: A Proposal for a Code of Affirmative Action in the Marketplace', *Journal of Business Ethics*, vol. 12.

Sethi, S. P. and Williams, O. F. (2001) *Economic Imperatives and Ethical Values in Global Business: The South African Experience and International Codes Today* (Notre Dame, IN: University of Notre Dame Press).

Toyota (1999) Toyota Group Human Resource Policy, 'Employment Equity Policy' (October).

Wessels, A. (1987) *Farmboy and Industrialist* (Johannesburg and Cape Town: Perskor).

4

Green Steel: A New South African Steel Company's Response to Internal and External Challenges

Elize Kotze

Introduction

The end of apartheid in South Africa in 1994 introduced new windows of opportunity for international and national organizations to take up the responsibility of restoring justice and fairness in the workplace. However, these new opportunities could not be separated from a number of challenges that faced businesses during this transition period. The first challenge they faced was to develop less authoritative management styles and more representative workforces. As a result of apartheid policies, the new workforce had an educational backlog, especially in technological training. Businesses were faced with the challenges of creating more employment opportunities for individuals from previously disadvantaged groups, and training these individuals for skilled and managerial positions, while competing in the turbulent global economy of the 1990s. The aim of this chapter is to gauge the responses of a newly established South African steel company to these challenges.

Saldanha Steel[1] is a state-of-the-art steel mill converting iron ore to liquid iron, and finally to hot-rolled steel at a plant located in Saldanha Bay, Western Cape. It is a mini-mill with a flat organization structure, leanly staffed with highly qualified, multi-skilled and flexible people. It focuses on its core business while support services are outsourced. It is an export-driven corporation and manufactures a high-quality product. Low costs, excellent quality and reliable delivery are seen as critical success factors. The production process is technologically complex, and calls for a highly qualified and reliable workforce, unequalled in the steel industry in South Africa.

The Saldanha Steel project was launched in 1996 by the South African Department of Trade and Industry as a joint partnership between the steel giant Iscor Ltd and the state-owned Industrial Development Corporation of South Africa (IDC). Its aims were threefold: to add economic value to the iron ore shipped from the harbour of Saldanha, to develop and create employment in an agriculture and fishing-based 'forgotten corner of the Western Cape'; and at the same time to manage the environment in a sustainable way. However, since its inception in 1996, the company has been faced not only with the general challenges of the average company operating in South Africa at the time, but also with a number of unique problems pertaining to the steel industry. These challenges ranged from responding adequately to opposition from environmentalists, to managing its young and heterogeneous workforce, addressing technical problems in the plant, adjusting to a drop of prices in the steel market and higher-than-expected interest rates, and coping with international protectionist policies that constrained the marketing of its products on the world markets.

Historical background

Saldanha Steel (Proprietary) Limited is situated on Saldanha Bay, South Africa's leading iron export port, 140 kilometres north-west of Cape Town. The Sishen-Saldanha railway line, linking the Port of Saldanha with the mineral-rich Northern Cape Province, was built in the 1970s for the export of iron ore, and more recently for other minerals such as copper. Work on the Saldanha Steel project started in 1996.

Prior to Saldanha Steel, fishing and agriculture – including wheat, livestock and sheep farming – dominated the economy of the West Coast. Over 80 per cent of South Africa's total fishing catch is landed on the West Coast, with some 17 per cent of that catch landed in Saldanha Bay (West Coast-Peninsula Transitional Council, 1996). Manufacturing in the area consists mostly of processing agricultural, marine and mining products by small- and medium-size businesses – the exception being Sea Harvest, a fish processing plant with about 3000 workers. Another relatively large project is Namakwa Sands, a smelter that processes ilmenite to produce a titania slag and pig iron for export.

The establishment of Saldanha Steel in 1996 brought one of the country's most expensive industrial developments to the West Coast. Already in 1974 a feasibility study had recommended the establishment of a plant for the production of semi-manufactured steel products at Saldanha. However, due to the world energy crisis at the time and the consequent drop in the demand for steel products, the project was shelved until early 1992. By then, new technology for the manufacturing of flat carbon steel, the coal/ore reduction or COREX process, replaced the traditional coke ovens and blast furnaces, resulting in a much more environmentally friendly plant. In April 1993 a feasibility study commissioned by Iscor and the IDC recommended that a plant be designed for the production of thin steel plates, catering to a niche in the export market for so-called ultra-thin hot-rolled coil. Saldanha Bay was chosen as one of two possible sites for the proposed steelworks. The environmental impact assessment, conducted by the Council for Scientific and Industrial Research (CSIR), selected a farm two kilometres from Saldanha Bay as the preferred site. In December 1994 Iscor and the IDC agreed to form a joint venture to implement the project. The local municipal authority approved the plan and in February 1995 applied to the provincial government for re-zoning of the property from agricultural to industrial land. A committee was appointed to review the CSIR environmental impact assessment. The World Wide Fund for Nature suppress conducted an independent study. All concluded that the plant could be located on the proposed site.

However, environmentalists were alarmed by the above decision and argued that insufficient attention had been given to the presence of the mariculture industry in the bay and the proximity of the wetlands site at the Langebaan Lagoon located about 5 kilometres from the site. Environmentalist groups were also concerned that the proximity of heavy industries to the Saldanha Bay shoreline would be detrimental to tourism. In October 1995 the Steyn Commission recommended that the Saldanha Steel Project be relocated to an alternative site 7 kilometres inland. Following many public debates, the provincial Ministry and Iscor compromised on a site 1.9 kilometres further inland. This site was also sanctioned by the WWF and the Ramsar Secretariat – the world's leading wetlands protection agency. The mill was commissioned in June 1999 at a total cost of about US$1 billion (Wesgro, 1999).

Challenges for Saldanha Steel

The first few years of the mill's operation (1998–2002) were characterized by numerous problems in five areas. First, the company had to struggle for financial survival. Unexpected changes in the global steel market caused a precipitous fall of export steel prices. Saldanha Steel was accused of dumping steel on the American and Canadian markets, which led to anti-dumping and countervailing duties being imposed upon the company as well. Serious technical problems, the result of a design error in the technology, caused a delay in production and increased financial problems. The third major challenge was to obtain a workforce of skilled technicians while implementing the new ANC government's racial criteria of employment equity. The market setbacks and technical problems increased Saldanha's fourth challenge, namely to keep to its original commitment to local job creation and socio-economic development. The fifth challenge concerned the environment: Saldanha Steel had promised 'globally competitive green steel' and strived to reach ISO 14001.

A struggle for financial survival

The business strategy for the establishment of Saldanha Steel was to create a differentiated, high-quality steel for export to world markets. However, the crisis in the world's steel market at the end of the 1990s put Saldanha Steel in a difficult financial position. The global steel market went through a period of oversupply towards the end of the 1990s, which was exacerbated by the Asian financial crisis. Hot-rolled coil producers were especially hard hit with prices below levels experienced during and immediately after the Asian crisis. These price drops led to a high level of uncertainty regarding forecasts. As well, by 2001 a turbulent US economy further lowered steel prices by more than 30 per cent to near 20-year lows (Berner, 2002). This market glut led to protectionist policies in the North American market. Between 1997 and 2001 about 25 US steel makers had gone bankrupt, many blaming their problems on a glut of cheaper imported steel. L. W. Gerard (2001), International President of the United Steelworkers of America, argued that 30 years of unfair trade had ruined the American steel industry, and that most competing countries were providing various forms of subsidies. He further raised the issue of national security and argued that a too strong dependency on foreign steel would restrict national security.

The US International Trade Commission (ITC), called in by Gerard, settled the dispute and concluded that the American steel market was indeed hurt by the glut of cheap foreign imports. More particularly, it concluded that South African exports had had a material impact on North American steel industries. The US then imposed a 'Final Anti-dumping Duty' of 9.28 per cent on Saldanha Steel's hot-rolled steel from August 2001 (Fraser, 2001a). In November 2001 a further countervailing duty of 5.76 per cent was imposed on Saldanha Steel's hot-rolled steel products being exported to the US. These duties made Saldanha Steel's financial position even more precarious.

The outcomes for Saldanha Steel of these adverse market conditions were an increasing level of debt and slower production increases, compared to what was initially planned. These conditions led to a restructuring of the ownership of the newly established plant. By June 2001 Saldanha Steel had compounded a debt of almost US$857 million. Since the beginning of 2001, long and intensive negotiations took place between Iscor and the IDC to re-capitalize Saldanha Steel to release this debt (Bruwer, 2001a). It was argued that this re-capitalization would enable Iscor to restructure into separately listed steel and mining companies. By early August 2001, Iscor was prepared to pay off its half of the debt (US$400 million), provided that the IDC did likewise. However, further financing of Saldanha Steel was not easy for the IDC. The Government of South Africa, the sole shareholder in the IDC, did not want to increase its exposure to steel. Although the increased use of Saldanha's production capacity grew more slowly than initially planned by May 2001, it finally reached 90 per cent of the design capacity of 100 000 tonnes per month. However, unexpected changes in the global steel market caused losses to the company of US$135 million and US$150 million in the 2000 and 2001 financial years respectively (Fraser, 2001b). In light of this uncertainty, it was decided to adjust downward the long-term projection of steel prices and to make an impairment provision of US$430 000 against the carrying value of the company's assets (Saldanha Steel, 2001a). Last, an analyst forecast that the earliest year a significant price increase could be reached would be 2003, and that 'Saldanha still has some bleeding to do until it sorts its costs out' (Bailey, 2001).

Newspapers echoed this tense financial situation and insinuated that if no solution could be found the company would have to close its doors, with an accompanying loss of jobs. This contributed to a general feeling of uncertainty among the company's employees. Job losses would also have been unacceptable for Government, since one of its aims was to maintain a viable steel industry in order to supply cheap steel to job-creating, down-stream manufacturers (Von Keyserlingk, 2001a). Towards the end of August 2001 there were indications that an agreement in principle had been reached on the merger of the IDC's 50 per cent stake into an unbundled Iscor steel company, which would retain the Iscor name (Fraser, 2001c). Further speculations had it that the whole South African steel industry could land in the hands of a foreigner, as the London steel group LNM had plans to acquire a dominant interest in Iscor (Bruwer, 2001b). The possibility of these larger structural changes stimulated further insecurity in the workforce.

Technical problems at the plant

Problems with the COREX technology further aggravated the situation of the new company, as they caused a delay in production. Hot spots had developed in the lining of the furnace that produced liquid iron from iron ore. This required the furnace to be shut down every six months for relining. This problem had also affected three of the four COREX plants in the world. Voëst-Alpine, the Swiss provider of the technology, was expected to pay for rebuilding the furnace (Von Keyserlingk, 2001b). This was scheduled for the first half of 2002 (Fraser, 2001a). The management of the company believed that these remedial actions would be sufficient to make the new technology fully effective over time.

The drop in world steel prices, the continuous accusations of dumping and the concomitant punitive levies, and the interruption of production due to the technical problems in the COREX all combined to threaten the company's survival. These developments, plus pessimistic newspaper reports speculating about the viability of the plant demoralized and de-motivated the workforce.

Building a new workforce

Saldanha Steel faced three challenges in building its new work force: (1) recruiting from local communities; (2) achieving demographic representation; and (3) training, managing and retaining previously inexperienced personnel.

During the project phase, the company committed itself to recruit locally and train at least 400 of the required 600 (projected to 800) permanent staff. In the end this turned out not to be completely feasible and the definition of 'local' eventually had to be extended, with the consent of the local Community forum, as many locals lacked the skills and training for recruitment into the new company. The second challenge concerned the creation of a demographically representative workforce in accordance with the Employment Equity Act of 1998. In August 1998 the *Saldanha Steel Express* reported that the company had set itself the goal of 50 per cent representation in all categories and on all levels by the fourth quarter of 2003. Saldanha Steel recruited intensively, even hiring Grade 12 pupils with mathematics and science in their curricula. The successful candidates were awarded bursaries to train at technical colleges and existing steel plants for periods ranging from a few months to 2 years. Some were sent abroad to steel mills such as Badische Stahl in Germany. Students from designated groups with exceptional potential were appointed in temporary coordinating positions, as an important step for future appointments as production superintendents. The third challenge arose from managing a largely 'green' workforce. Although the firm consisted in the first instance of a core group of experienced managers and expert technicians, most of the new employees were inexperienced. Further technical and managerial training under the guidance of experienced production and maintenance personnel provided the means to compensate for the recruits' lack of experience. In line with the company philosophy of multi-skilling, process experts were, for example, also trained in basic maintenance skills, while a strong complement of production experts were trained as millwrights (Wesgro, 1999).

As of September 2001, Saldanha Steel reported it had a total of 704 employees, 51 per cent of whom were white, 44 per cent of whom were coloured, while the remaining 5 per cent were either Indian or African (Saldanha Steel, 2001c). It should be noted that Saldanha Steel is located in a geographical area where there are traditionally few Africans and far fewer Indians, but many coloured inhabitants. To recruit blacks who are also from the local community has thus been difficult. An analysis of the number of employees on different occupational levels indicated that the company experienced similar problems recruiting managers from coloured and Indian groups.

Last but not least, the retention of the skilled workforce remained challenging, especially for the group of technicians who had benefited from 4 years of very expensive training with Saldanha Steel. The company found it difficult to retain the trained and experienced group of coloured and black workers, attracted by higher wages to other firms that were also trying to achieve employment equity. The company still attracts people, but has found it difficult to replace trained technicians from the designated groups.[2]

Training programmes at Saldanha Steel

Initially, training at Saldanha Steel was difficult. At the beginning of the project in 1996 the majority of the management team was based in Rivonia, in the province of Gauteng, 1500 kilometres north, with only a few in Saldanha, while the newly recruited employees were primarily locals. In January 1996 the first group of 120 trainees (followed by another 80 in January 1997) were sent for 2 years of technical training at the Iscor Training Centre in Newcastle, KwaZulu-Natal, some 1600 kilometres away to the east. Many of the Grade 12 trainees were fresh out from school – about 70 per cent of them being coloured – with high expectations about working conditions and remuneration.the only information they had received about the training programme came from an information brochure provided by the company. The first disappointment came when they realized that they were to be housed in hostels and not in accommodations similar to the picture in the information brochure, which showed a single guesthouse on the Newcastle premises. Soon other feelings of frustration and insecurity developed among the trainees who felt isolated and out of contact with management. At that stage, Saldanha Steel had not yet been established as a company: there was no organizational structure and the students did not know where they would eventually fit in, or what wages they would eventually be earning.

Communication between management in the north and the trainees in the east was largely inadequate. This too resulted in a loss of trust in management. One former trainee stated: 'For us, management was the equivalent of discipline and a fax machine.' Another one said: 'When management came to Newcastle, there had to be something wrong.' The perception was that management's visits were limited to disciplinary hearings or dealings with student failures – that the focus was strictly on the technical aspects of the training and not on the needs of the students. This frustration was aggravated by racial tension between a 70 per cent non-white majority and a 30 per cent minority of white students.

In April 1997 the students again complained about their accommodations, the hostel manager, the course content, the number of visits they were allowed to their hometowns on the West Coast and travel arrangements. Gradually, the polarization between management and the students turned into complete antagonism. The human resources manager at the time realized that the deterioration in relationships was heading towards a crisis. As there was no trade union yet accredited and consequently no one to negotiate on behalf of the students, an independent facilitator was contracted to mediate a process.

Fortunately the company's unpleasant experience with its first training intervention resulted in two positive outcomes. First, Saldanha Steel's management realized how important open communication was between employer and employees and established a workers' consultative body, the Consensus forum (CONFO). Second, the company broadened its training programmes beyond technical training per se to include the development of interpersonal and managerial skills.[3]

One of the most successful non-technical programmes was the certificate programme in Workplace Relations. Presented in conjunction with Technicon SA, the programme enabled graduates to be better prepared for labour affairs than many shop stewards and union members. When management realized the impact of the knowledge workers were gaining, the course was made compulsory for all supervisors and managers. The Conflict Resolution and Productive Problem Solving modules, being more general, developed skills that could be applied in a much broader environment than the workplace. These modules addressed the development of interpersonal and generic life skills, which are of essential importance in the South African context. As a result of the Workplace Relations Programme, CONFO members and other employees who took the course gained in their personal capacities. The fact that the course is accredited with a post-secondary institution also contributed to the individual's labour market qualifications, though this was a lesser goal; the functional training in specific work categories was probably far more empowering in this respect. The fact that Saldanha Steel workers were enticed for higher wages in other companies was proof that they were in a much better position to decide on their own career moves.

CONFO: A forum for worker empowerment

The initial training experience of the first group of technical staff in Newcastle, KwaZulu-Natal challenged the company's Human Resource Department. The physical distance between management in the north and the trainees led to a loss of communication that resulted in the loss of mutual trust. To address and redress these misunderstandings, the company contracted a private consultant, who led the company to institutionalize a worker consultative body where management and workers could meet on common ground.

In August 1997 about 50 elected and nominated employees (representative of the company at the time) gathered at Club Mykonos near Saldanha on the West Coast for a two-day workshop to discuss Saldanha's organizational structure, culture and value system, and the establishment of an institutionalized employee participation system. The only initial guidelines were that the steel plant would be based on the 'mini-mill philosophy', with a leanly staffed, flat organizational structure composed of a flexible, highly trained, and multi-skilled workforce, and outsourcing of all non-core activities. As a result, on 6 March 1998, the employee participation forum, CONFO, was created. On this forum, policy matters that affected employees, particularly human resources policies, were to be defined and jointly approved by management and employee representatives. CONFO operated independently from the normal line management structures and was facilitated by an external agency that specialized in employee participation. It was an autonomous body and was accountable only to the various constituencies it represented – not to line management. It was assumed that consensus could be reached because everyone was exposed to the same information. All financial and production figures were shared at CONFO, with the exception of strategic information or information deemed potentially detrimental to the organization. An attempt was made to have CONFO represent all the categories, shifts and departments, as well as the Chief Executive Officer, members of the senior management team and the officials of recognized trade unions. The Steering Committee could invite other participants as required, according to the agenda proposed. The monthly CONFO meetings served as an opportunity for Saldanha Steel and its internal stakeholders to participate in policy decision-making processes. Furthermore, it helped to equip participants with the competencies required to jointly determine the human future of the organization.

The forum was initiated before the workers had the opportunity to unionize. Individual workers subsequently joined various trade unions, but their numbers were never strong enough to reach the percentage necessary for the official recognition from the company.

CONFO had three permanent task groups: one for employment equity, another to monitor the company's medical aid scheme and a third devoted to the training programmes. Other teams were appointed on an ad hoc basis, focusing among other things on remuneration, organizational values, CONFO's constitution, housing arrangements and the relation of Saldanha Steel to the bigger Iscor group. Decisions were made on a basis of consensus. All participants, management and employees, were on an equal footing and were expected to agree to a single proposal after thorough investigation of all the relevant alternatives to the matter. No matter was put to vote. Consensus did not necessarily imply full satisfaction, but rather an overall acknowledgement of how reasonable the proposal seemed, and of the readiness to accept it. This mechanism has been successful in preventing conflicts within the workforce, in promoting the transparency and legitimacy of consensus-based governance and in developing acceptable remuneration and other policies.

To what extent has CONFO been able to prevent conflict? The answer is probably mixed. Overall, the forum claimed to have gained support from 70 to 80 per cent of the Saldanha Steel workers. Certainly no major labour agitation or work stoppage has taken place. On the issue of annual wage increases, CONFO set up a task force to benchmark wage policies with other companies in the steel industry. A suggested increase, based on the task force's findings, was brought to CONFO and after reaching consensus a final proposal was submitted to the Board of Directors. CONFO's annual wage proposals have been accepted unconditionally for the 4 years before the take-over by Iscor. However, CONFO avoided more controversial issues; it operated on a basis of information-sharing, consensus-seeking, constructive dialogue, problem solving and consultation. There were two occasions when the forum was not able to reach consensus: one pertaining to overtime, and the other regarding the agreement on a healthcare plan. In those instances, members had to return to their constituencies to once again discuss the identified problems before a consensus agreement could be reached.

CONFO has promoted the transparency and legitimacy of consensus-based governance within a major corporation. The aim was, among other things, to enrich the policy decision-making process with as much relevant information as possible. Forum participants were expected to disclose all relevant information during the discussion process in a highly transparent manner. Proposals and draft policies were tested from many different perspectives as CONFO endeavoured to accommodate all the divergent needs and interests in an inclusive fashion.

Third, consultations have affected employees in a number of ways. For example, as a result of discussions at CONFO, the company adopted the policy that remuneration levels would be based on the 75th percentile of the industry and that annual wage increases would be compared with other companies in the industry. CONFO resolved issues regarding the company's bonus system. Under the original arrangement, employees were to receive 50 per cent of yearly profits. As the steel mill was running at a financial loss, CONFO devised a new arrangement. Other remuneration issues that were successfully addressed by CONFO were the finalization of Provident Fund trustees and payment for overtime. Another working group investigated several different options for a medical scheme before recommending a policy for discussion.

The forum developed a set of policies for training programmes and industrial relations. They also spelled out a disciplinary code and grievance procedure that afforded employees effective redress on work-related matters, including racial or gender discrimination, abusive language, swearing and sexual harassment.

Saldanha Steel acknowledged that unequal distribution of work, careers and income levels had existed historically in South Africa. The company was required by law to address these imbalances, restore fairness in the workplace and establish a culture of equality and diversity. A task force for affirmative action (AA) drafted and revised the AA policy. After comments and recommendations by CONFO, the policy was accepted and enforced with subsequent company-wide workshops. CONFO reached consensus on a broad plan of action and established an AA monitoring group. The plan spelled out guidelines with respect to job requirements, promotions, staff development, removal of discrimination in all policies, procedures and practices, and performance management. It assigned priority to affirmative action over other human resources policies. In line with legislation, an annual progress report was submitted to the Department of Labour. To date, no disputes regarding affirmative action have been declared in the company.

Several mechanisms existed to facilitate the flow of information related to CONFO's discussions. The first and most important mechanism was direct feedback by a CONFO representative to his or her constituency. This was the main avenue of communication, and it was every CONFO representative's duty to arrange for such feedback sessions after each CONFO meeting. In addition, Saldanha Steel's senior management team met the day after every CONFO meeting to implement decisions made in the forum. The minutes were made available on the Intranet 48 hours after each meeting and copies of minutes were placed on all notice boards by the secretariat. The key points of matters discussed at CONFO were reported in the internal newsletter.

The CONFO initiative was a powerful intervention and it effectively shaped the character of human relations management at Saldanha Steel. The use of an external facilitator was a crucial decision. Participation seemed to enhance the belief that the collective opinion of employees should be heeded with respect. This posed further challenges to management's communication skills. One unforeseen effect of CONFO was that employees who were not directly involved in the forum as elected representatives sometimes felt excluded. Consequently, some of them brushed the concept aside as 'some place where management convey their messages' or where decisions of management were 'rubber-stamped'. Similar perceptions were also expressed in the monthly newsletter from time to time. Individual workers also complained sometimes that their representatives did not convey their opinions strongly enough (*Saldanha Steel Express*, 1999a) and that there was too little conflict at the CONFO (*Saldanha Steel Express*, 1999b).

CONFO representatives were well trained and well informed about the company and its dealings. This empowered them to represent employees at disciplinary hearings. Saldanha Steel's history abounds with examples of disciplinary charges 'lost' by supervisors due to CONFO representatives being better prepared than the supervisors laying the charges. A negative consequence of this was that supervisors lost face and self-confidence. It was finally decided that all supervisors should be involved in CONFO and receive the same training as CONFO members.

One CONFO member interviewed about workers' perceptions said that originally he was quite sceptical about the idea of participative management in the company, since this was not the traditional management style in South African companies. He was, however, co-opted into the discussion groups from which the forum was born. Asked why some workers did not feel that CONFO had value, he replied that there were actually two groups opposing the forum. There were a number of managers who considered that allowing workers to express their wishes, requests or demands was letting 'the tail wag the dog'. The other group consisting of workers with a trade union background preferred a more confrontational style and considered the forum as a 'club of management'.

CONFO played another very important role in the careers of previously disadvantaged employees. Through the AA monitoring group, CONFO kept an eye on the appointment, training opportunities and promotion of black and coloured workers, to ensure that they were fairly treated and that employees with potential were fast-tracked into higher organizational positions.

CONFO's workplace relations programme prepared its members extremely well to support themselves and their fellow workers in labour disputes at Saldanha Steel, such as cases of dismissal. In South Africa, any allegation of unfair dismissal is referred to the Council for Conciliation, Mediation and Arbitration (CCMA), an independent statutory body. CONFO did not get directly involved in unfair dismissals, since these were considered to be a line issue. Instead, CONFO helped create an internal appeal process with a three-day grace period. This made it possible for the worker to team up with CONFO-trained co-workers who had the theoretical and practical skills to assist in his or her defence. It also allowed time to bring forward new information that might possibly reverse a particular dismissal before seeking government mediation. So far only seven cases have had to be referred to the CCMA.

CONFO has made a remarkable contribution to the development of various company policies. However, strategic and financial matters are not within its authority, and consequently the forum does not have governance power in those areas. As far as appointments are concerned, the AA monitoring group has been able to exercise pressure with respect to employment equity.

Saldanha Steel's formal training programmes, such as the course in Workplace Relations, and the experience gained through participation in CONFO, have generated a healthy workplace that has brought advantages both to workers and to the company. Workers were more willing to cooperate because they understood their own positions within the broader organization; they appreciated that the employer–employee relationship was a matter not only of mutual trust, but also of mutual responsibilities. Such healthy workplace relationships were surely a help during the extremely challenging times when the company was struggling for financial survival.

Interactions with the local community

Interactions with the local community have taken place in three main forms: through the construction of the plant in 1995–96; through the integration of local businesses into the supply chain; and through training centres, such as the West Coast Development Centre and the West Coast Centre for Maths, Science and Technology .

Upon its inception, Saldanha Steel set a number of objectives with respect to its impact on the region. It hoped to create at least 20 000 jobs through outsourcing and new business creation over the first 10 years of operation. It expected to contribute towards the technical and entrepreneurial skills of local communities and promote the development of a cluster of competitive enterprises in the region. It promised to award a large portion of its corporate purchases to local small and previously disadvantaged businesses, and to assist with the formation of viable and self-sufficient new businesses that would, in time, create jobs and wealth. It said it would help to provide mentoring and business advice to new contractors with the aim of making these businesses competitive and facilitating their access to financing.

Creating jobs

During the planning and construction phases of the project, opponents of the steel mill argued that the full-time employment figures (a workforce of about 600) would hardly justify the huge capital investment. It was suggested that the capital might have been better invested elsewhere, for instance in direct support for small- and micro-enterprises active in the region's traditional activities such as fishing and agriculture and their transformation. However, the construction phase of the mill had a significant economic impact on the West Coast. Thomas (1998) reported that, during the 3-year construction phase, about US$165 million had been added to the Gross Regional Product of the West Coast, of which about US$49 million was paid out in salaries and wages to local people. Local business experienced a first-round injection of about US$105 million (over and above the downstream-effects to black-owned firms and black individuals amounting to US$17 million), including about US$1.4 million channelled through construction projects undertaken by West Coast black businesses. Approximately 72 new firms were established in the West Coast during the 1996–98 period.

However, the massive economic injection into the area also had a down side. First, the construction of the mill generated only temporary jobs and business opportunities. Upon its completion, job opportunities decreased from close to 9000 to just about 4000 and a considerable number of newly established businesses related to the mega-project faltered (Strydom, 2000). This short-term economic burst reproduced in Saldanha, according to Thomas (1998), a standard pattern of construction phases all over the world. A second effect of was a huge influx of semi-skilled and unskilled job seekers into the area, in numbers far exceeding what could be realistically accommodated. Once the project was completed, the high unemployment rate led to an increase in defaults on municipal water and electricity accounts, an increase in social unrest and an increase in criminal activity. These social costs obviously detracted from the value added by the project (Hein and Warie, 1998).

To what extent had Saldanha Steel foreseen the problem and what did the firm do to address it? The firm could have taken the attitude that it was only socially responsible in so far as its core business was concerned. However, in its business development philosophy, the company had stated that it accepted its role in developing and promoting a culture of entrepreneurship in the local community. Saldanha Steel committed itself to redressing past social imbalances by actively supporting and nurturing previously disadvantaged businesses. This policy dovetailed successfully with the goal of establishing a viable supplier base, especially for the company's engineering needs. In 2001 almost US$8 million worth of supplies were bought from previously disadvantaged businesses and, for the same period, almost US$20 million was spent in purchases from West Coast businesses in general. Saldanha Steel mentored these businesses and conducted regular audits to help them identify areas for improvement. Several of these firms, in the process, qualified for National Occupational and Safety Association (NOSA) safety ratings. Saldanha Steel's commitment to support local business was again confirmed during the shutdown period in the first half of 2002. In the course of the shutdown the company paid US$4 million to local suppliers. In addition, Saldanha Steel fostered the West Coast Business Development Centre, which the company created in February 1998 as a vehicle to promote the formation of local small enterprises, in cooperation with members from the local community and the Department of Economic Affairs. The Centre is a non-government organization, largely funded by Saldanha Steel as well as by membership fees and donations from the other corporate members. Other grants and aid come from the local government, the Department of Economic Affairs, Agriculture and Tourism, and the State Ntsika Enterprise Promotion Agency. But the Centre has a limited budget, which has seriously hampered its activities.

The Centre delivers its services through several programmes to support and develop prospective entrepreneurs, including a Business Skills Training Program, various Entrepreneurial Development Programs (a 5-week programme and a 9-month mentorship) that help participants to identify, develop and implement business ideas through an action-learning methodology based on their needs and experience. Other specialized workshops cover topics such as labour laws, cash flow management, market research, revenue services and first aid. In collaboration with the Saldanha-based South African Military Academy's Management Department, the Centre offers courses on Human Resources Management and Financial Management. The Centre has also offered courses and workshops on business counselling, information dissemination and the tendering process. Despite limited finances, the Centre also hosted an investment initiative conference and a small business expo. Within the first year (1998), successful joint ventures were established between local SMEs (Small and Medium Enterprises) and firms in Information Technology, in Wholesale Liquor Distribution, and in Chemical, Petroleum and Printing. Furthermore, business linkages resulted in the establishment of a catering company, printing company and a contract for specialist clothing, all managed by people from the previously disadvantaged groups. In 2000–01, contracts totalling US$1.5 million were awarded to SMEs through the business linkage programme. A furniture manufacturing project, sewing project and a fishing project were launched.

The West Coast Centre for Maths, Science and Technology

Because of the traditional reliance of the West Coast on its fishing industry, less importance was placed on formal schooling in mathematics and science. However, with the establishment of Saldanha Steel and other industries in the area, the value of skills in these subjects greatly increased. In 1998 Saldanha Steel initiated the establishment of the West Coast Centre for Maths, Science and Technology to train local students in these subjects. In February 2000 a managing trust was registered and officially launched with a US$28000 donation from Saldanha Steel and a US$14000 donation from Anglo American public limited company. This facilitated the conversion of a classroom at Weston High School, one of the previously disadvantaged schools for coloured pupils, to host the Maths Centre, equipped with 32 computers on a network, and a Master Maths computer-based programme.

Unfortunately, Saldanha Steel had to reduce its monetary assistance due to its own financial problems, which led to some instability in the operations of the Centre. The teacher recruited in August 1998 was retrenched at the end of 2000 and after a concerted effort to find financial support was re-hired on a part-time basis and at a reduced wage, until being re-appointed from April to December 2002.

In spite of these challenges, the school has achieved spectacular results. Previously, it only had a few pupils taking mathematics at the Grade 12 level. No student had achieved distinction in the final exams. However, in 2001, 12 pupils obtained an average of above 60 per cent and 4 pupils achieved distinctions in the Mathematics Higher Grade Exam. The school also stood out in many of the competition categories of the 2001 University of Cape Town Maths Olympiad and received a gold medal as the best newcomer school. In 2002, more than 30 pupils were enrolled for the Higher Grade; this number doubled in 2003.

Another benefit of the Centre was to bring children together from the previously racially segregated schools. This has positively affected relations between Weston High School, where students were predominantly coloured, and the 'white' school in town; several children from the latter attended afternoon classes at the Centre.

Producing steel in an ecologically sensitive area

Saldanha Steel is located less than 10 kilometres from the Langebaan Lagoon, a sensitive and fragile wetland area, which includes a wide range of inland and coastal habitats, from mountain bogs and fens and midland marshes to swamp forests and estuaries, linked by green corridors of stream bank wetlands. These wetlands have been recognized as being important for the regional ecology. The West Coast National Park at Langebaan on Saldanha Bay was added to the Ramsar list of Wetlands of International Importance in 1988. This status was further reinforced in 1995 by the Wetlands Conservation Bill tabled in Parliament. The Bill proposes the incorporation of the International Ramsar Convention into South African law in order to have certain areas protected from damaging activities (South Africa Yearbook, 1999).

As described earlier, environmentalists were alarmed by the decision to locate a steel mill near such an ecologically sensitive area as the Saldanha Bay-Langebaan Lagoon area. Their concerns were that the proposed site was chosen mainly according to economic criteria and that air and dust pollution from the steel plant and proposed solid waste disposal sites could affect the nearby fishing and agricultural industry and cause public health problems. There was also the risk that the plant would increase groundwater pollution, a danger for a domestic water supply aquifer. Other concerns were the potential social impacts of the steel plant, including the impacts on housing, social services, welfare and population growth on the wetland area.

Saldanha Steel has taken great care to honour its obligations under the environmental management plan that was agreed upon, both in design of the mill and in its monitoring mechanisms. It first designed a zero-discharge water system, and built a closed-circuit air-cooling system to reduce water consumption by about 30 per cent. It also built a storm water system consisting of three ponds. The first concrete pond was designed to capture the first 4 mm down-flush of rain water containing most of the dust deposited on roofs, roads and other paved areas. Water bypassing the concrete-lined pond was then collected in the plastic pond and the water recovered for use in the process. An unlined pond further downstream takes care of any excess water that cannot be accommodated in the other two. The plant processes all the COREX slag for use in the cement industry. In addition, COREX and MIDREX sludges and dust from the Conarc oven are granulated and either recycled into the process or sold off to the cement industry. The solid waste disposal sites and evaporation ponds have been equipped with leak detection systems *(Saldanha Steel Express,* 1999a).

Monitoring is another part of Saldanha Steel's environmental activities. A monitoring station has been built to check air quality for sulfur dioxide (SO_2) levels and PM10 dust (particles smaller than 10 micron). Groundwater quality is monitored through water samples taken every 3 months at the 28 boreholes drilled on and adjacent to the Saldanha Steel site. The boreholes cover strategic areas such as the slag disposal sites, the solid waste disposal site, the evaporation ponds, the raw materials storage area and the storm water collection pond *(Saldanha Steel Express,* 1999a).

Monitoring is continuously conducted by the Environmental Monitoring Committee (EMC) established by the Western Cape Government. This Committee praised the environmental performance of Saldanha Steel.

A report dated 7 December 1998 indicated that 'During the time of the construction of the plant the EMC has not received a single complaint from members of the public or any organization or body about environmental problems caused by Saldanha Steel. In view of the extreme antagonism by some people against the erection of the plant in its present locality, this is remarkable' (EMC, 1998). Later interviews with the same person confirmed that the Committee still had no serious concerns about Saldanha Steel's impact on the environment. Saldanha Steel received the ISO 14001 certification at the end of 2000.

Despite these efforts and achievements, problems with dust pollution remained and fuelled complaints in the local press at the beginning of 2000 (*Die Weslander*, 2000). The company publicly acknowledged the problem and admitted that it had underestimated the impact of the wind on the arid landscape. Saldanha Steel subsequently invested approximately US$1.2 million on dust suppression systems.

Conclusion: Achievements, adverse external conditions and lessons learned

Saldanha Steel started in adverse conditions. Turbulence in the world steel market, with price drops and punitive trade and tariffs measures, severely limited Saldanha Steel in reaching its original production projection figures. Technical failures further constrained production.

The three initial objectives of Saldanha Steel concerning its relations with the local community were (1) to create good employment opportunities for people from various racial backgrounds and various skills levels, to help them work effectively in spite of their lack of skilled work experiences and train them to work together effectively despite their different racial backgrounds; (2) to contribute to the economic development of the region, one of the forgotten areas of the Western Cape Province, while (3) building and operating a steel plant in an ecologically sensitive and fragile area.

Saldanha Steel managed to create a productive workforce and an open organizational climate. Management's commitment in this direction translated into a vast array of training programmes for recruits, employees and managers. One unexpected outcome of these programmes has been the challenge Saldanha Steel faces in retaining its qualified, trained workers, who are often hired away by competing companies. CONFO was a major contributor to the company's achievements, as it provided a forum for exchange of information between management and employees as well as a vehicle for maintaining a motivated workforce despite the challenging external circumstances. In addition, this forum provided a space for all employees, regardless of their sections and ranks, to voice their needs and concerns and to reconcile their often contradictory expectations with those of management. The forum thus succeeded in breaching the distinct line between management

---

and labour, urging that both sides had to 'think and act as owners'. Last, CONFO was a learning sphere in itself: as a non-confrontational, consensus-based mechanism, it helped develop interpersonal skills among workers and managers alike, and so shaped the organizational culture in a very important way.

Despite all the official commitments, training programmes and monitoring systems, employment equity remained a challenge. The company found it difficult to train enough people from designated groups (blacks and women) to get its staff profile into compliance with government expectations. True racial employment equity will probably be achieved more slowly than expected. The company had also committed itself to recruit a large percentage of its workforce from the local community, and has indeed created some employment opportunities. However, it had not successfully managed the influx of migrant workers during the construction phase. Despite Saldanha Steel's education and training initiatives, recruiting locally turned out to be more difficult than anticipated, as the working skills of many locals were tied to traditional occupations.

Saldanha Steel has done particularly well with the third dimension: it has complied with ISO standards and has created monitoring systems in response to critiques and local ecological concerns.

Three particularly interesting lessons of Saldanha Steel concern (1) working in the international markets, (2) the establishment of a company in a society in transition, and (3) the utilization of a worker consultation forum to promote consensus decision-making.

As a company adding value to nationally extracted base minerals through high quality steel production using advanced mini-mill technology, Saldanha Steel made good local and economic sense. While many steel companies positioned in a traditional mass-production mode in the steel market face a production glut, positioning one's product in a high-end niche is a promising strategy for competing successfully in the world market. Yet, despite the employees' sacrifices and high productivity levels, the company's fate was ultimately determined by external factors related to the global steel market.

The first difficult years of Saldanha Steel caused by the turbulent world steel market clearly suggest that competing internationally is challenging from the outset. The traditional trajectory of international corporations has most frequently consisted of starting locally, gaining a strong national market base, and, at a later stage, expanding to international markets. The promise of a global economy seems to offer the opportunity for firms to operate directly from their inception at the international or global level. Saldanha Steel adopted this international strategy directly, shortcutting the stage of national consolidation. Saldanha Steel may have expected international trade to be fairer, markets to be more open, international market opportunities to be more accessible. However, it paid a high price to learn that international markets are turbulent, instable and not as fair as expected. Retaliation takes place, quotas are set, tariffs established by most powerful players in the world's largest markets. These restrictions protect the national markets of developed countries – those very same countries that promote open markets and the establishment of free and fair trade.

The second lesson concerns the legacy of the old regime and of apartheid. Saldanha Steel was a new company. It did not exist under apartheid and was created 'from scratch' after apartheid was abolished. It had to comply with the new national policies aimed at creating a workforce numerically representative of the demographics of South African society. However, despite being a new company, Saldanha Steel adopted traits not dissimilar to those of a company established under the apartheid regime (see Chapters 3 and 5). An interesting lesson from the experience of Saldanha Steel is that even such a new venture largely 'espouses' the existing social, institutional, skill-base contexts in which it operates. Paradoxically, Saldanha Steel is new and green, but its internal challenges in human relations are similar to those of an 'old' apartheid-era corporation.

The last lesson refers to the company's efforts to make decisions by consensus. The CONFO model has excellent prospects for the creation of sound human relations, a motivated workforce and an ideal climate for human resource development. The downside, unfortunately, is that, as a participative management tool, the consensus-based forum remains a very time-consuming vehicle. Nonetheless, given the South African work culture and the unique challenges within the African context, the CONFO methodology has undoubtedly enormous potential for South African companies.

Notes

This research was conducted from 2000 to the beginning of 2002. I have drawn on various sources for this study: I conducted personal interviews with various members of the Saldanha Steel organization, as well as with representatives of other stakeholder groups, such as the West Coast Business Development Centre, the Centre for Maths, Science and Technology, the Environmental Monitoring Committee, and the external facilitator of the Saldanha Steel Consensus Forum during the period 2000–01. The information regarding CONFO was obtained in interviews with two former Human Resources managers, the Labour Relations manager and two of the first trainees, and also by attendance at one of the forum's meetings.

1. Saldanha Steel (Pty) Ltd is a South African company doing business on the national and international markets. At the end of 2001 Iscor Ltd took over the Industrial Development Corporation's shares in Saldanha Steel and it was subsequently integrated with Iscor. This restructuring meant that Saldanha Steel ceased to exist as an autonomous company. As this marks the end of an era in the company's history, it was decided to end the study at this point.

2. An interesting fact reported by the firm was that many young people who had resigned tried to get back into the company later on; accustomed to the value system at Saldanha Steel, they had difficulties adapting in less participatory companies.

3. The company's various training programmes include: (1) the Supervisory Development Program, a leadership training course which all supervisors attend 5 weeks per year, including some practical work; (2) Management training for middle and senior managers at Stellenbosch University; also a 5-day Leadership Development Course, which focuses on 'emotional intelligence', with follow-up courses in 2 consecutive years; (3) a frontline programme for secretaries and clerical personnel, which focuses on communication skills, office administration, language skills and career planning.

References

Bailey, S. (2001) 'Saldanha Struggles to Stem Bleeding', *Mail and Guardian*, vol. 17(23), August.

Berner, R. (2002) 'Metals and Machinery: Finally Forging Ahead?', *Business Week*, [website] http://www.businessweek.com/magazine/content/02_02/b3765625.htm, accessed 14 January.

Bruwer, P. (2001a) 'SA kap Bush oor staalkwotas' (SA rebukes Bush on steel quotas), *Die Burger*, 16 August.

Bruwer, P. (2001b) 'Groep wil Iscor koop. Suid-Afrikaanse staalbedryf kan in buitelander se hande beland' (Group wants to buy Iscor. South African steel industry may land in the hands of a foreigner), *Die Burger*, 11 October.

Die Weslander (2000) 'Welkom in ons "skoon" kontrei' (Welcome to our 'clean' region), 31 March.

EMC (1998): Environmental Monitoring Committee, Western Cape Province, 'Report of the Chief Executive Officer' (Cape Town).

Fraser, J. (2001a) 'Iscor Attacks Export Duty Move by US', *Business Day*, 20 August.

Fraser, J. (2001b) 'Saldanha Reports Loss of R1bn', *Business Day*, 16 August.

Fraser, J. (2001c) 'Iscor and IDC Reach "Breakthrough" over Saldanha', *Business Day*, 24 August.

Gerard, L. W. (2001) 'Face the Facts: Free Trade in Steel Just Won't Work', Editorial, *Financial Post*, 22 October.

Hein, R. and Warie, R. (1998) *The Economic Impact of the Saldanha Steel Project 1996–1998*. Unpublished Report for Saldanha Steel prepared by The Western Cape Investment and Trade Promotion Agency (Cape Town: Wesgro), September.

Saldanha Steel (2001a) *Audited financial results for the year ended 30 June*, 2001.

Saldanha Steel (2001b) *Report of Saldanha Steel to the Minister of Labour*, 2001.

Saldanha Steel (2001c) *Report for Saldanha Steel prepared by The Western Cape Investment and Trade Promotion Agency* (Cape Town: Wesgro).

Saldanha Steel Express (1999a): Monthly newsletter for Saldanha Steel employees, 'Globally Competitive Green Steel as Promised', February.

Saldanha Steel Express (1999b): Monthly newsletter for Saldanha Steel employees, 'Werknemers is honger vir inligting (Employees are hungry for information)', April.

South Africa Yearbook (1999) Republic of South Africa (Pretoria: GCIS).

Strydom, G. (2000) *Critical Success Factors for Entrepreneurs in Small and Medium Enterprises (SMEs) with Specific Reference to the West Coast of South Africa*. Master's thesis, University of Stellenbosch.

Thomas, W. (1998) Foreword in R. Hein and R. Warie, (eds), *The Economic Impact of the Saldanha Steel Project 1996–1998*. Unpublished Report for Saldanha Steel prepared by The Western Cape Investment and Trade Promotion Agency (Cape Town: Wesgro), September.

Von Keyserlingk, C. (2001a) 'Besluitloosheid sit Saldanha Staal se toekoms op die spel' (Indecision puts Saldanha Steel's future at risk), *Sake Rapport*, 5 August.

Von Keyserlingk, C. (2001b) 'Smith-kritici moet woorde sluk' (Smith Critics Must Withdraw Words), *Sake Rapport*, 19 August.

West Coast–Peninsula Transitional Council (1996) *Saldanha-Vredenburg Industrial Development Plan*, April.

Wesgro (1999) *Green Steel. A Big Impact*. The West Coast Report (Cape Town: Wesgro).

5

Old Wine in New Bottles: A South African Company Responds to the Challenges of a New Society

Elize Kotze

Introduction

The wine industry has been a major economic force in the Western Cape region of South Africa for nearly a century. By 1997 a total of 98 203 hectares was planted with wine grape varieties. Some 4664 farmers operated 79 wine estates, 69 cooperative cellars and 147 private wine cellars. (*SA Wine Industry Directory*, 2000, pp. 53–55). These producers had nearly 50 000 employees with 250 000 dependants living on the farms. The wine industry generated work for 215 000 people. One million metric tonnes of grapes were produced, 68 per cent of which was used for the production of natural and fortified wines and the rest for the distillation of brandy and wine spirits and for conversion into grape juice concentrate. An annual output of 1 billion litres made South Africa the seventh largest wine producer in the world (KWV, 1997, p. 4).

Wine production in this area has been going on for decades and a major force in its development has been the Ko-operatiewe Wynbouersvereniging (KWV or Cooperative Wine Growers Association), established in 1918. Until 1997, KWV was one of the largest wine companies of South Africa. It had been a regulating body for the South African wine industry until 1997 and it has a long history of being both a major exporter and employer in the Western Cape. The KWV sold wine to its members, national wholesalers and to international markets; it also offered a variety of technological and management services to wine farmers, wine cellars and the South African wine industry in general. As a cooperative it also held strategic investments on behalf of its members.

This chapter will describe how KWV, the traditional leader in the South African wine industry, responded to the social challenges it has faced since the end of the apartheid era in 1994. The chapter is divided into five sections.

In the first section I describe the company's historical development and its role as a producer cooperative during the period 1918–94. I also note how KWV responded to some of the moral issues that confronted it during the apartheid era. Second, I examine the company's response to political change during the last years of this era, in particular its association with the Rural Foundation. Third, I describe a number of significant changes in the organization and operations of KWV between 1996 and 2002. In the fourth section, I focus on one particular social issue that the company sought to address: the problem of alcohol abuse. Finally, in the last section, I offer some assessments of KWV's efforts to deal with ongoing problems of racial inequality.

Geography and history of KWV

The head office of KWV Group Limited, as the company is officially known (see Appendix), is located in Paarl, some 50 kilometres from Cape Town in the Boland region of the Western Cape. The Boland is an important agricultural region, with winter rainfall and a Mediterranean type climate. It is one of the world's finest viticulture regions and produces the bulk of the one million tonnes of wine grapes grown annually. Other wine growing areas are located in the Orange River Valley in the Northern Cape, along the Olifants River on the West Coast, the Cape South Coast and the Little Karoo.

The original 'Ko-operatiewe Wijnbouwers Vereniging' was established in 1918 as a national wine cooperative. In 1923 KWV, as it soon came to be known, was registered as a cooperative agricultural society. KWV was responsible for representing the interests of its members, the 500 to 800 owners of wine-producing farms, and for marketing their products at the best prices (Van Zyl, 1993, pp. 41–3). From its inception KWV was a thriving business. Its reputation among wine farmers increased constantly. KWV quickly established itself as the most successful agricultural cooperative in South Africa and one of the leading industries in the Western Cape (Van Zyl, 1993, p. 101). The South African government made KWV a regulatory agency for the wine market in South Africa. The cooperative stabilized the industry in the 1920s and the 1930s and its licence for the manufacture of wine was extended in 1940. In addition to fixing minimum prices for natural and fortified wines, KWV also introduced a production quota system to ensure a balance between supply and demand. These control measures enabled the wine industry to survive periodic crises in the international markets, creating stable conditions for the Cape wine industry and ensuring its independence from government subsidies, unlike most of the other South African agricultural sectors.

As a successful wine exporter over the latter half of the twentieth century, KWV brought millions of rands into the economy of the Western Cape, enabling it to keep up with the changing patterns of liquor consumption in the post-war period, as well as with the latest cultivation and production methods. It successfully built a stable work force, with good working conditions and ample social security for its mainly white employees. KWV pursued technical expertise in both the making and marketing of wine and related products. It was a modern company, facilitating the continuous modernization and improvement of the Cape wine industry. The knowledge and skills KWV had painstakingly acquired over decades enabled it to survive the international trade sanctions brought to bear against the apartheid regime in the 1980s.

Nonetheless, the organizational structure created by the cooperative reflected the social characteristics of South African society. In short, KWV was an altogether typical South African company of the apartheid era – an era, according to Terreblanche (2002), characterized by white political and economic domination, land deprivation for blacks and restrictions on black labour. KWV operated in compliance with segregation and the institutionalized inequality of the apartheid regime, following the standard apartheid regulations and practices for blacks.

A central component of the apartheid system was to restrict the education and training of black people so as to create an 'African' population that would serve as 'hewers of wood and drawers of water' (Terreblanche, 2002, p. 47). KWV was a microcosm of this broader South African society characterized by the supremacy of the white workforce over workers of colour. The cooperative did not promote any black or coloured employees into managerial positions. KWV's managers, who shared the belief that blacks were not competent to hold such positions, assumed that the poverty and underachievements of the blacks resulted from shortcomings in their character and personality (Terreblanche, 2002, p. 52) and overlooked the role of discrimination in maintaining the poverty of the blacks.

Historically, agricultural land in South Africa had been unevenly distributed among the respective population groups, with the whites having the lion's share. The Native Land Act of 1913 set out certain specified areas, totalling just over 9 million hectares – less than 15 per cent of the land – for the exclusive use of black Africans, who already occupied these areas. Although 5 to 8 million hectares were added as 'released areas' by the Bantu Land and Trust Act of 1936, this legislation also prohibited the sale of land outside these areas to blacks (Nattrass, 1981, p. 70). The Act also stipulated that Africans could not be involved in sharecropping, tenant farming and squatter farming in 'white' South Africa. At that stage other people of colour were still in an advantageous position compared to black Africans. However, when the National Party took office in 1948, their position was degraded through a rigid definition of coloured ethnicity and by making numerous apartheid laws applicable to them as well (Terreblanche, 2002, p. 267). The restrictions on ownership of land had a direct effect on the ownership and benefits of the wine industry. Membership in KWV was exclusively reserved for owners of wine farms and thus automatically excluded coloured people, who were not allowed to own property in white areas.

Conditions for workers on South African farms have always been poor. In 1995 the average monthly cash wage on Boland farms was US$50, supplemented by payment in kind, which included the rental value of land and housing, clothing, shoes, transport, rations and medicine. The education level of these workers was on average about 5 years, but illiteracy and non-numeracy were pervasive (Karaan and Tregurth, 1996, p. 63). A 1998 study further found that 21 per cent of 247 farm workers could not even sign their own names (London *et al.*, 1998a). There were also significant levels of malnutrition, poor housing, alcohol abuse, lack of personal hygiene and spousal abuse (Te Water Naude *et al.*, 1998). Health indicators suggested a high incidence of disease among farm workers and their families, of which tuberculosis, foetal alcohol syndrome and low birth weights were among the most prevalent. Many of these health and social problems can be traced back to the *dop* or 'tot' system, a system in which wine was also given to workers as part of their payment (London *et al.*, 1998b).

The practice of handing out wine to farm workers as a work incentive dates back to the early years of white settlement in the mid-seventeenth century. By the 1680s the indigenous people were induced to enter service on white farms and in the towns through payments of tobacco, bread and wine (Scully, 1992). The growth of the wine industry brought an increased demand for manual labour, which led to the emergence and intensified use of the tot system. Employers provided wine rations to farm workers at regular intervals during the working day (Department of Trade and Industry, 1997). Eventually farm workers accepted these 'tot' rations as an integral part of their employment. (There are cases involving farm workers leaving an employer who did not include the tot in their remuneration.) For wine farmers, the system provided a market for low-grade alcohol products and, at the same time, a 'home-grown' farm product that could be used to reduce labour costs (Scully, 1992). The 1928 Liquor Act curtailed but did not abolish the tot system. It was only in 1961 that the Act was amended to outlaw payment in alcohol as part of the wage (Scharf, 1984). The *free* dispensation of wine, however, was not addressed.

Through this system alcohol played a pivotal role in social and economic relations on the farms. The tot system cut down the outlay of cash wages, while farmers managed to secure an inwardly focused workforce linked to the farm by ties of alcohol dependence. 'As an insidious means of attempting to dominate and control a rural underclass, the tot system had few equals' (Scully, 1992, p. 57). Prior to the end of apartheid, the tot system was one of the most contentious moral problems KWV had to deal with.

Despite its failure to address the problems of white supremacy, landlessness and discriminatory labour practices, KWV made some laudable efforts to ameliorate the effects of poverty and alcohol abuse among its own workers, as well as those on the wine farms. By 1997 KWV was contributing annually more than US$2.2 million towards development of the wine-lands community (KWV, 1997, p. 15). However, in the early nineties the organization still had a paternalistic, do-good approach towards social problems in the area; white domination in the wine industry was not seriously questioned and limited career opportunities for people of colour were not addressed within the apartheid framework of the time.

The last years of apartheid: New social policies – the Rural Foundation

Until 1996, the most important player in the empowerment of disadvantaged people in the wine industry was the Rural Foundation, a coordinating body for social support programmes founded in the 1970s and formally established in 1982. It was through this body that KWV sought to implement social responsibility initiatives.

The foundation was funded through the membership fees of farmers, contributions by donors (including KWV), South African government grants and donations from public agencies in Germany and the United Kingdom. In 1993–94 the central government contributed R11.2 million (Rural Foundation, 1993–94, pp. 4–5). In 1994 the Rural Foundation had 204 employees who sought to reach the rural communities through a variety of developmental programs. Areas of intervention included several social empowerment and responsible drinking programmes on farms in the Boland. One initiative concentrated on the eradication of the tot system. The foundation also worked to improve the living conditions of workers and establish health clinics on selected farms.

The mission of the Rural Foundation was to facilitate a dynamic process of community development in such a way that the people on farms developed the will and skills to determine their own future and improve their quality of life. In practice, communities established development associations. Membership in these associations was voluntary and associations remained autonomous, being able to choose whether they wanted to be affiliated with the foundation or not. Affiliates elected members to its regional and national branches, and full-time community developers were appointed to coordinate the process. Although the hiring of personnel was done by the foundation, communities always made the final selection. The community workers initiated and organized the various programmes for a given community and also trained a number of part-time workers, who were employed and paid by the farmers.

The foundation played a supportive and facilitating role by providing expertise, technology, personnel, finances, training, facilities and lobbying upon request. Its research and development service operated in nine different areas, including developing literacy, pre-school care (in 1994 about 16 000 children were accommodated at about 1000 pre-school centres) and leadership development. Beyond these capacity-building activities, the foundation also had a bursary scheme to support post-secondary professional training and higher education. Although most of the foundation's activities were concentrated in the South-Western Cape, it provided services throughout the country (Rural Foundation, 1993–94). At its peak the foundation was working on approximately 4000 farms through 131 regional offices.

In 1994 the Rural Foundation was the only national organization working on farms; it was also the only organization of this kind in which employers were also involved. Consequently the foundation had a very high profile and soon became subject to transformation. At first the new government and in particular President Nelson Mandela supported the developmental programmes offered by the foundation. Mandela even publicly expressed sincere appreciation for KWV's contributions at the 1996 annual general meeting of the former KWV:

> Linked to your strong labour force, this industry could be a development model for other industries. We are aware of the imaginative initiatives launched in the industry to help those who have previously been denied access to acquire land or shares in existing enterprises. In these initiatives there is great promise for progress. (KWV, 1997, p. 15)

Unfortunately, the foundation did not survive the winds of change. This was due primarily to two factors. The first concerned the controversy around the previous government's Population Development Programme (PDP), a major source of funding for the foundation. A large segment of the population believed that the actual goal of the PDP was to curb the population growth among blacks. In its reorganization of the civil service the Mandela government moved the PDP from the Department of Health to the Department of Social Welfare. PDP funding to the Rural Foundation consequently decreased; foreign sponsors also reduced their support, in part because the foundation seemed to be too closely associated with the apartheid philosophy of the former National Party. These budget cuts led the foundation to scale down its activities.

The second factor was that some stakeholders felt that the foundation was too paternalistic and that it encouraged worker committees among the farm workers in order to keep the unions out (Bibb and Bendix, 1991, p. 43). Finally the Mandela government stopped its contributions altogether, and the foundation was liquidated in 1997. For a short while its work continued under the auspices of the Centre for Integrated Rural Development (CIRD), primarily funded by Germany. Only about 10 members of the Rural Foundation continued to work for CIRD; the rest were retrenched. Interestingly, many of these original Rural Foundation employees continued their work, and are still working in the field as private advisors to farmers' groups.

At the time the Rural Foundation closed its doors, KWV was fully financing two of its projects: a school and a health care project. The school project concentrated on training teaching assistants for pre-school education. The healthcare project involved the training of healthcare workers for selected farms, including 12 months of training for ten nursing sisters at the Paarl Hospital until the end of 1996. The downsizing of the Rural Foundation had a negative effect on KWV's targets for education and health care. Many at KWV regarded the termination of the Rural Foundation as a short-sighted decision, detrimental to the farming communities. A farm worker of the Tulbagh area reflected on the issue as follows:

> The termination was not good. Everything came to a standstill. That was the worst thing that could happen. We had an open relationship with the farmers. Everything fell flat, because there were no more formal leaders or a formal communication channel. It is difficult to work through individuals. We were left behind in a vacuum ... No, we are not yet back where we previously were. There is still a lot of work. (*Translated from Afrikaans by the author*)

KWV in the post-apartheid era, 1996–2002

In 1997 KWV was converted from a cooperative into a public corporation. The objectives of this conversion were to implement a better marketing profile, to foster fairer and more equitable foundations for future profit-sharing and to develop a more favourable position to create and accumulate capital. Control of the newly established corporation remained in the hands of the wine growers (Jonker, 1997, p. 1).

The transformation within KWV should, however, not be interpreted as a mere reaction to legal requirements in the new South African context. Many serious changes were implemented well before the new legislation. By the early 1990s KWV had already begun to explore several ways to fulfil its corporate responsibility to add value to the region and its people. It made contributions to the region and to society at large in several ways, using different agencies, institutions and trusts as vehicles to achieve its objectives.

Equal access to land and training

A number of efforts have been made to address the problem of inequality in the region. First, in 1999 KWV, working with the Ministry of Agriculture, helped to establish the South African Wine Industry Trust (SAWIT). This consisted of representatives appointed by the Minister of Agriculture (the chairperson and six members) and by KWV (six members). SAWIT had two major objectives: one was a business objective, to be carried out by the Business Support Company (BUSCO); the other objective was social, to be carried out by the Wine Industry Development Company (DEVCO), to assist with the establishment of new farmers from previously disadvantaged groups and to support farm worker communities. KWV made available

US$58 million over a period of 10 years, to be divided between BUSCO (55 per cent) and DEVCO (45 per cent).

Until 2002 DEVCO had been involved in two main projects: the Lutouw Farm Project near Lutzville, Northern Cape and the Wine Education Fund. The Lutouw area is favourable for the production of quality wines for export. DEVCO bought a US$290 000 share in a 420-hectare wine farm and gave its 30 workers a 40 per cent interest. The remaining shares are held by the two original owners (50 per cent) and four private shareholders (10 per cent). SAWIT will keep the workers' shares in trust until the project becomes profitable; the workers will then be able to buy back their shares. DEVCO will also facilitate the training of these new farm owners. The Wine Education Fund facilitates the entrance of people of colour into the wine industry as wine makers, viticulturists and marketers. In 2000, almost US$400 000 over 3 years was budgeted for this fund. Eight to twelve students have been enrolled every year.

A second area in which KWV was involved was in targeting aid funds. The Farm Workers Association received some limited financial support from DEVCO. As of July 2001, the Association had been allocated about US$18 000 to organize themselves, but it did not receive the full amount (Le Roux, 2001). This was a typical catch-22 situation: SAWIT would not transfer funds to an unorganized association and the farm workers could not organize themselves without funds. The former Rural Foundation might have helped the workers to organize; but it no longer existed.

There were also other unresolved matters between the farm workers and SAWIT. The workers believed that priority should be given to helping some of them establish themselves as new wine farmers, not only because that fit with the mandate of the new era but also because they possessed both relevant experience and technical knowledge. They argued that as most of SAWIT's funding came from the wine industry (KWV), the funds should be put back into the wine industry. This was seemingly not a priority for SAWIT. DEVCO's allocation of funds between 1999 and 2001 reflected several projects outside the traditional wine growing area and as far away as the Free State.

SAWIT also had other problems. The board was divided about DEVCO's goals. This difference of opinion clearly ran along political lines. Government representatives seemed to support empowerment projects in traditional black communities; the KWV representatives, however, wanted money spent in the traditional coloured communities associated with the wine industry. One result of this inability to come to terms about DEVCOs goals was that the allocation for the settlement of new farmers was not fully spent during the previous financial year. The balance was transferred to BUSCO for scholarships for black students (LeRoux, 2001).

A third area of KWV activity was its involvement as a founding member and shareholder in the New Farmers Development Company (NewFarmers), which became operational on 1 March 1995 (*SA Wine Industry Directory*, 2000, p. 28). By 2001 it had eight projects, ranging in size from 180 hectares of olive trees in Paarl, Western Cape, to 2.2 hectares of hothouse tomatoes in Badplaas, Mpumalanga. NewFarmers helps participants from developing communities gain access to loans as well as government settlement grants. The development company supports projects with high potential for economic success for farmers to pay back the loans in due course. The farmers pass through orientation programmes designed to develop their business skills. NewFarmers also help them with packaging their products and export marketing (NewFarmers, 2001; *SA Wine Industry Directory*, 2001, p. 57).

A fourth initiative in which KWV attempted to address the problem of inequality was the establishment of Winetech in 1996. This organization was designed to coordinate research, training and technology transfer in the wine industry. Winetech is now a network of participating institutions and individuals with a strong interest in improving the competitive position of the South African wine industry. The organization focuses on training staff at all skill levels to develop and integrate expertise and technology in business strategy. It also supports the entry of resource-limited producers into the wine industry and makes appropriate technology available for their development. KWV serves on the executive council of Winetech and contributes considerable financial support to its activities (*SA Wine Industry Directory*, 2001, p. 47).

A fifth initiative was started in 1998, when KWV helped to establish VinPro, a service organization for South African wine farmers. It represents them on all relevant industry-related governmental forums, producer associations and related groups or activities. Through VinPro, KWV provides a consulting service for viticulture, viniculture, financial planning, general management and training of new farmers. All services to small farmers are free of charge (LeRoux, 2001).

In sum, since 1994 KWV has begun, albeit slowly, to respond to the new challenges related to its social responsibilities toward the region and the country. Through several modest efforts, it has helped blacks and coloureds to start new farms or improve their conditions as farm labourers. Through SAWIT, it has provided eight to ten scholarships per year so that blacks and coloureds can receive training in wine farming. It has attempted, though not altogether successfully for a variety of reasons, to help farm labour organizations. Through DEVCO and NewFarmers they invested in a half-dozen new small farms – devoted mostly, however, to fruit and vegetables. WineTech, devoted chiefly to research and development, had scant impact on black and coloured farmers and farm workers, even though it sought to help all wine farmers, especially the smaller operations. These initiatives have been modest. They barely acknowledge, much less address, the inherited inequities in land holdings and employment opportunities in wine growing areas of the Western Cape.

Efforts to change labour practices

KWV has made numerous efforts to change unequal relations at the workplace through new statutes, training programmes and a human resources forum. The company helped to establish the Wine Industry Labour Code in 1992, 5 years prior to formal legislation. The code encouraged fair and modern labour management practices, such as reducing the number of unfair dismissals, recruitment and promotion equity, reasonable service benefits and freedom of association. While management felt they had made reasonable progress towards fair labour practices, many critics disagreed. They asserted that KWV hired mostly white people for vacant posts before the Labour Act came into force on 1 June 2000. They also felt that KWV rarely promoted people of colour from within the organization, but appointed others from outside the company.

Many of KWV's labour programmes were targeted at its own workforce. These programmes include an ABET (Adult Basic Education and Training) literacy programme; multi-skilling projects where employees learn to operate different types of machinery, enabling them to earn higher salaries; management programmes; and bursary schemes for tertiary education. The union representative regarded this programme very positively and emphasized that previously disadvantaged people could now enrol in management courses at a post-secondary institution at KWV's expense.

In 1997 KWV reported that it spent an average of 16 days per worker for training and developmental activities, in line with the government's National Qualifications Framework. Emphasis was placed on establishing a culture of participative management, healthy labour relationships, empowerment of supervisors, performance management, life skills, business principles and management of diversity (Jonker, 1997). The Human Resources Department's report of January 2000 indicated that 683 people out of 900 were sent on intervention courses in the previous 6 months. In August 2001 KWV employed 551 males, of whom 358 were coloured, 39 were black and 154 were from the white population group. There were 209 female employees, consisting of 90 coloured, 9 black and 110 white employees. It should be taken into consideration that KWV is located in an area where, traditionally, there have not been many black people, although their numbers have increased lately.

Generally, however, white male employees benefited more from training opportunities while black and coloured employees and the unions alike felt that they rarely led to promotions, since the senior positions were already occupied by qualified whites. The union was especially upset that there were so few openings, even among clerical positions, most of which were already filled by white people before the Act came into force. The Managing Director recognized that many employees from previously disadvantaged backgrounds had not yet reached their full potential. To rectify this, he had a budget to identify, recruit and appoint a limited number of such persons even though there might not be a vacancy at that particular time. This would then give them the opportunity to develop further and eventually be promoted. Despite all these training and development initiatives at KWV, many black and coloured workers did not experience any real change in terms of their own advancement in the company. In 1997, in an effort to foster better relationships among workers and between workers and management, KWV created a cross-functional, cross-hierarchical forum representing all of the company's stakeholders. It was given the name Astera, meaning 'reach for the stars'. Astera's mission is to discuss matters of current affairs, to respect the opinions of all stakeholders and to contribute constructively to the promotion and achievement of consensus. It is expected to formulate, recommend and monitor the implementation of human resource policies. Astera has discussed policies on all important personnel issues such as remuneration, employment equity, sexual harassment, employing people with disabilities, HIV/AIDS, substance and alcohol abuse, smoking and private work. On a monthly basis, issues and information regarding appointments, promotions, transfers and training, especially with regard to issues of gender, race and the physically challenged are discussed at Astera. In addition Astera has become a sounding board and forum for consultation on management strategy, as stipulated by the Employment Equity Act. Astera strives towards consensus decision-making. If consensus cannot be reached, the constitution provides for a formal procedure, which includes a 'cooling off' period, facilitation, mediation and advisory arbitration. When Astera was established all practices, policies and codes of the company were submitted to the forum for scrutiny and the recruitment and selection policies were rewritten completely.

The history of Astera is almost synonymous with the career of Nosey Pieterse, one of Astera's founding members and a driving force at KWV. Previously involved in the liberation movement and in trade unions, Pieterse was appointed as Group Industrial Relations Specialist on 1 July 1997. Immediately he found numerous problems in the company, not only relating to racial tension, but also between workers and a perceived authoritarian management structure. Workers claimed that their input was not acknowledged and the workplace was not democratic. Matters were further complicated because the two unions active at KWV, the National Council of Trade Unions (NACTU) and the Congress of South African Trade Unions (COSATU), were in dispute with management over recognition of the unions and wages. Already in 1996, management attempted to improve the situation by contracting a firm of facilitators to establish a communication forum. Unfortunately this was not successful and the unions walked out. A large number of grievances remained in abeyance.

Pieterse's first priority was to solve a wage dispute. An agreement on wages was reached at the Council for Conciliation, Mediation and Arbitration

(CCMA), despite work stoppages and marches. To address his second priority, the dispute around the recognition of the unions, Pieterse identified the problem as the way management handled grievances and disciplinary procedures. Towards the end of 1997 he developed a four-day workshop on industrial relations open to everyone in the company, including management, stewards, supervisors and workers. The workshop achieved moderate consensus. The unions finally supported the creation of Astera as a workplace forum, as long as it would not have a non-statutory status, or otherwise interfere with the unions'statutory mandates. Things became less complicated when NACTU lost several members and management cancelled the company's agreement with them in 1999. The company then had to deal with only one union.

Both management and employees were initially sceptical about Astera. Workers feared that the forum might co-opt employees into management objectives. To prevent this, several clauses were incorporated into Astera's constitution to prevent Astera from discussing any substantive matters, such as wages, grievances or disciplinary hearings, which ordinarily were the prerogative of the union. The parallelism between Astera and the union was jealously protected: the union was careful not to let the functions of the two organizations be confused, because the cooperative approach of Astera was in contrast to the traditional confrontational style of the trade union. This strategy created a sense of trust in Astera among the members of the trade union. On the other hand management was also initially very critical and felt that the forum was encroaching on management functions. The facilitator was often asked who was running KWV, management or Astera? In 1998, KWV management was asked to discuss its financial position at an Astera meeting. Although they were initially very uncomfortable, they soon realized the value of this exercise, when the union, having been made aware of KWV's financial situation and management's plans, made no wage demands. This moment led to a shared recognition of the value of transparency and trust. Interviewed in 2001, Pieterse commented that when he started at KWV there was absolutely no communication between the two parties, or if there was any, it was very negative. 'Now,' he added, 'it is very positive and they feel part of the decision-making process; not only is this true for organized labour or the trade union members, but also for the rest of KWV as well. It's more a bottom-up approach than a top-down approach.'

Astera convinced KWV management that codes and policies could and should be instituted to cover all facets of life in the workplace. The company currently has a fairly comprehensive set of workplace codes and policies covering employment, training, grievances and discipline, the use of alcohol, sexual harassment, company car policy, quality control and procurement. All these codes were initially discussed and agreed upon in Astera. As a result, KWV had in place a wide range of employment codes well before the June 2000 deadline set by the government's Employment Act. KWV introduced these standards several years before they were mandated by the government. The codes have made a significant difference for all the stakeholders connected with the company, labour relations have improved and there has not been a strike for 10 years. Astera, as a place where all stakeholders are represented, has played an important role in developing, communicating and gaining support for these codes and policies. The company also distributed the codes and policies on its Intranet. The Director of Human Resources believed that the availability of standard policies made things easier. 'They can always go back to the policy guideline to solve the problem. If people disagree with the policy, it (the policy) has to go back to Astera to be investigated.'

Promoting responsible alcohol use

KWV has made a commitment to promote responsible alcohol use. The company's contribution in this regard should be seen against the background of the history of liquor in South Africa as an integral part of the history of segregation and apartheid. Liquor was alternately made available and prohibited as a means of economic and social control and was used to attract and retain workers on farms, mines and urban industry (DTI, 1997). To what extent is the tot system still prevalent? Sources on both sides differ and it is difficult to obtain clear and reliable information. Those who estimate that as few as 1 per cent of the farms maintain the practice, define 'tot' as giving workers wine during working hours – a part of their remuneration. Others, who estimate that the practice continues on at least 20 per cent of the farms, define 'tot' more broadly as free wine given to workers on the farm. Regardless of these differences, the system in fact is still practised on some farms in the wine regions. Nevertheless, KWV has taken a definite stand against the tot system. In its newsletter to producers in September 1996 the company stated:

> The responsible and moderate use of wine with food at the end of a day's work is part of a healthy and civilized lifestyle. KWV, on the other hand, considers the tot system as an unacceptable, obsolete and illegal practice ... KWV is willing to support projects which are aimed at eradicating the tot system ... where it is still being practised. (KWV, 1996, p. 1)

This strong stand has been translated into action. KWV's standard producer's contract (in effect since 1999) stipulates that it will cancel the agreement if the producer is accused and found guilty of contravention of the Liquor Act of 1989, which outlawed these practices.

An unanticipated consequence of the prohibition of the tot system has been the emergence of unlicensed and illegal liquor outlets, called shebeens. The liquor sold at these outlets is often of dubious quality and expensive, especially over weekends, which leaves many workers with less money for their households. In 1997 KWV initiated a campaign to address the shebeen issue. It accused the government of taking little concrete action (LeRoux, 2001). The secretary of the Farm Workers Association admitted that the provision of wine to farm workers was a politically sensitive issue, suggesting that the wine industry should distance itself from the debate, monitor the situation and act where individual farmers transgressed. Nonetheless, some farmers are still finding new ways to maintain old practices.

On the other hand, there are farmers who find ingenious ways to transform this system in ways that benefit their workers. For instance, one of the farms in the Stellenbosch district began to bottle a certain percentage of the harvest under the name of its farm workers. It is sold on behalf of the workers, who are then free to use the income according to their own needs. It should also be noted that KWV instituted an alcohol and drug policy for its employees including raising awareness on the dangers of alcohol and drugs as well as paying for treatment of addicted employees or their dependents at the Toevlug Rehabilitation Centre in Worcester.

KWV has also taken a proactive stand in addressing alcohol problems at the national level. First, in 1981 together with major producers and distributors of alcoholic beverages in South Africa, KWV helped to establish the Social Aspects of Alcohol Committee. In 2000, this inter-industry group was renamed the Association for the Responsible Use of Alcohol (ARA). By 2001, KWV was contributing more than 22 per cent of the ARA budget. ARA's mission is to protect the rights and freedoms of its members to trade and promote the responsible use of their products. Members of the ARA pledge to conduct their affairs with integrity and in compliance with all relevant regulations.

Makan (2000) describes how ARA has engaged in various activities related to alcohol issues in various forms. First, through its advertising, packaging and media rules established as early as 1981 with standards more stringent than those of the Advertising Standards Authority, ARA members agreed to emphasize age restrictions in the sale of their products. Second, ARA has pioneered research on alcohol-related issues, focusing especially on the effective prevention of alcohol abuse. With the University of Cape Town, it established in 1996 the Foundation for Alcohol Related Research (FARR), today one of the world's leading research organizations on research studying foetal alcohol syndrome. Third, ARA has drawn up a human resource policy framework that deals with 'alcohol and personnel'. Intended for its members as well as for employers in other industrial sectors, this framework includes guidelines on appropriate staff induction programmes, continuing education on the dangers of alcohol abuse, potential risks from exposure to alcohol products, a policy on employee and staff abuse of the company's own alcoholic products, employee assistance plans and policies dealing with the consequences of alcohol abuse, driving while under the influence of alcohol and imbibing while on duty (Makan, 2000). Last, ARA has worked closely with international organizations, including the World Health Organization, on substance abuse problems.

ARA believes that, in the long term, the only effective means of ensuring the responsible use of alcohol is by empowering people with adequate and correct information. It has done so by instituting three comprehensive education programmes for young people. For students in grades 1 through 12, the very successful Horizon Lifestyle Education Project, a comprehensive lifestyle education programme, reaches 100 000 pupils annually. ARA has long campaigned for life-skills education to be made part of the regular school curriculum, and these subjects will be officially incorporated to the school curriculum in 2005 (Makan, 2000). Older youth are targeted through the Buddy Programme on university and college campuses. This programme concentrates on issues of drinking and driving. Since 1998, the Buddy campaign has run as a complement to the government's comprehensive Arrive Alive road safety campaign. ARA also supported and funded workshops for the ANC Youth League to develop a policy on substance abuse prevention. In 1996 ARA helped to establish the Institute for Health Training and Development by the South African National Council on Alcoholism and Drug Dependence. The primary objective of this institute is to train community health workers.

Along with five other major wine producing wholesalers, KWV helped to develop the Wine Foundation in 1989. The foundation has sought to provide generic wine education to non-wine consumers, to provide health and social responsibility information to potential wine consumers and to broaden South Africa's consumer base. Today, as the other wholesalers have withdrawn from the Wine Foundation, it is funded entirely by KWV. Based in Johannesburg, the foundation targets particularly senior students at post-secondary institutions to emphasize the responsible use of the product and the consequences of alcohol abuse (*SA Wine Industry Directory*, 2001, p. 26). Through the printed media and radio, the foundation reaches a broader audience. For instance, in December 2000, 18 million listeners were reached through broadcasts focused on the black population.

KWV has responded to issues of alcoholism in a number of additional ways. It has helped to fund the Toevlug treatment centre in Worcester. Through SAWIT, it helps to facilitate an educational project targeting school children in the Lower Orange River area in the Northern Cape. For many years KWV has been sponsoring a life-skills project of the United Reformed Church for roughly 120 000 pre-school children in the Western and Eastern Cape (LeRoux, 2001).

Conclusion: Old wine in new bottles

KWV has received various awards for its social as well as for its commercial achievements. In addition to two export achievement awards in 1998 and 1999, KWV International's social responsibility initiatives merited the Department of Trade and Industry President's Award in 1999 and led to its placing in the top five on the Mpumelelo Top 100 Companies listing in 2000.

Throughout most of its history, KWV has been an internationally connected business, as most of its wine production has been exported. In addition, given its sheer size, KWV remains central in the landscape of the Western Cape Province, where it has contributed to shaping political life, society and the economy for most of the twentieth century. From its inception in the 1920s to 1990, KWV 'enforced' an apartheid-like social system that reproduced the inequalities legislated by South Africa's apartheid regime. KWV executives had close ties with the National Party government until the end of apartheid. The stability and closeness of these relations benefited both cooperative members and the government. For government, this advantage was twofold: it used KWV expertise to build a long lasting regulatory body for the wine industry, and, in contrast with other agricultural sectors, it never had to give regular subsidies to the wine producers. These relations also benefited the wine farmers, who gained considerable political influence on matters related to the public regulation of their industry. They also helped white farmers maintain the system of domination over the coloured and black farmers, who continued to be excluded from land ownership and access to technical skills. Not surprisingly, KWV's close relationship with the previous regime has been a main cause for the strained relations between KWV and the new ANC-led government since 1994.

During the 1970s and 1980s KWV acted in small ways to mitigate some of the worst by-products of apartheid. Government involvement through the Rural Foundation, established in the 1970s along with KWV, representing the wine industry, attempted to reform the system. Under post-apartheid legislation, most of KWV's reforms have been about changes in the workplace, including internal labour relations (especially through Astera) and training opportunities for KWV staff, regardless of their ethnicity. KWV was working on many of these reforms even before the new legislation was enacted. As a whole, KWV has shown commitment to implementing the Employment Equity Act, despite differing responses to the Act from management and workers. Our research suggests that, while management seemed almost too eager to explain the company's progress in terms of the Act (and to explain away issues that were still causing concern), workers and the union representative felt that progress was too slow, but were convinced that the new labour law would eventually rectify the discriminations of the past. Lastly, KWV has publicly committed itself to eradication of the tot system from its suppliers' practices. In addition, it continues its sponsorship of education and counselling to children, students and farm workers on the responsible use of alcohol.

As for access to managerial/leadership positions and land redistribution, KWV has made very little progress. Although training opportunities are open to all, and formal and legal restrictions on the upward mobility of black and coloured workers have been removed, managers and leaders are still predominantly white. Some land has been redistributed, but the number of new non-white farmers is a drop in the bucket: less than 3 per cent of all land has been redistributed in the 1994–2001 period. At this pace, the objective of the national land reform of redistributing 30 per cent of the land by year 2014 will only be reached by the beginning of the twenty-second century (*The Economist*, 2001).

An interesting lesson from the experience of KWV is that some of the primary reasons for its success in the apartheid period have become the core obstacles in the new context. At the local level, KWV must address ongoing problems of racial inequality as well as the persistence of the now illegal tot system. KWV must also continue to distance itself from its historic ties to the National Party regime – still an obstacle to amicable working relations with the post-apartheid ANC government.

These strained relations have particularly been an obstacle in making SAWIT function effectively as an autonomous organization funded, but not controlled, by KWV. At the time of this study there was tension between representatives from KWV (which contributed the finances but had only limited say in the spending) and the other SAWIT board members who came from different spheres of society, not necessarily associated with the wine industry, and who have had limited interest in SAWIT. This is a serious predicament for KWV, for though it is not the only decision-maker and cannot be held solely accountable for SAWIT's lack of visible progress to date, its efforts are nonetheless being judged by the tangible outcomes of its association with SAWIT.

It is understandable that KWV's relationships with the trust and with the government representatives on the board have been tense. After all, it was the government that initiated SAWIT. Yet because KWV's investments in the trust have not paid the expected dividends, KWV has not received the full support that it deserved from government agencies, given the financial contribution it has been making. At the same time, this unsatisfactory relationship with SAWIT was only one cause among many for ill feeling between KWV and the government. Many of the issues between them encompassed larger problems experienced by the agricultural industry in general.

Since the end of apartheid, KWV has no doubt attempted to act as a good corporate citizen. It has proactively amended its own labour policies, ended overt discrimination and provided training programmes; it has repudiated the tot system, provided opportunities for non-white farmers and financed the SAWIT trust as a framework for progressive agricultural policies. But the effects of its efforts to deal with inherited inequalities have been miniscule. The irony is that KWV has *always* been a 'good corporate citizen'. Given its historic role as a pillar of the Western Cape economy, KWV has always closely identified with and supported government policies, whatever government was in power – the National Party in 1948 no less than the ANC in 1994. Indeed, in the apartheid era KWV was once a model of corporate social responsibility within the apartheid context. That for so long it never seriously challenged the assumptions of apartheid is not lost on its critics, to whom KWV's well-meant but still somewhat paternalistic responses to the post-apartheid era seem no more than small gestures, not signs of a serious and forthright attempt to address the fundamental changes facing the nation.

The one major lesson to be learned from the history of KWV is that good corporate citizenship means more than putting old wine into new bottles. Conformity with existing government policies may define a corporation's moral terrain and provide the stability necessary for it to thrive; but it does not follow that those polices are just towards the population, the corporation's employees, dependents, suppliers and even customers. In South Africa, corporations that have adopted the changes brought about by post-apartheid policies find that they must also assess, from a new perspective, their own practices during the apartheid era.

Appendix: Profile of KWV

KWV Group Limited is a publicly held company controlled by the South African wine farmers. It has 390.5 million class A shares, 74 per cent of which are issued to wine farmers, and 1.6 billion class B shares held by KWV Cooperative Limited. The latter is owned by the wine farmers, each of whom has a share and equal voting rights. Control by the primary producers in the company is further entrenched in that the directors of KWV Cooperative Limited, who are elected democratically by its members, appointed the Board of Directors of KWV Group Limited (KWV, 1999, p. 10). In addition to its other functions, KWV Cooperative runs a service organization for the benefit of wine farmers, called VinPro, which represents them on all relevant forums and provides consultation in viticulture and viniculture, cellar management and harvest estimates. It furthermore provides a voluntary surplus removal system, assists with generic promotion and publishes the *WineLand* magazine and the annual Wine Industry Directory (*SA Wine Industry Directory* 2000, p. 34).

KWV Group Limited has three subsidiaries: KWV South Africa (Proprietary) Limited, KWV International (Proprietary) Limited and KWV Investments Limited. KWV SA is the group's production arm: it procures, processes and supplies the products of the vine to its wholesale and/or retail customers.It has a 21-hectare cellar complex in Paarl as well as production facilities and depots in Worcester, Robertson, Vredendal and Upington. More than 50 per cent of the brandy marketed in South Africa originates from KWV distilleries. KWV International is a global marketing and trading company, responsible for the export of the group's products to world markets. The company's overseas marketing and distribution subsidiaries are

Eggers & Franke in Germany; Edward Cavendish and Sons in the UK; 57 Main Street Inc in the US; and La Concorde Wines in the Netherlands. KWV Investments is listed on the JSE and owns 50 per cent of the associated company Rembrandt-KWV Investments Limited, which in turn owns 60 per cent of the issued share capital of Distell Limited. Further information may be obtained at http://www.kwv.co.za/structure.htm.

Notes

Research for this study was conducted from 2000 to the beginning of 2002, drawing upon various sources. In 2000–01, I conducted 18 personal and three telephonic interviews with various members of the KWV organization and other stakeholder groups, such as former officials of the Rural Foundation, the Farm Workers Organization and the SAWIT. Interviews averaged 60–90 minutes and were taped. The majority of the interviews were transcribed. Archival data, including annual reports of the company and of the foundation, as well as unpublished documents of the Association for the Responsible Use of Alcohol (ARA) were also used. Newspaper articles completed my data collection.

References

Bibb, P. and Bendix, W. (1991) 'Corporate Social Responsibility in the Present South African Socio-economic and Political Context', *Industrial Relations Journal of South Africa*, vol. 11(1), pp. 43–59.
DTI (1997) Department of Trade and Industry, Government of South Africa, *Liquor Policy Paper*: http://www.polity.org.za/govdocs/policy/liqourpol.html 01/01/09.
The Economist (2001) 'The Bare Necessities, Survey: South Africa', vol. 358(8210), 24 February, pp. 4–5.
Jonker, L. N. (1997) Chairman's Address, 27 August.
Jonker, L. N. (Undated) Supreme Court of South Africa, Ko-operatiewe Wynbouersvereniging (1st Applicant), KWV Groep Ko-operatief Beperk (2nd Applicant) and The Minister of Agriculture of the Republic of South Africa (Applicant in the application for leave to intervene), Case No 13333/96, Statement of Information: Letter from Chairman to Members, p. 1.
Karaan, M. and Tregurth, N. (1996) *A Human Development Profile of Farmworkers in the Western Cape* (Stellenbosch: Rural Foundation).
KWV (1999): KWV Group Limited, *Group Financial Report* (Paarl, South Africa).
KWV (1997): KWV Group Limited, *A Tradition of Quality* (Suider Paarl: Logo Print).
KWV (1996) *Produsente nuusbrief (Newsletter to producers)*, September.
London, L., Meyers, J. E., Nell, V. and Thompson, M-L. (1998a) 'Health Status among Farm Workers in the Western Cape – Collateral Evidence from a Study of Occupational Hazards', *South African Medical Journal*, vol. 88(9), pp. 1096–101.
London, L., Sanders, D. and Te Water Naude, J. (1998b) 'Farm Workers in South Africa – The Challenge of Eradicating Alcohol Abuse and the Legacy of the "Dop" System', *South African Medical Journal*, vol. 88(9), pp. 1092–95.
Makan, C. V. (2000) *Industry Association for Responsible Alcohol Use* (ARA), Unpublished document, 22 March.
Nattrass, J. (1981) *The South African Economy: Its Growth and Change* (Cape Town: Oxford University Press).

NewFarmers (2001) NewFarmers Development Company Limited, untitled document (August).

Rural Foundation (1994) *Jaarverslag (Annual Report) 1993–94* (Paarl: Paarlse Drukpers).

SA Wine Industry Directory (2000) (Wynberg: Ampersand Press).

SA Wine Industry Directory (2001) (Wynberg: Ampersand Press).

Scharf, W. (1984) 'The Impact of Liquor on the Working Class (with Particular Focus on the Western Cape). The Implications of the Structure of the Liquor Industry and the Role of the State in this Regard.' Unpublished Master's thesis, Department of Criminology, University of Cape Town.

Scully, P. (1992) 'Liquor and Labour in the Western Cape, 1870–1900' in J. Crush and C. Ambler (eds), *Liqour and Labour in Southern Africa* (Athens, OH: Ohio University Press), pp. 56–77.

Te Water Naude, J., London, L., Pitt, B. and Mahomed, C. (1998) 'The "Dop" System around Stellenbosch – Results of a Farm Survey', *South African Medical Journal*, vol. 88(9), pp. 1102–05.

Terreblanche, S. (2002) *A History of Inequality in South Africa, 1652–2002* (Pietermaritzburg: University of Natal Press).

Van Zyl, D. J. (1993) *KWV 75 jaar (KWV 75 years)* (Paarl: KWV).

6
Preparing to Mine: The Rio Tinto Venture in Madagascar

Frederick Bird

Introduction

In 1986 Rio Tinto (RT), one of the world's largest mining companies, undertook through a Quebec-based subsidiary to develop mining operations that would exploit the 'black sand' heavy-mineral deposits of iron–titanium ore (ilmenite) along several beaches on the south-east coast of Madagascar. Once this mine becomes operational, RT estimates that it could supply up to one-tenth of the world market for titanium dioxide for about 60 years.

By March 2004 RT had not yet made a decision to proceed. It had spent over US$45 million in exploratory studies, which included prospecting, social and environmental investigations, test work and consultations. About US$10 million of this amount was spent in Madagascar. RT recognized that Madagascar had an unusual – and unusually vulnerable – environment, which would have to be treated with respect. It recognized as well that its operation might greatly affect the peoples living in the area of the mining fields. Many of these had had limited contact with modern markets and industry, and RT would have to manage its operations in ways that respected these peoples and their ways of life.

Rio Tinto is a large multinational enterprise with headquarters in the UK and Australia. It owns shares of more than 60 mines and processing plants in over 40 countries, and directly employs more than 50 000 workers. It was one of the original members of the UN-sponsored Global Compact initiative. As an international mining giant operating in socially and environmentally sensitive areas, Rio Tinto has understandably been the target of criticism. Over the past several decades its operations have occasioned protests, unrest and opposition in a number of countries. It has been accused of dumping toxic tailings into water supplies in several areas, including its mine in West Papua, New Guinea, where the local Amungmne tribal council sued Freeport McMoRan and RT, joint owners of the mine, for environmental damage, forced displacements and acts of violence by security guards (WWF International and IUCN, 1999). RT has been criticized for endangering local habitats in Australia. In Kalimantan, Rio Tinto was accused of displacing several hundred families, who claimed that they were not adequately compensated. Workers in RT mines in Namibia allege that they were carelessly exposed to excessive levels of uranium. The list of complaints is extensive (APHRN, 2000; Kennedy, 2001; Whiteman and Mamen, 2002).[1]

The proposed development of a mine in Madagascar, given the vast island's unique biodiversity and extreme poverty, has raised concerns both far and near. In the mid-1990s, the environmental organization Friends of the Earth organized protests in opposition to the proposed mine. In 2001 they prepared a critique of the social and environmental impact assessment prepared by RT (Nostromo, 2001). Although generally welcoming the opportunities associated with the mine, some people in the neighbouring areas, part of the Anosy region, have expressed concern about several possible features of the mining operation. These include the likely rise in food and housing prices, the impact of the proposed port on marine life, the risk to several rare plant and animal species and the anticipated threat to traditional ways of life. Still, most groups in Madagascar seem to look forward to the opportunities associated with the Rio Tinto mine, which is expected to create 600 regular jobs and nearly 1000 indirect employment opportunities. Many hope that the mine and particularly the proposed multi-use deep-sea port will spark other forms of economic development in the south-east corner of the island, including transport opportunities, free-trade zone activities, tourism and increased fishing, as well as other businesses opportunities (Mitchell, 2000).

In 2005 RT will decide whether to proceed with the mine. If it decides to proceed, it will then begin construction. Hence, in this chapter I am not analysing an existing mine but rather preparatory procedures as an international firm gets ready to commence mining operations in an impoverished and environmentally challenged area of a very poor, environmentally unique and politically tense country. RT has spent 18 years and considerable amounts of money exploring this possibility. What can we learn from the way RT has approached this particular operation?

I will initially review the history of RT's involvement in Madagascar. I will then reflect on this history by addressing three questions.

First, how has RT prepared itself to address a number of very serious environmental challenges? As a part of the mining process it will initially destroy trees in an area where the rates of deforestation are already excessively high. The mining process itself uses considerable amounts of water in an area where the majority of people have only limited access to clean water. It will also be mining in an area that is home to some rare fauna. How has RT equipped itself to manage these concerns?

Second, to what extent is RT prepared to deal with a number of inevitable social tensions that will arise? Because no one directly inhabits the lands that RT plans to mine, the firm does not face the kinds of issues it would if mining required them to dislocate large numbers of people. Other issues have nonetheless arisen. For example, as it develops the mine, it will affect the traditional occupational patterns of fishing and harvesting wood. It will bring modern, technologically advanced equipment into a region dominated by traditional culture and subsistence farming and fishing. It will inevitably affect the way in which town councils and village elders deliberate and the issues they will have to consider. It will have an impact on how different ethnic groups in the area interact. What steps has RT taken to meet these challenges?

Third, how has RT prepared itself to deal with the considerable economic impact of its operations? As it begins offering jobs, it may attract many more applications than there are positions. Many of these applicants may have travelled long distances in search of work; if unsuccessful applicants remain in the area unemployed and idle, will RT assume responsibility for them? As the firm begins paying and housing workers, it may cause the local economy to inflate, making food and housing more expensive for local residents. What preparations has RT undertaken so that the economic impacts of this mine help develop not destabilize the local economy? How does RT expect to manage its affairs so that the economic benefits of the mine are not appropriated by a politically and economically elite minority but are more generally dispersed through the population?

Historical review

In 1960 Madagascar achieved independence from France, which had colonized the island in 1886. The world's fourth-largest island, Madagascar is inhabited by about 15 million people divided into 18 different ethnic groups, most of whom speak Malagasy. Madagascar is extremely impoverished: 80 per cent of the people are involved in subsistence farming, and per capita annual income in 1995 was US$260, down from US$324 in 1975. The foreign debt grew from US$1.2 billion in 1980 to US$4.4 billion in 1998. The government has been paying US$4 million per week in interest on foreign debt – twice as much as it spends on public health and education. The population growth rate is very high; so is infant mortality, and 40 per cent of children under 5 suffer from malnutrition. Only 4 per cent of the rural and 54 per cent of the urban population has access to clean water. Forty-six per cent of the population over 14 years of age are illiterate.

Madagascar is home to a number of species of plants and animals not found anywhere else in the world: every known species of lemur, 80 per cent of all reptile and amphibian species and 53 per cent of all bird species are represented on the island. As the population of the island has increased, they have destroyed the existing forest at very high rates to supply wood and charcoal for construction and especially local cooking stoves; 85 per cent of the original forests have been felled (ITM, 1999; QMM, 2001).

Politically, Madagascar has a history of instability and corruption among government officials. A popular uprising made the country ungovernable for several months in 1992, and again 10 years later in 2002.

The Anosy region, in which the black sands are located, is especially impoverished. Its population of 360 000 is sub-divided between Antanosy (40 per cent), the Antandroy (37 per cent), and other smaller ethnic groups. The small port city of Tolanaro (formerly Fort-Dauphin) has a population of 50 000. An airport has served the area since 1991, but the roads remain precarious. The schools are in poor condition and student absentee rates are very high.

Prospectors originally discovered ilmenite in Madagascar's coastal black sands in the 1950s. The black, crystalline mineral is iron titanium oxide ($FeTiO_3$), which when smelted produces titanium dioxide (TiO_2), the lustrous, bright-white pigment used in modern paints, plastics, paper, textiles, cosmetics and food colouring. In 1986 Rio Tinto took a formal interest in the area as a mining site. At present RT estimates that the heavy-mineral sand deposits on the three beaches are sufficient to sustain mining operations for 60 years. Together with the Office des Mines Nationales et des Industries Stratégiques (OMNIS), a government agency, Rio Tinto began prospecting. Rio Tinto's operation were conducted by QIT Fer et Titane Inc (formerly the Quebec Iron and Titanium Company), a wholly owned subsidiary, headquartered in Montreal. In 1998 this firm, together with OMNIS formed QIT Madagascar Minerals (QMM), owned 80 per cent by the Rio Tinto subsidiary.

In 1989 QMM began to undertake studies to explore how its proposed mine might affect the social and natural environments in which it planned to operate. For assistance in these investigations, RT sought out a number of groups in Madagascar and in North America, Europe and Australia. It contacted zoological and environmental organizations, including the Missouri Botanical Gardens in St Louis and the Smithsonian Institution in Washington, DC. It hired a team from the Université du Québec to conduct anthropological studies (GRAIG, 1990) and worked with universities in Madagascar as well. By 1992 QMM had produced a number of reports related to its proposed mining operations and their probable social and environmental impacts. With this information in hand, RT began to negotiate a legal and fiscal framework agreement with the Government of Madagascar.

QMM determined that the richest heavy-mineral beach deposits were in three locations: the largest was in Mandena, just north of Tolanaro; the second and third beaches, St Luce and Petriky, were located further north and south. Although very few people lived in the areas where the black sands were located, only small tracts of land remained where the original littoral forest continued to grow. In order to extract the ilmenite from the black sand beaches, QMM would have to destroy all remaining vegetation in mining areas and to dig up the land thoroughly. All the sandy soil in ore-bearing areas would then be mixed with water and fed into spirals to physically separate the light silica sand from the heavier mineral grains, which constitute about 5 per cent of the original mixture. The remaining 95 per cent of the sand can then be restored to the excavated areas. The heavy minerals are then further refined, separating the ilmenite from small amounts of zircon and trace amounts of silica monazite. The silica and monazite are mixed with the silica sand that is returned to the beaches, while the ilmenite and zircon are exported to factories, where the titanium dioxide is subsequently extracted from the ilmenite. Immediately following mining, the excavated areas would be replanted and rehabilitated.

QMM recognized that the threats of continued deforestation were very high. Villages were hauling hundreds of loads of wood out of forested areas every day. They were also burning wood for charcoal, which they either used or sold in town. Independent studies indicated that in 20 years most of the remaining littoral forests were likely to disappear. QMM recognized that their proposed mining operations would further aggravate this situation if something were not done. The situation was getting worse as families from other parts of the Anosy region moved into the area. Overall QMM thought it could eventually address these issues both, one, by helping the local population to use forests more conservatively and, two, by quickly rehabilitating the areas mined with fast-growing trees, like eucalyptus, that could provide sustainable source of wood for the local population. The initial environmental studies pointed to the fact that there was a shortage of good clean water in the Tolanaro area (GRAIG, 1990). QMM recognized this problem but did not initially develop any strategies in response to help the region address this issue.

QMM initially proposed not to upgrade the existing port at Tolanaro but to build a new port facility primarily for their activities at Evatraha, which is north of the city on the other side of the Mandena mining area. QMM proposed to locate its ilmenite separation plant near the proposed port. Transportation costs would be lower at this site and the port activities would interfere less with existing living patterns. Still, there was a small village not far from the port site that would be affected.

With these proposed plans in hand, over the next several years representatives from QMM began a wide series of consultations with various experts and interested parties. These included members of the Anosy Regional Development Committee, the country's ministry of environment, as well as representatives of the councils and elders in Tolanaro and all the neighbouring villages in the project area. It also consulted with NGOs, institutions and university experts. At this stage of their pre-development investigations, it faced resistance and opposition in several forms. Environmental groups like Friends of the Earth opposed the plans. Many local residents remained sceptical of the promises of land rehabilitation. 'We have seen pictures of the dredging machine', said one villager. 'You won't be able to recreate Petriky for a long time after that. What wood will we use for the next 47 years?' A villager at Evatraha complained about the proposed port: 'The sea won't be able to get through to the river and we won't be able to fish' (WRM,

1999). At this stage, the World Bank agreed to offer financial assistance for project engineering studies.

By the mid-1990s QMM had reached several preliminary decisions. First, if the company was to adequately address the complex social and environmental challenges facing the project and the region, it needed to do more than hire outside experts to study the problems and make recommendations. QMM therefore decided to establish full-time environmental and social teams to consult with the affected parties, identify potential ways to address the issues and then proceed to research and test the solutions. Many of the professional staff for those teams were hired from social and environmental NGOs working in Madagascar. By 2004 more than 70 full-time employees, all but two of whom were Malagasy, were working on social and environmental programmes.

Second, QMM decided that it had to approach the deforestation issue more directly. It was not enough to exhort the local population about conservation measures and develop models demonstrating how the damage caused by mining would be overcome through subsequent rehabilitation. QMM decided to get directly involved in conservation and in planting fast-growing trees outside the mining areas. In each of the three mining areas it also decided to devote to conservation (and therefore not mine) targeted lands where original littoral forest was still intact. It developed and staffed an ecological research centre. It undertook detailed studies of rare flora and fauna found in the mining areas. Together with NGOs and local officials, it contributed to several health, educational and recreational projects. It helped to install fresh-water wells for local villages.

Third, QMM began to consider other possible sites for port facilities, so that the port could be used by other businesses in ways that would promote economic development in the region, and at the same time limit the port's impact upon the Evatraha villagers.

QMM began to develop its financial and operational plans for the proposed mine. In 1998 the Government of Madagascar ratified a legal and fiscal framework agreement with QMM. This agreement provided a number of tax benefits. QMM would be exempt from corporate taxes for the first 5 years of active operation and then pay at a reduced rate for 5 additional years before paying regular rates. For any investments after this date the company would be eligible for tax credits of up to 75 per cent of the sums invested. It would be exempt for a decade from any real estate taxes for building and land improvements. It would pay royalties at 2 per cent of FOB value of the product, a rate that was subsequently adopted by the government for all similar mining operations. This is just one of many cases where QMM helped the Government of Madagascar update its legislation in line with international standards and thereby make the country more investor-attractive.

The 1998 Framework Agreement specified that QMM had to submit a social and environmental impact assessment (SEIA) by May 2001. Beginning in 1998, QMM initiated a thorough programme of consultations at the local, regional, national and international level, as well as with social and environmental experts, on the project and the terms of reference for the SEIA. These terms of reference were then submitted to the Government of Madagascar for approval before the SEIA work actually began. QMM then commissioned a new and much more detailed social and environmental impact assessment. In May 2001 QMM submitted it to the national environment ministry for formal approval. This report was quite different from the anthropological and environmental studies undertaken a decade earlier. Unlike the earlier reports, this one focused almost exclusively on the Mandena section of the mine. This report, however, was far more comprehensive and far more detailed. Every feature of the larger operation, from the type of mine to the way roads were built, from the management of water resources to sources of power, from hiring policies to cultural exchanges, was evaluated and compared with possible alternatives. These alternatives too were evaluated with respect to technical, economic, social and environmental considerations, as well as to their impact on regional development. The result was a multi-dimensional analysis that estimated the time, costs, resource implications and impacts for all aspects of the proposed mine, from initial construction to the eventual closure of the mine decades in the future. Following a thorough technical evaluation and public consultation process by National Environmental Office, the government granted QMM an environmental permit in November 2001. The permit was keyed to an Environmental Management Plan that listed the mitigation and enhancement measures QMM was required to implement at each phase of the project.

By 2001 QMM had altered its plans for the mine in several ways. It decided to develop a much nearer and more versatile port at Ehoala, south of Tolanaro. Port construction and operations at the site would not interfere with existing residences or agriculture. It was very near the airport and the main highway running through the region, making it much more accessible for other uses, from tourism to agricultural export activities. QMM decided to build the port at this site to reduce possible social disruption and to facilitate possible economic development. It decided as well to seek public funds to help meet the extra costs for its construction. Because it had decided to locate the port further from the mining site, QMM had to consider alternative ways of transporting the ore from the mine site to the port. It decided to build a separate road that bypassed the city of Tolanaro. It made this decision because it did not want the trucks hauling ore to add to traffic congestion in the town.

QMM also examined the water issues much more thoroughly, to see how the mining operation might use and recycle vast amounts of water in an area where fresh water was scarce. To meet this challenge, it decided that it would make sense to build a weir across the meandering, swampy and partly brackish river that led from a lake to the ocean. This weir would turn more water in the lake and river system into fresh rather than brackish water, making it useable for the mining process without damaging the Mandena flora. It would also make it possible for the town of Tolanaro to draw more of its water supply from this source.

By 2002 the Madagascar government, the regional planning committee and QMM began to consider the idea of granting a concession to QMM to build and operate a public port with an expanded role at Ehoala. Recognizing the proposed port as an opportunity to spur economic development, the three stakeholders began looking into its potential as a strategic transfer point for container shipping in the Indian Ocean. Developing a container port would greatly add to its activity and create a large number of additional jobs. The government was interested in exploring these possibilities for generating employment and revenues. This expansion could also increase the willingness of the government and the World Bank to fund part of the US$50–100 million estimated cost of the port.

In 2003 the Government of Madagascar and the World Bank initiated a new Growth Pole project in Madagascar and selected Tolanaro as one of the sites for this collaboration. Tolanaro will be the focus of much more attention by the Government of Madagascar and various donors, in particular the World Bank, which has tied its investment to measures integrating the port facility with social and economic development in the Anosy region. This means that support will be provided for regional and urban planning, along with the necessary funding to establish administrative capacity to deal with the issues associated with economic development. Financial support for expanded power lines, fresh water supplies and improved roads will aid local residents and attract other new investors. The growth pole project will also result in additional investments for agricultural improvements to feed the anticipated growing population (QMM, 2003b, c, d).

If the proposed port facility is developed as now envisioned, it will significantly affect the social and economic life of Tolanaro. The population of the urban area is expected to greatly increase, putting additional pressure on social and physical infrastructures and the environment. These changes will affect housing and consumer markets, social interactions and politics in ways that have not as yet been fully anticipated. To further explore possibilities, in 2002 QMM entered into an agreement with USAID to work with local groups to support regional and town planning to integrate the economic, environmental and social aspects of potential developments. They will also collaborate on regional sustainable natural resource management, including conservation and plantations, to promote aquaculture, provide food and income to local villagers and minimize the risk of the spread of HIV/AIDS as the region develops.[2]

Once Rio Tinto gives the green light to the project, it will take 3 years to construct the basic port facilities, roads, separation plant, weir, power lines and other physical infrastructures required to make the mine operational. QMM has estimated that the cost of construction would reach about US$400 million. It has promised that 35 per cent of the construction workforce would come from Madagascar.

In order to reach this point, Rio Tinto and its subsidiary, QMM, had to act as more than just a cost-minimizing, engineering-dominated mining company. It had as well to consider and address a wide range of issues that required both expert knowledge and considered judgment with regard to management of ecological systems, protection of rare and endangered species, community economic development, integration of infrastructure development with poverty reduction goals – a full range of social, cultural, political and economic issues.

Rio Tinto invested in these diverse studies, consultations and community projects not only because it judged these to be in its best interests – that it must make a major investment ahead of time in order to understand from every angle and manage the risks it would probably face once the mining operation began – but also because it actually had the resources to do so. Smaller firms might not have been in a position to invest so much money, time and effort before making an investment decision. These very thorough social and environmental impact assessments were also tied to World Bank funding requirements for the proposed port. Moreover Rio Tinto faced a huge reputational risk if its mining operations in Madagascar were to seriously upset the area's precarious ecological balance. Environmentalists worldwide would be alarmed and outraged; but Rio Tinto also had an economic interest, given the current rates of deforestation on the island, in discovering ways to proceed that might ultimately improve the local environment.

The potential wealth of the mining venture was a reputational risk of another sort, since it would not do for the company and a few local partners to get rich but leave the local population as impoverished as or worse off than before. On the other hand, this same potential is part of the reason why RT has been able to spend much more time exploring possibilities in Madagascar. The entire project is a long-term investment. RT estimates that the world market for titanium dioxide will remain saturated until about 2009 or 2010 (QMM, 2003a). No doubt Rio Tinto decided that it could afford such extensive preliminary investigations because the black sands of southeastern Madagascar were likely to yield a steady flow of income for a very long period.

Environmental challenges

Whether as a result of NGO protests, World Bank requirements, a desire to avoid negative public exposure pressure – or simply as part of a broadly conceived estimate of its own best interests – QMM realized that it faced serious environmental challenges if it were to proceed with its proposed mines. The mining operations themselves would destroy the forests, grasslands and swamps located where the mineralized sands were to be mined. Besides threatening wildlife habitats, the mine would use vast amounts of fresh water to extract and separate the ilmenite and other valuable minerals from the sands, in a region where water resources were limited. QMM recognized that it would be facing several lesser environmental challenges, such as adverse impacts from its roads, plants and docks. It knew as well that in the process of separating the ilmenite from mineral sands it would also separate out small amounts of monazite, a rare-earth mineral containing the radioactive element thorium. This would be returned to deposit areas and re-mixed with the sands. In the process, however, some mineworkers might be exposed to radioactivity; QMM would thus need to have adequate protective measures in place.

QMM recognized that it could only proceed with the mine if it found reliable and publicly acceptable ways to address these challenges. The means it used to meet these challenges had to be scientifically credible, economically feasible, and capable of soliciting the commitment and cooperation of the people living in the area. The schemes it has thus far proposed to address these concerns seem to meet many of these criteria, with some noticeable exceptions, which we will discuss.

QMM's responses to the deforestation problems are noteworthy. Under the environmental clauses of its permit, the company is obliged to greatly increase the forested lands. This, it has recognized, is not a simple matter: every day about 200 people from Tolanaro and about 250 families from the nearby villages enter the Mandena forest to cut wood for charcoal. Overall they consume extensive amounts of wood per year. They also harvest medicinal plants from forested areas. Outside the mining areas, forests were being cleared by crude slash-and-burn methods for farming. Given the social and cultural momentum furthering these practices, and the likelihood of protest from environmentalists and villagers alike if its practices were perceived to be destructive, QMM decided to reverse the deforestation trends long before it made any decision about whether to mine. QMM accordingly decided to initiate tree-planting projects outside the mining area and to set aside conservation areas where forests would be protected both from mining and from harvesting by villagers. QMM also committed itself to rehabilitation of the excavated lands as soon as possible following mining of a particular area: as one area of the deposit was being excavated, the area recently mined would be restored and replanted.

In order for these schemes to work, it had to gain the cooperation of the local people currently harvesting wood in these areas. Had RT not entered the picture, their wood consumption, according to independent estimates, could lead to the complete destruction of the remaining littoral forest within several decades. The situation was aggravated during the past decade as different local groups increased their competition for access to the forests in the Tolanaro area. QMM's challenge has been to find ways of empowering these people to manage the forests in a sustainable manner. A condition of this empowerment is the mutual recognition of the long-term importance of conservation of key zones and plantations and harvesting of other zones. This process is complicated by the additional challenge of encouraging the local population to convert from the better-performing charcoal made from slow-growing native forest trees to the poorer quality plantation charcoal made from fast-growing trees. In order to foster cooperation, QMM has held dozens of consultative discussions with the villagers and the authorities.[3]

QMM has responded to other environmental challenges in comparable ways. It has hired experts to identify any rare or endangered flora or fauna in mining areas and explored ways of ensuring its protection. It has sought to determine whether any species were native only to the mining areas. It has committed itself to observe internationally recognized standards in protecting workers potentially exposed to monazite dust. As it has considered alternative ways of undertaking every aspect of its operations, from the location of quarries to building of roads, from the site for accommodations for workers to the type of port facilities, it has attempted to measure environmental impacts. It has worked hard not to overlook some possible problems.[4]

Over the past decade QMM has given considerable thought to fresh water issues. Its plan to build a weir down river from Lake Ambavarano helps address this problem but occasions other problems. The weir will reduce the area that has been used for various kinds of salt-water fishing. Without the weir, the lake waters become brackish at certain times, making the lake a less suitable source of water for the townspeople in Tolanaro. The weir will not only allow QMM to pump water out of the lake for the mineral separation process, but will also provide more fresh water for the townspeople. The mining operations will not reduce water supplies to the town since the water from mining will be largely recycled. As QMM eventually moves its mining operations north and south, it will need to locate additional water supplies for its own operations. Just as it has adopted a long-range strategy around deforestation, it will similarly need to adopt a set of long-range strategies concerning existing or potential fresh water shortages.

QMM recognized that construction of the weir might result in an irreversible ecological change, as cutting the flows of brackish water in and out of the inland waterways could make it impossible to fish those areas for salt-water shrimps, eels and crabs. This change will adversely affect the livelihood of some villagers. QMM hopes to offset this loss through remediation efforts, focusing principally on various forms of aquaculture, including small-scale farming of fresh-water fish and enhanced methods of shrimp production in the salty zone below the proposed weir. Since the fish population in the current water system has declined significantly over the past decade due to progressive over-fishing, the aquaculture programme, supported in part by USAID, should help improve the lot of the villagers dependent on the water systems.

Environmental groups have criticized QMM's social and environmental impact assessment (SEIA) for failing to consider how to respond to possible worst-case scenarios: vehicle and ship accidents, fires, excessive flooding of mining zones or droughts reducing fresh water supplies (Nostromo, 2001). Clearly, these are contingencies that the company is well advised to consider, especially in Madagascar, which has recently experienced both excessive flooding and drought.

Overall, QMM has solidly committed itself to understanding and to addressing the environmental challenges this mining operation faces. So far, it has organized its operations to leave few ecological footprints. Its commitment to identify and address these concerns prior even to construction is indeed exemplary, and mirrors the attention which various international NGOs and mining watch groups have likewise devoted to environmental issues in Madagascar. As we will see, in many ways the environmental challenges are likely to be easier to manage than a number of the corresponding social and economic challenges facing this proposed mining operation.

Social challenges

In its reports and studies, the QMM has identified a number of social issues. It has recognized, for example, that villagers are accustomed to harvesting reeds for weaving as part of their traditional way of life; 80 per cent of the women are involved in this activity. QMM has accordingly planned its future operations so that the villagers can continue to harvest reeds from swampy areas. The firm promises to rehabilitate swampy areas that are excavated, so that these practices can be maintained. However, for a number of years particular locales will be inaccessible. The firm has also considered the ways its operation will affect local housing; it recognizes that new housing must be constructed for workers and in a way that will limit possible tensions that might arise between workers coming from outside the area and current local inhabitants. This, in turn, raises the even more challenging question of overall interactions between local residents, foreign workers and Madagascar nationals migrating to the Tolanaro area from other regions. Although the town itself is already relatively cosmopolitan, it remains to be seen how far the presence of these diverse groups, with the different income levels, group loyalties and different lifestyles may lead to social friction and unrest. This is a real and complex issue that QMM has begun to study in cooperation with the Regional Development Committee and the Government of Madagascar.

Other social issues are less easily defined. For example, there is a major concern about access to the lands that will be used for mining. Traditionally the local populations have treated these lands as common property, invested with a complex web of economic and cultural meanings. They were the haunts of various revered and feared spirits. They were pharmacies in the wild, supplying various medicinal plants. They served as a kind of large, shared backyard, an extension of people's homes from which they could obtain food, fuel and construction materials – a natural extension of their villages. Their relationship to these lands was not strictly utilitarian. The proposed mining operations would dramatically alter the relationship of the local residents to these lands. Their access to the lands would be temporarily blocked in some places; for short periods of time the lands would be torn up and rendered unrecognizable. It is more than likely that many residents will experience these changes as profoundly alienating (Whiteman and Mamen, 2002).

QMM has responded to this issue by working to establish community land agreements with local authorities. Under these community land agreements, called *Dinas*, villagers who currently have no title to the land would gain the legal right to its use in exchange for their participation in its management in a sustainable manner. In the Mandena area, such an agreement was ratified in 2002. Similar agreements for the Ste-Luce and Petriky zones are planned for 2004 and 2005.

QMM has also recognized other aspects of these interwoven concerns. It has gone out of its way, for example, to set aside and protect identifiable sacred spots, especially tomb sites. It has made extensive efforts to inform neighbouring residents about projected developments so they will be less shocked by eventual changes. It has continued to allow people to enter most of the lands in order to fish and to harvest wood, reeds and medicinal plants. Nonetheless, issues regarding the meaning of the lands to people are subtle and not just a matter of pragmatic arrangements. QMM will no doubt have to devote more energy and thought to preparing itself to be responsive as new but as yet unclearly defined concerns emerge.

In many ways the major social challenge facing QMM concerns the impending interactions and possible social tensions between two quite different ways of life. Up to now, most people on the south-east coast lived by subsistence farming. They lived as extended families. Most were malnourished, illiterate and impoverished. QMM will introduce a markedly different lifestyle. Over a thousand people will be earning incomes that will give many of them real purchasing power for goods and services. Some of the highest wage earners will be outsiders with foreign lifestyles and manners – whether foreigners or Madagascar nationals from other regions. The old ways of life are likely to be devalued or at least questioned. Family tensions are likely to increase. Many local residents are likely to spend their extra earnings in ways that do not always benefit their households, but may actually make things worse. In short, Anosy natives will in all likelihood face the historic social upheavals that occur to a greater or lesser extent wherever communities undergo the various phases of industrialization.

QMM has thus far demonstrated that it is at least aware of these problems. It has sought to address some aspects of the larger mixture of potential difficulties. It has already initiated literacy and training programmes so that local residents will be able to qualify and compete for jobs at the mine. It has held dozens of consultations and listened as local people voiced their concerns. Still, much more needs to be done. These issues are multi-dimensional and ongoing.

How well QMM addresses these challenges depends in large part on how successfully the firm can develop genuinely collaborative relations with groups representing diverse villages, communities and peoples in the Anosy region. It will, no doubt, seek to avoid the difficulties faced by a RT subsidiary that recently sought to develop a mine on Zimboanga peninsula in the Philippines. That firm, Tropical Explorations Philippines Incorporated (TEPI), held initial public hearings in 1996 at which local residents largely voiced their opposition to any proposed mine. TEPI viewed these initial encounters as simply preliminary consultations; it hoped in time to persuade the indigenous groups to see how the mine's operation could be beneficial to them. TEPI was indeed able to gain interested cooperation from several sizeable groups but most groups simply boycotted further meetings. Local churches and bishops spoke out against the mine. TEPI was never able to establish any ongoing collaborative relations. In 1999 it decided to withdraw from the area.

Establishing viable collaborative relations with local populations requires a combination of social skills, willingness to listen, patience and good luck. QMM has sought to communicate with local groups through hearings, announcements and consultations, and by developing models of responsible forestry. In 2002, the local National Environmental Office and the local Prefect established a Liaison Committee, with QMM's support, to allow local interest groups to obtain regular information on the mining project and to provide a forum for debate and recommendations from the local population. Establishing this committee was one of the obligations stipulated in the management plan that accompanied the 2001 Environmental Permit. Membership on this committee is divided between the public sector, the private sector and civil society and one of the current issues the committee has tackled is how to maximize the local benefits from the planned economic development. It makes sense for QMM to seek out additional partners from among the burgeoning number of local NGOs with whom they could collaborate. QMM will have to discover ways of helping local groups develop their capacities to communicate, to realize their own objectives, as well as to work with – which may mean, at times, to challenge – the mining company as it proceeds with its operations.

Economic challenges

The major economic challenge facing QMM is to discover effective ways to ensure that the wealth created by the mine not only produces satisfactory rates of return but also appropriately enriches the people of Madagascar, especially those living in the Anosy region. How can this operation be managed so that it genuinely helps to reduce the poverty of this very impoverished country? How can QMM maximize the economic benefits to the region? How can the company maximize the number of people hired locally, instead of workers from other parts of Madagascar or from abroad? How can QMM maximize its purchases from Madagascar suppliers so as to create secondary economic benefits?

Although the expected economic development from the mine and the port will create employment, some potentially negative economic impacts associated with a large-scale development must also be addressed by QMM and the government. These challenges are probably most clearly stated in negative terms. How can QMM develop this operation to avoid exacerbating economic inequalities between the project's stakeholders who stand to gain through taxes, royalties, salaries and wages, and other groups or individuals who will not directly benefit? How can QMM proceed so that the increased demands for consumer goods, food and housing occasioned by higher wages in the Tolanaro area do not excessively inflate local prices to the disadvantage of existing residents? What steps can QMM take so that a fair share of national revenues produced by taxes and royalties accrue to the benefit of the Anosy region, rather than being appropriated by a political or economic elite, as so often has happened with mineral wealth in other countries? These are important and not easily answered questions (Auty, 1993; Ross, 2001).

QMM has already considered a number of these issues. Madagascar laws require that the government return to the affected areas 70 per cent of royalties earned from these kinds of investments. It recognizes that, if not handled appropriately, opening the mine might give rise to unmanageable levels of speculative migration as people look for possible job opportunities. This is a very real problem. Gemstone discoveries elsewhere in Madagascar have occasioned influxes of thousands of opportunistic miners, far in excess of the available resources. QMM hopes to deal with problems of this sort in several ways. It will overtly discourage migration of job seekers, and will attempt initially at least to train and hire selected workers in advance of the launch date for construction work; it will do the same for the mining operations. Nonetheless, this issue may become aggravated. It is not clear how it plans to respond if speculative migration becomes excessive, though it is always possible that associated projects, such as the port development, will offer alternative sites for employment.

QMM hopes to deal with several of these economic challenges by fostering regional economic development of the area. QMM has worked with a local NGO to develop a micro-credit system in Tolanaro area. It intentionally decided on the type and location of a port so that it could be used for other purposes. The current port concept will include one berth for minerals and large bulk exports and other berths to promote regional and national trade and development. QMM hopes that the existence of a new port in the area will encourage those who want to export additional quantities of local goods from sisal and granite, to fish or farm produce. It hopes that the new port will encourage more tourism by allowing cruise ships to stop at Tolanaro. By encouraging these developments, QMM hopes that additional households will be able to grow their incomes without having to depend directly upon QMM operations. If plans for expanded port usage go forward, the area will witness not only a dramatic expansion of job opportunities but also increased urbanization, sizeable population movements, increased and uncertain pressures on consumer and housing markets, as well as possible expression of social unrest. Responsibility for addressing the consequences of these changes will lie with federal, regional and municipal governments. However, QMM along with donors and local NGOs will necessarily be called upon to collaborate with the public sector so as to ensure that these economic and social changes add to the general good. The World Bank too will take its share of responsibility by helping to create a more attractive investment climate in Anosy as one of Madagscar's growth-pole regions.

Once construction and operations begin, QMM as well as the government and the World Bank are expected to take further action along these lines.

Conclusion

To all appearances, the Rio Tinto–QMM mine will be developed in ways that add value to Madagascar, the people of Anosy and Tolanaro. While it is too early to assess actual operations, it can be said that Rio Tinto has so far made it clear that it acknowledges the responsibility to address a wide range of environmental and social issues for which it is likely to be held publicly accountable. Despite mistakes and missed opportunities in other developing countries, it appears that RT is committed to ongoing learning; this is certainly to be hoped, since in the environmentally and socially fragile setting of south-eastern Madagascar, the firm is likely to confront unexpected problems and challenges for which the long pre-project assessment has not yet fully prepared it.

Acknowledgements

This study is based on consultation of publicly available documents on the proposed project and discussions with Daniel Lambert, president of QMM, who directs this project for RT from offices in Montreal and Antananarivo. It is also based on readings about this operation listed in the works cited (see especially QMM, 2001 and QMM, 2003a, b, c, d). I am grateful to Emmanuel Raufflet and Gail Whiteman for their comments on earlier versions of this chapter.

Notes

1. For the purposes of this discussion I will not attempt to gauge the validity or extent of these criticisms. I refer to them in order to indicate that RT has been vocally criticized for its operations and has been especially concerned in Madagascar to operate in ways that allow it to avoid or be able to address possible criticism.
2. HIV/AIDS represents a potential rather than a current issue. The rise in the rates of those affected with HIV disease has been associated with mining areas in southern Africa. As a result USAID agreed to partner with QMM to address this issue.
3. Environmental groups such as Friends of the Earth and Conservational International have criticized QMM's report for overstating current deforestation trends and being overly optimistic about their own reforestation plans (Nostromo, 2001).
4. Friends of the Earth have called attention to what they regard as several flaws in QMM's environmental surveys, which, they argue, failed to look at the impact of the operations on marine turtles and increased carbon sequestration (Nostromo, 2001).

References

APHRN (2000) Asian-Pacific Human Rights Network, 'Human Rights Feature', Article 623. www.corpwatching.org/campaigns/PCD.jsp?articleid=623

Auty, R. M. (1993) *Sustaining Development in Mineral Economies: The Resource Curse Thesis* (London and New York: Routledge).

GRAIG (1990) Groupe de Recherche et d'Analyse Interdisiplinaire en Gestion de l'Environmrent, *Social Analysis Report* (Université de Québec à Montréal).

ITM (1999) Instituto de terco mundo, *The World Guide* 1999/2000 (Oxford: The New Internationalist Publishers).

Kennedy, D. (2001) 'PT Kelian: A Case Study of Global Operations', http://www.corpwatch.org/campaign/PCD.jsp?articleid=622, accessed 18 February 2003.

Mitchell, A. (2000) 'Could This Child's Struggles to Survive Help to Spark a Wave of Extinction that Threatens Humanity? A Special Report from the Vanishing Forests of Madagascar', *The Globe and Mail*, 15 April 2000, pp. A11, A14, A15.

Nostromo Research (2001) 'The Case Against QMM/Rio Tinto in Madagascar' read at: www.minwesand communities.org/Company/foemadagascar.html.

QMM (2001): QIT Madagacar Minerals SA, *Ilmenite Project: Social and Environmental Impact Assessment*. Presented to the Office Natiuonal pour l'Environment de Masdagascar, May 2001.

QMM (2003a) 'Projet Ilmenite: Rapport de Faisabilite', QIT Madagascar Minerals S.A. and l'Office des Mines Nationales et des Industries Strategiques. Submitted to l'Office des Mines Nationales et des Industries Strategiques, 14 May 2003.

QMM (2003b) 'Projet Ilmenite: En Route vers un Developpment Durable', August 2003.

QMM (2003c) 'Port d'Interest National Tolanaro', November 2003.

QMM (2003d) 'Projet Ilmenite: Rapport de Faisabilite: Rapport d'Etape, deposited with l'Office des Mines Nationales et des Industries Strategiques, November.

Ross, M. (2001) 'Extractive Sectors and the Poor', An Oxfam America Report.

Whiteman, G. and Mamen, K. (2002) 'Examining Justice and Conflict between Mining Companies and Indigenous Peoples: Cerro Colorado and Ngabe-Bugle', *Journal of Business and Management*, vol. 8(3), pp. 293–310.

WRM (1999) World Rainforest Movement, 'Madagascar: Communities Defend Rainforest Against Rio Tinto', WRM Bulletin No. 22, 22 April. www.wrm.org.oy/bulletin/22/madagascar.html, accessed 15 January 2003.

WWF International and IUCN (1999) World Wide Fund for Nature and The World Conservation Union, *Metals from the Forest: Mining and Forest Degradation*, Special Supplement in *Arborvitae* (newsletter), January.

7

Hard Times Recalled: The Child Labour Controversy in Pakistan's Soccer Ball Industry

Farzad Rafi Khan

Introduction

'Timeo Danaos et dona ferentes.' These words in Virgil's *Aeneid* (2:49), translated proverbially as 'Beware of Greeks bearing gifts', are uttered by the priest Laocoon seeing the colossal wooden horse that had appeared outside the walls of Troy – a pretended token of peace but concealing forces that would destroy the city. Today his words are an apposite reminder that one should be wary of 'great expectations' proffered by outsiders, especially when couched in idealistic or utopian terms. This is sound advice, as this chapter will demonstrate, in interpreting the dynamics and utopian promises of corporate social responsibility in 'developing' countries.

This chapter explores the origins and consequences of an international exercise in corporate responsibility undertaken by the soccer industry to phase out child labour from its production processes in Sialkot, Pakistan. In the mid 1990s, the international media exposed the use of child labour by the soccer ball industry. Children, as it would turn out, were involved in stitching soccer balls along with their parents in their village homes. In reaction to this adverse publicity campaign and consumer rage, the industry put together an initiative to remove children from the soccer ball production process. This initiative came to be known as the 'Project to Eliminate Child Labour in the Soccer Ball Industry in Pakistan'.

The project was launched chiefly to placate Western consumers and preserve the reputations of the leading brands in the sports goods industry. It thus ended up paying little attention to the local context and the needs of the child soccer ball stitchers and their families. Instead, the project made removing child labour from soccer ball stitching its primary objective. It paid little attention to the goal of creating wealth for the local community by way of ensuring sustainable livelihoods that would meet families' basic needs without those families being forced to send their children to the external labour market. The overriding flaw in the initiative was to conceive of child labour in isolation, as if it existed in a social and economic vacuum. The local reality, however, was far complex, for child labour was intricately enmeshed in the social fabric of the local community, particularly the household economy of the poor. By tugging at one thread, the fact of child labour, without seeing how deeply it was interwoven with other parts of the local economy (e.g. home-based women's employment) that would be pre-judicially affected by such interventions, Western consumers and the sports goods industry, together with the international and local NGOs that worked on the project, ended up unravelling the entire social fabric of the soccer ball stitchers' household economy. Incomes were savaged, particularly the liveli-hoods of women soccer ball stitchers, a large proportion of whom ended up suffering severe social and economic trauma.

Pakistan: A brief introduction

The area now known as Pakistan has long been inhabited, boasting the ruins of many ancient civilizations. As a modern nation-state, however, Pakistan came into being as an independent country on 14 August 1947.

At the time of independence, Pakistan was considered by *Time Magazine* to be 'an economic wreck [with serious social unrest]' (Zaidi, 1999, p. 84). Since 1947, Pakistan's real GDP (adjusted for inflation) has grown, with slow-downs in the 1970s and 1990s, at an annual average rate of about 5 per cent, a rate sufficient to keep pace with the country's equally explosive popula-tion growth rate of about 4 per cent (Statistics Division, 2003a, pp. 11, 76). To have an annual 5 per cent real growth in output over a period spanning more than half a century is quite impressive. Pakistan today also has more diverse industrial base than at the time of its creation. The country now produces a wide spectrum of items, from soccer balls to mangoes, for export markets.

Agriculture, which dominated Pakistan's economy at its inception, now contributes about a quarter of GDP; it is still the largest sector in terms of employment accounting for approximately 42.1 per cent of the country's workforce (Statistics Division, 2003b, p. viii). The relative decline in agricul-ture's contribution to the economy has been matched by the ascendancy of the industry and services sectors of the economy. Industry accounts for a quarter of the national output, while the services sector now accounts for half of the country's GDP (*The Economist*, 2003, p. 40). The output from all of three sectors translates to a per capita income for Pakistan of US$400 (Statistics Division, 2003c, p. 487).

This development, however, has not greatly helped the vast majority of the Pakistani population. After over five decades of economic growth that saw 8 of the 17 wealthiest billionaires and millionaires in Pakistan being retired military officers or their sons (Zaidi, 1999, p. 439), the social register reads grimly as follows:

> In Pakistan, 42 million people or roughly 30 per cent of the population are income poor; 47 million adults or 62 per cent of the adult population cannot read or write, 76 per cent of the female population is illiterate; 8 million children are out of school; 61 million people or 45 per cent of the population have no access to safe drinking water; 54 million people or 40 per cent of the population have no access to even basic health services; 72 million people or 53 per cent of the population have no access to sanitation; 9 million children under the age of 5 or 38 per cent of the under 5 population are malnourished. (Haq, 1999, p. 3)

Sialkot: An overview

Relative to the rest of Pakistan, Sialkot is quite prosperous. By virtue of its agriculture and its industry, Sialkot ranks as the fourteenth highest district out of 91 districts in Pakistan in terms of the human development index (Hussain, 2003, p. 12). Still, we see plenty of squalor in Sialkot; in fact that is the word used to describe the district by a recent US Department of Commerce report (2000, p. 207) which otherwise (unsurprisingly) eulogizes the dynamism of Sialkot's private sector. Another report, equally gushing in its praise of Sialkot's 'culture of enterprise', mentions briefly and somewhat euphemistically in passing that 'Sialkot's road and other infrastructure [*sic*] are primitive and choked' (Ghani, 2002). Only 2.6 per cent of the villages, where more than 70 per cent of the population live, have a piped water supply (US Department of Commerce, 2000). Drainage facilities are available in only 27 per cent of the villages (APFOL, 1999, p. 3). Only half of the roads in the villages are asphalt (Save the Children, 1997); of these, the majority are in poor condition and often become flooded and impassable with a slight amount of rain. The new wide-lane roads bypass most of Sialkot's population; the roads in the inner-city areas where the working classes live are in a state of complete neglect.

Most of Sialkot's population cannot afford basic healthcare or have access to basic health facilities (APFOL, 1999, p. 7). Public schooling is in disarray. According to a survey by Save the Children (1998), 'most of the schools were lacking in basic amenities including drinking water, toilet facilities and blackboards. Many teachers were absent and SMCs [school management committees comprising teachers and parents] were either nonexistent or inactive' (p. 10). The female literacy ratio in Sialkot, though better than the national average, is still unforgivably low at 51.5 per cent, dropping further to 45.5 per cent for rural females (Bureau of Statistics, 1998).

Municipal services are equally non-existent. There are only three traffic policemen to regulate more than 18 000 vehicles registered in Sialkot (US Department of Commerce, 2000; Dawn, 2003a). These resource-starved municipal services are also overwhelmed by the stresses brought about by industrialization. Thanks to the boom in leather exports over the last two decades, there are now 163 tanneries just around the city itself. They are, 'a consistent source of pollution, generating contaminated waste water' (US Department of Commerce, 2000). Instead of responding to this environmental degradation by helping to build a wastewater treatment plant, the private sector is responding to this crisis by building a multi-million-dollar international airport that perhaps will be used by less than 1 per cent of Sialkot's population. The fruits of economic expansion have, with some minor exceptions (e.g. all the villages have electrification, albeit with a highly unreliable electricity supply) (Dawn, 2003b), not significantly touched the lives of the vast majority of Sialkot's population.

The soccer ball industry before the child labour crisis

Soccer balls came to be produced in Sialkot in the late nineteenth century by firms there that were producing a variety of sports goods from cricket bats to hockey sticks for British India, and had decided to add soccer balls to their production lines. Sialkot's reputation as a sports goods manufacturing centre soon spread to other parts of India. British soldiers and missionaries would send their damaged sports items for repairs. Siakot's tennis rackets were in high demand, even though they were somewhat rough-and-ready in quality. By 1880, the tennis racket industry was organized along religious lines. The *mistris* (artisans) were Muslims; the middlemen who interfaced between them and the British clientele were predominantly Hindus and Sikhs. These middlemen would send Sialkot's sports goods to the rest of the British Empire, including England. Production in those days was conducted on a cottage-industry basis, with the manufacturing of rackets taking place in the workers' homes.

In 1888, two Sikh brothers, Ganda Singh Uberoi and Jhanda Singh, opened Uberoi Limited, the first sporting goods factory in Sialkot. They started off with a half dozen men manufacturing cricket bats using the willow found amply in the Kashmiri forests nearby (Apna Sialkot, 2003). They soon added other product lines such as 'tennis and badminton rackets, hockey sticks, polo sticks and assorted balls' (Weiss, 1991, p. 123). The Uberoi factory, on account of its commercial success, became the dominant design for organizing sports goods production in Sialkot. Cottage-based manufacture gave way to factory organization, with Sikhs and Hindus owning the factories. They also 'arranged for the raw materials and quality control, while Muslim craftsmen did the actual manufacturing' (Weiss, 1991,

p. 123). Along with adults, children came to work in these factories as apprentices to adult master craftsmen, learning the craft of skilfully producing sports goods. As a former child worker and later successful entrepreneur, Bashir Ahmad, recalls:

> For three years I worked at Uberoi's factory, during my childhood. When I was a little boy and I would have the *takhti* [school slate board] around my neck, they would put me to work when school would finish. At that time we continued to learn for seven years from our teachers at the factory. (Weiss, 1991, p. 123)

Another account explains the organization of labour in these factories at that time:

> A system of apprenticeship was started and workers in Sialkot were trained to follow English methods. Apprenticeship indentures were not actually employed but boys were taken on for a couple of months or so, to judge of their suitability and were paid 3 to 4 annas a day; their parents were then asked if they agree to the boys being bound for three years; they were then specialised in light work such as stitching balls and as they grew they were pushed up into higher grade work in the same line. After the first period they usually signed on again and were put on to piecework and were finally graded into classes. Many boys left after six years and many stayed on for 14 or 18 years. (Apna Sialkot, 2003)

These factories began innovating their production processes by importing European industrial technology, entering into joint ventures with British firms and hiring British engineers as consultants. For example, Uberoi Limited imported a boiler engine from England for its factory in 1913 – the first factory in all of Punjab to be powered by a machine source (Weiss, 1991, p. 123). Around this time, it also employed the services of English experts who introduced many patents and improvements to the factory production process (Apna Sialkot, 2003).

The industry received a massive boost with the advent of the First World War, when sports goods production in Europe came to a stand still and Sialkot began to fill the production void. Sialkot goods began to be found not only in the British Empire but also in countries such as Japan and the US. Thus, by the 1920s, Sialkot workshops were producing a wide variety of sports goods, from tennis rackets to polo sticks and soccer balls, sold internationally. Its export success drew the notice and admiration of the colonial administration. In 1922, one Sayed Sahib[1] was awarded the British Empire Export Award for supplying footballs to the British Army (Ghani, 2002). The sports goods industry comprised factories that were quite small in scale, mostly comprising units employing between five to eight workers (Weiss,

1991, p. 124). The industry continued on this pattern of scale and owner-ship until it experienced sudden and massive changes brought about by Partition in 1947.

Ownership changed hands after 1947 when the subcontinent was parti-tioned into two countries, India and Pakistan. Sialkot came to be part of Pakistan. Not wanting to live in a Muslim-dominated country, Hindu and Sikh owners migrated to India; the entrepreneurial vacuum created by their departure came to be filled by Sialkot natives hailing from its educated Muslim urban middle class, such as Anwar Khawaja who set up one of the first post-partition sports goods factory in Sialkot in 1952. Though owner-ship changed, the industry kept on organizing its production on factory lines, as opposed to the earlier cottage-based system.

The industry continued to innovate, benefiting from an industrial policy that favoured capital accumulation and from a transfer of technology from its European customers, who decided to outsource all their production requirements to their Sialkot suppliers. In 1968 Sialkot produced its first (Fédération International de Football Association) FIFA-approved ball. Though it was beginning to move up the value chain, the industry was hit by a labour relations crisis in the early 1970s.

In 1972 Zulfiqar Ali Bhutto came to power as prime minister of Pakistan with a populist mandate in the wake of East Pakistan's 1971 declaration of independence as a separate state (Bangladesh). Bhutto's political campaign, which he would largely betray later, promised to remove class-based inequal-ities and usher in an era of worker and peasant rights (Burki, 1980). His pop-ulist rhetoric radicalized the working classes; and though he suspended fundamental rights and the constitution, he nevertheless encouraged labour as well as collective action against private industrial interests.

The 1970s in Sialkot saw plenty of strikes and union activity (Weiss, 1991). Unions began making numerous demands, from higher pay and better work-ing conditions to bonuses and increased representation. At the same time the government passed labour-friendly laws.[2] Factory owners reacted to this state-supported labour activism in a way that neither the government nor the unions had anticipated: they decentralized operations, sending stitching operations, in which most of the labour in a soccer ball factory is employed, back to their homes and villages. They 'cottaged-out' stitching, in other words, sending raw materials through a chain of contractors and subcon-tractors to the homes of workers in villages and collecting the finished soc-cer balls from their contractors, just as was done in the infancy of the soccer ball industry nearly a hundred years before. Workers were dispersed, so that labour could not be easily organized and mobilized. Unions could not be eas-ily re-united. From the owners' point of view, it was a brilliant counterstroke.

Cottaging-out work, apart from its effects of disbanding the unions, was also advantageous to manufacturers as it enabled them to evade imperfectly crafted labour laws that largely applied to factories having salaried employees

(RDC, 1996). The stitchers were hired on a contract, piece-rate basis, and by this artifice many of the benefits of Bhutto's progressive industrial laws were inapplicable to them (APFOL, 1999).

In spite of a tumultuous environment of labour agitation and strikes taking place all over Pakistan, the soccer ball industry continued to prosper gaining international market share. Up to the early 1970s, big brands like Adidas (according to one of its longest-serving suppliers) used to source from Spain where soccer balls were stitched in prisons. The Spanish government began discouraging this practice in the early 1970s, just when the Sialkot manufacturers were returning to cottaging-out; a constitutional amendment in 1978 banned the use of prison labour for commercial purposes. But Adidas and other major brands had waited for this constitutional amendment; they had already begun to search for alternative sources. Sialkot entrepreneurs had been making efforts to obtain contracts from Adidas since 1970, regardless of the changes that were taking place in Spain. In late 1974, when they approached the founding owner of Adidas, Adi Dassler, they found, to their surprise, a sympathetic audience. In 1975 two Sialkot companies entered into agreement with Adidas. Three years later, when Adidas won the bid to supply the soccer ball to the 1978 World Cup in Argentina, it was Sialkot that made the famous Adidas 'Tango' ball. This brought Sialkot to the most prestigious realm of the international soccer universe. Soon other international brands started sourcing from Sialkot. When Nike decided to make soccer balls in 1995, it came straight to Sialkot and sourced exclusively from there.

By 1995, just before the onset of the child labour crisis, Sialkot was turning out 60 to 80 per cent of the world's football production (Cummins, 2000). The industry had also become more concentrated: out of possibly hundreds of local soccer ball firms in Sialkot, only a handful among the top 10 had more than 100 employees (the majority had fewer than 50); yet these top 10 firms, according to a major Sialkot soccer ball exporter interviewed for this study, controlled 60 to 70 per cent of all soccer ball exports (APFOL, 1999). The number of people employed in the industry varies from estimate to estimate: an ILO study estimated the soccer ball workforce in 1995 to be around 100 000 (Awan, 1996, p. 5), while a corporate publication put the figure at 75 000 (Saga Sports, 1998).[3] The stitching workforce estimates also vary from 30 000–65 000 (Awan, 1996: 5; IMAC, 2003).

Throughout this time (i.e. up to 1995), the decentralized, village-based organization of soccer ball production remained in place, with the cottage industry spreading out within a 10-mile radius of Sialkot city. Panels (the individual hexagon- and pentagon-shaped pieces that make up a soccer ball) were prepared in the factories; then, through an elaborate chain of subcontractors, they were taken to some 1600 villages surrounding Sialkot, where they were stitched together, mostly in homes. An insignificant number of balls were stitched in shacks called workshops that were owned by the subcontractors (HRCP, 1995; RDC, 1996). Figure 1 illustrates the soccer ball production chain.

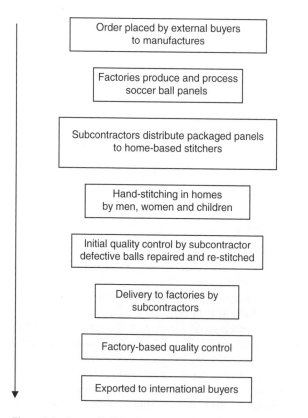

Order placed by external buyers
to manufactures

Factories produce and process
soccer ball panels

Subcontractors distribute packaged panels
to home-based stitchers

Hand-stitching in homes
by men, women and children

Initial quality control by subcontractor
defective balls repaired and re-stitched

Delivery to factories by
subcontractors

Factory-based quality control

Exported to international buyers

Figure 7.1 Soccer ball production process before child labour crisis

Source: Adapted from Save the Children, 'Info – Pack (date not given)'.

Women constituted a significant percentage of the stitching workforce; estimates vary from 30 to 58 per cent (Save the Children, 2000; IMAC, 2003). Similarly, estimates of children involved in stitching range from 5000 to 17 000, though the more reliable ILO estimates place the figure at about 15 000 (ILO, 1999; Husselbee, 2001, p. 133).

The local industrialists supplying international brands (e.g. Nike) prospered in the soccer ball export trade, building opulent office buildings with gleaming glass façades that might well rival the glamour of high-tech industrial parks in North America or Europe. Such riches, contrary to the promise of 'trickle-down' economics, did not reach the soccer ball stitchers. Theirs was a life of grinding poverty, where what Marx called 'the dull compulsions of living' pressed all hands, including children, into stitching soccer balls to make ends meet. Wages, depending on a host of factors, from the quality of balls being stitched to the stitchers' proximity to the contractors or factories (with those further away receiving lower wages), varied from Rs45–100 (i.e., approximately US$1.42–US$3.16) for a full day's work (Save the Children, 1997, p. 23). A stitcher could assemble at most three to four balls per day and the ball rate ranged from US$0.47–US$0.79[4] (ibid). A first-quality soccer ball in the West would retail for upwards of US$100; less than one dollar would go back to the stitcher household that produced the ball. Given that the average household size in Sialkot was about 8 persons and that almost half the stitching households had only one breadwinner, the stitching families barely (if at all) eked out a living (Saaed, 1998, pp. 18–19). All worked long hours, whenever possible; for example, women would stitch in the spare time between their household chores and tending to their children (RDC, 1996; Save the Children, 2000a).

The child labour crisis begins

In the 25 years preceding 1995, Sialkot's soccer ball industry rarely attracted the notice of the international media. Some articles praised the important contribution the soccer ball industry was making to Pakistan's economic development, earning vital foreign exchange. B. Crossette's article in the *New York Times*, 'Soccer Balls Sustain Pakistan Town' (Crosette, 1990) highlighted the economic and entrepreneurial prowess of the soccer ball industry. The article portrayed stitching work in idyllic terms: a tranquil village industry where 'youngsters' learn their trade sitting in the shade at the feet of a master craftsman, earning US$28 a week – which, the writer hastened to add, was 'a good wage in Punjab' and providing much needed income for the families of the boy apprentices. The common motif of these stories was that the entrepreneurial energies of the soccer ball industry and the skills of the stitchers (including young boys working in their village homes) were helping to build a better, more prosperous Pakistan.

This comforting message would undergo a dramatic shift. On 6 April 1995, CBS broadcast a news documentary on the soccer ball industry in Sialkot (CBS, 1995). The documentary investigated and addressed the question of whose hands stitched the soccer balls. The hands that stitched the soccer balls, according to the CBS story, were those of children as young as 6 years old working in dark and dank one-room workshops without electricity or water. The poverty of the children and of their working conditions was starkly displayed in the images that were aired nationally in the US. The CBS story had forcefully brought to the fore the unsettling irony of poor children at work so that 'rich' American kids could play.

On several counts, the CBS story failed the test of journalistic rigour. First, CBS made allegations that children earn less than adults. However, no evidence was provided except for the questionable testimony of their interpreter who, not being a native of Sialkot and lacking in-depth knowledge of the soccer industry, could hardly be counted upon and actually failed (as we shall shortly see) to give an accurate portrayal of the work situation in Sialkot. CBS overlooked certain key questions that, if asked, would have seriously challenged its claim that children were being paid less than adults for the same work. Could this rate differential be because adults worked on higher-quality soccer balls requiring more strength for sewing stitches, and therefore earned more money per ball?[5] Alternatively, could the wage differential be explained by the different types of stitching operations performed?[6] Children were usually involved in operations, due to their limited physical strength, that earned lower rates – sewing the initial parts, rather than the whole ball. By treating stitching as a monolithic, homogeneous and undifferentiated work, ignoring its nuances and complexities (wage rates contingent on the combination of types of stitching work and types of soccer balls), the report misleadingly implied that since the stitching work was the same, the apparent fact that children were getting paid less than adults must mean that children were being employed in the industry because they were a cheaper labour resource. At this time, this seemed to justify a widely held popular stereotype that often does not hold upon closer empirical scrutiny about why children are found working in the developing world. Though the report at the beginning mentioned that stitching was done in surrounding villages, the interview with the child stitcher took place in a workshop. Other footage of children at work in Sialkot showed them in workshops, giving the incorrect impression that this was the primary workplace for most Sialkot children. In fact, most of the children stitched balls at home. But that was not the version that was aired. The factually questionable CBS story was picked up by the other mass media both in the US and abroad, where it was further embellished and distorted.

The media campaign worked. On 28 June 1996 with official endorsement of the US department of Labour and prominent politicians (e.g. Joseph Kennedy II), a campaign was launched to bring an end to child labour in the soccer ball industry. The campaign came to be known as the 'Foul Ball Campaign' coordinated by the International Labor Rights Fund (a Washington-based labour advocacy group) in cooperation with a network of labour, consumer, religious, sports and child advocacy groups (US Department of Labor, 2003). The campaign called on everyone from youth soccer leagues to school administrations to put pressure upon industry to stop using children in the production of soccer balls.

In Pakistan, the local Sialkot soccer ball manufacturers could not understand some of the baseless allegations of inhumane working conditions being levelled at them by the international media. They were not so innocent of the other allegations (such as exploitative wages), which they conveniently ignored in a rush to paint themselves as self-righteous victims of sinister international conspiracies. The national press carried headlines such as 'Western propaganda on child labour doing great harm to economy' (Malik, 1996).[7]

The project: A solution for child labour

The somewhat fantastic conspiratorial explanations of the child labour controversy swirling in Sialkot did not prevent the soccer ball exporters and their industry from working to devise a solution to this problem (Riddle, 1997). As soon as the child labour issue first erupted in April 1995, the global soccer ball industry began holding a series of meetings in Europe and North America, as well as conversations with world government organizations such as the ILO and international NGOs such as Save the Children, to seek their help on how to address this issue.

At a press conference on 14 February 1997 as part of the SuperShow in Atlanta, Georgia, the global soccer ball industry unveiled its solution to the child labour crisis that had been plaguing it for almost 2 years. The industry announced that a project would be jointly established by the Sialkot Chamber of Commerce and Industry (SCCI), the United Nations Children's Fund (UNICEF) and the International Labour Organization (ILO) to phase out children from Pakistan's soccer ball industry over the next 18 months. The project's board principles were articulated in the Atlanta Agreement co-signed by the SCCI, UNICEF and ILO. Their aim was to eliminate child labour in the soccer ball industry in Pakistan. The project's objectives were based largely (though not solely) on ILO conventions 138 and 59, which essentially prohibit employment of children under the age of 14. The agreement stated that for the purposes of the project, ' "Child Labour" shall be deemed to be present in Pakistan whenever children under age 14 are working in conditions that interfere with schooling, or that are hazardous or otherwise injurious to their physical, mental, social or moral well-being' (Save the Children, 1997, p. 63).[8]

The project had two goals: the first was the elimination of child labour in soccer ball production, to be accomplished in an 18-month period; the second was the 'elimination of child labour in other local industries' in Sialkot (ibid.). This was viewed as a long-term goal to be worked upon after the attainment of the primary goal. Implementation of the project began in October 1997. The Atlanta partners, working with local NGOs, implemented its prevention, monitoring and social protection programmes. It was decided to phase out child labour by shifting stitching, the activity in which children were involved, to monitorable 'stitching centres' – factories or workshops that, unlike village homes, could be easily accessed by ILO monitors to verify that no children were involved in stitching soccer balls. The social protection programme was to take care of the displaced child stitchers and their affected families by providing alternative income opportunities, largely through micro-credit schemes and vocational training (e.g. tailoring). The children were to be provided with an education, either by enrolling them in government schools or by setting up one- to three-room education centres where they would be educated up to grade 5 level, attending school for a few hours a day. These education centres were called Non-Formal Education Centres (NFEs).

The project's score card: Winners and losers

As of 2004, the project is now in its seventh year of operation and has generated several consequences for Sialkot. The consequences can be discussed in relation to the three main stakeholder groups that were involved directly with the project: the Sialkot industry, NGOs and, of course, the stitchers.

For Sialkot manufacturers, the project has helped them to phase out child labour. According to the ILO, over 95 per cent of all soccer ball production in Sialkot is now child-labour-free (IMAC, 2003). By helping to phase out child labour from the production processes, the project has enabled local manufacturers to maintain their dominant world market share of the soccer ball industry. At one point around the fall of 1996, when international condemnation was reaching its peak, Sialkot soccer ball manufacturers (including Nike's supplier, Saga Sports) had seriously considered the demise of their industry with their products being banned from European and North American markets (Zubeiri, 1996; Mir, 1996). At present, largely due to the project, this fear has been banished. Manufacturers have also gained considerable experience in handling social responsibility crises. Instead of denying criticisms outright, as some of the Sialkot manufacturers did when the child labour crisis first erupted (*Business Recorder*, 1995), they now constitute fact-finding missions through the Sialkot Chamber of Commerce and Industry (SCCI) consisting of not only themselves but also third parties. This was clearly seen in 2002 when Global March alleged that children were still largely involved in soccer ball industry (Roy, 2002). The Sialkot industry quickly established a fact-finding mission, which included local members of Global March, who incidentally had not been involved in the study that had made those charges (Mirza, 2002). The fact-finding mission marshalled sufficient evidence to dismiss the allegations as being quite baseless.

These benefits to the industry, however, have come at a cost. According to the only detailed study done of the project's effects on manufacturing, it appears that manufacturing costs have risen by about 10 per cent for the manufacturers, without a commensurate increase in the prices they receive from their international customers (Cummins, 2000). These higher costs can be attributed to the outlays involved in establishing the new stitching centres and the higher wages that manufacturers began paying in 1998 to entice adult male stitchers to work there. This cost increase has meant that the Pakistani soccer ball industry, which already was losing market share to China for lower-quality balls, has now, according to Cummins (2000), effectively been priced out of the lower-quality ball market. The project has nevertheless helped them maintain their dominant market share in higher quality balls, where the real profit margins are. Therefore, overall, we can say that the project has been beneficial to the manufacturers.

For the NGO community, the project has been a blessing on many fronts. Local NGOs such as Sudhaar (a Lahore-based education NGO) and international organizations such as Save the Children can take substantial credit for their work as part of a project that has been hailed in the highest circles of officialdom as a model for dealing with social issues involving industry. Lastly, according to interviews with Pakistani NGO staff, the project seems to have added to the capacity of their organizations. For example, staff members at Sudhaar stated in interviews that they have a higher skill set, thanks to the training they received in various project techniques (e.g., participatory rural appraisal procedures) from their donors (e.g., Save the Children). Further experience based on this training will certainly benefit the individuals and the organizations in implementing other such projects. For example, a local NGO employee of Bunyad Literacy Community Council (BLCC), one of the Pakistani NGOs who worked on the child labour project, now finds that work on a similar project in Sialkot's surgical industry has led to far less chaos and anxiety than the soccer ball child labour project entailed.

Not all NGO staffers interviewed were so sanguine about their organizations' enhanced capacities and skill sets. Some felt the gains had been too few and far between. The project, they said, had had far greater potential for adding local capacity (such as in-depth database management and training) than it actually managed to deliver; only a few organizations benefited substantially. This complaint was heard most often from members of Sialkot-based NGOs, who criticized the international donors for allegedly giving the lion's share of the project's limited training opportunities to their NGO partners based in Lahore. Thus some parts of Pakistan's NGO community were left with a feeling of having been discriminated against – unhappy that they had not been involved in the child labour solution as fully as they could have wished to be.

There are other similarly distasteful feelings that the project has generated, which are more widely shared – notably, a strong feeling of cynicism, particularly among the NGO field staff who interacted directly with the soccer ball stitchers. This feeling has largely grown from contradictions in the project's outcomes and the way they have been euphemistically reported to outsiders. For example, take UNICEF's crowning project achievement, referred to constantly by UNICEF and the SCCI: 100 per cent school enrolment of all children in the Sialkot district aged 5 to 7 years. Apart from UNICEF, most NGOs are highly sceptical of this figure: if 100 per cent of children in that age bracket are in proper government schools, then how, they ask, does one explain the incidence of those children learning in their non-formal education centres? The answer, as these NGOs inform us, lies in UNICEF's statistical practices. UNICEF could only make its 100 per cent claim because of the way it defined enrolment: any child who was registered at any point in time in a school would be considered enrolled for the whole year – even if the child were to drop out the next day.

Such behaviour by UNICEF and other NGOs has made lower-level employees of these organizations question the motives and sincerity of the NGOs. In their interview conversations, many of them view the child labour project as one giant *kagazi karawai* – an Urdu expression meaning organizational work where everything looks pretty on paper while reality holds altogether a different story. In interviews with lower-level staff, instances of apparent corruption were often attributed to *kagazi karawai*: NGO executives, it was suggested, exploited the project as a resource-extraction tool to funnel donor money to their private ends. These employees complained that the purported beneficiaries – the stitchers – received only a fraction of the project funding allocated in their names, while NGO higher-ups spent the lion's share on executive salaries, foreign trips and expensive office vehicles. One NGO social mobilizer and educator commented:

> [NGOs] hide all the money they are getting in their [i.e., stitchers'] names. If everyone [stitchers] was paid what has been spent in this project, they would all be driving pajeros. For every one dollar goes to people ten dollars are consumed in overhead. (24 September 2003)

While some of these claims may be exaggerated, NGO employees' perceptions are real enough[9] and must be taken into consideration – especially since these perceptions of resource wastage tend to sap the positive energies of the NGO project community seeking to aid the child stitchers and their families.

Though the NGO community, institutionally speaking, claims the project as an unqualified success, this euphoria is not shared by the NGO workers, especially the lower-order field workers, whose mood is one of guilt mixed with cynicism producing such angry statements as the following: 'True my salary is tied to NGO sector but I do not feel good about the way it is operating. Top managers make Rs150 000 (US$2500) to Rs200 000 (US$3333) (Field staff make on average about US$100). The most profitable business in Pakistan is NGO!'.[10]

This mood becomes even more understandable when we take into account the project's consequences for the stitchers. A total of 1703 stitching centres have been constructed as of July 2003 (IMAC, 2003). These centres vary in their scale and are almost wholly either all-male or all-female centres. Most are one-room workshops with a capacity of 4 to 5 stitchers while a few are like miniature airplane hangars that can seat over 500 stitchers. Some of these larger centres provide transport facilities, meals and subsidized ration stores for stitchers, facilities that previously were not available. Also, stitchers have benefited from higher wages, intended to lure them from home into the stitching centres.

Similarly, the NGO community can claim success in that their income generation and education programmes have benefited child stitchers and their families (10 October 2003). These alleged project benefits, however, have materialized only for an insignificant portion of stitchers. Take for example, Save the Children's micro-credit programme. By April 1999 only about 12 per cent of the families that received micro-credit were stitching families (PCC meeting, April 1999). When the project was completed in September 2001, the project evaluation report showed that less than 30 per cent or so of the families that received micro-credit under the project were stitching families (Crawford, 2001, p. 16). Similarly, Save the Children's vocational training benefited about 400 stitchers (Crawford, 2001). Even if we take the smallest estimate of the stitching work force to be during the 1990s about 15 000 (Ghani, 2002), it seems that less than 3 per cent of the workforce received vocational training. If we include the vocational training by other NGOs, for example, BLCC and the Punjab Rural Support Programme (PRSP), the figure trebles, at best – still less than 10 per cent of the stitching workforce, based on the most conservative estimates (PRSP, 2002; IMAC, 2003). If we assume that the stitching workforce was most likely around 60 000 (Awan, 1996), then it seems that vocational training from all sources reached at best 3 per cent of the stitching workforce.

As for education, the projects that the NGOs developed and implemented were geared for making child stitchers literate. According to IMAC (2003), 10 000 children went through these projects. However, this figure is open to question. How many of these schemes were *kagazi karawai*? The work of one NGO that claimed to have imparted literacy to 7000 children (IMAC, 2003) was questioned by many employees of other NGOs. One of them produced invoices as evidence that the NGO in question had severe financial irregularities and that its reports could not be trusted at face value. Moreover, the figure tells us little about how many of these children were child-stitchers and what percentage of the total number of child-stitchers was comprised by these stitchers. One NGO's internal database suggests that about 66 per cent of children made literate under these schemes were stitchers. This means that at most 7000 child stitchers were made literate, less than half of the 15 000 child stitchers in Sialkot District estimated by an ILO midterm project evaluation report (PCC meeting, 28 January 1999). As for children enrolled in government schools, the UNICEF figure of 100 per cent enrolment for children aged 5–7 years has been shown to be quite dubious; moreover, though figures are not available, there is strong evidence that significant numbers of children enrolled soon dropped out of the school.

With the income generation and education programmes having largely missed the bulk of stitching families that were affected by the project, the lot of the stitchers seems not to have improved in any substantive way by all the NGO work carried out in their name. As for higher wages, they are paid only to those working in stitching centres. The women largely, due to home-based obligations, cultural and personal security reasons, refused to go to these centres. Women found home-based stitching far more convenient, first, because it enabled them to do their household chores, socialize and save time from commuting. Said one interviewee: 'Most of us would prefer work at home. What happens when we come to the centre and a guest comes?' (10 October 2003). Another says: 'We could stitch more at home. Here can only stitch during centre times. Here we stitch less. Before we could work at home and stitch in spare time. Now lose time commuting which could be used for stitching' (10 October 2003). Even one woman stitcher, who, unlike most female interviewees, liked working at the stitching centre because of health facilities and cheap groceries provided by her employer nevertheless left her job there because she had a hard time commuting to the centre.

Commuting problems are linked to another aspect of what 'home-based stitching-convenience' means to women stitchers – that is, privacy. By working at home the women avoid exposure, as soccer ball stitchers, to the slurs and derogatory comments made by their fellow villagers, particularly men, as they make the daily commute to centres.

> If we go to factories, people say nasty things about us. [They say] Putting red lipstick, going out, what do you have in mind. [We] do it [stitching] out of necessity. Common feeling [in villages] is that if one cannot do anything [one is useless] then stitch. No respect in village. (12 October 2003)

The fact is that the wider village culture of Sialkot soccer ball stitching is looked down upon as a lowly activity (PRSP, 2002). One woman stitcher, nostalgic about home-based stitching, sighed, 'Before you could earn with respect at home' (10 October 2003). Home-based stitching also provided women protection from the threat of physical or sexual abuse. One former Save the Children officer, a Sialkot village resident himself, pointed out that the potential threat of sexual harassment, realized in a few cases (including rape) made women overwhelmingly refuse working at centres, even at the pain of severe economic deprivation. Sexual abuse at the workplace too was a pivotal issue that led those involved in the project to argue against large monitorable centres and in favour of all-female stitching centres based in or near the villages of women stitchers. As he recollects:

> [During early days] subcontractors complained to us that they are being pulled in opposite directions. Industry wants work done in centres. But social pressures from workers, asking that women work should be given at home. We got this feedback [from subcontractors] about issue [of women wanting to work at home].
>
> Then there was near that [area of subcontractors referred to above], a big stitching centre of Saga Sports that provided pick and drop facilities. We

told women why not go there. But women were being exploited there, sexually. [The centre] had all male staff. Had middle woman would act as middle person. [She would] get girls to agree and then [the girls] taken to head office. This information went back to villages. Women not want to work. They reacted by stopping to come.

[We] got this information from female staff who were establishing school councils for female girl schools. Of course Saga Sports and Nike had to show centre operational. So brought girls from Gujurat [a nearby district]. Then we found out [about the sexual exploitation of women stitchers]. But kept this issue [to ourselves]. Did not share it [with other NGOs]. This feedback we did not show to industry for fear they would harass females [sexually abused women stitchers] for telling us. (24 September 2003)

Sexual molestation also occurred in other companies, but Saga Sports (Nike's chief supplier) was quite notorious in this regard, even though in other respects it was an excellent employer, providing state-of-the-art workplace facilities for its workers.

The women stitchers who made the hard trek to the stitching centres form at best maybe 20 per cent of the pre-project female stitching workforce (Awan, 1996; IMAC, 2003). The remainder who refused stitching centre work, whether out of self-respect, home obligations or prohibition by their men folk, have paid a terrible economic price. They have found themselves at a sharp edge of a pincer movement. At one end they are losing the cheaper ball orders to China (Cummins, 2000), which can produce them at lower rates; on the other end, for higher quality balls, they are losing business to the stitching centres. Caught in these economic pincers, they must compete with one another for the fewer balls that are now stitched at village homes, driving wages down even further – much to the satisfaction of those unscrupulous subcontractors, who further press home their exploitative advantage. A woman stitcher interviewed at her home angrily told me:

Wages are poor. We have children. Work hard to earn bread. We get money on times [from subcontractor] sometimes. Ten years [I have been] stitching. If I protest, there are 1000 people willing to stitch. [Subcontractor will] say fine. You do not want to work, [I will] give it to others. (11 October 2003)

Another woman stitcher described the drastic drop in orders in the following way: 'Before we used to get two balls, now get one ball. If before we get one ball, now make half' (11 October 2003). Yet that woman stitcher was relatively fortunate, having lost only 50 per cent of her pre-project production levels. Others have fared worse.

Though wage rates initially increased for male stitchers at the centres, they were not enough to compensate for the loss of income suffered by women and children now unable to stitch. In absolute terms, household incomes fell. Though, NGO personnel dread speculating on this matter, most of them estimated in interviews that average household incomes have fallen by around 25–30 per cent in absolute terms.

The aftermath of the child labour crisis has seen the difficulties for stitchers rising. Even the male salary increases have been more than wiped out by the five years of double-digit inflation. Wages have not been raised since 1998; coupled with the lost incomes of women and children, households have seen their already-marginal purchasing power eroding even further. No wonder then that NGO employees have felt that whatever good will that had been built between them and the stitcher community is beginning to vanish, or that quite a few stitchers register resentment at having their miseries opportunistically used by the project organizations to enrich themselves. The following outburst from two stitchers, who were interviewed together, powerfully captures the fragility of their existence that the project has so menacingly savaged:

> *Stitcher 1*: We stitch to feed ourselves. Sometimes get no work for two, three months... Listen, see this kid of mine. He is without clothes. That is our situation. I have nine children to feed. Not have time to go around organizing because I need to work every day to eat everyday.

> *Stitcher 2*: NGOs, what benefit have they provided us? Make a NFE [non-formal education centre] and then say, 'We will pay master's [i.e. teacher's] salary.' Next month say to us, 'You pay. Six people per [school] committee. 1200 Rupees. Not that much [for you stitchers].' But what is the point of you then, if you want us to do self-help. Why are you here? You are here to earn big money. So many teams [foreign delegations] visited our NFE and they [NGOs] must have charged them much. Must have prepared big bills. Not interested in us. (6 October 2003)

Conclusion: Lessons of *Hard Times*

From the above case study, we can postulate certain, albeit tentative, understandings. International business is rooted in *both* the developed and developing world. The international community wanted international business to end child labour at once, while parents and the children in Sialkot were more interested in securing living wages. Of course, this Gordian knot of cultural contradictions could be cut by paying living wages to the adult stitchers. This would afford them the resources to educate their children and remove the children from the labour market, while meeting the international community's demand for production free of child labour.

For the three organizational sectors involved in this case – the international brands, their Sialkot suppliers and the NGO community – the case tells us the importance of meeting and working closely with those at the grassroots (e.g. the stitching families). Such local involvement would give such actors exposure to local context so that they can devise socially responsible engagements, without the sort of undesirable negative consequences that resulted when construction of stitching centres ignored the concerns and values of women stitchers.

What about codes of conduct and international labour standards? The lesson we can gain from the case is that international brands must pay attention to the spirit of these international labour codes – the 'good' or 'end' or 'values' that international standards are attempting to realize in a real social and economic *context*, whether it be the reduction of poverty, the improvement of education, the raising of wage levels, the prohibition of forced labour, or the well-being of children. By thinking about valued outcomes and ends, international business, if it so desires, will be in a position to see when conformity to the letter of the code (e.g. zero child labour presence in the workplace) can lead to a negation of its ultimate objective (e.g. well-being of the children) so that it can take necessary measures to ensure that its socially responsible behaviour is able to realize the valued ends for which it is enacted.

As for the international human rights groups and concerned citizens in both the developing and developed worlds who wish to check the abuse of human dignities in the pursuit of commerce, what this case has depicted so strikingly is that activism that is poorly conceived can be worse than no activism at all. Prior to the activism on child labour, the Sialkot families suffered from stagnant and exploitative wages. The activism that aimed merely to abolish child labour resulted in a drop in household incomes. If society is to expect international business to act responsibly for development, understood in the widest possible sense of the word, then it does not help to have sensationalist activism that gets its facts wrong, as was the case here. One should act on one's decent impulses. However, that practice of solidarity needs to be tempered with judiciousness, so that when activism intervenes with courage and intelligence, it will do so in a manner that restores dignity to those who are in want of it, rather than worsening their plight through interventions poorly conceived and rashly executed. Activism also, like the corporate community, must pay heed to the local context.

Incorporating local content into initiatives geared at making business more responsible, whether they originate from outside or within the business community, may, however, be quite a challenge. Such initiatives these days are negotiated far from the local sites in international arenas involving multiple transnational players from major corporations to human rights groups. This intensely transnational nature of present day corporate social responsibility initiatives has the danger, as sadly realized in this case, of being removed from and, hence, marginalizing the local stakeholders. In our soccer ball child labour case, key decisions were made and the blueprint for the project was articulated in Geneva, Zurich, London, Atlanta and Munich.

The agreement that ushered in the child labour elimination project was the 'Atlanta' agreement not the Sialkot agreement. Imagine how odd it would look if an equally intrusive project, one that would disrupt something so private as the household division of labour in a major North American or European city, was called the 'Sialkot Agreement' where all the key decisions were made by individuals neither from Europe nor North America. At no time during the project's conception and implementation were the stitchers consulted in any substantive way. They needed steady work, a good pay and adequate latrines. The female stitchers had household responsibilities and were opposed to working in desegregated environments where they would have had to interact with males outside their families. All of these needs were effectively ignored by the project's self-appointed social engineers, who performed a vivisection on the stitching community under the pressure of Western consumer sentiments.

Neither Western consumer activism nor the corporate response to it should ignore the contingent features, let alone the context, of the local site where such action is to unfold. One size does not fit all, as we have clearly seen. In the absence of local context, content and input into decision-making, what other results could one expect to befall on stitchers, particularly children and women? Reflecting on the Sialkot outcomes, the stitchers and their families would most likely agree with Thoreau: 'If I knew someone was coming over with the expressed intention of doing good, I would flee' (Fisher, 1997, p. 439).

The early sensationalist and flawed media reporting in the Western press seemed to have simply grafted the worst Dickensian child labour nightmares still dimly held in their late-industrial civilization's collective consciousness, onto Sialkot. Though the child labour situation was grim in Sialkot, it was not *Oliver Twist*. In a strange 'twist', however, the chain of events unleashed by the media outcry brought about changes in Sialkot that recall yet another novel and character of Charles Dickens. In effect, the whole soccer ball child labour reform, with its cast of characters from Pulitzer prizewinners to local NGO activists, ended by constructing a project that resurrected Gradgrind, perhaps the most memorable character from Dickens's *Hard Times*. In Coketown, where the banker and mill owner Bounderby bleeds his workers dry, telling them: 'the institutions of your country are not your piece-work, and the only thing you have got to do, is, to mind your piece-work,' Gradgrind has turned utilitarian educator – 'with a ruler and a pair of scales, and the multiplication table always in his pocket ... ready to weigh and measure any parcel of human nature'. On these principles he runs a school where the children are taught only 'facts' – the system sweating their minds, if not their bodies. The NGOs of the child labour elimination project in Sialkot succeeded also in setting up schools quite a bit like the one Gradgrind established – cheerless, one-room affairs filled with emaciated faces 'grinding at the mill of knowledge' while little was done to alleviate the material suffering of the children and their families. That Gradgrind would be resurrected, all thumbs and no fingers, as seen by the poorly targeted interventions, which benefited only a minority of the affected stitching families – resurrected largely by the so-called grass roots NGOs – is an irony worth noting. The child stitchers and their mothers who, as a result of the Sialkot interventions were denied work and saw their household income plummet, with little being done to alleviate their loss, would be hard put to read anything other than 'Hard Times' into this story.

Notes

Research for this case study was funded by the Canadian International Development Agency (CIDA) and the Social Sciences and Humanities Research Council of Canada (SSHRC). I began the study in November 2000 and completed it by October 2003. Three field trips were made to Sialkot, Pakistan in December 2000–January 2001, February–April 2003 and July–October 2003. These field trips enabled me to obtain primary and secondary documents and conduct interviews with male and female soccer ball stitchers, including children, who were affected by the child labour issue, as well as with NGO staff working locally on the soccer ball child labour elimination project in Sialkot. Approximately 115 people participated in these interviews. Of these, 51 were women stitchers and 36 were NGO personnel. The average length of interviews was about 80 minutes.

1. The name 'Sayed' apparently is Muslim; thus suggesting that the dominance of the industry by non-Muslims, though very great, was not total.
2. In 1992, for example, Bhutto's government enacted the Workers Children (Education) Ordinance which required the employer to provide free education to two children of each worker (APFOL, 1999, p. 11).
3. Such a wide variation in estimates is due to the part-time and 'flexible' nature of the contracting work. In a World Cup year, more hands are brought into the industry to meet the additional demand, and the figures swell to the maximum figure indicated above; in a downturn year, they gravitate towards the lower limit.
4. Conversions from Pakistani rupees are based on the average rate of exchange upto all prevailing in April 1995.
5. Wage rates differ on the type of ball being stitched. There are basically three types of balls:

   - Valati (meaning 'foreign' or 'English') is a high-end, grade A ball used for professional and club matches.
   - Lahori ('from Lahore') is a lower-end, Grade A ball used for club matches, amateur clubs and general retail.
   - Desi ('local') is a Grade B ball used for general retail and promotional purpose.

   Valati balls command the highest wage rates while the Desi balls have the lowest wage rates. Wages are paid at piece rates; in 1995 the range was from 18 rupees for Desi balls to about 35 rupees for Valati balls.

6. There are at least five types of stitching operations:

   - Thread waxing (primarily done by children);
   - Stitching individual panels (primarily done by children and women);
   - Stitching half a ball (done primarily by children, women and some men);
   - Stitching that joins two halves of a ball (done primarily by some children, but mostly by women and men);
   - Stitching the last six panels (called putting a 'bhan' on the ball). This is the most intricate part of the stitching process and it is largely done by men, though a small number of women and children also do this work. (Kazmi and Macfarlane, 2002)

   Wages would depend upon how many different stitching operations a worker performed; naturally whole-ball stitching commanded the highest wage rate.

7. Many of these 'conspiracy theories' (often couched in extreme jingoistic terms) were directed at India rather than at the West – an absurd notion on the face of it, given their own child labour issues (Schanberg, 1996).

8. This definition of child labour is a far more elaborate one than the definitions used in ILO (conventions 138 and 59), which consider child labourers as contingent on age (14 years). The Atlanta definition incorporates the age factor but then adds a host of other factors into its understanding of what constitutes child labour that go beyond the ILO conventions that are alluded to in the agreement.

9. In researching this study, information on internal costs for programmes being delivered under the project could be obtained only from one NGO known in the community to be more or less fiscally responsible. It would appear that office overheads consumed about 70 per cent of the budget of a programme aimed at improving education facilities for child stitchers. As for actual financial irregularities or evidence of fraud, one senior NGO executive showed this researcher from his personal files a number of invoices that clearly showed (to put it politely) massive irregularities on the part of the NGO that had prepared them. In one instance, a doctor's bill for visiting a village contained the amount of Rs275. In a clearly a different handwriting a number '1' was added to the amount in figures yet the amount in words read 'Rupees two hundred and seventy five only', indicating that this was likely the original amount. This senior executive claims that when he brought such discoveries to the attention of the concerned donor, he was given a dressing-down: 'Boss in Islamabad says, "Everybody does it. What is your problem!" He [the "boss"] is now in Geneva.' (15 September 2003)

10. Conversion is based on average exchange rates prevailing in October 2003.

References

APFOL (1999) All Pakistan Federation of Labour, 'Workers Behind the Label: A Study of Working Conditions in Sialkot' (Rawalpindi: APFOL).

Apna Sialkot (2003) 'History of Sports Industry in Sialkot', *Apna Sialkot* [website] [accessed 30 December 2003] http://www.apnasialkot.net/about_sialkot/history_of_sialkot_industry.asp.

Awan, S. A. (1996) 'Child Labour in the Football Manufacturing Industry' (Sialkot: Directorate of Labour Welfare, Punjab, in collaboration with International Programme on the Elimination of Child Labour (IPEC) of the International Labour Office).

Bureau of Statistics (1998) Punjab Development Statistics 1998 (Lahore: Government of Punjab, Pakistan).

Burki, S. J. (1980) *Pakistan under Bhutto, 1971–1977* (New York: St Martin's Press).

Business Recorder (1995) 'Footballs Can't Be Sewn by Children', *The Business Recorder*, 26 June, p. 3.

CBS (1995) 'Children at Work', CBS 1995 [retrieved 24 November 2003]. Available from Lexis-Nexis Electronic Database.

Crawford, S. (2001) *Lessons Learned from the Project to Protect the Rights and Livelihoods of Working Children in Pakistan* (Edinburgh: Edinburgh University).

Crossette, B. (1990) 'Soccer Balls Sustain Pakistan Town', *The New York Times*, 8 October.

Cummins, E. (2000) *The Pakistan Football Stitching Industry* (Islamabad: Save the Children Fund).

Dawn (2003a) 'Sialkot: Three Cops Control Sialkot's Traffic', *Dawn* [Internet Edition] [retrieved 2 January 2004] http://www.dawn.com/2003/12/29/local31.htm.

—— (2003b) 'Sialkot: "Foul play" in Zakat Distribution', *Dawn* [Internet Edition] [retrieved 4 March 2004] http://www.dawn.com/2003/11/23/local36.htm.

The Economist (2003) 'Pakistan: Country Profile' (London: Economist Intelligence Unit).

Fisher, W. F. (1997) 'Doing Good? The Politics and Antipolitics of NGO Practices', *Annual Review of Anthropology*, vol. 26, pp. 439–64.

Ghani, J. (2002) 'Sialkot – A City at Work' [retrieved 1 January 2004] http://www.the-south-asian.com/March2002/Sialkotper cent201.htm.

Haq, K. (ed.) (1999) *A Profile of Poverty in Pakistan* (Islamabad: Mahbub ul Haq Centre for Human Development).

HRCP (1995) Human Rights Commission of Pakistan, *Child Labour in Pakistan: Sialkot Kasur* (Lahore: HRCP).

Hussain, A. (2003) Pakistan National Human Development Report 2003: Poverty, Growth and Governance. (Islamabad: United Nations Development Programme (UNDP)).

Husselbee, David. 'NGOs as Development Partners to the Corporates: Child Football-Stitchers in Pakistan.' In Deborah Eade and Ernst Ligteringen (eds), *Debating Development: NGOs and the Future*, 127–44. Oxford: Oxfam International, 2001.

Kazoni, B. A. and Macfarlane, M. (2002). 'Elimination of Child Labour', (Unpublished manuscript: Warwick).

ILO (1999) International Labour Organization, Update Sialkot (newsletter), May (Sialkot: ILO) unpaginated.

IMAC (2003) International Monitoring Association for Child Labour, Fact Sheet of the Sialkot Soccer Ball Programme, July 2003 (Sialkot: IMAC).

Malik, N. (1996) 'Western Propaganda Against Child Labour Doing Great Harm to Economy', *The Business Recorder*, 8 April, p. 4.

Mir, A. (1996) 'Threat of FIFA Ban Jolts Football Industry', *Inter Press Service (Pakistan)*, 11 October.

Mirza, A. M. (2002) Physical Scanning of the Soccer Ball Stitching (Sialkot, Pakistan: Sialkot Chamber of Commerce and Industry (SCCI)).

PCC (1999): Project Coordination Committee, Minutes of the 21st Meeting, 29 April (Sialkot: PCC).

PRSP (2002) Punjab Rural Support Programme, 'Provision of Micro-Credit and Skill Training to the Soccer Ball Stitching Families in Sialkot: Midterm Report (January–December 02)' ILO–PRSP partnership p. 13 (Sialkot: Punjab Rural Support Programme – Sialkot).

RDC (1996) Raasta Development Consultants, 'An Assessment of the Working Child in the Soccer Ball Industry, Sialkot' (Karachi: Raasta Development Consultants).

Roy, P. (2002) 'Outside Sialkot: Child Labour in the Sporting Goods Industry: The Global March Against Child Labour', Report (New Delhi: Global March against Child Labour).

Riddle, J. (1997) 'Sports Industry Tackles Child Labor Issue', *Sportshop/Newsbulletin*, January/February, pp. 1–2, 14, 16.

Saeed, A. T. (1998) *Women's Stitching Centres: Exploring Avenues* (Public Document) (Sialkot: Save the Children (UK)).

Saga Sports (1998) 'SAGA as leader of Change', *Saga News*, May.

Save the Children (1997) *Stitching footballs: Voices of Children* (Islamabad: Save the Children Fund).

—— (1998) Social Monitoring Report (January–June 1998) (Islamabad: Save the Children (UK)).

—— (2000) *Milestones Reached: Partners working so that children won't have to* (Public Document) (Islamabad: Partners of the Sialkot Child Labour Project).

—— (2000a) *Social Monitoring Report (January–March 2000)* (Public document) (Islamabad: Save the Children (UK)).

Schanberg, S. H. (1996) 'Six Cents an Hour', *Life*, vol. 19(7), pp. 38–46.

Statistics Division (2003a) *Pakistan 2003: Statistical Pocket Book* (Islamabad: Ministry of Economic Affairs and Statistics, Government of Pakistan).

—— (2003b) *Labour Force Survey 2001–2002* (Islamabad: Ministry of Economic Affairs and Statistics, Government of Pakistan).

—— (2003c) *Pakistan Statistical Yearbook 2003* (Islamabad: Ministry of Economic Affairs and Statistics, Government of Pakistan).

US Department of Commerce (2000) 'International Market Insight Reports: Sialkot City: A Commercial Profile', Global News Wire 2000, October 2003. Available from Lexis-Nexis Electronic Database.

US Department of Labor (2003) [Bureau of International Labor Affairs], 'Soccer Balls' [retrieved 14 November 2003] http://www.dol.gov/ilab/media/reports/iclp/sweat4/soccer.htm.

Weiss, A. M. (1991) *Culture, Class and Development in Pakistan: The Emergence of an Industrial Bourgeoisie in Punjab*, Westview Special Studies on South and Southeast Asia (Boulder: Westview Press).

Zaidi, S. A. (1999) *Issues in Pakistan's Economy* (Karachi: Oxford University Press).

Zubeiri, S. (1996) 'Pakistan's First Child-Free Hand Stitched Soccer Ball Centre Opens', *Agence France Presse*, 26 November.

8
The Formation of Business Practices in South Korea

Joseph Smucker

Introduction

Why South Koreans embraced industrialization and economic development with such zeal remains somewhat conjectural. This was certainly not foreseen among development experts 50 years ago. In this paper I highlight a number of factors that provide some clues to understanding South Korea's unique course of economic development and conclude with some observations about emerging questions of equity and social justice. I begin with a brief description of the effects of geo-politics on South Korea following the end of the Second World War. Next, I describe the cultural and ideological themes that appear to have provided the rationale for both the motivation and the justification for the dislocations and privations endured by Koreans in the course of economic development. I then describe the way in which successive governments influenced the course of development. The role they played in the financial sector and their relationship with the large business conglomerates are important ingredients in this account. In the fourth and final section of the paper, I review a number of issues that deal with the social costs of South Korea's development. These are issues that are now in the forefront of any consideration of socially responsible business practices.

Geopolitical considerations

Korea has a very long and rich history with records going back beyond 200 BCE. Its geographic position has served as a pathway for military, diplomatic and cultural incursions from China and Manchuria in the north and from Japan in the south. For much of its history it consisted of three kingdoms often involved in various alignments or 'investitures' with China. Beginning in CE 918 it was ruled by one united dynasty, the Koryo dynasty, which, from 1231 until 1392 was forced into a state of vassalage to Manchuria as a result of the 'Mongol Conquest'. The Yi Dynasty that followed in 1392 ruled until its demise in 1910 with the conquest by Japan, which then annexed

Korea as a province (Osgood, 1951, pp. 157–210). Korea returned to its independent sovereign status at the end of the Second World War in 1945.

Immediately after the end of the Second World War in 1945, the Koreans installed a provisional government, committed to socialist ideals. This government was replaced by American occupation forces in the south and a government directed by the Soviet Union in the north. At the time of this division, most of the important industry was located in North Korea close to sources of minerals and hydroelectric power, while a more culturally conservative and poorer agriculture-based society existed in the South.

The provisional government in its pursuit of land reform, a strong voice for labour and social welfare, had been committed to policies that included the removal of the entrenched landed gentry. But American occupation forces, fearing the spread of communist regimes, replaced the provisional government with the nationalistic but conservative and authoritarian government led by Syngman Rhee.

Believing that there was some support for socialist regimes among the general population in South Korea, North Korea launched an attack in 1950. The invasion evolved into an extremely destructive war that lasted 3 years. Military aid from the Soviet Union supported North Korean troops and armed forces from China joined the North Korean army in fighting a coalition of American and South Korean troops along with armed forces and materiel from other United Nations allies. Since the signing of the armistice that ended hostilities in 1953, the US government has lent at least benign support for subsequent authoritarian regimes. South Korea has continued to occupy a front-line position in the defensive strategy of the US, first as an outpost of the West during the Cold War and then as a defensive bulwark against the communist state of North Korea. American troops have been stationed in South Korea continuously since 1953.

In the years immediately following the end of hostilities of the Korean War, South Korea, already poor before the war, was left extremely impoverished. In 1962, the gross national product per capita in South Korea was the equivalent of only US$87. Indeed, many American policy advisors at that time regarded South Korea as an area permanently dependent on its agricultural sector and having little chance for advanced industrialization. Nevertheless, the South Korean economy did profit from American economic aid and from the manufacture and sale of goods and services to American military forces. The involvement of the US in the Vietnam War increased demand for South Korean goods, especially basic materials such as textiles and concrete. American payments to South Korean military forces that served in that war contributed additional economic benefits.

In addition to the economic aid it received from the United States, South Korea's economy was and continues to be influenced by its geographical proximity to Japan. Despite considerable hostility toward Japan as a result of its long period of military and economic hegemony, aggressive Korean entrepreneurs, often with the aid of the government, developed intricate business networks and cross-holdings not unlike the Japanese *kereitsu* system. Further, South Korean governments adopted Japanese strategies for stimulating industrialization and directing the course of economic development. Indeed, economic ties between the two countries were formally established by the Park regime in 1965.[1]

Japan has been a major source of technology and has also provided a model for entry into American and more recently, European markets. American and European markets as well as the Japanese market have been of major importance for South Korea, since encouragement of export-oriented industries has been a major component of its governments' development strategies. Not only are these regions important as consumer markets, they are also important as sources for information about developments in technology and strategies in sales promotion. Foreign buyers provide information on product design and quality. They often provide training not only in technological skills but also in cost control and accounting procedures (Hobday, 1998, p. 55).

The role of culture

One of the puzzles of the rapid economic growth of South Korea is the population's acceptance of the many privations they have endured during the development process. Further, it is not clear why, the authoritarian governments have not also been 'rent seekers'?[2] Why did the state continue to invest in human, social and economic capital rather than consume the surpluses (Amsden, 1989, p. 64; Fields, 1995, p. 239)? How does one account for a development process that has been marked by favouritism, nepotism and kickbacks, and yet has enriched the population in economic terms? How have employers got away with requiring labour to work more hours per week than in any other industrialized and industrializing country? A clue to arriving at some answers may well be found in the interwoven nature of South Korea's cultural attributes and institutional structures.

Observers of economic development in different countries have been struck by a set of common attributes among the cultures of China, Hong Kong, Japan, Singapore and Korea. Many have ascribed these attributes as manifestations of a 'Confucian ethic' (D. J. Kim, 1996; Lie, 1998; Lim, 1999, p. 182). It is not that these attributes describe a necessary condition in accounting for motivations; nor are they entirely sufficient in their explanatory efficacy. Rather they are elements of public ideologies that *articulate* motives and that *justify* and *legitimate* the extraordinary human efforts devoted to rapid industrialization. Their effectiveness rests on perceptions of social conditions and explanations for their existence. In the case of those perceptions of social injustice they provide formulae for change. In arguing the case for the role of Confucianism, the stress should be on *elements* of the

Confucian philosophy rather than its entire corpus.[3] Indeed, the interpretation and application of Confucian principles differs somewhat among these countries. B.W. Kim, for example, argues that Confucianism was more an attribute of the elite in traditional Korean society, while being more pervasive among the general population in Japan (B. W. Kim, 1992, pp. 66–87).

South Korea also has a relatively large contingent of Christians, encompassing a third of its population (Lie, 1998, p. 141). Christian groups have often been in the forefront of dissident movements, both during the Japanese occupation and in association with labour movements since the Korean War. Buddhism also remains a visible presence. Indeed, for centuries, Confucianism has existed compatibly with Mahayana Buddhism in Northeast Asia. Still, the existence of these and other groups has not diminished the Confucian emphasis on collective welfare, whether defined in terms of family, clan or nation.

A general description of the elements in the Confucian ethic would include the importance of hierarchical order, the priority of group allegiance over personal wants, the importance of the family as an arena for proper socialization, a high value placed on education and scholarly training and a positive outlook toward worldly involvement. Further, there tends to be a fusion between the private and public spheres. The development of one's character is not so much a matter of perfection of the self as it is a consequence of one's contribution to the public welfare (Ching, 1977; Ch. S. Kim, 1992, pp. 13–14). Additionally, the concept of public welfare is not boundary-free but may be defined by a variety of jurisdictional limits ranging from family and clan to region and nation.

In the history of Confucian thought the priority of loyalties has provoked some dilemmas. There have been occasions when Confucian scholars have cited the danger of narrow family and kin loyalties in undermining loyalty and service to the ruler and hence to the larger collectivity. A contemporary expression of this dilemma is Earley's observation that in relationships in which each transaction requires a response of equal value, unrelieved states of indebtedness in contractual relations will lower levels of trust and often result in a general neglect of the public welfare. In exchange systems in which it is recognized that repayment can be made to other members of a given group rather than to the original provider, wider expressions of trust and concern for the general social welfare are fostered (Earley, 1997, p. 129).

Complaints about placing priority on sectarian loyalties at the cost of public welfare have a long history in Korea. Nevertheless ties of reciprocity and loyalty remain strong, not only to kin groups but also to school associates and geographical regions of one's birth.[4] These latter types of social ties might be viewed as 'fictive' clans. An example of these ties and the more generalized exchange relations described by Earley (1997) is reported by D. J. Kim (1996) who notes the importance of kinship, region and school in recruiting engineers to the firm he was studying. Employees are encouraged to view the firm as clan-like. Kim cites one engineer who, in commenting on his accomplishments in establishing a Korean plant in the US, said: 'I feel like I am doing something for the honour of our clan and our country' (Ch. S. Kim, 1992, pp. 68–9). Important in this comment is the notion of bringing honour to a generalized but finite social group: the clan and the country. There is no mention of taking satisfaction in one's own *personal* achievement.

Clan-like social networks provide the referent points for achievement and they form the basis for patterns of trust and commitment. When they are interpreted as linkages to social honour they can provide a powerful basis for collective effort (Hahm, 1999). In the West, social networks also play a major role in the economy, but these tend to be instrumental and self-serving and are transitory in nature (Powell and Smith-Doerr, 1994, pp. 388–9).

Loyalty to the ruler is a central tenet of Confucianism. Loyalty to an unjust ruler poses a dilemma. In aligning the priorities of loyalty, however, the welfare of the collectivity takes precedence over the ruler. The Chinese Confucian scholar, Ssu-ma Kuang (1019–86), who was also a government minister, wrote that ministers who were members of the ruler's kin group should counsel him in an effort to correct him; ministers without such kinship ties should not attempt such counsel but should resign if the ruler fails to reform (Ching, 1977, pp. 197–8). This illustrates an ongoing tension in the practice of a Confucian ethic and explains an apparent paradox in Korean society. Themes that stress harmony, social order and social honour can also justify political oppression and authoritarianism. Confucian values may emphasize service for the collective welfare, but they also can encourage favouritism, nepotism and 'crony capitalism'.

Confucianism itself does not hold economic activity in high regard. But neither do the doctrines of Christianity nor its Protestant expression. Max Weber, of course, applying the concept of 'elective affinity', attempted to demonstrate the perverse effects of Protestantism – of how the non-worldly preoccupations of the Protestant justified and encouraged the actions of the frugal capitalist (Smucker, 1980). While Confucian collectivist values appear to be diametrically opposed to the self-oriented attributes of Puritan beliefs, as Weber describes them (Weber, 1958), when viewed against an environment dominated by military threats from the North and economic threats from advanced capitalist economies, they provide a potent mixture of motivational themes based on collective survival. The fusion of private welfare with the public good has been used to powerful effect by authoritarian governments and business interests. In establishing their legitimacy, successive authoritarian governments have emphasized themes of group loyalty, interdependence, individual sacrifice and the idea of ensuring survival through economic strength.

To these cultural attributes of South Korea, some commentators add the concept of '*han*', defined as a theme of grievance or *resentment* (Ch. S. Kim,

1992, pp. 15–19; Lie, 1998). The concept is said to derive from a history of suspicion toward foreigners and, more specifically, an underlying sense of resentment against the long periods of foreign rule. As an economic and social theme, *han* denotes an unleashing of effort to outperform and supersede the accomplishments of foreign economies. Expressions of *han* might be found in the long hours of the working week, and in the education system, where competition is fierce and middle-class parents often supplement their children's public school education with extra hours at evening education 'institutes'. Massive structures such as the new airport at Inchon or the large, luxurious hotels of Seoul, or the broad modern highways, elevated above the valleys in the country – all seem to be tangible expressions of claims to excellence and triumphalism against previous periods of servitude.[5]

Another expression of this orientation can be seen in an inspirational book written by Kim Woo Choong, founder of the huge business conglomerate or 'chaebol', the Daewoo Corporation. Kim states in his book that he wishes to 'share his devotion to self-sacrifice' and goes on to note how he created the largest building in Korea, and built the world's largest dock at the Okpo shipyards, as well as the world's largest garment factory (W. Ch. Kim, 1992). At the time of the book's publication, Daewoo, with sales of US$25 billion, owned some 22 companies in sectors ranging from textiles and heavy industry to electronics, pianos and hotels. Mr Kim claimed that he had no interest in getting rich, only in helping Korea and described himself as a 'neo-Confucian' who wishes to surmount the traditional Confucian bias against merchants and businessmen (W. Ch. Kim 1992; Hamilton and Biggart, 1988).

Constructing the business environment: Government–business relations

In general, governments play a crucial role in market economies in defining and protecting property rights, in interpreting and defending the legal standing of contractual relations and in establishing and guaranteeing rules of governance (Wade, 1990; Fligstein, 1997; De Soto, 2000). There are wide variations in the ways in which governments have carried out these roles, whether as active agents of development or as the watchful referees of competing players in the market place. Furthermore, although the principal economic actors in 'late-developing' countries have an advantage in learning from earlier developed countries, they are also extremely vulnerable to exploitation from the more developed countries. Pursuing the goals of economic development while warding off foreign control and exploitation requires carefully considered decisions of strategy (Busch, 1999).

Successive governments in the Republic of Korea have been extremely active in providing the terms and setting the goals of economic development. The strategies they have pursued have resulted in unique constellations of power and influence in both the economy and in civil society. The most notable of these constellations has been the oscillating relationships between the South Korean business conglomerates *(chaebol)* and the state.[6] Remaining in the background of these movements has been, until the recent past, strong governmental control of civil society. Elaboration of the significance of these and related features is the focus of the account that follows.

First steps in reconstruction and development

At the end of the turmoil following the Second World War and the end of the Japanese occupation, the Rhee administration embarked on economic reforms designed largely by American advisors. Banks previously owned by the Japanese were turned over to the government and plans were in place to set up an independent central bank. Reconstruction of South Korea's economy was based on principles of import substitution. Following the Western orthodoxy of economic development at that time, the idea was to establish a viable, largely self-sufficient agricultural base accompanied by industries such as textiles that employ simple technology and low-wage labour. There is some evidence that the Americans would have been content to simply maintain a stable, agriculturally based economy in South Korea rather than have it embark on the risks of rapid economic development (Lie, 1998, p. 23). But the exigencies of the 1950–53 Korean War destroyed much of this original vision and altered irreversibly the course of industrialization and economic development.

During the Korean War, the South Korean government exerted tight controls over manufacturing enterprises and financial institutions. After the war the government continued to play a very active role in controlling the direction and pace of economic development. It returned to the original import-substitution plan of development. It directed much of the foreign financial aid to preferred enterprises in selected industrial sectors. Special discount rates and pre-authorized loan approvals were used to achieve these ends. Those industries receiving priority in investment funds were textiles, chemical products, food, machinery and metal products (Choi, 1993, p. 260). The devastation of the war also facilitated large-scale land reforms and the demise of the *yang-ban* (landed gentry).

A close relationship between Rhee's government and favoured entrepreneurs initiated a patronage system that set in motion the eventual development of family-run cross-industry conglomerates, the chaebol.[7] These conglomerates also developed their own networks of suppliers and banks. The Rhee government justified its control over the economy and its strictures over civil society as a necessary part of its defensive strategy against North Korea. But widespread opposition to the corruption and increasingly repressive civil policies of the Rhee government resulted in student-led revolts and weakened support from the US. In 1960 President Rhee resigned and took refuge in Hawaii.

The largely ineffective attempts at democratic reforms by the elected government of Chang Myon, which followed the Rhee regime, ended a year later with a military coup and the installation of General Park Chung Hee as president in 1961. Legitimizing the coup as a populist-based movement and following a policy of what might be called 'authoritarian reform', the Park regime shifted the emphasis of economic development to an export-led model. But the government also maintained many of the controls required for import substitution. Like Rhee before him, Park's tight control over economic development was justified as a defensive measure against the constant threat of renewed conflict with North Korea. Economic development was not merely something to pursue in its own right.

The Park regime continued the pattern of government influence through the control of the financial sector. It proceeded to nationalize commercial banks by repossessing the bank shares, most of which were held by the owners of the chaebol, whom the government accused of 'illicit wealth accumulation' (Choi, 1993). The Bank of Korea now was controlled by the state and the Ministry of Finance was put in charge of financial policy. Specialized banks were set up to service specific economic sectors. These banks also proved to be an effective means to gain political support for the regime. For example, specialized banking services for the agricultural sector helped gain support from farmers for government policies. Meanwhile, nearly all of those business persons who had initially been accused of unlawful behaviour during the pronouncements of reform in the early days of the Park regime, either received only symbolic punishments or reprimands, or were not punished at all. They were co-opted by the government in its development plans and rewarded by various forms of government protection and favouritism.[8] This pattern of threats followed by promises of cooperation by major business leaders was to continue in subsequent government regimes. The increasing size of the chaebol provided successive governments with efficient paths of influence. But, they also could provide the means for powerful opposition to government policies.

The Park government clamped down on the nascent labour movement by declaring all existing labour organizations illegal and reconstituting the labour federation, putting it under central control and organizing it into industry-based divisions.[9] An effort by labour organizers to create an alternative union federation failed under government opposition. With these developments, the Park government created, in effect, a corporatist structure, controlled by the government but subject as well to the growing influence of the chaebol. At the same time, labour protests have remained a constant undercurrent. The self-immolation of the worker, Chon Tae-il in 1970, prompted by his commitment to force public attention on the government's arbitrary application of labour standards, has served as a symbolic reminder of the years of hardship endured by labour and the uphill battles of the labour movement as a whole (Ahn, 1996, p. 115).

By the 1970s American aid began to decline. Subsequently, the government turned to private foreign loans to finance its series of 5-year plans. State-run agencies like the Economic Planning Board ensured that the major part of these funds was directed to export-oriented firms in selected industries. In addition, tight restrictions on the import of consumer goods were imposed, as were restrictions on foreign direct investments. The government also subsidized the importation of production technology. Special tax breaks were made available to favoured business interests and preferential allocation of credits were also included in these government policies. The Park government also used public funds to subsidize the risks of large-scale investments in industries that it targeted for growth (Matthews and Ravenhill, 1994, pp. 60–5; Lim, 1999). While these policies stimulated rapid growth, it is also likely that they reduced incentives for independent accountability of individual banks and other private financial institutions.

In 1965, despite popular opposition, Park normalized relations with Japan as part of his aggressive policy to secure not only loans and portfolio capital investments but also to gain technology and technological expertise through joint ventures and foreign direct investments. The immediate effect was the infusion of about US$800 million worth of public loans, grants and commercial credits. Direct investment from Japan increased from US$1.2 million in 1965 to US$27.1 million in 1969. Accompanying these investments was a steady increase in the diffusion of technology and management expertise (Jun, 1995; Lie, 1998, p. 60).

An additional consequence of this relationship was the creation in the early 1970s of Japanese electronics assembly plants in South Korea. South Korea was an attractive location for these plants, not only because of its proximity to Japan but also because of the availability of a low-wage, highly disciplined labour force. In 1976, 50 per cent of South Korea's electronics output came from foreign or jointly owned factories, nearly all of which were Japanese. These investments also facilitated the transfer of technology. Korean corporations such as Samsung and Lucky Goldstar gained technology through licensing and subcontracting arrangements with Japanese firms like NEC and Sanyo (Hobday, 1998, p. 52).

The very strong dependence on foreign capital increased with large-scale investments from foreign financial institutions. The South Korean government acted as guarantor for these loans. In addition, the large chaebol used their diverse company holdings to acquire loans by using each company to serve as equity for the other.[10] By the late 1960s, however the Park government was already under pressure from both the US and the International Monetary Fund to curtail the risks of rapid growth and seek greater economic stability. This resulted in the potential bankruptcies of scores of firms. But in the restructuring process that followed in the early 1970s, the government in effect bailed out the troubled firms by directing the banks to convert the loans to equity or to reschedule the loans. The banks were also instructed to supply additional funds to these firms to meet the immediate demands for repayment (Choi, 1993, p. 29). These measures provided temporary solutions, but from the perspective of foreign advisory bodies, they also perpetuated a highly vulnerable, although admittedly fast growing, economy, dependent on deals cut between the state and favoured entrepreneurs. In 1971, in the wake of declines in foreign investment funds, the South Korean government devalued its currency (the won) by 18 per cent causing considerable distress to those firms indebted to foreign creditors. Many firms turned to unregulated money markets for their capital requirements.

In 1972, at the beginning of what has become known as the '*Yusin*' period ('revitalizing reform') and with the introduction of even greater state intervention in the economy and civil society,[11] the government continued to meet growing debt problems by forcing the conversion of loans to equity holdings and by encouraging the growth of 'non-bank' financial institutions. In addition, it began a programme of channelling funds toward the development of heavy industry including steel and shipbuilding and the chemical industry. The Park government also began placing increased restrictions on the Japanese direct investments in electronics manufactures, including the withdrawal of existing tax benefits. As a result, Japanese firms withdrew, while Korean firms took over most of electronics production and introduced their own brand names into world markets.[12] These policies were accompanied by militaristic control that kept labour costs low and suppressed any expressions of dissent (D. J. Kim, 1996; Lie, 1998, p. 76). In effect, the whole of civil society was regimented into an 'army' of producers working an average of 55 hours per week.

Holders of savings accounts and private moneylenders were hit hard by government controls in the financial sector. The government also created the Corporation Disclosure Promotion Law in a professed effort to protect shareholders. But very few firms adhered to this law and the government did not pursue their compliance. Further, the strength and influence of the chaebol increased as they acquired controlling shares of non-banking financial institutions (Choi, 1993, p. 31). As inflation rates climbed, a growing proportion of internal investment funds were diverted to land speculation rather than to productive industries (D. J. Kim, 1996, pp. 84–97; Lie, 1998, p. 149). At the same time, there were sporadic episodes of labour riots and growing opposition from students and voices from the middle class against the severe restrictions of civil liberties that, in 1979, included martial law in all the major cities (Lee, 2000).

President Park was assassinated in October 1979 by the head of the Korean Central Intelligence Agency (KCIA). In the midst of the ensuing power vacuum, the country was racked by labour unrest and by massive demonstrations of students and workers demanding greater civil liberties and improvements in working conditions. The most notorious of these uprisings occurred in May 1980 and has come to be remembered as the Kwangju

Uprising. As an act of protest against the arrest of the popular dissident Kim Dae-jung and other prominent opposition figures, a massive demonstration erupted in the historic city of Kwangju, a university town in the lower southeastern part of the Korean peninsula. In a face-off with the South Korean army, the protest was put down; an estimated 200 demonstrators lost their lives. Under the leadership of General Chun Doo Hwan, the government invoked stronger repressive measures against the press, incarcerated voices of opposition and strengthened its control of the military establishment.

General Chun assumed the presidency and, in an effort to gain greater public legitimacy, attempted to embark on a policy of controlled liberal reforms. He also announced his intention to destroy the 'hegemonic pact' between the state and big business (Moon, 1994; Lie, 1998, pp. 122–3). Chun's professed intentions were to uproot and purge elements of 'cronyism' between members of the Park government and representatives of big business. However, in a pattern reminiscent of the early days of the Park regime, the Federation of Korean Industries, the collective voice of the chaebol, fended off the aggressive stance of Chun and in return, pledged their loyalty to his government. Indeed, this alliance between authoritarian government and big business, although often fraught with conflict, explains much of the unique pattern of economic development in the Republic of Korea.

Chun's government did attempt to stabilize the economy through monetary measures and it continued in its efforts to gain the support of the growing middle class although it also invoked measures to control domestic consumption. It continued to provide economic support to selected firms in heavy industry, ship building, shipping and overseas construction (Amsden, 1989, pp. 139–55; Moon, 1994, p. 147; Lim, 1999, pp. 126–34). The government also made renewed efforts to reign in the seemingly reckless expansion policies of the chaebol. The chaebol through their association, the Federation of Korean Industries, firmly opposed a monopoly regulation law, tighter credit controls and efforts by the government to rationalize industrial expansion (Moon, 1994, p. 147). But even when government policies were successful, their effects were often perverse. When the government began privatizing commercial banks as part of an effort to stimulate competition, the chaebol simply bought out the banks and added them to the vast proliferation of non-banking financial institutions under their control (Moon, 1994, p. 150). Unable to resist the combined influence of the chaebol, the Chun government reverted to previously used tactics: favouring and supporting those firms and organizations that were more cooperative and actively supportive.

Meanwhile, the growing militancy of the labour movement prompted the government to revise existing labour laws by making it even more difficult for workers to organize and by restricting the scope of any worker organization to the jurisdiction and control of individual enterprises. The effect of this was to create more opposition from labour and to create more mass support for an independent workers' movement. Militant demonstrations, strikes and labour disputes continued throughout the Chun regime. In 1987, the last year of Chun's administration, the government made moderate moves toward liberalizing labour laws by relaxing some of its restrictions on organizing unions, except in the government and defence sectors. In fact, these actions were merely part of a pattern of waffling between enforcing strict controls and attempting to placate voices of dissent. Near the end of its term, Chun's government itself was racked by revelations of past loan scandals (Lie, 1998, p. 124).

Despite the political and civil turmoil throughout the authoritarian reigns of Park and Chun, the economy remained very much in the control of the government–chaebol nexus. Investments in the Korean industrial infrastructure continued and during Chun's presidency, the first surplus in the balance of payments was registered. At the end of his seven-year term, there was a relatively peaceful transition to a new regime headed by the elected president, Roh Tae Woo.

Advanced development and contemporary issues

Tension between the state, big business and a restive labour force continued during the era of the Roh Tae Woo government (1987–92). Roh did introduce significant political reforms: direct elections replaced federal appointments to local governments, and the government announced its support for greater freedom to organized labour and to the press (Moon, 1999, p. 8). This relaxation of control resulted in the emergence of new and diverse political groups.

The Roh government also attempted to rein in real estate speculation and to tighten up the enforcement of tax collection. It sought to restrict the scope of diversified expansion by the chaebol and it tried to invoke policies that would make corporate transactions more transparent (Moon, 1994, p. 154). Roh's hope was to win the support of the rising middle class while attempting to contain the power and influence of the chaebol. However, the growing current account surpluses, which had been viewed as a positive national achievement, contributed to an increase in funds flowing to real estate and stock market speculation. These flows, in turn, resulted in skyrocketing land prices and housing rents and widening disparities between the rich and the poor (Moon, 1994, p. 154). In 1989 appreciation of the price of land was 35 per cent greater than the increase in local aggregate income earned by all urban workers in the same year. Attempts to increase taxes on idle lands merely resulted in building 'unnecessary and often unsightly "improvements" 'and 'exacerbated a shortage of materials and skilled labour that might otherwise have been used for genuinely needed construction' (Lee, 2000, pp. 373, 378).

Thwarted ambitions of the middle class and continued deprivation among the working class found political expression in the growing polarization in orientations of political parties. Meanwhile, the Roh government reduced its subsidies to the large conglomerates while lending support to smaller business enterprises in an effort to stimulate greater market-oriented competition.

At the end of Roh's term in 1992, the opposition candidate, Kim Young Sam, with Kim Dae-jung, the well-known dissident, running a close second, won the first free election involving multiple political parties. Previously, a member of Parliament during the regime of General Park Chung Hee and an outspoken critic, Kim Young Sam had been under house arrest for two years. Now, as the newly elected president, he, like the presidents before him, began his first days in office vowing to institute a programme of reforms. By filling his cabinet positions with prominent intellectuals, Kim signalled the end of military rule in the government. Indeed, in 1995 both former presidents Chun and Roh were arrested and sentenced to death (later commuted) for 'abuse of power' (Lie, 1998, p. 155).

Because of its economic and trade successes in the past and its emergence as a major world player in the production of key products such as electrical goods, automobiles, steel and ships, the Kim administration faced more formidable negotiations with its major trading partners, especially Japan and the US, over terms of trade and technological transfers. Although the exploitation of labour had been a correlate of Korea's competitiveness in the past, labour costs continued to rise to a level where it was no longer a low-cost producer in labour-intensive industries (Ahn, 1996; Lie, 1998, p. 156; Mo and Moon, 1999).

In response to these developments, the government encouraged South Korean producers to increase investments in research and development and to pursue the manufacture of high value-added goods. The chaebol became more aggressive in their attempts to diversify and penetrate foreign markets beyond those of the US and Japan. Korean-owned factories spread increasingly to offshore low-wage areas. At the same time, foreign firms and governments, particularly those from the US and Western Europe, exerted increased pressure on Korea to liberalize its trade restrictions, to permit more foreign direct investment and to make its corporate structure more transparent and open to foreign shareholders.[13] The ongoing power struggles between government and big business continued during this reformist era. The chaebol continued to operate through tight social networks and opaque business practices. Relations with government agencies were also based on social ties reinforced by the threat of massive economic disruption should government policies allow a conglomerate to fail. On the other hand, government agencies could contain the power of the chaebol by imposing various government sanctions, including charges of tax evasion. In 1997, in a second, free, multi-party election, Kim Dae-jung was elected president on a platform promising to continue with a programme of economic and social reforms along with efforts to expand relations with North Korea. His election came during the same year that severe financial crises, now known in Korea as the 'IMF crisis', struck both South Korea and nearly all of the other economies of north and southeast Asia.[14]

Kim had a long career as a dissident. He was an outspoken critic of the regimes of Syngman Rhee, Park Chung Hee and Chun Doo Hwan and spoke out against the military regimes and their effects on civil society. For this he had been accused of being a Communist and an enemy of the state. He had endured 14 years of exile, house arrest, death threats and imprisonment.[15] Kim's was one of the leading voices in speaking for the rights of labour and for protection of small farmers. He was especially vehement in his criticism of growing disparities of wealth and the opaque practices of the chaebol. Following his election, he attempted to follow a course of reconciliation with North Korea.[16] He also pardoned his former political enemies, including Chun Doo Hwan, who during his regime had sought to sentence Kim to death.

The immediate task of the Kim government was to deal with the sudden collapse of the economy and to respond to the demands of the IMF. In order to obtain a record-breaking US$55 billion rescue package from the IMF, the government had to sign a 3-year arrangement in which it agreed to drastic changes in its governance of the economy. Included in the recommended changes were a suspension of some 15 of the 30 merchant banks carrying huge non-performing loans until they met the necessary criteria for capitalization, liquidity and transparency in management; more transparent financial data to be provided by firms with the use of independent external auditors; an oversight body to monitor bookkeeping practices of the financial ministry and the chaebol; greater foreign access to Korean financial markets with an increase in the limits of foreign ownership of listed shares to 55 per cent by the end of 1998; an end to restrictive trade practices; raising taxes and tightening monetary policy; and promoting greater labour market flexibility by easing lay-off and dismissal restrictions (El Kahal, 2001, p. 37; Federation of Koran Trade Unions, 2001).

One result of the government yielding to many of these demands was the bankruptcy of the huge Daewoo chaebol. Other chaebols, most notably Samsung and Hyundai remain in the throes of restructuring. But, like his predecessors, Kim's efforts at reform were met with strong opposition from the conglomerates. The by-now-familiar process established in previous administrations, of threats, retreats and negotiations between the government and the Federation of Korean Industries continued. The government under Kim's administration did allow concessions. Back-tracking on its directive on equity investments, it offered exceptions to the rule if investments were intended to aid in corporate restructuring and the enhancement of core businesses (*Korea Herald*, 2001a; *Korea Times*, 2001). In addition, business associations sought more flexibility in rules regarding debt-to-equity ratios. The government also made concessions to this request.

From the financial reformists' point of view the government was still too ready to use questionable interventions in the economy. For example, banks were frequently required to make poor risk loans at the government's bequest. Poor risk ratios were (and continue to be) far higher for Korean-owned banks, subject to government directives in their loans policies, than they are for the few foreign-owned financial institutions (*Korean Herald*, 2001b).

In sorting out the causes for the losses suffered by the Korean economy, the OECD cited three fundamental weaknesses:

1. Low levels of profitability and high levels of debt were endemic to the corporate sector. Huge debt burdens were carried by the chaebol, made possible by their equity in cross-holdings and cross-loan guarantees among the companies under their control. Such a system was perpetuated by the belief that these corporate structures were simply too large to fail.
2. The financial system was not independent of government control. Governments determined the allocation of capital; but the allocation process lacked a thorough system of credit analysis and internal risk controls.
3. In 1993, following the enactment of more liberal policies with respect to overseas borrowing, corporations and financial institutions built up huge levels of foreign debt with little attention focused on credit and exchange rate risks (OECD, 2000, p. 28).

Expansion rather than cost and profit concerns seemed to be the preoccupation of South Korean companies and governments alike.

Opaqueness and protectionism are still seen by Western-dominated monitoring agencies as continuing problems. In 2001 PricewaterhouseCoopers found South Korea to have 'the most opaque standards of accounting and corporate governance of the 35 countries it surveyed' (*The Economist*, 2001, p. 69). When the Daewoo chaebol collapsed in July 1999, it was revealed that it had debts of US$80 billion. The Korean state prosecution agency charged that Daewoo had hidden debts of some US$34 billion. By inflating its assets, it borrowed about US$7.5 billion from banks while illegally channelling US$20 billion to a secret account in London. Daewoo's founder, Kim Woo Choong fled the country. Meanwhile, the national assembly proceeded to pass harsher laws designed to curb misleading and fraudulent accounting practices (Ibid, p. 69–70).

New accounting rules introduced by the Kim government still failed to meet international standards. Minority shareholders still had too few rights. While the finance ministry planned to introduce a bill allowing class-action suits designed to protect shareholders, this would apply only to companies having assets of more than US$2 billion. Only about 12 firms would be affected by this proposed law.

Writing in *The Economist*, Andreas Kluth reported that South Korea had the poorest quality of corporate governance among the Asian economies. Only China was worse than South Korea in the ranking on 'transparency'. Kluth also reported that 'the companies that inspired the most optimism in the early days of the recovery have since proved the most disappointing', having made investments with 'no apparent regard for economic return and, collectively, running up debts five times the size of their equity' (Kluth, 2001, p. 9).

Despite the efforts of the government to force the chaebol to 'sell assets, reduce their debt loads, produce more transparent balance sheets and appoint independent directors on their boards' (Kluth, 2001, p. 9), they have had little effect. The chaebol have remained only partially reformed although the increased presence of foreign-owned firms in South Korea has put competitive pressure on them for further reform. Meanwhile, government agencies remain active in supporting those firms and industries that it regards as crucial players in what might be viewed as a 'next level' of competitive activity in world markets. At the same time, the South Korean government also began to encourage more independent paths of growth for firms in the small- and medium-sized business sector. These firms have traditionally been the main suppliers to the large chaebol (Moon, 1999, p. 17).

In 2001 the economy suffered an additional shock. Economic downturns in the US and Japan had severe negative effects in South Korea, occurring at the same time as a rise in consumer prices. With exports accounting for 38 per cent of the gross national product, any reductions in exports to world markets have a serious effect on the Korean economy. The decline in market demand for the telecommunications and computer industries has been especially devastating for South Korea, where memory chips for computers once accounted for 37 per cent in value of total exports (*Chosun Ilbo*, 2001a).

South Korea has also been faced with trade barriers from developed countries, particularly the US. Korean steel products have been hit hard with punitive tariffs from the US, as has the microchip industry (*New York Times*, 2002, 2003). Many Koreans believe that it is ironic that the US, which continually reminds the world of the merits of free markets, has been the most aggressive in applying protective tariffs and in its readiness to accuse other nations of unfair trade practices.[17]

The South Korean government has reduced its role in the financial sector, and a number of banks have been taken over by private, foreign interests. Banks have also changed their marketing practices, concentrating more on individual investors rather than corporate accounts. But while many innovations have been introduced, they have not always had beneficial consequences for the population. The introduction of credit cards, for example, has resulted in one of the highest proportions of individual bankruptcies among market economies (*Chosun Ilbo,* 2002a, b; *Korea Times,* 2003a).

Meanwhile, the re-emergence of a threatening voice from North Korea has divided the population. The older generation tends to view these threats as heralding a return to a garrison-like existence. The younger generation, on the other hand, tend to believe that the economic might of South Korea will continue, and that despite the sabre-rattling of North Korea reunification is only a matter of time. Many of this generation resent the presence of American troops and believe that the two Koreas can resolve their animosities without outside help.[18]

Kim Dae-jung's party continued in power with the election of Roh Moo-hyun at the end of 2002. What is significant about this election is that it was won without the financial support of the chaebol. Rather, Roh's campaign depended heavily on the support of individual voters, especially those in their twenties and thirties. Roh, who passed his law exams without benefit of a university education, is seen as a voice of reform not only in the structure of the economy but also in civil society. These reforms include his avowed intention to take seriously the concerns of organized labour.

Even though labour has made large gains in income in absolute terms, relative to the value of their production, workers have fallen behind. The pressures from the IMF and from private investors to change the ways in which South Korea has managed its economy, in addition to the challenges of marketing high-value goods in advanced industrialized countries, have added the spectre of increasingly insecure employment to the already relatively poor working conditions (*Korea Times* 2003b; see also Kim and Lee, 2000). Employment is now less secure as firms seek more 'flexibility' in their use and deployment of workers. The paternalistic Confucian model of management–labour relations is being threatened by Western models that offer little employment security (Ahn, 1998).

In 2003 the new Roh government announced its intention to enact legislation more supportive of labour. But labour relations continue to be hostile and confrontational. This is further abetted not only by the turbulence of changes in the structure and policies of business firms but also by the failure of the government to follow through on its own promises to move swiftly to enact more comprehensive support for improved working conditions and improved social welfare programmes, including more comprehensive coverage for the unemployed.

Economic development and civil society: Current issues

Since the 1997–98 financial crisis, state policies, once described by foreign experts as severe in their impact on civil society but 'enlightened' in the economic sphere, have been heavily criticized. Government interventions that in the past were thought of as being productive and appropriate have more recently come to be seen as instances of cronyism and corruption. Monetary policies praised in the past as maintaining stable interest rates and pegging the Korean won to the US dollar have been redefined as creating an over-valued currency and heightening a debt crisis. What foreign observers once viewed as flexible but prudent fiscal policies have come to be seen as lax and preferential. Meanwhile, policy uncertainties have replaced what was once regarded as relatively stable relationships between public and private sectors (El Kahal, 2001, p. 30; *The Economist*, 2002a).

Within Korea, a more vocal middle class is less receptive to the solemn calls for sacrifice in the cause of defence against threats from the North. Arguments that long hours at work are a reasonable price to pay for a future of higher living standards have become more muted in the midst of public debates over questions of equity and social justice. Family networks are no longer able to absorb the costs of unemployment and underemployment nor can they absorb health costs and the costs of retirement. This has prompted calls for more comprehensive, publicly funded social welfare programmes. Significant proportions of the middle class also have joined organized labour in calls for greater 'democratization' and greater transparency in governance in both the state and private industry. Within business firms, hiring and promotion on the basis of merit are competing with traditional network systems and associated rewards of loyalty and trust.

It is with this increase in individual autonomy that issues of fairness and equity, on one hand, and individual rights and social security, on the other, have become more salient. Both Koreans and foreign commentators have cited these changes as factors heightening the public's concern over

1) cases of corruption or 'questionable payments';
2) the impact of foreign direct investments upon national autonomy;
3) income and wealth inequities;
4) justice in private as well as public sector governance;
5) social welfare and labour policies; and
6) civil liberties.

I shall consider each of these issues briefly.

The concept of 'questionable payments' covers a broad array of behaviour that expresses some degree of inequity, whether through bribes, influence peddling and favouritism or various forms of extortion. Western observers (e.g. Hinkleman and Genzberger, 1994) have often cited the presence of 'corruption' in South Korean business and politics. But the problem also occupies a prominent place in the Korean media. While questionable payments of various kinds certainly are not unknown in Western societies, the frequent exchange of gifts and favours associated in South Korea with the social dynamics that accompany business relationships makes its forms of expression far more ambiguous. In a sense, one might argue that the various networks have served as checks and balances against excessive rent-seeking by any single agent involved in the process of economic development. The informal social networks, sustained in part by 'gift-giving', served to make authoritarian governments more tolerable and more effective (see Huntington, 1968). Nevertheless, concerns about corruption are very salient in public opinion. More than 70 per cent of South Koreans think that corruption is a serious problem and 61 per cent agreed with the statement that 'in Korea, there is nothing one cannot solve with money' (*Chosun Ilbo*, 2003b).

The practice of gift-giving and providing entertainment while conducting business remains a subtle and seductive art. While these practises have not been a major hindrance to obtaining foreign loans, they are obstacles to foreign direct investment where ownership of an enterprise remains with the foreign investor (Wei, 2000, pp. 347–54). Indeed, it is the usual practice of foreign firms when negotiating with Korean companies, to do so through 'brokers' who understand the social protocol of establishing trust and who may require gifts or payments as symbols of honoured relations. Still, the use of such brokers may impede the current movements toward greater transparency in negotiations and governance. On the other hand, in Korean society the creation of personal trust in contractual relations is crucial; gift giving and operating through trusted intermediaries are means of creating and sustaining that trust.

One of the conditions imposed by the IMF for aid in overcoming the 1997–98 economic crisis was the requirement that South Korea open its economy to more foreign direct investment. Previously, in 1996, as a condition of its membership in the OECD, South Korea was required to be more receptive to foreign ownership of investments. The Foreign Investment Promotion Act, enacted after the 1997–98 financial crisis, states that all business sectors, in principle, are to be liberalized with restrictions applicable only in cases implicating 'national security, public order, public health, environmental preservation, or social morals' (MOFE, 2003). Nonetheless, many foreign firms have experienced considerable frustration in negotiating and implementing their direct investments. Examples include the protracted negotiations of General Motors in the takeover of Daewoo's automotive division; the lengthy negotiations and their final breakdown over Micron's attempt to buy out Hynix (a Hyundai-controlled semiconductor manufacturer); and the lengthy negotiations between Bombardier with the city of Pusan over the construction of a public transit line.

There are a number of technical reasons why direct investments have proved to be so difficult. These include the problems associated with licensing arrangements of vital technology; the intricate relationships among companies within the chaebol system; and the huge debt loads and opaque accounting practises of the target firms (*The Economist*, 2002b). In addition, the cultural differences in the methods and interpretations of negotiations are often difficult to resolve. For example, though Western negotiators tend to focus only on favourable *economic* returns, personal and social honour and a sense of 'winning' (or at least upholding one's status – not losing face) have been crucial bargaining elements in the Korean style of negotiations. Still, though profits tend to be low among the chaebol, their assets are extremely attractive for foreign investors and potential take-overs of Korean companies have caused considerable apprehension among the populace.

Income and wealth disparities have become a particularly sore point not only with respect to wage labour but also because of the growing disparities between a wealthy elite and the middle class (Leipziger, *et al.*, 1992). Individuals, especially younger adults no longer accept the old maxim, 'develop first, share later'. There is no question that the entire population has benefited from the economic returns of industrialization. Gross domestic product per person, expressed as purchasing-power parity with the US, is nearly US$20 000, which is about US$6000 less than the euro area (*The Economist*, 2003, p. 6). It is rather that some have benefited much more than others.

Citizens' groups, students' groups and organized labour have become increasingly vocal in their demands for greater equality. Findings from the national survey conducted by Samsung Economic Research Institute and Seoul National University, cited earlier, indicate that 59 per cent of those in the survey thought that 'conflict between the haves and have-nots in Korean society were very serious'. Sixty-four per cent agreed that 'Korea gives too much recognition and financial rewards to the winners' (*Chosun Ilbo*, 2003b). Past assurances from managers and government officials that low labour wages were necessary in order to be competitive in world markets are no longer accepted amidst an economic environment dominated by increasingly lavish life styles of the affluent.

Within firms, compensation has typically been based on seniority and to a lesser extent, merit. In the past, the emphasis has been placed on maintaining 'harmony' among workers within a firm. As we have already seen, the increased intensity of competition has increased pressures to move toward wage scales based on merit. This shift, of course, while raising issues about allocation rules, also challenges traditional notions of honour and respect.

Most analysts of the financial crisis of 1997–98 place a major share of the blame on a management style that emphasized expansion of assets and international marketing while neglecting adequate profit margins. Before the crisis, large conglomerates were viewed with some awe in their daring and risk-taking. Following the crisis, the same companies were faulted for mismanagement. Typically these companies have borrowed excessively and have made investments with little regard for economic return. In 1999, the collective debts of Korean firms were more than five times the size of their equity (Kluth, 2001, p. 9). There have been very few checks and balances in monitoring the costs of grand projects by the managers of the chaebol. This was partly a result of the involvement and backing of government agencies. But, as we have seen, a succession of governments has been unable to control many of the excesses of these conglomerates. With the collapse of many Korean enterprises, most notably the Daewoo chaebol and a number of prominent banks, calls for greater transparency and accountability are very much in the public domain. Pressures for reform have also come from foreign investors, many of whom had thought that the financial plight of many Korean companies would make them relatively inexpensive acquisitions.

Issues of governance *within* business firms are also subjects of public debate. Within Korean enterprises, advancement by employees into more responsible positions has typically been by seniority and demonstrations of company loyalty. Implicit here is the importance of trust and reliability to management dictates. Typically, managers have exerted authority while leaving the details of the work process to their subordinates. But with the increasing presence of foreign business interests and the increasing influence of foreign-trained Korean managers, these patterns of management are being challenged by new management styles and new systems. Merit, rather than loyalty and seniority is increasingly used for hiring and promotion. Ministry of Labour figures show that the percentage of firms using merit-based pay scales increased from 5.7 per cent in 1996 to 21.8 per cent in January 2001 (KPMG, 2002, p. 21). There is evidence that many recent university graduates would prefer employment with a foreign firm based in Korea because they believe that these firms are 'more likely to hire and promote workers strictly according to the workers' ability' (*Chosun Ilbo*, 2003a). These changes and preferences have been unsettling for those who have worked within the traditional system of social networks, social deference and social reciprocity.

Finally, it can no longer be assumed that the extended family can absorb welfare costs, including the costs of unemployment. Thus there have been increased demands for more comprehensive government welfare legislation. Opponents of these reforms argue that the additional costs will price Korea out of the world market, where Korea has held an advantage because of its low labour and social welfare costs. Those arguing for reforms point out that despite its economic growth, productivity rates for Korea have remained relatively low and higher social expenditures will be more than repaid through higher productivity when accompanied by management reforms (Martin and Torres, 2001).

Meanwhile, underemployment and unemployment rates have been increasing, in part because of increasing use of non-standard employment practices. Employment uncertainty, corruption and perceptions of unjustified inequality may account for the findings of one survey that claimed that more than 70 per cent of South Koreans in their twenties and thirties claim they would emigrate 'if given the chance' (*Chosun Ilbo*, 2003b).

Civil liberties remain a central concern among the general population. But there is also concern for the practice of social responsibility and accountability. These issues are most dramatically portrayed in the conflicts between the government and the media over questions about what constitutes freedom of expression and what constitutes responsible reporting.[19] While the media may expose irregularities in the government and among business enterprises, there have been occasions when it too has used questionable methods in its news-gathering activities. Because personal honour within the maze of social networks remains a strong motivator, public exposure becomes a powerful tool for both punishment and retribution. For example, a favourite tactic of the government in its response to negative reports in the press is to level charges of income tax evasion against the offender.[20]

Conclusions

While it might be argued that economic development implies a perpetual state of change and transition, the changes now facing South Korea seem to herald a new stage. Korea has moved from manufacturing low value goods and components within a protected economic environment to producing high value goods and services in open and highly competitive and unstable markets. The ponderous family-controlled chaebol dependent on low-wage labour can no longer compete effectively in innovation-driven markets (Chung, *et al.* 1997, pp. 221–37, 244–60). This transition also requires new linkages with foreign producers and new modes of entry into foreign markets. These changes have forced a reassessment of past assumptions about the relationship between economic development and social development – between sacrifice for the sake of a more affluent future and social justice in the immediate present. But there are severe restraints in bringing about desired changes. As Rodrik (1999) has pointed out, 'international capital markets are quick to punish countries that pursue policies that are perceived to be incompatible with macroeconomic sustainability' (p. 8).

Rodrik also notes that as technology for the production of goods and services becomes more standardized and diffused internationally, variations in norms, values and institutions become increasingly subject to economic assessments as factor endowments or as elements in comparative advantage. The costs of maintaining those unique social arrangements that are not economically efficient become more difficult to justify in strictly economic terms. But there is the danger of substituting assessments based on economic returns for those based on social justice and practices which have served economic objectives, such as low wages and long working hours, may become difficult to dislodge (see Sen, 2002). These and related issues are now in the forefront of public debate in South Korea as assessments are made over what practices are to be preserved, what are to be discarded and what are to be embraced (see Weller, 1999). Both Korean and foreign executives need to be sensitive to these issues if they are to act in a socially responsible manner.

Notes

I wish to offer my special thanks to Ahn Bu Young for facilitating my visit to South Korea in May 2001 and for his role in arranging interviews. I also wish to thank Ahn and Jay Kim for sharing their insights into Korean culture, and for their long-term friendship and support. I am grateful to Duane McMullan at the Canadian Embassy in Seoul and Peter Katz of CMC Electronics for providing me with contacts in South Korea who willingly shared their insights into Korean business practices. Finally, I wish to thank Steven Lehman for hosting my stay in Taegu.

1. Park himself had been educated in Japan and was greatly influenced by Japan's post-war strategy of economic development. There was also the expectation that Japanese technological expertise could be useful for Korea. Finally, the US, which encouraged and supported the agreement with Japan, was reducing its flow of aid to South Korea, and the Park government was well aware it would need to find new sources of financing.
2. Amsden (1989) notes that the Korean model was not simply a government policy choice but rather the outcome of 'a long process of social change. ... [A]t the heart of the model were subsidies offered by the state to private enterprise in exchange for higher output of exports and import substitutes. ... [T]he state used its power to discipline not just workers but the owners and managers of capital as well. A larger surplus was extracted, and this was invested rather than consumed' (pp. 63–4).
3. B. W. Kim, using regression models of effects on earnings functions, argues that the strong relationship between age and earnings that is sustained after human capital, screening, hierarchical and agency effects are taken into account, supports his argument that Confucian principles of honour, loyalty and respect for age are very much in evidence in the reward system and management of Korean firms (B. W. Kim, 1992, p. 130).
4. Loyalties to regions, schools and kinship ties are striking. Moon (1994) cites the linkages among administrative personnel in Samsung Industries to Kyungbok University in Taegu. Daewoo drew its management almost entirely from the graduates of Seoul National University. The key companies controlled by Hyundai are managed by the sons of its founder. The public bureaucracy is not immune to the importance of ties either. Graduates of Kyunggi Senior High School occupy the influential positions in the public sector. Most of the advisors to President Kim Dae-jung came from his home province.
5. Koreans' resourcefulness is legendary: after the War, one could see house roofs made from flattened tin cans, shopping bags and baskets woven from army field communications wire, footwear fashioned from rubber tires, women's pantaloons sewn from army blankets, eating utensils and bowls forged from brass shell casings.
6. The pattern of government–business relations in Taiwan provides a nice contrast to Korea. Following its retreat to Taiwan from Chinese communist forces, the Kuomintang government of Chiang Kai-Shek, consisting of mainland Chinese and confronted by a business sector controlled by Taiwanese, initiated an economic policy that sought to limit the power of large business interests. Instead, it protected its political base of power by favouring small- and middle-size enterprises. These smaller enterprises stimulated exports in their role as parts suppliers to

foreign firms. Amsden (1990) points out, however, that the government was not averse to supporting selected large firms in the early stages of development. And, more recently the government in Taiwan has lent support to larger firms. In contrast, Korean governments, beginning with Syngman Rhee and continuing until the late 1990s, encouraged the growth of large-scale enterprises as a means to create powerful economic allies who were able to draw on their large economies of scale and diversity of resources in competing in world markets for both component parts and finished goods.

7. The Chinese character for 'chaebol' means cluster of fortune. The conglomerates operate without a holding company. Rather, it is typically the case that owners and their family members operate out of one of the companies included in the conglomerate (Kirk, 1999, pp. 10–11). According to Lie (1998), state patronage made possible by American foreign aid was primarily responsible for these huge conglomerates. The founder of the Samsung chaebol, for example, got his start in the 1950s through government patronage, securing loans to construct a huge sugar refinery, which then served as equity to procure loans for holdings in other sectors (Lie, 1998; p. 34; Hobday 1998, pp. 57–8).

8. Business leaders who did not support the Park government were severely punished. The government forced Samhak, a major chaebol in the 1960s into bankruptcy and its owner, who had backed the dissident Kim Dae-jung in the 1971 presidential election, was convicted of tax evasion (Lie, 1998, p. 94).

9. The vast majority of workers employed in the light, export-oriented industries were women – a fact that served to justify low wages and poor working conditions. In effect, female labour was in the vanguard of the labour movement. Nonetheless, gender-based disparities in working conditions continue to be a matter of concern among social reformers.

10. Samsung provides a good example of the evolving pattern of chaebol holdings. It began in 1938 as a trading company dealing in fruit and dried fish. In the 1950s it invested in the production of sugar, and subsequently developed holdings in wool, textiles and other consumer products. These holdings were made possible by subsidies Samsung received under the government's import substitution policy. By the end of the 1950s it had expanded its holdings into fire and marine insurance; through 1960s and 1970s it acquired interests in media, property, retailing, paper, consumer electronics, construction and aerospace. In 1977, it invested in semiconductors and telecommunications (Hobday, 1998, pp. 57–8). Samsung is now a major world competitor in the manufacture of DRAM chips and flat computer monitors. In the era of restructuring following the 1997–98 crisis, it took the lead among the chaebol in directing its focus toward what it perceives as its core industry, microelectronics and announced planned divestitures and layoffs of unprecedented size.

11. General Park introduced new constitutional amendments. The changes resulted in an increasingly authoritarian government, ruling through frequently used martial law and political intimidation. Nevertheless, the government pursued economic policies designed to hasten the process of economic development, including concerted efforts to build up local rural economies. These amendments also made it possible for Park to stay in office for life.

12. In the period from 1976 to 1985, employment in foreign subsidiaries fell over 30 per cent, despite 50 per cent growth in electronics sector employment (Hobday, 1998, p. 53). This period also witnessed a major corporate exit by the Japanese: firms like Matsushita, Sanyo and NEC terminated their joint ventures

with Korean firms during the 1980s. However, having learned the ropes of technology-driven production from their Japanese partners, the Korean firms embarked on their own production and marketing operations.

13. In fact, FDI increased dramatically between 1998, when US$5.74 billion were invested in manufacturing and US$2.94 in services, and 2000 when US$7.12 billion were invested in manufacturing and US$8.57 billion in services (KPMG, 2002, p. 2).

14. The precipitating event of the crisis in Korea was the collapse of semiconductor prices on world markets in 1996. During the 1990s the manufacture and sale of semiconductors played a leading role in Korea's economic growth. The already highly indebted corporations became extremely vulnerable to the economic uncertainties and this vulnerability spread to the financial sector. Bankruptcies increased by 50 per cent and 7 of the 30 largest chaebols collapsed in 1997 (OECD, 2000, p. 28).

15. Two years of Kim Dae-jung's political exile – 1983–84 – were spent as a visiting fellow at Harvard University's Center for International Affairs. During this time he published the monograph 'Mass-Participatory Economy: Korea: Road to World Economic Power' (D. J. Kim, 1984). This publication maps out Kim's analysis of the extent of the social costs accompanying military rule and programmes of forced development.

16. In October 2000 Kim Dae-jung was awarded the Nobel Peace Prize for his efforts at reconciliation with North Korea and for his record as a human rights activist.

17. In the case of the microchip industry, the United States charged that Hynix, the company that the American firm Micron had previously tried to take over, was being unfairly subsidized because the principal bank providing loans to Hynix was itself relying heavily on government loans, while at the same time awaiting a buyout from another Korean bank.

18. I wish to thank Ahn Bu Young and Kim Jong Goon for alerting me to this generational divide.

19. See 'Who's Reforming Who?' (*Chosun Ilbo*, 2001b).

20. Particularly damaging have been the allegations of bribery and influence peddling against the adult sons of president Kim Dae-jung (*Korea Herald*, 2002a,b). There have also been allegations that the Hyundai chaebol gave over US$500 million to the North Korean government to 'facilitate' talks with the South Korean government and to win private concessions for a tourist enterprise.

References

Ahn, P. S. (1996) 'Mature Industrialisation and Democratisation: The Role of Korean Trade Unions in a Double Transition', University of Newcastle Upon Tyne: PhD dissertation, Faculty of Law, Environmental and Social Sciences.

Ahn, P. S. (1998) 'The Role of Trade Unions in the Economic Crisis of Korea', House of Culture, International Conference: Calvin versus Confucius, 7–10 May (Berlin).

Amsden, A. (1989) *Asia's Next Giant: South Korea and Late Industrialization* (New York: Oxford University Press).

Amsden, A. (1990) 'South Korea's Record Wage Rates: Labor in Late Industrialization', *Industrial Relations*, vol. 29, pp. 77–93.

Busch, M. L. (1999) *Trade Warriors: States, Firms and Strategic-Trade Policy in High-Technology Competition* (Cambridge: Cambridge University Press).

Ching, J. (1977) *Confucianism and Christianity: A Comparative Study* (Tokyo: Harper Row).

Choi, B. S. (1993) 'Financial Policy and Big Business in Korea: The Perils of Financial Regulation' in S. Haggard *et al.* (eds), *The Politics of Finance in Developing Countries*, (Ithaca: Cornell University Press), pp. 23–54.

Chung, K. H., Hak, Ch. L. and Ku, H. J. (1997) *Korean Management: Global Strategy and Cultural Transformation* (New York: Walter de Gruyter).

De Soto, H. (2000) *The Mystery of Capitalism* (New York: Basic Books).

Chosun Ilbo (2001a) 'Perils of Shrinking Exports (1): Exports Stymied by Downturns in US, Japan', 1 May, *Digital Chosun Ilbo* [website] http://www.english.chosun.com/service/archives.html, last consulted 20 December 2003.

—— (2001b) 'Who's Reforming Who?', 21 September.

—— (2002a) 'Banks Mired in Household Debts: FT', 20 November.

—— (2002b) 'Savings Ratio Falls to 20-Year Low', 11 December.

—— (2003a) 'IBM Korea Most Coveted Workplace', 10 February.

—— (2003b) 'Young People Want Out, Survey Says', 23 April.

Earley, P. C. (1997) *Face, Harmony and Social Structure* (New York: Oxford University Press).

The Economist (2001) 'Korean Murk', 31 March, pp. 69–70.

—— (2002a) 'Monsters Still, But Prettier', 5 January, p. 63.

—— (2002b) 'Dead Deals Walking', 9 February, pp. 51–2.

—— (2003) 'Keeping the Lights On: A Survey of South Korea', 19 April, pp.1–16.

El Kahal, S. (2001) *Business in Asia Pacific: Text and Cases* (New York: Oxford University Press).

Federation of Korean Trade Unions (2001) 'Industrial Relations and Increasing Globalization,' Unpublished paper (Seoul: International Relations Bureau, Federation of Korean Trade Unions).

Fields, K. J. (1995) *Enterprise and the State in Korea and Taiwan* (Ithaca, NY: Cornell University Press).

Fligstein, N. (1997) *Markets, Politics and Globalization* (Stockholm: Almqvist and Wiksell International).

Hinkleman, E. G. and Genzberger, C. A. (1994) *The Portable Encyclopedia for Doing Business with Korea* (San Rafael, CA: World Trade Press).

Hahn, C. (1999) 'The Confucian Tradition and Economic Reform', in J. R. Mo and Ch. I. Moon (eds), *Democracy and the Korean Economy* (Palo Alto: Stanford University, Hoover Institution Press), pp. 35–54.

Hamilton, G. and Biggart, N. W. (1988) 'Market, Culture and Authority: A Comparative Analysis of Management and Organization in the Far East', *American Journal of Sociology*, vol. 94, Supplement, pp. S52–94.

Hobday, M. (1998) 'Latecomer Catch-up Strategies in Electronics: Samsung of Korea and ACER of Taiwan', in C. Rowley and J. Bae (eds), *Korean Businesses: Internal and External Industrialization* (London: Frank Cass), pp. 48–83.

Huntington, S. (1968) *Political Order in Changing Societies* (New Haven: Yale University Press).

Jun, Y. W. (1995) 'Strategic Responses of Korean Firms to Globalization and Regionalization Forces: The Case of the Korean Electronics Industry', in D. F. Simon (ed.) *Corporate Strategies in the Pacific Rim: Global Versus Regional Trends* (London: Routledge), pp. 135–65.

Kim, B. W. (1992) *Seniority Wage System in the Far East: Confucian Influence Over Japan and South Korea* (Aldershot: Avebury).

Kim, Ch. S. (1992) *The Culture of Korean Industry: An Ethnography of Poongsan Corporation* (Tucson: The University of Arizona Press).

Kim, D. I. and Lee, J. H. (2000) 'Changes in the Korean Labor Market and Future Prospects', in K. Judd and Y. K. Lee (eds), *An Agenda for Economic Reform in Korea* (Palo Alto: Stanford University, Hoover Institution Press), pp. 341–73.

Kim, D. J. (1984) 'Mass-Participatory Economy: Korea: Road to World Economic Power', Monograph (Cambridge, MA: Center for International Affairs, Harvard University).

Kim, D. J. (1996) *Mass-Participatory Economy: Korea's Road to World Economic Power* (New York: Harvard University and University Press of America).

Kim, W. Ch. (1992) *Every Street is Paved with Gold: The Road to Real Success* (New York: William Morrow & Co.).

Kirk, D. (1999) *Korean Crisis* (New York: St Martin's Press).

Kluth, A. (2001) 'In Praise of Rules: A Survey of Asian Business', *The Economist*, 7 April, pp. 1–18.

Korea Herald (2001a) 'Chaebol to Submit Deregulation Proposals Today', 14 May, *The Korea Herald* [website] http://www.koreaherald.com/archives/result_detail.asp, last consulted 20 December 2003.

—— (2001b) 'Foreign Banks Record Higher Net Profits', 18 May.

—— (2002a) 'GNP Again Calls on Prosecutors to Arrest President's Second Son', 9 June.

—— (2002b) 'Prosecution Interrogating Friend of President's Second Son Over Suspicious Money Transactions', 12 June.

Korea Times (2001) 'Parties, Government Agree to Push Ahead With Corporate Reform' 21 May, *The Korea Times* [website] http://times.hankooki.com/service/listmore/kt_archive.php?media=kt&page=1&strSec=&strItem=&type=, last consulted 20 December 2003.

—— (2003a) 'One Out of 13 in Their 20s Faces Bankruptcy', 23 April.

—— (2003b) 'Korea Outgrows Economic Development Model', 26 October.

KPMG (2002) KPMG Samjong, 'Foreign Direct Investment in Korea', *KPMG Samjong* [website] www.aspac.kr.kpmg.com, accessed 20 December 2003.

Lee, T. I. (2000) 'Republic of Korea (South Korea)', *The American Journal of Economics and Sociology, Supplement: Land-Value Taxation Around the World*, vol. 59(5), pp. 371–83.

Leipziger, D. M., Dollar, D., Shorrocks, A. F. and Song, S. Y. (1992) *The Distribution of Income and Wealth in Korea* (Washington, DC: The World Bank).

Lie, J. (1998) *Han Unbound: The Political Economy of South Korea* (Palo Alto: Stanford University Press).

Lim, Y. (1999) *Technology and Productivity: The Korean Way of Learning and Catching Up* (Cambridge, MA: The MIT Press).

Martin, J. P. and Torres, R. (2001) 'Korean Labor Market and Social Safety-Net Reforms: Challenges and Policy Requirements', in F. Park, Y. Park, G. Betcherman and A. Dar (eds), *Labor Market Reforms in Korea: Policy Options for the Future* (Seoul: Korea Labor Institute).

Matthews, T. and Ravenhill, J. (1994) 'Strategic Trade Policy: The Northeast Asian Experience', in A. Macintyre (ed.), *Business and Government in Industrialising Asia* (Ithaca, NY: Cornell University Press), pp. 29–90.

MOFE (2003): Ministry of Finance and Economics, Republic of Korea, 'Liberalization of FDI in Principle – 4 April', *MOFE* [website] (updated 20 December 2003) www.mofe.go.kr, accessed 20 December 2003.

Mo and Moon (1999) 'Epilogue', in J. R. Mo and Ch. I. Moon (eds), *Democracy and the Korean Economy* (Palo Alto: Stanford University, Hoover Institution Press), pp. 171–98.

Moon, Ch. I. (1994) 'Changing Patterns of Business–Government Relations in South Korea', in A. Macintyre (ed.), *Business and Government in Industrialising Asia* (Ithaca, NY: Cornell University Press), pp. 142–66.

Moon, Ch. I. (1999) 'Democratization and Globalization as Ideological and Political Foundations of Economic Policy', in J. R. Mo and Ch. I. Moon, (eds), *Democracy and the Korean Economy* (Palo Alto: Stanford University, Hoover Institution Press), pp. 1–34.

New York Times (2002) 'Bush Puts Tariffs of as Much as 30 per cent on Steel Imports', 6 March.

——— (2003) 'U.S. Tariff on Hynix Chips Draws South Korean Protest', 20 June.

OECD (2000) Organization for Economic Cooperation and Development, *OECD Economic Surveys: Korea* (Paris: OECD Publications).

Osgood, C. (1951) *The Koreans and Their Culture* (Tokyo: Charles E. Tuttle).

Powell, W. W. and Smith-Doerr, L. (1994) 'Networks and Economic Life', in N. Smelser and R. Swedberg (eds), *The Handbook of Economic Sociology* (Princeton, NJ: Princeton University Press), pp. 368–402.

Rodrik, D. (1999) *The New Global Economy and Developing Countries: Making Openness Work* (Washington, DC: Overseas Development Council).

Sen, A. (2002) 'How to Judge Globalism', *The American Prospect* (Winter), pp. A2–6.

Smucker, J. (1980) *Industrialization in Canada* (Scarborough, ON: Prentice-Hall).

Wade, R. (1990) *Governing the Market* (Princeton, NJ: Princeton University Press).

Weber, M. (1958) *The Protestant Ethic and the Spirit of Capitalism* (New York: Scribner).

Wei, S. J. (2000) 'Local Corruption and Global Capital Flows', *Brookings Papers on Economic Activity* (Washington: Brookings Institution), vol. 30(2), pp. 305–54.

Weller, R. (1999) *Alternate Civilities: Democracy and Culture in China and Taiwan* (Boulder, CO: Westview Press).

9
Managing for Whom? Foreign Ownership and Management of Korea First Bank

Joseph Smucker

Introduction

This paper raises a number of issues in defining the social responsibilities of managers of foreign firms. It is one thing to argue that they must act responsibly in preserving, if not improving, the quality of life in their host country; it is quite another to know what standards to employ in pursuing these ends, and how priorities should be established.

In this chapter, I attempt to illustrate the dilemmas confronting managers in an economy that operates differently from the economic model in their home country. I describe a number of events following the first foreign takeover of a South Korean bank. This takeover itself was significant because it represented what appeared to be major changes in the way in which banks traditionally functioned in South Korea. These changes were the result of a set of comprehensive demands imposed on South Korea by the International Monetary Fund (IMF) as part of the conditions for receiving a rescue loan of US$55 billion during the financial crisis in 1997–98.

I first describe the events leading up to the takeover. Next I describe the changes in bank practices introduced by the American CEO and their positive evaluations by the Western business press. I contrast these assessments with the more critical views of the Korean press. I offer some reasons for the sudden resignation of the CEO, and I then describe subsequent developments under the bank's new American administration.

Precipitating events

One of the principal ways in which the government of South Korea was able to foster the rapid advance of the Korean economy and facilitate the growth of the large conglomerates or 'chaebol' was through its close ties with Korea's financial institutions (Amsden, 1989; Moon, 1994; Fields, 1995; Ku, 1997; Hirschman, 1999; D. Kim, 1999; Johnson *et al.*, 2000; OECD, 2000b; *Chosun Ilbo*, 2002c). For example, the federal government was always represented on the banks' boards of directors. It acted as the guarantor of loans for favoured projects that kept the highly leveraged chaebol operational. It also used these roles as channels of influence by which it could reward or chastise business interests.[1] Banks, in turn, passively followed government policies and, prior to 1997, continued to operate with low profitability and poor returns as measured by returns on assets, returns on equity and capital adequacy ratios (OECD, 2000a, pp. 264, 273). But prior to the financial or liquidity crisis of 1997–98, few observers of Korea's rapid pace of economic development questioned the effectiveness of this arrangement; instead, Western financial commentators lauded the high rate of Korean savings, the control of currency flows and the policy of investing in production for export rather than for internal consumption or for quick financial returns. Profit margins for banks were not viewed as especially important as long as funds were being actively employed in productive enterprises. Further, the government had been praised for its rigour in ensuring that this pattern continued even though there were strong voices raised against the costs to civil liberties of these policies.

Although there had been a few setbacks in the course of Korea's economic development since the Korean War, the liquidity crisis that struck in 1997–98 was unprecedented in its destruction. There were a number of causes for this crisis, which first struck Asia and reverberated into Russia and Latin America (China, with its tightly controlled economic policies, largely escaped these aftershocks). A major factor was the collapse of currency values, as huge sums of capital from Western countries sought more favourable investments in the world market. Following the devaluation of the baht in Thailand, currency traders began taking advantage of these falling values. Nervous investors then began to withhold investments that they regarded as too risky in yielding acceptable returns and to call in loans, rather than renew them, as they had done in the past. The spread of these effects to Korea caused the bankruptcies of a number of prominent highly leveraged conglomerates in Korea as well as the near collapse of its financial institutions. As a result, the Korean government was forced to seek aid from the International Monetary Fund.[2] In accepting its request, the IMF required the Korean government to meet a number of conditions designed to restructure the Korean economy along more Western, open-market lines, so as to make the banks more autonomous but also more independently accountable, and in addition to require higher standards of loan processing, provide for bankruptcy procedures – and permit foreign direct investment in the banking industry.[3] In effect, what had once been praised as a unique arrangement for rapid economic development was now seen as a fatal weakness (Kirk, 1999; Chopra *et al.*, 2001).

In response to the IMF demands, the Korean government allowed a number of banks to fail; others were merged. Two other banks, Seoul Bank and Korea First Bank,[4] were nationalized with the intent to sell the government's controlling interest to foreign investors. The last-mentioned of these, Korea First Bank (KFB), is the focus of this chapter.

KFB had been a major player in the economic development of South Korea. Originally established as the Chosun Savings Bank in 1929, it had played a key role in the economic development strategies of the Park regime after the Korean War. During the 1980s and 1990s, it was considered to be the premier bank in South Korea. In 1996, it and its subsidiaries constituted the largest financial group in Korea (Huang and O'Neil-Massaro, 2002). It gained its prominence by serving as one of the principal financial institutions serving the giant chaebol. But if its strength lay in its close ties to the chaebol, KFB was also the most vulnerable to collapse following the liquidity crisis of 1997. Foreign investors had called in their short-term loans, leaving the chaebols bereft of investments for their continued long-term expansionary projects – not that the chaebols were short of assets to back up these loans: the problem was rather that they lacked liquidity, while the banks, KFB especially, lacked the resources to meet the cash payments demanded by foreign investors.

Faced with the bank's imminent failure, the Korean government assumed full control and recapitalized it in preparation for its eventual takeover by private interests. Through its own Korea Deposit Insurance Corporation (KDIC), the government invested 3.5 trillion Won (US$3.2 billion) in the bank and then contributed another 38 billion Won (US$34.5 million) and purchased over 3 billion Won (US$2.7 million) of the banks assets.

Since no Korean bank had the resources to buy out KFB, the Korean government concluded, with the encouragement of the IMF (which probably would not have opposed its liquidation) that it should be sold to foreign interests. The IMF set a deadline of November 1998 for the sale. The IMF assumed that foreign ownership would introduce new management skills to the Korean banks and that this would be a step towards achieving reforms in the financial sector, including improvements in governance and profitability. In addition, it would further the IMF objective of liberalizing trade and capital flows while reducing the influence of both the chaebol and the government on financial institutions.

In September 1999, after nearly 2 years of intense negotiations with Newbridge Capital, an American investment firm, the Korean government through its agencies, agreed to Newbridge's purchase of 51 per cent of KFB (*Chosun Ilbo*, 1999; *Korea Times*, 1999). The final terms of the agreement specified that the government, through KDIC, would play a major role in covering 'non-performing' and defaulted loans, and would continue its involvement for 3 years following the conclusion of the purchase agreement. KDIC continued to hold 49 per cent of the bank's shares. As part of the restructuring scheme, it is scheduled to withdraw its involvement in the bank during 2004.

Newbridge Capital was founded by two private American equity firms in 1994. It opened offices in the major financial centres of Asia and specialized in buying controlling interest in companies that had been divested, were undergoing restructuring or were in less favoured industries. Its strategy was to build value in its purchases and make them profitable before selling them.[5] In the early 1990s Newbridge concentrated its activities on the People's Republic of China, where asset prices were relatively low, due to the Chinese government's policy of restricting foreign capital inflows. In the rest of Asia, because of the huge amounts of available foreign investment capital, assets had become comparatively costly.

Following the financial crisis of 1997–98, Newbridge quickly sought investment opportunities in a market that had seen the value of assets drop dramatically low in price. It bought out an Indonesian electronics manufacturer and was looking for more buyout opportunities. One of the original partners of Newbridge had considerable experience in restructuring banks in the United States; with this experience behind it, Newbridge saw an opportunity to make a profitable investment in Korea First Bank.

Following the conclusion of the extensive negotiations, Newbridge took effective control of KFB in January 2000 (for an account of the difficulties experienced by foreigners attempting to invest in, or buy out Korean firms, see *The Economist*, 2002a,b). It installed its own Chief Executive Officer, Wilfred Horie, an American who had previous experience in Japan, representing the interests of another American investment company, Associate First Capital Corporation (*Chosun Ilbo*, 2000a,b). Horie was soon hailed by the international business community for his ability to institute policies that not only were reviving the bank's fortunes but also changed a rigid bureaucratic structure and challenged assumed inviolable cultural business norms and long-standing government interventions in business operations (*BusinessWeek Online*, 2001a; *American Chamber of Commerce in Korea Journal*, 2001; see also *Chosun Ilbo*, 2000d).[6]

In taking over the bank, Horie redirected its focus from commercial to retail banking, with most operations aimed at small- and medium-sized businesses and individual clients. No longer would it play a major role as financial agent for the giant chaebol. In making this change, Horie introduced US-style mortgages, private banking for individuals, quick cash loans and a broader range of credit card products. He also emphasized 'brand-building' in an effort to capture and retain a larger share of the retail market. Considerable effort was made to improve customer service, with the implementation of the staff motto 'Smile, serve and sell'. Horie in marked contrast to the traditional deportment of Korean executives, personally sought out potential customers, socialized with all levels of personnel in the bank and made himself readily available to the press.

Horie was also lauded by the foreign business press for his revolutionary approach to staffing and human resource policies. In an effort to change the rigidly bureaucratic nature of the bank administration, he laid off 170 managers through early retirement incentives, he hired 60 new personnel (from

1600 applicants) and charged them with becoming 'agents of change' responsible for initiating new administrative procedures.[7] In the meantime, American personnel from Newbridge Capital were appointed to the key positions of chief credit officer, chief financial officer and chief technology officer. The presence of these foreign personnel in top management positions was highly unusual in the Korean banking industry (*BusinessWeek Online*, 2001a).[8]

In addition to these revolutionary changes, Horie was also able to win over an initially hostile labour union by his frankness, openness and ready accessibility. Relations were further smoothed by his presence at company-wide social events and by his monthly luncheon meetings with the head of the bank employees union.

Along with further innovations that made the administration of the bank more transparent, new accounting procedures were brought into play so that accurate running accounts were instantly accessible. In the past, such records were often fully known only at the end of the fiscal year. All of these new approaches in the banking industry seemed to serve dramatic notice that many of the cultural imperatives and powerful networks that had governed organizational administration in the South Korean banking sector could be changed, or at least circumvented (*Korea Herald*, 2001d).[9] Further, banks in this new approach were to become profit centres themselves rather than merely serve the needs of the chaebol.

Horie reached his greatest fame when he resisted government pressures to purchase company bonds in order to keep failing conglomerates afloat. This act not only signalled a more independent role of the bank but also announced the bank's profit-oriented objectives. A specific case was the government's attempt to pressure KFB into cooperating with other financial institutions to provide financing for Hynix Corporation, a computer chip manufacturer and a subsidiary of the Hyundai chaebol.[10] Horie was lauded by the international financial press for taking this stand and for stating quite boldly, that the bank's primary objective was to maximize its profits rather than serve as a social welfare agency or serve 'the national interest'. Indeed, a number of publications hailed his actions as responsible for breaking the long-standing submissive relationship of Korean banks to government agencies.[11] Horie further challenged the government financial supervisory body when he instituted a policy requiring a monthly 2000 Won commission (about US$1.80) from clients who had less than 100000 Won in their accounts (US$91.00). He defended this policy by declaring that it was improper for banks to retain small accounts that did not yield profitable returns (*Korea Times*, 2001a).

Under his direction, the bank, which lost 10 trillion Won (US$9 billion) in 1999 made a 200 billion Won (US$181.8 million) profit by October 2001. Its return on assets improved from −3.21 per cent to 1.55 per cent over the 2-year period. Its return on equity went from −52.8 per cent in 1999 to 28.33 per cent in 2001 (*Business Asia*, 2001).

Despite the positive reports of Mr Horie's performance as a bank executive, the Korean media were quick to offer a supplemental interpretation of his success (*Chosun Ilbo*, 2000c, 2001a,c,d,e; *Korea Herald*, 2001a,b,c). It was pointed out that under the terms by which Newbridge Capital took over Korea First Bank the government would compensate Newbridge for losses on normal loans until 2001 and until 2002 for 'workout' loans to companies in the process of restructuring. In return, KFB was to share part of the 'responsibility' for supporting struggling companies during the restructuring period. In addition, readers of the Korean press were reminded that the bank received a total of some 15.8 trillion Won (US$14 billion) in public funds at the time of sale to Newbridge Capital of which 6.5 trillion Won (US$5.9 billion) had been repaid by January 2001. Furthermore, the bank continued to receive government support. KFB continued to be backed by the Korea Deposit Insurance Corporation, which owned 49 per cent of the bank's shares. The government agency's chief role was to purchase the bank's bad loans and provide support funds for allowances against bad loans. It was to serve this insurance function until the year 2004, when the bank was to be totally privatized (*Chosun Ilbo*, 2001a). Despite these misgivings, however, there is no question that Horie was able to set the agenda for a more autonomous banking system and played a significant role in reducing the often graft-laced ties between government officials and private industry.[12]

National objectives and foreign interests: Dilemmas facing the CEO

In October 2001 Wilfred Horie surprised the banking industry by announcing his resignation (*Chosun Ilbo*, 2001g; *Korea Herald*, 2001e; *Korea Times*, 2001b). The probable cause of his resignation was Newbridge Capital's displeasure over new exposure of Korea First Bank to possible non-performing loans. Despite Horie's refusal to join other banks in granting Hynix financial support, Hynix was able to follow through on its corporate restructuring in preparation for a future sale. Several months later Hynix was in negotiations with Micron, an American firm, for its purchase. Knowing this, KFB now agreed to lend Hynix the equivalent of US$77 million as part of a US$615 million syndicated loan. This meant that with past loans before Horie's arrival the bank's exposure to Hynix alone totalled US$212 million (*BusinessWeek Online*, 2001b; *Chosun Ilbo*, 2001f). But no one had anticipated the rapid fall in computer chip prices, and there were no definite signs that the impending acquisition of Hynix would not take place. With the downturn in the computer chip market and the growing likelihood that Hynix would not be bought out, the bank's exposure represented a serious risk to Newbridge Capital (see *Korea Herald*, 2001h).

In addition, it was believed that Newbridge Capital was disappointed with the pace of restructuring at the bank and the fact that the bank had already accumulated some US$339 million in bad loans. All this after the bank had a 'clean' balance sheet when Horie took over, following the government injection of US$12 billion. Further, the bank's strategy of moving into the highly competitive mortgage market was being questioned, since this market was already dominated by four of the largest banks in South Korea (*Korea Times*, 2001b; *BusinessWeek Online*, 2001b).

Following the announcement of Horie's resignation, a number of Korean commentators expressed concern that the influence of foreign interests, such as Newbridge Capital, could thwart the restructuring aims of the South Korean government. In the particular case of Hynix, they believed that the government was correct in keeping it afloat in order to ensure it was well positioned for meeting an eventual return of increased market demand for computer chips (*Korea Herald*, 2001f,h).

Further concerns about national interests were raised when it was revealed that Horie had received stock options a year prior to his resignation amounting to 4.12 million shares at 9834 Won per share. The labour union at Korea First Bank had previously voiced its opposition to these stock options, claiming that these would deprive other employees unfairly of the bank's profits. The government in fact did move to prevent the realization of these options by invoking its revised securities laws, which require employees to serve at least 2 years before exercising their rights and then only upon retirement (*Korea Herald*, 2001g). Then, in July 2002 the Financial Supervisory Commission, a government agency, sent a 'reprimand' to Horie and another past president of the bank for their approval of loss-provoking loans (*Chosun Ilbo*, 2002d), which under the original takeover agreement the government would still be obliged to cover.

Commentaries in the foreign business press interpreted Horie's departure in a positive manner, citing his resignation as evidence that bank presidents were now beholden to their major shareholders and should not be expected to continue in office as agents involved in networks of influence and intrigue. Those who argued for the reform of Korea's financial sector and business practices in general maintained that profit motives, regardless of their source, represented a 'cleansing' process for a system formerly dependent on empire building, opaque financial accounting and government subsidies (*BusinessWeek Online*, 2001b; see also *The Economist*, 2001).

Other commentators (mostly Korean) took a different stance, arguing that the interests of foreign investors were not necessarily in Korea's best interests, especially during the economic and social upheaval that accompanied the restructuring process. In some accounts that attempted to interpret the significance of the choice of Horie's successor, concerns were raised that Newbridge Capital was only interested in maximizing returns on its investment and that it would sell out its stake as soon as it could realize a desired profit – or else cut its losses (*Chosun Ilbo*, 2001i). In any case, the benefits of the sale, they argued, would be lost to Korea.

Robert Cohen, the new CEO who replaced Horie, had served as vice-chairman of Republic National Bank of New York; as a director of Korea First

Bank, he had been in charge of the risk control and financial restructuring committees (*Korea Times*, 2001b; *Korea Herald*, 2001g). The appointment of a risk management expert as CEO reinforced speculation that Newbridge's interests might be at odds with the ultimate goals of the government's restructuring programme, which, it was hoped, would benefit the Korean economy (*Korea Herald*, 2001b; *Korea Times*, 2001c).[13] The *Korea Times* (2001c) also reported that Cohen was attempting to 'wipe out the short-term "hedge fund" image' of Newbridge Capital. According to the *Korea Times* article, Cohen's inaugural speech outlining his reorganization strategies, appealing to the need for 'transparent management' and 'growth-oriented strategy', failed to allay fears among many observers that a sale was being planned. Certainly the KFB employees' union representatives were openly suspicious of Newbridge's motives, stating publicly their belief that Newbridge was interested only in short-term gains while it organized the bank into an attractive saleable commodity (*Chosun Ilbo*, 2001h,j; see also 2002a,b).

Following the installation of Cohen as CEO, conflicts between Korea First Bank and the government became pronounced. In March 2002 it was reported that KFB had requested compensation from the government for losses under the 'put-back option agreement'. This agreement, signed at the time of the takeover of the bank, required KDIC to buy back bad loans over the 3-year period following the signing. A *Korea Times* editorial commenting on this stipulation raised the question whether KFB management had exercised due caution in its loan policies. The author cited recent figures showing the bank's poor performance relative to the other major Korean banks. Further, according to the author, the value of the stock option rights of the bank's managers did not seem consistent with their own performance during the previous 2 years (*Korea Times*, 2002a).

In May 2002 the press reported that, contrary to an agreement with Hynix involving a restructuring pact made prior to the KFB's takeover by Newbridge, the bank was attempting to recover part of that debt (*Korea Times*, 2002b). This news was followed by the revelation that the government was taking disciplinary action against a number of KFB executives and employees, who allegedly were responsible for losses over the previous 5 years. Even Wilfred Horie, the previous CEO, was sent a 'cautionary warning' (*Korea Times*, 2002d). This was followed by further media announcements that government supervisory and investment agencies were filing lawsuits, seeking reparations for previous bad loans made by a number of banks, including KFB, that were covered by public funds (*Chosun Ilbo*, 2002d,e).

In the case of KFB the claim that, as part of the Newbridge takeover agreement, the government was responsible to insure losses against bad loans, was countered by the government's implicit charge that the bank, knowing this, had been irresponsible in its loan policies and executive compensation packages. These practices, the government declared, could not be condoned, since it was responsible for recovering the public funds it had made available during the restructuring period. In fact, the government was facing increased public criticism for continuing to inject public funds into the banks and for failing to recover all or part of these funds more promptly (*Korea Times*, 2002c; see also Karasulu, 2002, p. 107).[14]

The government proposed that the banks be responsible for about 30 per cent of the public fund losses as part of a collective effort to help pay for restructuring costs. But this was criticized by both the banking industry and business interests, who feared that this would reduce the profit margins of banks, while raising interest rates for business firms.

Wilfred Horie's resignation and the conflicts between KFB and the government illustrate a dilemma of growing importance for managers of firms operating in foreign countries – especially countries going through periods of severe structural change as has been the case in Korea. Broadly put, the dilemma is one of meeting diverse and often conflicting demands on the business enterprise. Certainly the organizational innovations introduced by Horie increased the transparency of the bank's administration and moved it towards greater independence and accountability. These changes were consistent with the more general requirements of the IMF (OECD, 2000a). Horie's unabashed announcement that he intended to make the bank 'profitable' would seem to meet the interests of Newbridge Capital. At the same time, it is hardly likely that Newbridge was envisioning itself as an agent of reconstruction for the benefit of the South Korean economy. Thus when Horie sought to provide loans to the Hynix Corporation he probably thought that not only was he serving the cause of reconstruction, while regaining some lost support from the government, but in doing so Newcastle would benefit in the long run. But the parent company was not to be so patient in realizing its returns, and the deal was aborted. These actions made it clear that the bank was to adopt a profit-maximizing role, more consistent with the current practices of Western, especially American, market principles.

The conflict between KFB under Cohen's administration and the government was also a conflict between Newcastle's interests and the interests of the government. In seeking to make KFB a profitable enterprise, Newcastle also sought ways to maximize its returns on the assumption that the government would cover loan losses. But in doing so, it was encouraging the use of public funds for its own private benefit. While purportedly serving the interests of the bank, it was violating its own market principles by taking advantage of government financial resources.

Foreign direct investment, by its very nature, is likely to create conflict between national interests and the interests of foreign investors. Stallings (1990) argues that 'the purpose of foreign capital is to further the interests of those who provide it. Development of the host country is a fortuitous side effect at best, which will only come about if the host government maintains enough autonomy and control to guarantee that the benefits are shared between providers and recipients of foreign capital' (p. 84).

Current pressures from the international financial community on South Korea to open its economy to greater foreign direct investment have increased the array of conflicting interests both in the business community and in civil society as a whole (Joh, 2001). Managers of foreign firms are faced with the problems of reconciling the claims of shareholders in their home countries, claims which are consistent with a model of capitalism in which financial interests reign supreme, with the unique requirements of Korean society. Failure to find an acceptable path through the diverse and often contradictory claims regarding both the allocation of returns and the method of allocation is likely to lead to a 'costly and drawn-out' resolution process (Karasulu, 2002, p. 109; see also Choi, 1993; Hollingsworth, 1997; Rodrik, 1997, pp. 3–5; D. Kim, 1999; and Johnson *et al.*, 2000).[15]

In November and December 2003, as the deadline drew near for the government's complete withdrawal from supporting banking operations, commentators predicted increased foreign investment and the likely sale of a number of Korean banks, including KFB. The *Korea Times* reported that major foreign shareholders in eight commercial banks, including KFB, raised their holdings from 12.5 per cent at the end of 2002 to 21.7 per cent in November of 2003. Foreign held shares in one bank, Korea Exchange Bank increased from 32.6 per cent in 2002 to 65.75 per cent in October of 2003. The article further reported that Citibank, HSBC and other foreign financial institutions were keen to take over additional banks, including KFB (*Korea Times*, 2003a). Rumours of the impending sale of KFB continue, and in all likelihood it is only a matter of time before this takes place.

Meanwhile, Korea First Bank has remained a viable, though much smaller, enterprise. But the fact that it is controlled by a foreign investment firm; that the announced objectives of the owners is to create value for its shareholders, most of whom are foreign, challenges a source of considerable Korean pride in having built a vibrant, strong economy. It strikes at the very tenets of the Confucian, communitarian culture which had given legitimacy to the central role the government had played in this process.

Conclusions

This brief account illustrates a number of dilemmas facing a CEO of a firm operating in a foreign country. First, market economies differ not only with respect to the role played by governments but also with respect to the priorities governing economic behaviour. To administer a firm in a socially responsible manner in a foreign country, managers need to be aware of these differences. Strategies that emphasize large profit margins and high returns for investors may be inappropriate in a country involved in enlarging its productive capacity, as had been the case in South Korea (Marglin, 2003). Second, even if these strategies are appropriate, socially responsible managers of foreign firms need to ensure that adequate returns remain within the host country. Korean critics of foreign ownership fear that the benefits of their country's many decades of Spartan discipline and single-minded drive towards economic development may be lost to foreign interests (see *Korea Herald*, 2003a,b; *Korea Times*, 2003a). Third, while it may be obvious that greater transparency in governance, and improvements in organizational efficiency, among other significant structural changes, must be brought about as economic development proceeds, these changes need to be adopted gradually, with minimal disruption and in conformity with the most beneficial expression of local cultural norms. Fourth, to gain acceptance as a socially responsible entity in a host country, a foreign firm needs to be acutely aware of existing social inequities and needs to engage in activities aimed at reducing them. Firms cannot ignore the consequences of how their gains are allocated (Friedmann, 1992, pp. 27–30; *Korea Times*, 2003b). Finally, what needs to be stressed most of all is a cautionary note that social justice is not served if preconceived notions of the 'correct' objectives of economic enterprises are imposed upon foreign cultures having different institutional configurations and different cultural priorities (Fligstein, 1997; Djelic, 1998; Naim, 1999; Stiglitz, 2002).

Acknowledgement

I wish thank Mr Duane McMullen, Minister-Counsellor of the Canadian Embassy in Seoul, for facilitating my research in South Korea in the Spring of 2001 and for calling my attention to this particular case. I also wish to thank Myung Joo, Political and Economic Officer of the Canadian Embassy, for her extremely valuable role in providing me with contacts and leads during my sojourn in Korea. Others who have contributed to my perspective on this and related papers on Korea include Ahn, Bu Young, Kim, Jong Goon and Chong, Chong Mo. I owe additional thanks to Anders Muller for his contributions to relevant literature; and finally to Fred Bird and Emmanuel Raufflet for their critical comments.

Notes

1. For a historical overview of government involvement in the financial sector, see Choi (1993). From the early 1960s through the late 1980s the strategies for economic development often resembled major military mobilization plans.
2. For accounts of the specific causes of the crisis see OECD (2000a), p. 28, *The Economist* (2001); El Kahal (2001), p. 24.
3. Kim, Dohyung (1999) argues that Korean government did not merely accept the IMF conditions carte blanche. It believed that to do so would have resulted in a very severe contraction of its economy. In the financial sector the government purchased non-performing loans and provided money for the recapitalization of key businesses. But it also allowed the collapse of non-viable financial institutions and it opened up the possibility of foreign participation in domestic commercial banks.

4. In April 1999, because these two banks had exhausted all of their capital, the government ordered them to stop making any new loans. Meanwhile, in the restructuring process, the number of commercial banks was reduced from 26 to 17 and the number of banking employees was reduced by one-third (OECD, 2000a, pp. 291, 264). The vulnerability of the banking sector in general had always been high relatively due in large part to the active interventions of the government. But the collapse of the Daewoo chaebol in 1999 dramatized the alarming extent of their exposure to loan defaults.

5. In its statement of 'philosophy' Newbridge states that 'Newbridge actively seeks investment opportunities in those industries that stand to benefit from economic growth and Asia's recovery, or in rapid-growth industries, such as technology.' It also claims to be 'a strong supporter of growth through acquisition' (www.newbridgecapital.com).

6. Much of the description to follow is based on accounts appearing in the internet English publications of the South Korean newspapers *Chosun Ilbo*, *The Korea Herald* and *The Korea Times* during the years 1999 to 2003.

7. Horie claimed that these were not layoffs but rather choices made by personnel: 'no unemployment, only re-employment'. Personnel could choose to stay employed if they were willing to learn new skills and adapt to new changes, or accept 'an attractive retirement package' (*American Chamber of Commerce in Korea Journal*, 2001).

8. Since then other banks, principally those with a sizeable proportion of foreign stockholders, have made similar changes. One of the most 'socially' revolutionary changes has been a shift away from internal promotion to increased hiring of senior personnel from outside the bank organizations. Especially hard-hit by these changes are middle-aged, middle-management employees (see *Chosun Ilbo*, 2002c).

9. Mosakowski (2000) notes that some of the most successful entrants into foreign cultures have simply ignored the foreign culture and relied upon their own model. But she also points out that for this to succeed a number of conditions must prevail. These include some degree of upheaval in the relevant industrial sector; transparency in the rules of the 'new game'; adequate rewards for those who adopt the new policies; and fervent commitment of the innovator to the new strategies.

10. Horie did agree to participate in extending export credits to the troubled Hyundai Electronics, in response to requests from the Korean government's Financial Supervisory Commission, to help stabilize financial markets that were still in trouble in January 2001 (*Korea Times*, 2001a).

11. *Business Week* included Wilfred Horie among those it selected as 'Asia's best and brightest' (*BusinessWeek Online*, 2001a).

12. In 1996, for example, the then president of Korea First Bank was arrested for allegedly receiving bribes in granting loans to failing companies. There were also widespread suspicions that government bureaucrats played an active role in facilitating these loans (*Chosun Ilbo*, 1996).

13. The *Korea Herald* quotes a government Financial Supervisory Service official as being 'worried' that KFB under Cohen would reverse the decision to grant loans to Hynix or 'get into conflict with the labour union which suspects Newbridge of attempting to sell off KFB after raising enough money through the bank'.

14. According to the author of the *Korea Times* article, 'The public rage is growing over the tremendous sum of public fund losses...Civic group members and critics accused the government of trying to force taxpayers to shoulder almost all the burden, claiming that the tax authorities are likely to increase tax revenues to cover the

losses.' Karasulu (2002) in his report to the IMF, notes: 'The extensive public focus on revenue generation in Korean privatization efforts may have overshadowed other important objectives' (p. 114). He offers the opinion that 'Although the recovery of public funds should remain an objective in the privatization process, management of expectations is equally important to deter a public perception of fire-sales' (p. 115).

15. On the other hand, one can also point to cases where the Korean model of management has been totally inappropriate in other cultures. Anecdotal accounts of Korean managers operating as if their Mexican or Vietnamese employees were part of a disciplined army sacrificing their time for the good of the firm reveal an equivalent failure to be sensitive to host-country models of labour market behaviour.

References

American Chamber of Commerce in Korea Journal (2001) 'Banking on Korea: Face to Face with Wilfred Horie, President and CEO, Korea First Bank', September–October.

Amsden, A. (1989) *Asia's Next Giant: South Korea and Late Industrialization* (Oxford University Press).

Business Asia (2001) 'Korea First Bank Only Fully Foreign-Owned Bank', 15 October.

BusinessWeek Online (2001a) 'The Stars of Asia', 2 July.

—— (2001b) 'Banking: Raising the Bar Can Hurt. Korea First's CEO Ushered in Accountability, Now He's Out', 19 November.

Choi, B-S. (1993) 'Financial Policy and Big Business in Korea: The Perils of Financial Regulation', in S. Haggard, Ch. H. Lee and S. Maxfield (eds), *The Politics of Finance in Developing Countries* (Ithaca, NY: Cornell University Press), pp. 21–54.

Chopra, A., Kang, K. H., Karasulu, M., Liang, H. and Ma, H. P. (2001) 'From Crisis to Recovery in Korea: Strategy, Achievements and Lessons', *IMF Working Paper 01/154* (Washington, DC: International Monetary Fund).

Chosun Ilbo (1996) 'A Closer Look at the Hyosan Scandal', 3 May, *Digital Chosun Ilbo* [website] http://www.english.chosun.com/service/archives.html, last consulted 20 December 2003.

—— (1999) 'Newbridge Inks Deal to be the Official New Owner of KFB', 23 December.

—— (2000a) 'KFB Directors Resign En Masse', 20 January.

—— (2000b) 'Horie to Lead New Era for Korea First Bank', 23 January.

—— (2000c) 'KFB Overly Generous to Staff at Taxpayers' Expense', 6 April.

—— (2000d) 'KFB Posts First Quarterly Profit in 3 Years', 12 May.

—— (2001a) 'Diverse Evaluations on KFB Performance', 20 January.

—— (2001c) 'FSS Likely to Issue Warning to Korea First Bank', 25 May.

—— (2001d) 'Debate Rages Over Root of KFB's Success', 24 June.

—— (2001e) 'Korea First Bank to Shed Workers', 24 August.

—— (2001f) 'Korea First Inspected Over Exposure to Hynix', 18 October.

—— (2001g) 'Korea First Bank CEO Horie to Step Down', 23 October.

—— (2001h) 'Public Fund-Injected Banks Barred from Pay Increase', 24 October.

—— (2001i) 'Korea First Bank to Trim Mid-Level Staff', 9 November.

—— (2001j) 'Newbridge Does Not Aim at Quick Profits: KFB Head', 27 November.

—— (2002a) 'Korea First Open to Merger: KFB President', 10 January.

—— (2002b) 'Korea First Bank to Trim Staff', 23 February.

—— (2002c) 'Banks Undergoing Change' (3-part series), 24, 25, 30 April.

—— (2002d) 'Watchdog Censures Korea First Bank', 26 July.

—— (2002e) 'Watchdog's Lawsuit Action Rattles Banking Sector', 6 August.

Djelic, M. L. (1998) *Exporting the American Model: The Postwar Transformation of European Business* (Oxford University Press).

The Economist (2001) 'In Praise of Rules: A Survey of Asian Business', 7 April, pp. 1–18.

—— (2002a) 'Dead Deals Walking', 9 February, pp. 51–2.

—— (2002b) 'Takeovers in South Korea', 4 May, p. 61.

El Kahal, S. (2001) *Business in Asia Pacific: Text and Cases* (Oxford University Press).

Fields, K. J. (1995) *Enterprise and the State in Korea and Taiwan* (Ithaca, NY: Cornell University Press).

Fligstein, N. (1997) *Markets, Politics and Globalization* (Stockholm: Almquist and Wiksell International).

Friedmann, J. (1992) *Empowerment: The Politics of Alternative Development* (New York: Blackwell).

Hirschman, D. (1999) 'Development Management Versus Third World Bureaucracies: A Brief History of Conflicting Interests', *Development and Change*, vol. 30, pp. 287–305.

Hollingsworth, J. R. (1997) 'Continuities and Changes in Social Systems of Production: The Case of Japan, Germany and the United States', in J. R. Hollingsworth and R. Boyer (eds), *Contemporary Capitalism: The Embeddedness of Institutions* (Cambridge University Press), pp. 265–310.

Huang, Y. and O'Neil-Massaro, K. J. (2002) 'Korea First Bank (A)', Case study 9-701-022, 13 March (Boston: Harvard Business School).

Joh, S. W. (2001) *Korean Economic Crisis and Corporate Governance System* (Seoul: Korea Development Institute).

Johnson, S. *et al.* (2000) 'Corporate Governance in the Asian Financial Crisis', *Journal of Financial Economics*, vol. 58(1–2), pp. 141–86.

Karasulu, M. (2002) 'Bank Privatization in Korea: Developments and Strategies', in IMF, *Republic of Korea: Selected Issues, IMF Country Report No. 02/20 (Feb)* (Washington, DC: International Monetary Fund), pp. 101–15.

Kim, D. (1999) 'IMF Bailout and Financial and Corporate Restructuring in the Republic of Korea', *The Developing Economies*, vol. 37, pp. 460–513.

Kirk, D. (1999) *Korean Crisis: Unraveling of the Miracle in the IMF Era* (New York: St Martin's Press).

Korea Herald (2001a) 'KFB Heading for Collision with KDIC Over Stock Option', 19 March, *The Korea Herald* [website] http://www.koreaherald.com/archives/result_detail.asp, last consulted 20 December 2003.

—— (2001b) 'Korea First Bank Unionists Demand Stock Options', 14 April.

—— (2001c) 'Bank Unions Complain Foreign Managers' Style', 19 April.

—— (2001d) 'Experts Call for New Organization Model for Firms', 19 October.

—— (2001e) 'CEO of Korea First Bank Tenders Resignation', 23 October.

—— (2001f) 'Uncertainty for Hynix May Follow Horie's Resignation', 25 October.

—— (2001g) 'KFB Board Appoints Cohen as New CEO', 29 October.

—— (2001h) 'Hynix Loans Not Cause of Horie's Resignation', 31 October.

—— (2003a) 'Foreign Stakes in Banks Top 26%', 2 December.

—— (2003b) 'Money Man Warns of More Hostile Takeovers', 4 December.

Korea Times (1999) 'US Takeover of Korea First Bank Completed', 23 December, *The Korea Times* [website] http://times.hankooki.com/service/listmore/kt_archive.php?media=kt&page=1&strSec=&strItem=&type=, last consulted 20 December 2003.

—— (2001a) 'KFB Changing Fast Under Profit-First Management', 29 January.

—— (2001b) 'KFB Head Horie Resigns; Cohen Likely Successor', 25 October.

—— (2001c) 'KFB Head Tries to Wipe Out Negative Image of Newbridge', 30 November.

Korea Times (2002a) 'Put Back Option of Korea First Bank', 3 March.
—— (2002b) 'KFB Recovery of Hynix Loan Raises Ire of Other Creditors', 5 May.
—— (2002c) 'Banks' Profitability Feared to Worsen: Burdened by Public Fund Losses', 4 July.
—— (2002d) 'Two Former Presidents of Korea First Bank Penalized', 26 July.
—— (2003a) 'Foreign Holdings In Banks Jump', 2 November.
—— (2003b) 'Are Foreign Funds Poison or Medicine for Banks?', 7 November.
Ku, H. J. (1997) 'Business–Government Relations in Korea', in K. H. Chung and H. Ch. Lee (eds), *Korean Management Dynamics* (New York: Praeger), pp. 11–26.
Marglin, S. (2003) 'Development as Poison: Rethinking the Western Model of Modernity', *Harvard International Review*, (Spring), pp. 70–5.
Moon, Ch. I. (1994) 'Changing Patterns of Business–Government Relations in South Korea', in A. MacIntyre (ed.), *Business and Government in Industrializing Asia* (Ithaca: Cornell Univesity Press), pp. 142–66.
Mosakowski, E. (2000) 'Strategic Colonialism in Unfamiliar Cultures', in P. C. Earley and H. Singh (eds), *Innovations in International and Cross-Cultural Management* (Thousand Oaks, CA.: Sage Publications), pp. 311–38.
Naim, M. (1999) 'Fads and Fashions in Economic Reforms: Washington Consensus or Washington Confusion?', *International Monetary Fund* [website] (updated 26 October 2003) http://www.imf.org/external/pubs/ft/seminar, accessed 26 October 2003.
Newbridge Capital (2004) 'Philosophy', *Newbridge Capital* [website] (updated 29 March 2004) http://www.newbridgecapital.com/philosophy.html, accessed 29 March 2004.
New York Times (2001) '2 Rival Chip Makers Consider Joining Forces', 4 December.
OECD (2000a) Organisation for Economic Cooperation and Development, *Pushing Ahead with Reform in Korea: Labour Market Reform and Social Safety Net Policies* (Paris: OECD).
OECD (2000b) Organisation for Economic Co-operation and Development, *Economic Surveys: Korea* (Paris: OECD).
Rodrik, D. (1997) *Has Globalization Gone Too Far?* (Washington, DC: Institute for International Economics).
Stallings, B. (1990) 'The Role of Foreign Capital in Economic Development', in G. Gereffi and D. L. Wyman (eds), *Manufacturing Miracles: Paths of Industrialization in Latin America and East Asia* (Princeton, NJ: Princeton University Press), pp. 55–89.
Stiglitz, J. (2002) *Globalization and Its Discontents* (New York: W.W. Norton).

10

A Brief Account of Mexico's Experience with International Businesses

Emmanuel Raufflet

Introduction

The presence of international businesses in Mexico has a long and conflicted history. Over the course of the twentieth century, arguments among the general population and officials regarding the effects of foreign direct investment on national development have oscillated between praise and criticism. Some have praised and welcomed international businesses, picturing them as engines of economic growth and as vehicles for transferring technology – both of which, they claim, are indispensable to national development. Others have vilified the multinational enterprises, portraying them as foreign exploiters of Mexico's workers and its natural resources and blaming them for the misfortunes in Mexico's economic development.

This chapter reviews the processes and outcomes of international businesses in Mexico. I argue that central to these developments is the nature of the exchanges between the governments of Mexico and international businesses. I assume here that specific national policies will influence the nature of international investments as well as the behaviour of international businesses once they are present within the country. Some of these policies will encourage cost-minimizing corporate behaviours while others will foster the creation of economic, human and social assets. In return, these forms and types of international investments will influence the nature of the country's economy and society. The outcomes of these two-way relationships in Mexico should provide some insights into the contributions and limitations of international businesses in developing areas.

There are two central characteristics of Mexico's experience with international businesses. The first is that Mexico's economy, despite having become export-driven and open, largely remains 'low tech'. It is positioned at the low end of the world value chain. Most of its exports are components or raw materials that contribute to the manufacture of finished goods outside the country. Mexico has not reaped the benefits of a century-long relationship with international businesses and has failed to develop a strong national innovative capacity, and to create an industrial base that grows and develops technology in a sustainable way. The second argument is that Mexico's failure to build this capacity is due to the emphasis of successive governments on three main objectives: (1) building a large-scale material infrastructure, such as transportation systems, rather than developing institutions that foster and support innovative capacities; (2) supplying employment for an abundant and low-skilled labour force rather than developing opportunities for skilled labour and promoting a knowledge-generating education system; and (3) the prioritizing of industrialization over agricultural development. Overall, there has been little emphasis on long-term social and technical capacity building. I define capacity building as the ability to generate innovations in a way that minimizes the costs of environmental degradation while raising living standards and the quality of the life for the majority of the population.

This chapter contains three sections. In the first, I introduce some paradoxes in Mexico at the turn of the millennium. I particularly emphasize Mexico's Janus face: while being the world's tenth largest economy, it remains a country vulnerable to the vagaries of both international and national events. As well, over 50 million of its population live in poverty; of these, around 30 million live in extreme poverty. In the second section, I present the stages in the complex and irregular history of economic development in Mexico since the late nineteenth century. The governments of the Porfiriato era (1877–1910) favoured elite foreign direct investment. The revolutionary and post-revolutionary era (1910–40) preferred nationalization and indigenization of foreign firms. The strong state-intervention era (1940–80) severely restrained the roles of international businesses and set the conditions for what has been described as the 'Mexican economic miracle', a three-decade-long period of political stability and steady economic growth. More recently, since the 1980s, Mexico has again opened its economy to foreign direct investments. Overall, the patterns of these policy changes towards international businesses have been abrupt and sweeping. It has been as though the country leaders have failed to anticipate the changes and have responded to crises rather than anticipated them. A lot of improvisation seems to have prevailed over the relations between the country and its international investors. This pattern of managing change has been one of the causes for the lack of any effective social and technological capacity building. In the last section I present some tentative lessons for other developing areas based on Mexico's experience with international businesses.

Paradoxes of Mexico at the turn of the millennium

In 2001, with a population of 97 million and GNP of US$621 billion, Mexico had the world's tenth-largest economy. A special point of pride for Mexicans is that in that same year their country overtook Brazil, the other Latin American giant (with US$502 billion GNP), making Mexico's the largest economy in

Latin America (*The Economist*, 2002a). In addition, Mexico has an impressive record of international trade agreements. It is a member of the World Trade Organization (WTO) and the North American Free Trade Agreement (NAFTA). It has free trade agreements with the European Union and with most Latin American countries. It is the only Latin American member of the Organisation for Economic Cooperation and Development (OECD).

Mexico's economic achievements have been praised at various times during the twentieth century. Between the late 1940s and the mid 1970s, with average growth rates of 6–7 per cent, its sustained economic achievements were often referred to in both the popular and academic press as 'the Mexican miracle'; Mexico's fast-paced industrialization and its abundant natural resources led development analysts to think that its industrialization was more promising than Korea's or Taiwan's (Lowe and Kenney, 1999). By the end of the 1970s, the discovery of new oil reserves in a context of rapid inflation of world oil prices seemed to represent its ticket to modernity and the resources necessary to prolong its miracle (Haber, 1989). Later, at the beginning of the 1990s, under Carlos Salinas de Gortari's presidency (1988–94), Mexico was praised for its ability to adapt its economy: Salinas's government opened boundaries, stabilized state deficits, gradually dismantled a complex web of protective trade barriers and privatized state-owned companies, including state-owned banks. Persistent rumours in 1993–94 said that Salinas, the main artisan of this liberalization and stabilization process, would be a good candidate for the leadership of the WTO.

However, these periods of optimism have often been interrupted by deep and unexpected crises. The prosperous economic miracle that extended from the 1940s to the 1970s ended with the financial crisis in the 1980s. The value of the peso plunged from 22 to a dollar to 70 in 1982 and reached 925 to a dollar in 1988. Hyperinflation struck the country for the next 6 years. Growth was nil and real salaries went through an 8.6 per cent decline in the 1980s. Why? As Haber (1989, p. 11) describes it, the Mexican economic miracle (1940–70) had produced an unhealthy industrial structure, with firms dependent on high tariff barriers and with a low innovative capacity. The crisis of the 1980s saw the end of this model.

The next attempt to build a new model was Salinas' *sexenio*[1] (1988–94), which, in 1995, led to one of Mexico's worst political and economic crises. It caused a further devaluation of the peso by 30 per cent. Mexico was 'saved' by an exceptional International Monetary Fund (IMF) emergency package of US$50 billion (*The Economist*, 1995), strongly supported by the Clinton administration in the US. Moreover, internal conflicts and imbalances contradicted the image of 'progress and development' the country aimed to project to the world. The day Mexico entered NAFTA (1 January 1994), a Zapatista[2] insurrection exploded in the Southern state of Chiapas in protest against poor agrarian conditions and the exclusion of the Mayan population from access to land and livelihood opportunities.

These crises have reduced the benefits of economic development policies for most Mexicans. The average purchasing power of a Mexican household fell by 30 per cent between 1980 and 2000. In 2002, 45.9 per cent of all households could not cover the cost of total basic needs (*The Economist*, 2002b). There are strong regional discrepancies between the North, which is increasingly connected with the economy of the US, and large rural areas of the South, characterized by high levels of emigration and rural underdevelopment. Similar discrepancies exist between the technologically connected and globalized cities and the remote, hardly accessible rural areas deprived of livelihood possibilities.

Most of Mexico's economy remains neither innovative nor 'high tech'. While Mexico does export a large percentage of its GNP, most of these exports are either 'low tech' manufactured goods or unprocessed raw materials. Manufacturing represents 87 per cent of Mexican exports and oil 10 per cent. Maquiladoras, the mainly low-tech, labour-intensive plants at the low end of the international value chain, produce 54 per cent of all manufactured goods (*The Economist*, 2002a, p. 22). Although oil represents 10 per cent of its exports, Mexico also needs to import more sophisticated types of petroleum products. Pemex, *Petroleos Mexicanos*, the state owned oil company, relies on often-outdated production technologies. As a whole, Mexico ranks fifty-third in national innovation capacity (Porter and Stern, 2001). Lastly, remittances from Mexican workers living in the US represent the most important source of foreign currency inflow; this amounted to over US$6 billion in 1999 (*The Economist*, 2000). In all, growth has been impressive in quantitative terms, less so in qualitative ones.

In summary, Mexico at the turn of the twenty-first century is a country of fascinating contrasts: it has an open economy and yet is positioned as an overall low-cost producer in the international supply chain. It is an economy highly sensitive to external turbulences, prone to deep economic and social crises, yet with a resilient fabric of small- and medium-sized enterprises. If the quest for progress and development was a motto for the last century, the form and the outcomes of progress do not resemble the initial expectations and promises of the masterminds of development. Due to their central role in the history of economic development in Mexico, an examination of international business relationships provides an interesting lens through which to understand its national trajectory. In the following section, I examine the changing relations between international businesses and the country during the twentieth century.

Mexico and international business (1877–2003)

This section presents the cycles of exchanges between Mexico and international businesses within the broader context of national economic and social policies during the period from 1877 to 2003. These eras are summarized in Table 10.1. It presents the dominant economic paradigms and international businesses-related policies.

Porfiriato (1877–1910): Laissez-faire and elite investment

The Porfiriato era (1877–1910) comprised three decades of political stability dominated by General Porfirio Díaz. The general economic paradigm was laissez-faire. The Mexican government invited foreign investors and provided them with incentives to build an infrastructure, including transportation. Government planners saw this as a key prerequisite for developing the market economy within the country.

The form of exchanges between the government and the international businesses was the following: The government expected international businesses to help construct transportation and communications infrastructure, which in turn would expand consumer goods industries. The government would thereby gain control over the national territory while creating and opening up markets. The government provided international investors with incentives, such as tariff protections and the guarantee of steady supplies of natural resources and labour. Concessions were often obtained through presidential decrees and laws favourable to investors (Connolly, 1997). As the investments in infrastructure and the development of internal markets were long-term, investors expected stability and guarantees of returns (Haber, 1989).

At the turn of the twentieth century, many international investors in Mexico were absentees who channelled their money through Paris-based banks or foreign investment firms such as the Geneva-based Société pour l'Investissement au Mexique (Mexico Investment Corporation) or Paris-based banks. Individual investors included wealthy entrepreneurs such as the retail and textile families from Southeastern France known collectively as 'Barcelonnettes', US citizens such as Tomas Braniff, Spanish investors and foreign 'empire builders' such as the giant British firm of S. Pearson & Sons Ltd (the Porfiriato's main public works contractor, builder of the Port of Veracruz and the Gran Canal de Desague in Mexico City). These international players were often associated with the local and national elite composed of Mexico City's 'white' upper-class Spanish *criollos* and members of the family of Porfirio Díaz. Close ties with the *caudillo* and the elites provided the main guarantee for the security of investments in the country.

The construction of the transportation infrastructure, supported by this long-term investment policy, contributed to opening the country to further foreign investments. In 1873, Mexico possessed only 573 kilometres of railways and it took about 12 months to transport machinery 350 kilometres from the port of Veracruz on the Gulf of Mexico to the mining centre of Pachuca, 94 kilometres from Mexico City. Poor transportation and communication represented a major constraint for any economic activity and for effective government control of different parts of Mexico. International

Table 10.1 Institutional cycles and foreign direct investment in Mexico

	Eras			
	Porfiriato (1877–1910)	Revolution and Post-revolution (1910–40)	The Mexican economic miracle (1940–82)	Opening the economy (since 1982)
Paradigm of economic development	Laissez-faire economics inside protected boundaries	• Land reform and nation-building • National corporativist state apparatus	• Import substitution strategy • State-led industrialization	• Openness and international integration • International trade agreements (NAFTA since 1994)
Expectations vis-à-vis international business	• Infrastucture • Markets • Import technology • A basis for consumer and production goods markets	Constrain and limit their influence on the country	Import and create technological capabilities not available from Mexican firms	Fiscal incentives
Foreign investment incentives	• Investors provided with de facto monopolies and long-term leases or concessions • Closed borders in growing consumer markets	• International business seen as obstacle to nation-building • Nationalization of natural resources	• FDI constrained – except for technology and specific consumer products • Mexicanization of international businesses	• Low paid labour force • Open borders and proximity to the USA • Access to natural resources
Structural development policies	Protection of large monopolies by high tariffs	Gradual small-scale nationalization or indigenization of firms	State-led, large-scale industrialization	Foreign direct investments.

investments made it possible to increase the railways to 5000 kilometres in 1882 and to 19 000 kilometres in 1910 (Haber, 1989, p. 15). The effects of the new transportation infrastructure on the broader economy were also far-reaching. It created new markets both within the country and abroad. National silver production rose from 606 000 metric tonnes in 1877 to 2.3 million metric tonnes in 1910, and there was a threefold increase in production for the whole mining sector during the same period. Oil production rose from 5000 barrels in 1900 to over 8 million barrels in 1910. Increased opportunities for the commercialization of agricultural products in the national market also led to large production increases (Haber, 1989).

This form of industrialization benefited Mexico City, the neighbouring State of Mexico and the region of Monterrey (Garcia Luna, 1998). It also led to the formation of industrial enclaves around the factories. Management–employee relations were governed by a form of paternalism, a reproduction of the master–servant relationships that existed on the haciendas (Espejel, 1994).[3]

These exchanges between the *caudillo*, the elite and international investors had mixed outcomes. One the one hand, transportation and urban infrastructure improved and industrial output and trade increased. The centenary of Mexican independence in 1910 in Mexico City was a celebration and international recognition of General Porfirio Díaz for transforming Mexico into a model for Latin American countries (Krauze, 1997). But this wave of optimism was short-lived. Less than 6 months later, revolution erupted simultaneously in the North and in the state of Morelos – reflecting inequities and tensions that these policies had created. In the rural areas, where more than 90 per cent of the population lived, there had been virtually no benefits from these early efforts at industrialization. Subsisting on farming in rural areas where 9 out of 10 farm labourers were excluded from land ownership and vulnerable to harvest fluctuations, the majority of the population lived on the verge of starvation (Warman, 2001) while foreign investors owned more than 150 million hectares (Pearce, 2002). Furthermore, in 1910, international businesses controlled a significant part of the natural resources, such as silver, gold, oil and land, as well as most of the production of consumer goods (Anaya Perez, 1998). These imbalances, endemic poverty and poor harvests in 1907–09 led to the 10 years' turmoil of the 1910–20 revolution – a period so complex economically as well as politically that its impact on Mexico's international investors remains a controversial topic among historians to this day.

Revolution and post-revolution (1910–40): Small-scale and nationalizing

Revolutionary and post-revolutionary governments emphasized small-scale production and national ownership. Land was redistributed to small farmers and natural resources were nationalized. National interests dominated the political agenda. Consequently, the three subsequent decades were on the whole unfavourable to international businesses, which were perceived as capitalistic and exploitative of both workers and natural resources (Krauze, 1997; Pearce, 2002). They were also viewed as serving only the interests of the Porfirian elite resulting in social and economic inequalities.

The administration of Lázaro Cárdenas (1934–40) epitomized the post-revolutionary, nationalist spirit. It used various strategies to restrain the domination of international businesses and to affirm national control over resources and production capacity. For example, it nationalized the oil extraction industry, thereby removing foreign control. Following a 2-year conflict between the Mexican Oil Workers Union and 17 British and American oil producing companies that led to a ruling of the Council of Conciliation of Arbitration favourable to workers, the Standard Oil Company issued an ultimatum to the workers and to the government, expecting that the government's limited capacity to act would lead to an acceptance of the ultimatum (Pearce, 2002). President Cardenas, in an address to the nation on 18 March 1938, announced the response of his government to this ultimatum:

> The far-reaching decision of the Mexican government is to recover the oil wealth that foreign enterprises have been exploiting. I call for the support of the people not only for the recovery of oil ... but also for the dignity of Mexico, that foreigners think they can ridicule after having obtained great benefits from our natural resources. (Krauze, 1997, p. 232)

Foreign investors were compensated and Pemex, *Petroleos Mexicanos*, was established as a state-owned company. Its mission was to 'rationally take advantage of petroleum and its derivative products' and to contribute to the sustainable development of the country. Through the years the national government has used about 60 per cent of Pemex's profits to balance national budgets.

A second strategy the Cárdenas government used to limit the influence of foreign businesses in the country was to create competitors against foreign companies that had monopolistic or oligopolistic positions in specific markets. For example, in 1936, in the pulp and paper sector, it established *Productora y Importadora de Papel SA de CV* (PIPSA), a state-owned company, to limit the domination of the San Rafael Company over newsprint supply. Third, it restricted the form of foreign and national capital ownership. International investments were controlled by the Secretary of External Relations. Finally, in the name of the defence of national workers from foreign investors, it often supported Mexican workers on strike and their claims for the enforcement of labour rights and improved conditions of work in foreign-owned firms. The government benefited from the establishment of trade unions as it was then able to insert them into the national corporativist system.[4]

The system itself relied on the *Partido Revolucionario Institucionál* (PRI) (Institutional Revolutionary Party), the overwhelmingly dominant political party, which would rule Mexico until the dawn of the millennium; the *Confederación de los Trabajadores Mexicanos* (CTM) (Confederation of Mexican Workers); and the for workers and on farmers' unions (Cordova, 1972). These revolutionary and post-revolutionary governments set the institutional basis and the conditions of political and social stability for a major economic leap forward.

State-led industrialization and import substitution (1940–82): The economic miracle

The ensuing *four* decades of social and political stability are generally known as the age of the Mexican 'economic miracle'. In a climate of unchallenged PRI-dominated political stability, the country experienced a steady high rate of economic growth for 4 decades. This Mexican model of development relied on state-led investments and implementation of an 'import substitution strategy' involving:

1. Creation of the necessary industrial and economic structure to serve the fast-growing national market;
2. Restricting the role of non-Mexican firms to areas in which Mexico did not have expertise or the funding necessary to develop the industry;
3. Tariff barriers to protect the nascent national industry;
4. Emphasis on serving the national market – as opposed to a strong export-orientation;
5. Significant intervention by the Federal State as an investor and project initiator (Haber 1989; Pearce, 2002)

State-led investments were often major infrastructure projects, such as large industrial plants, transportation and irrigation projects. High tariffs closed the borders to foreign competitors (Haber, 1989). This model restricted the role of international businesses to products and technologies that could not be supplied by national producers. In these times of rapid economic and demographic growth, serving the national market took precedence over the development of exports.

In this era, a succession of presidents shaped the country's growth path within this state-led import substitution development strategy. Miguel Alemán (1940–46) emphasized the development of electricity, transport, communication and energy, built dams for electricity and irrigation purposes, and established many of the country's important businesses in the production of consumer goods. Adolfo Ruiz-Cortines (1947–52) completed some of Alemàn's large but uncompleted projects. Adolfo Lopez Mateos (1953–59) distributed about 30 million ha to farmers' communities and expanded social security to rural areas (Pearce, 2002).

Industry grew at an average of 7.2 per cent per year in the 1940–70 period (Krauze, 1997). At the beginning of the 1970s Mexico's future looked as promising – if not more so – than the so-called East Asian 'tigers'. For instance, the consumer electronics sector was growing at full speed: by 1970 there were 16 television manufacturers, 30 manufacturers of radio and audio equipment and 120 supplier firms – most of them fully Mexican-owned and serving a national market that was in constant expansion (Lowe and Kenney, 1999, p. 1428).

These decades of spectacular growth had, however, led to increasing imbalances between regions, as well as between groups in society. From a regional standpoint, Mexico City and the neighbouring state of Mexico was the area that benefited the most from these investments. Opportunities for livelihood in the countryside were limited, and many rural inhabitants had to go either to Mexico City or to the US in search of a living. As a result, the metropolitan population grew from 3 to 5 million between 1950 and 1960; by 1980 it had reached 15 million. But large areas of the country, such as the states in the south, remained poorly connected and excluded from the 'miracle'. Furthermore, from the standpoint of capacity building and innovation, this development approach led to few innovations over the long term; instead it sheltered an industrial sector that was not competitive in international markets. In his study of the relations between the state and entrepreneurs in Mexico, Haber (1989) shows that entrepreneurs were more dedicated to getting further state protection from foreign competitors than to new product innovation and development. Lobbying strategies replaced product/market-based strategies in the concerns of many business leaders. At the same time, trade unions – one of the pillars of the state – were reluctant to change and to engage in negotiations regarding productivity issues and improving the competitiveness of their firms (see Chapter 11). Overall, this model led to extensive quantitative growth rather than intensive development toward higher-quality production. At the end of the 1970s, after more than eight decades of prioritizing an industrial development model, Mexico still earned the bulk of its foreign currencies from petroleum, the services sector (in the form of tourism-related incomes) and remittances from Mexican workers who had emigrated to the US. Paradoxically, after decades of emphasizing industrial development, Mexico was far from being competitive in exporting high value-added goods.

By the end of the 1970s the economic model was exhausted. As Haber (1989) has pointed out, the industrialization of Mexico was fundamentally unsound. It relied on tariffs; productivity was often low; machinery was often obsolete, since there had been little re-investment. Under the presidency of José Lopez Portillo (1976–82), the state of the country's finances went from bad to worse. In 1976, at the beginning of Portillo's term, the flight of capital, the inability of Mexican products to compete with foreign products, government subsidies to agricultural products and devaluation of the peso increased the national debt to US$50 billion (Pearce, 2002). The discovery of large oil reserves in the Gulf of Mexico in a world context of fast-growing oil prices gave the illusion that the economic miracle could be sustained. This was shattered however, by the 1982 economic crisis, which led to a further devaluation of the peso. The debt crisis of 1982, precipitated by the combination of falling oil prices, rising world interest rates and excessive government spending, strained the country's fiscal capacity (Gunther and More, 1994). During the following years, hyperinflation struck and unemployment increased. In 1985 disaster struck in the Mexico City earthquake, which caused 10 000 to 30 000 deaths and the destruction of property amounting to US$4 billion (Pearce, 2002, p. 312). The earthquake also caught the government unprepared; yet despite a shortage of adequate equipment to move the tonnes of fallen concrete and stone in the streets, the Ministry of Foreign Affairs announced that Mexico did not need assistance from foreign countries – a statement that caused widespread public resentment.

Between economic and natural disaster, the 1980s are known in Mexico as the 'lost decade' (Krauze, 1997). Large sections of the middle class suffered from the economic decline, and poorer groups became further impoverished. The optimism of the 1970s was gone.

Opening the economy (1982–2004): Maquiladoras and new international investment

The beginning of President Miguel de la Madrid's term was marked by the 1982 economic crisis. During his time as president (1982–88), he saw a 40 per cent drop in the living standards of his people and a continuous devaluation of the peso. His government's borrowing requirements grew to massive proportions, approaching one-sixth of the economy's output in 1986 and 1987. Mexico's limited access to international capital markets implied that the bulk of these borrowing needs had to be satisfied internally (Gunther and More, 1994). The deterioration of the Mexican economy called for structural reforms, which caused a high level of social and political unrest. One such reform was the announcement of a quick transition towards the opening of the economy and free trade. This meant a new role for international businesses: they were expected to create employment and open up specific natural resources for extraction while enjoying freedom from national protectionism.

Carlos Salinas (1988–94) was elected in controversial conditions, which reflected the strong erosion of the PRI-led regime (Pearce, 2002). The PRI had been continuously in power since its inception in the early 1930s. Once 'elected', Salinas moved swiftly to privatize large state-owned companies, such as the monopolistic telephone company (Telmex), banks, the state television network, airlines, highways and sugar mills. In 1994 the number of state-owned firms was reduced to 27. Salinas managed to renegotiate loans with the IMF, balance the state budget by cutting government spending and fight inflation through an anti-inflation pact with industry. Inflation declined from 160 per cent in 1987 to less than 10 per cent in 1993 and the New Peso, as a symbol of this newly gained stability was launched (Pearce, 2002). Last, he signed the NAFTA treaty in 1992, which became effective on 1 January 1994.

Mexico's new development model relies on international businesses and tight economic integration with the US. A dominant form of international business in this scheme are the 'maquiladoras',[5] foreign-owned companies that use intensive labour (mainly women) in low-tech industries, such as textiles, to produce goods that are re-exported to the US and Canada. Most maquiladoras are located in the northern part of the country. At the turn of the millennium, the maquiladoras' earnings accounted for 10.4 per cent of the economy, 2.9 per cent of employment and 43.7 per cent of national exports (*The Economist*, 2002a).

However, this high dependence on the maquiladoras limits Mexico's capacity to build a national system of innovation that would include cutting-edge educational institutions and research centres. First, analysts have highlighted the fact that the maquila model has not resulted in any significant technological transfer. *The Economist* (2001) cited three reasons for this:

1. Most of the plants established on this model in Mexico are labour intensive units, with limited technology transfer.
2. Maquiladoras have most often operated separately from the rest of the local economy, which has restricted the possibility for technical or technological spin-off (Grunwald, 1989).
3. There is evidence that a significant number of maquiladoras are located in Mexico for the short term, and may migrate to other areas of the world where labour is cheaper.

A second reason for the many negative effects of the maquiladoras is that they are extremely vulnerable to the vagaries of the US economy. Since the beginning of the US economic recession in 2000, maquiladora employment has decreased by almost 300 000, or 23 per cent, compared to 2000 when it created 1.3 million jobs (ibid.). In all, there has been little technological gain or transfer. The durability of the model has been questioned even further as many more maquiladoras – 500 in 2002 and 2003 – closed down in Mexico. Most of these operations have moved to areas with even cheaper labour markets, such as the People's Republic of China and Vietnam, where wages are as low as US$2 per day – a 75 per cent saving over the average Mexican worker's daily US$8 wage. The lost jobs represented over $US1 billion of lost income for Mexican workers in 2000.

This tight integration with the US economy achieved through the NAFTA treaty since 1994 has also affected the land itself. Subsidized US agricultural products have been increasingly imported into Mexico. Mexico's grain imports – including maize – have increased by 220 per cent between 1994 and 2001 (Sanchez Limon, 2002). The share of agriculture in the economy has declined from 6.4 per cent in 1992 to 5 per cent in 2002. The only agricultural sector that has increased its production is flowers and related products (Sanchez Limon, 2002). The future of the *ejidos*,[6] the main form of farmers' communities is challenged (Warman, 2001). There is evidence that NAFTA has exacerbated inequalities between rural and urban areas, while weakening the competitiveness of Mexican agriculture (Dresser, 2002; Sanchez Limon, 2002).

Lessons from the Mexican experience

The pattern of exchanges between Mexico and international business has led to a low-tech, resource-extraction form of investment rather than development of a knowledge-based, capacity-building economy. The two policies that in the twentieth century have promoted Mexico to foreign investors have done so by promoting its pool of human and natural resources. In the Porfiriato era (1877–1910) it had been hoped that through these policies there would be an expansion of consumer goods products on the national market and the export of natural resources. In recent years (since 1982) it has been hoped that Mexico would succeed as a platform for assembling products for re-exports. Neither of these schemes has promoted Mexico as a potential source of competencies and innovation skills to be built over a long period of time. The future will reveal whether or not this latter pattern will eventually evolve. The current evolution of the maquila model, however, does not encourage optimism that it will create a greater capacity for innovation.

What can we learn from the history of the exchanges between the national government and international businesses in Mexico? What lessons are relevant for other developing areas? I offer three observations.

The changing face of international businesses

At a historical and descriptive level, the Mexican experience with international investment reveals the changing face of international businesses and investors over the twentieth century. At the turn of the century, investors were either wealthy individual entrepreneurs associated with the national elite or absentee investors who channelled their investments through foreign firms such as the Société pour l'Investissement au Mexique based in Geneva. Connections with local elites provided additional guarantees for the security of long-term investments in the country. These long-term investments built an infrastructure that expanded and served the indigenous national market. Firms like the San Rafael Corporation built hydro plants, roads and railroads, indispensable for their activities, for industrial development and for the creation of markets (Garcia Luna, 1998). By contrast, now both large and small firms in Mexico operate at the *global* level. International businesses are either maquiladoras in the Northern part of the country, that serve the US market or they are multinational corporations that serve the domestic market.

The presence of international businesses today seems much more elusive than their counterparts of a century ago. First, networks of ownership have become much more difficult to trace. Second, the maquiladoras, capitalizing on cheap labour, are oriented toward direct, short-term benefits. They have few long-term interests in Mexico as such, and thus cannot be counted on to remain in Mexico.

National, local and technical contributions of international businesses

International businesses have contributed to the building of infrastructure, such as roads, railroads, urban centres and enclaves in areas endowed with abundant resources. They contributed to building intra-firm technical capabilities. This contribution was evident during most of the twentieth century. One example is the San Rafael pulp and paper company, which imported heavy machinery and brought in technicians from more advanced countries (see Chapter 11). San Rafael is referred to in Mexico as 'the mother of pulp and paper companies'. As a hotbed of new pulp-and-paper-related techniques, the San Rafael Company was the training ground for many leaders in the industry. Companies of that generation that made similar contributions to Mexico's development include Fundidora Monterrey, San Ildefonso, Buen Tono and Atlixco, among others (Haber 1989, p. 65).

However, international businesses contributed only marginally in more remote areas. They fostered geographically unbalanced development. They did not contribute to building the skills required for anticipating new markets or developing new technologies.

A knowledge-based economy waiting to be born

The price of not building a knowledge-intensive economy has been high in Mexican society in several respects. First, the majority of the population remain in precarious socio-economic conditions. International investments and the 'subordinate' (Lowe and Kenney, 1999) insertion of Mexico in the international economy have exacerbated inequalities in various periods. These periods include both the Porfiriato era (1877–1910) and the last few decades in our time when the economy was opened up to foreign investment. NAFTA has further increased social and economic inequalities (Lopez Villafane, 1997; Sanchez Limon, 2002). Second, the social price of these missed opportunities has been emigration, especially to the US. In 1990 the number of people of Mexican extraction living in the US was estimated at 13.5 million, 4 to 5 million of whom were born in Mexico. By the end of 1996 an estimated 2.7 million illegal immigrants from Mexico were living in the US. Between October 1999 and September 2000 1.6 million people were apprehended by US border patrols (*The Economist*, 2002a). There are 8 million Mexican-born people living in the US, representing 28 per cent of all immigrants living in the US. These numbers include more than 1.2 million deportable Mexican aliens.

The chapters dealing with Mexico in this volume will discuss in detail some of the issues introduced here. Chapter 11, dealing with the history of the San Rafael pulp and paper company, will highlight the rewards and costs of an 'early multinational firm' for its surrounding community and for the country as a whole. In Chapter 12, Anders Riel Muller describes the challenges arising from changing patterns of market relationships in coffee production in the States of Veracruz and Oaxaca.

Acknowledgement

I am grateful to the participants of the workshop of the research project held in Montreal in October 2002. In addition I would like to thank Pedro Moctezuma Barragan, Frederick Bird, and Joseph Smucker for valuable comments on this paper. Errors, opinions and omissions are my responsibility.

Notes

1. *Sexenio,* 'a six-year period', refers to the Mexican presidential term of six years or (by metonymy) the year in which the president is elected.
2. On New Year's Day 1994, the Zapatista National Liberation Army (EZLN) seized control of several towns in Chiapas. The Zapatista movement, which remains a political force in Mexico, takes its name from the Mexican revolutionary Emilano Zapata (1879–1919).
3. Mexico's pre-revolutionary haciendas were a system of vast land grants (some covering entire states of the present-day country), many dating from the sixteenth century, to private aristocrats and orders or the Church. Each was a complex, interdependent society under the landowner or padrón, who wielded vast arbitrary powers over his Indians, slaves, *peons* (fieldhands) and *campesinos* (tenant farmers). Except for the great coffee plantations of the south, the haciendas were not primarily agricultural: ranching and stock raising were often the central economic activity, and some haciendas included working mines. The haciendas were abolished in 1917, but land redistribution has never been entirely completed and powerful remnants of the system persist in some parts of the country even today.
4. In this book, 'corporativism' and 'corporativist' have been retained in context as the being the appropriate historical terms, as well as to prevent confusion with the more recent sense of 'corporatism' denoting a trend in legislation or policy that favours the transnational interests of corporations rather than citizens or communities. Under Mexico's corporativist system, society is organized in sectors (*gremios*): industrial workers, farmers, white-collar workers (*burocratas*), the army, teachers, professionals and business leaders or entrepreneurs. Coordinated and organized along lines of common interest, each sector has very limited contact with the others; rather all have a strong dependency on the central government.

The government has used this division of society by sectors to allocate positions and resources and play one group against another (Krauze, 2003, p. 29).

5. Mexican corporations operating under an in-bond (maquila) programme approved by the Mexican Secretariat of Commerce and Industrial Development (SECOFI). A maquila programme entitles the company to about 100 per cent foreign investment participation in capital *and* management, as well as duty-free imports of equipment, materials and computer systems. However, the company must post a bond that all such imports will remain in the country *temporarily*. The maquiladora's products (whether temporarily imported parts or finished items) are exported directly or indirectly, through sale to another maquiladora or exporter (Gonzalez Baz, 1996). A maquiladora is thus de jure and de facto a non-permanent economic participant.

6. Federally owned lands granted for farming and ranching purposes to legally constituted small communities.

References

Anaya Perez, M. A. (1998) *Rebelion y revolucion en Chalco – Amecameca (1821–1921)* Vol. 2 (Mexico: Instituto Nacional de Estudios Historicos de la Revolucion Mexicana, U.A. Chapingo).

Connolly, P. (1997) *El contratista de Don Porfirio, Obras publicas, deuda y desarollo desigual* (Mexico: Fundo de Cultura Economica – UAM – Colegio de Michoacan).

Còrdova, A. (1972, reed. 1998) *La formacion del poder politico en México* (México: Ediciones Era).

Dresser, D. (2002) 'TLC: lo blanco, lo negro, lo pendiente', *Proceso*, 1363, 22 December, pp. 52–3.

The Economist (1995) 'To the Rescue', 4 February, p. 13.

The Economist (2000) 'A Survey of Mexico: After the Revolution', 28 October, pp. 1–16.

The Economist (2001) 'Country Profile Mexico', (Economist Intelligence Unit), 1 March.

The Economist (2002a) 'Country Profile Mexico', (Economist Intelligence Unit).

The Economist (2002b) 'Country Report Mexico', (Economist Intelligence Unit), 4 October.

Espejel, L. (1994) 'San Rafael, una enclave' in A. Tortolero (ed.), *Entre lagos y volcanes: Chalco Amecameca, pasado y presente* (Toluca: el Colegio Mexiquense) pp. 481–520.

Garcia Luna, M. (1998) *Los origenes de la industria en el Estado de México (1830–1930)* (Toluca: Gobierno del Estado de México).

Gonzalez Baz, A. (1996) 'What is a Maquiladora?' [online document] http://www.udel.edu/leipzig/texts2/vox128.htm (Last modified 3 June 1996).

Grunwald, J. (1989) 'Opportunity Missed: Mexico and Maquiladoras', *The Brookings Review*, vol. 9(1), pp. 44–8.

Gunther, J. W. and More, R. R. (1994) 'Money, Credit and Fiscal Policy in Mexico's "Lost Decade"', *Financial Industry Studies*, vol. 5, December. pp. 1–21.

Haber, S. H. (1989) *Industry and Underdevelopment, the Industrialization of Mexico, 1890–1940* (Palo Alto: Stanford University Press).

Krauze, E. (1997) *Mexico, A Biography of Power, A History of Modern Mexico* (HarperCollins).

Krauze, E. (2003) *La Presidencia Imperial* (Mexico: Tusquets).

Lopez Villafane, V. (1997) *Globalizacion y regionalizacion desigual* (Mexico: Siglo XXI Editores).

Lowe, N. and Kenney, M. (1999) 'Foreign Investment and the Global Geography of Production: Why the Mexican Consumer Electronics Industry Failed', *World Development*, vol. 27(8), pp. 1427–43.

Pearce, K. (2002) *Mexico, a Traveller's History* (London: Cassell).

Pemex (2003): Petroleos Mexicanos, 'La Empresa', *Pemex* [website] (updated 10 December 2003) *http://www.pemex.com/index.cfm/action/content/sectionID/1/catID/5/ index.cfm?action=content&sectionID=1&catID=5*, accessed 10 December 2003.

Porter, M. E. and Stern, S. (2001) *National Innovative Capacity: The Global Competitiveness Report 2001–2002* (New York: Oxford University Press).

Sanchez Limon, M. (2002) 'La miseria del campo, la globalizacion y el TLC', *Epoca*, vol. 23 December, pp. 16–18.

Warman, A. (2001) *El campo mexicano en el siglo XX* (Mexico: Fondo de Cultura Economica).

11
The Mixed Blessings of Paternalism: The Case of San Rafael (1893–1991)

Emmanuel Raufflet

Introduction

The San Rafael Paper Manufacturing Company (Compania de la Fabricas de papel de San Rafael y Anexas, S.A.), a multinational enterprise (MNE) that dominated the pulp and paper industry in Mexico for most of the twentieth century, is located in the village of San Rafael. The village itself is located within the Municipality of Tlalmanalco at the foothills of Iztaccihuatl Volcano, 40 kilometres southeast of Mexico City. In this chapter I document the evolution of this early MNE in its local social context. I examine what occurs when a manufacturing firm – large-scale, rationally organized in its labour and production methods – a prototype of modernity interacts with a traditional rural agricultural community, with its localized social structures and subsistence economy. What social and economic transformations occur when these two apparently opposite worlds meet? What configurations of MNE–local community relations then emerge? How do these configurations later evolve?

In attempting to answer these questions, this chapter documents how an international company has dealt with two dilemmas associated with managing firms in developing areas. The first dilemma concerns productivity and the organization of labour. This case study shows how the company created an effective local labour force over a period spanning nearly a century. It explains how, beyond training per se, relations between management and labour crafted the competencies and rigidities of the organization over time. The second dilemma documented here concerns the relations between the firm and the local community. San Rafael, in its sheer size was a towering organization in the region. It built an enclave and fostered patterns of social relations that were centered on the company. In so doing, it developed the region materially and socially. However, San Rafael also created a structure that was not responsive to national and international, as well as to technological and market changes. The long period of time during which the company had dominated the community, resulted in relations of dependency from which the local community has not been able to extricate itself.

Over its 98 years of existence, the San Rafael Company had three configurations of firm–community relations. In the first configuration, discretionary authority of the company management was based on a *traditional paternalistic relationship* (1893–1936). Dialogue between state-supported trade union and management established the backbone of the second arrangement, the *corporativist- paternalistic configuration* (1936–70). A gradual erosion of this model characterizes the third period, the *brittle paternalistic configuration* (1970–91).

The traditional paternalistic configuration (1893–1936)

Founded in 1893 by a group of foreign investors including Tomas Braniff, Henri Tron, Léon Honnorat, Jules Beranda, Léon Olivier, H.C. Waters, and national investors including José Sanchez Ramos, Luis Barroso Arias, and Porfirio Diaz Jr. (Arango Mirana, 1997, p. 36), equipped with imported modern machinery, endowed with abundant natural resources and protected by high import tariff barriers, the San Rafael mill soon became the leading pulp and paper producer in Mexico. Growing from 120 workers in 1900 to 500 in 1910 and more than 1000 in the early 1930s, San Rafael, the main producer of newsprint, enjoyed a monopoly until the 1930s (Espejel, 1994).

Compared to its competitors, the San Rafael firm represented an industrial powerhouse, a key investment and technological breakthrough in the Mexican industrial landscape. Its Swiss-made machinery, driven by 15 water-powered turbines, had a capacity of 12 metric tonnes a day – about three times that of all of its national competitors combined. It further strengthened its position in 1904 by acquiring El Progreso Industrial, a smaller but modern plant located close to Mexico City (Haber, 1989, p. 97). The establishment of the San Rafael company represented 10 per cent of all the investments made in the state of Mexico (the area around Mexico City) in the last decade of the nineteenth century (Garcia Luna, 1998). It built 16 kilometres of underground canals through the Iztlaccihuatl mountain to secure its water and hydroelectric supply, acquired the San Rafael–Mexico City railway company and established control of local haciendas to access land and pulpwood forests (Huerta Gonzalez, 1994).

At the local level, haciendas were then the cornerstone of social and economic local life. Due to high land concentration, most farmers worked and lived as labourers (*peones*) on the haciendas (Huerta Gonzalez, 1994, p. 284). For instance, in 1891 only 8 per cent of the farmers in Tlalmanalco owned land. Although labourers and their families were provided a survival livelihood, including housing (*caserio*), a salary and credit in hard times, they were tied to the hacienda through debts to rural stores (*tiendas de raya*). These stores, the only sources of basic items and staple food, sold their products at steep prices and labourers and their families were not allowed to leave if they had a debt (Huerta Gonzalez, 1994).

Gradually adapting the all-encompassing characteristics of the traditional hacienda to the requirements of the new manufacturing configuration, San Rafael took over the hacienda's pivotal role in local social and economic life. Elements of continuity between the pre-existing configuration of relations between the hacienda and its tenants and the newly established firm and its workers included (1) the central role of a single ruling family in company and local life; (2) for the paper mill workers, an inherently precarious relationship to the company, dependent on the benevolence of management but without stable labour contracts, incomes or title to the land where they built their houses; and (3) the slow emergence of a mixed agricultural-industrial work identity.

With respect to the role of the family, the La Macorra family in San Rafael soon became emblematic of the mill's management. In the early years of the paper mill, various factors contributed to their gradual identification with the traditional *hacendados*. Born in Spain and trained as a forestry engineer, Don José de La Macorra was general manager of the company from 1897 to 1936. His son Don Fernando succeeded him and remained at the head of the company from 1936 until his retirement in 1968. Various La Macorra relatives also occupied managerial positions in the company. Like the traditional *hacendados* (landowners), the family lived in the *casco*(main residence) of the Hacienda de Zavaleta, located close to the mill. These facts created a symbolic continuity between the management of the old hacienda and the new San Rafael.

The second and most striking feature of this continuity concerns the nature of relations between the San Rafael management and the local workers. If the management expected workers to be loyal, the inducements the latter received were framed as the 'favours' or 'benevolent initiatives' of the general director to workers. On the one hand, the company referred to labour contracts as *convenios de servidumbre* ('servant's agreements'). These contracts required that workers be loyal, without restraining the firm's possibility of hiring or firing workers according to industrial needs (Huerta Gonzalez, 1994, p. 276). As many landless farmers had little choice but to work in the paper mill to earn their livelihood, they gradually built their houses on company land, without the assurance of permanent employment with the San Rafael Company, or of ownership of the land where they built their houses. While management imposed these precarious working conditions, Don José led initiatives to alleviate the difficulties of workers' lives. He started and financially supported mutual solidarity funds (*mutualidades*) and charities whose services included support for ill and elderly workers and their families. The general manager, as protector and honorary president of these funds, had the right to be informed about all decisions made regarding allocations and could veto any decision. In a letter written in 1922, José de

La Macorra, the general director stated he had 'launched these initiatives with much willingness to please and much pleasure so as to do good around me in the big family' (José de La Macorra, cited in Huerta Gonzalez, 1994, p. 277)

The general director presided over the celebrations sponsored by the factory and made the local social sphere another area for displaying his initiatives and generosity. A former worker recalled an advance in holiday customs during the 1920s:

> For patriotic holidays they used to build a tent up there by the mill. On September 16 (National holiday), that year, the tent collapsed under heavy rain. Don José got soaked. The same night, he stood up and said, 'I promise that next year we will have a celebration hall.' And that was it. 1 peso a week was taken away from the workers' wages, and the following year the celebration hall was ready. Don José then inaugurated it. (Interview, 10 August 1999)

In sum, in adopting the attributes of the traditional *hacendado* to establish the firm and the new community, the management created a sense of continuity between the old prevailing configuration of relations and the new industrial context. However, a challenge for management was to transform the working skills of farmers into skills needed by industrial workers.

In the early days of the company, all the workers were also farmers, and they maintained their links with the agricultural activities that were central to their traditional way of life. They cultivated a plot of land, tended their animals – and worked in the pulp and paper mill. Farm income was a guarantee for times when work at the mill was insufficient. In the first 30 years almost all workers were from Tlalmanalco or nearby municipalities.

Within the paper mill, management policies were marked by a constant tension between paternalism and authoritarian rigor in worker–manager relations. While managers were invited to workers' gatherings and celebrations, such as baptisms or first communions, they also remained the chief enforcers of discipline at the workplace. If the traditional *hacendado* had expected his workers and *peons* to be loyal, the managers in charge of labour in the mill expected workers to be loyal *and* 'disciplined, silent, methodical, less violent and (to engage in) nothing spontaneous. In other words, to become mill workers' (Espejel, 1994, p. 503).

Recruitment and retention of skilled labour were constant concerns for the San Rafael management. Because of the paucity of technical trades locally, skilled labour had to be imported from other parts of Mexico and from Europe. European engineers supervised the construction of the hydraulic equipment in 1890–94; Swiss and German engineers installed the manufacturing facilities (Lenz, 1990). Some of them later established Loreto y Pena Pobre, San Rafael's main competitor. Company reports from the 1920s also repeatedly mention that José de La Macorra, the general director, travelled to Europe to visit pulp-and-paper plants and recruit engineers. The firm constantly sought out ways to keep their skilled labour, offering favourable working conditions and providing them with some of the features of urban life, such as quality housing, leisure and entertainment opportunities such as a local mini-casino and a social /leisure club for single engineers established in 1905. These skilled tradesmen were *personal de confianza*, technicians of the same class as including middle and senior management, had stable labour contracts. The company's first housing efforts were directed at them. In 1900, management authorized the construction of 25 houses for single men, mainly engineers (Huerta Gonzalez, 1994, p. 290). In 1904, the *casino cosmopolita*, an accommodation and entertainment centre for bachelors, was built (Arango Miranda, 1997, p. 50).

Prior to the arrival of the factory, forests and water were goods that belonged to the community, under the jurisdiction of the municipality. However, various presidential decrees (1893, 1897) and government agreements (1897) bypassed these communal rights and accorded usufruct of the forest and water to the factory. Local inhabitants contested the 1893 presidential decree that had given an exclusive water and timber concession to the factory. However, the company's influence largely prevailed over the interests of the small, mainly rural group; local farmers soon lost any rights to use local natural resources (Huerta Gonzalez, 1994).

The 1910–19 revolution affected San Rafael pulp and paper operations in various ways. Epidemics hurt communities, the local population decreased and forests were damaged Because of insecurity created by the Emiliano Zapata's rebel forces, the mill was not able to access and manage its forests for 4-years (1914–18). This led to the destruction of plantations and the annihilation of forest management efforts the company had initiated after 1900. In the 1920s, the mill began to recruit workers from more distant areas and to repair its facilities damaged during the Zapatistas' 4-year occupation. It took from 1920 to 1921 for 'normal' working conditions to return. The 1917 constitution established the workers' rights to strike and to unionize and decreed an eight-hour working day. These rights, however, were ignored by the management of San Rafael, and were not enforced.

As an indirect response to these new labour rights and as a strategy to defuse workers' claims, San Rafael gradually built a model village, 'whose climate of modernity contrasted with the mainly rural landscape of the region' (Espejel, 1994). In 1923, it established the *Club Deportivo San Rafael* (San Rafael Sports Club), which later became one of the country's leading sports associations. It opened the Tienda Grande, a uniquely modern shopping centre, in 1928; the Casino Obrero, a social club for workers, in 1929; a school for adults and a dispensary for workers and their families in the 1930s. After 4 decades of construction, a company document (San

Rafael, 1931) depicted the wealthy enclave in these terms:

> It is a veritable city in constant growth, it has its own market, stores for the sale of groceries, clothing, shoes and other utilities and household goods which life demands; barber shop, complete steam rooms, Russian, Turkish shower and tub baths, free medical, pharmaceutical and nursing attention, all installed according to what hygiene prescribes. Workers have their own chapel, casino, billiard room and dance hall, with pianolas, phonographs and radio; a library well stocked with books of all descriptions, magazines and periodicals; a musical section that maintains the *Orquesta típica* de San Rafael, composed of 50 professors and workers from the mills who present concerts periodically; a great well-decorated Celebration Hall especially built for theatre performances, gymnastics and movies, public meetings, banquets, etc, with a capacity for more than 3 000 people. (p. 96)

Labour relations were depicted in idyllic terms:

> The company works in this manner and lives without strikes or conflicts in complete harmony and openness with its employees. In return it offers stimulation and educative solicitude. A suggestion contest was established and it is held annually. Each innovative idea or procedure for the improvement of the different phases of work is awarded a prize. (p. 97)

In sum, the first 43 years (1893–1936) of management–labour relations in San Rafael were traditional, paternalistic relations. Management took over the configuration of relations that existed in the haciendas prior to the creation of the company, both in terms of symbolic and material attributes. At the symbolic level, the founder's family lived in the same place the *hacendados* had lived before, importing and adapting the hacienda-like configuration of social relations to the industrial context. Meanwhile, the material relations between management and workers were based on exchanges of precarious living and working conditions for workers, for benevolent welfare activities, funded and conducted by management. In this early period, workers maintained strong ties with the land and its cultivation. The considerable improvements of the material and social conditions of the village of San Rafael in the post-revolutionary period (1920–36) were the outcomes of a strategy to continue these paternalistic relations while avoiding the enforcement of labour rights promulgated by the 1917 Constitution and claimed by local San Rafael workers.

The corporativist-paternalistic configuration (1936–70)

The 1917 Constitution had established workers' rights to strike, to unionize and to work eight hours a day. In 1922, a group of workers established the first trade union to enforce these rights and went on strike. A former worker, who was 17 in 1922, remembers:

> When I started, salaries were so miserable. Then we all got together and went on strike to demand an increase of 75 per cent. And after four months we got it. We also got school supplies for schools and housing for workers. All that was obtained because we were from the Revolutionary Trade Union. (Interview, 17 July 1999)

The corporate annual report's mention of the management reaction to the list of claims presented by workers during the 1922 strike reveals the paternalistic attitude of the management:

> In October, workers presented a list of demands while the general director José de La Macorra was in Europe. A fair and satisfactory solution was found. Our company has accepted, as it always does, the workers' justified demands and has rejected the unjustified ones. (Annual Report, 1923)

This short statement from the 1922 annual report strongly suggests that the management of San Rafael defined 'legitimate' according to their own criteria, regardless of the content of the 1917 constitution, while part of the constitution, the eight-hour working day and the right to unionize was still not enforced in San Rafael. As such, management was reluctant to enforce these new workers' rights. Yet the following year, 1923, the firm recognized the local section of the Central Revolucionaria de los Obreros Mexicanos (CROM), a management-controlled union, as the workers' only representative. In 1936 a second strike broke out in support of wage hikes. However, the motives of workers went beyond salary issues. In the trade union statement, there were vehement and bitter attacks on the main representative of the paternalistic configuration. The following excerpt of this 1936 open letter addressed to President Lázaro Cardenas, the founder of the national corporativist regime, argues against the current management representative on nationalistic and anti-capitalistic grounds:

> The undesirable Spaniard José de La Macorra has exploited and humiliated more than 3500 Mexican workers over more than 30 years. Due to its location in the foothills of the mountains, it has always been difficult to have the federal authorities intervene into the factories. (Sindicato Unico, 1936 p. 2)

Beyond its vehement, nationalistic rhetoric, this letter reveals the workers' expectations: a tighter integration into the corporativist state to counter the power of the dominant local family, help enforce workers' rights and improve workers' bargaining position with the paper mill. The strikers invoked nationalistic values, calling for the protection of Mexican workers to guard against the foreign 'invader' – who, ironically, had been living and working in the community for about 4 decades. The strike lasted 4 months. Some trade union leaders were killed in conflicts between the two trade unions: CROM, a 'white' union, that is, largely co-opted by the San Rafael management; and the 'red' or radical Confederación de Trabajadores de México or Mexican Workers' Confederation (CTM). Cardenas sent his personal secretary to mediate. Eventually, management accepted most of the workers' grievances.

From this incident, the founding section of the CTM, the local section of the national trade union, emerged as the counterweight to the San Rafael management.[1] This new union, independent from the management, negotiated a new contract which recognized the workers' rights, established by the 1917 constitution. This formed the basis for subsequent annual negotiations, in the course of which further clauses were added.

With this new labour contract and the firm's dominant position in the Mexican market, this configuration of relations remained stable for the next few decades. With 3000 workers, the San Rafael mill was then the largest pulp and paper company in Mexico and a leader in Latin America. It also gradually became a Mexican owned firm, as Mexican industrialists acquired equity from foreign investors. By 1950 it was a fully-owned Mexican company.[2]

By providing workers with above average salaries and housing, sponsoring sports, cultural activities and patriotic and religious celebrations, the factory sustained a 'privileged enclave', a 'model village' with benefits for workers and their families. Between 1936 and 1970, around 860 houses were built by the company (Arango Miranda, 1997). An internal department of the Company took care of their maintenance. A former worker (1945–80) recalls:

If a light bulb in our house was broken, we just had to call the factory and it was replaced the following day. For free. San Rafael took care of everything'. (Interview, 13 July 1999)

Another San Rafael inhabitant says:

We (at San Rafael) were a model village. We used to have the best patriotic celebrations in the whole Republic (Mexico). We had sports clubs and cultural associations … We realized how lucky we were when we went to other villages. San Rafael was clean, tidy and wealthy. People were educated. Everybody depended directly or indirectly on the factory. (Interview, 20 July 1999)

Indicators confirmed the positive effects of the factory in the development of the village of San Rafael, compared to the rest of the region. For instance, in 1950 the literacy rate in San Rafael was 64 per cent compared to

50 per cent in the rest of the state of Mexico. The common diet of a San Rafael family offered more variety than the average diet in the rest of the State. The factory provided lifetime, secure employment to workers based on the contract. The former secretary of a trade union says:

> I started working at 16. As a son and brother of workers, I had priority – almost the right – to get a job there. The factory used to come to the local secondary schools to recruit us before graduation. Money at the factory was good. Working there solved all the economic problems of raising a family. (Interview, 10 January 2000)

If daily and interpersonal interactions between workers and managers are remembered as being generally convivial, yearly negotiations over the company-wide labour contract were moments of tension between the representatives of the factory and leaders of the trade union. Annual union–management negotiations centred on pay and working conditions. Conversations never dealt with the position of the company in its markets or with production issues.

If the factory sponsored local life, the trade union leadership oriented the affairs of the municipality. Of the 14 men who served as mayors between 1935 and 1970, eight were union members – some being former general secretaries. The affiliation to the CTM implied a tighter integration into the national corporativist regime. Being a predominantly industrial municipality, Tlalmanalco was part of the industrial part of the country in the national division of political power between the industrial, agricultural and urban sectors of the corporativist regime. As a consequence, the CTM, which represented the workers of the main local industrial employer, appointed the PRI (Partido Revolucianario Institucionál) municipal candidate who was invariably elected during the years, 1936 to 1991.

The generation change in the leadership of the factory also brought a new style of leadership. Within the boundaries of the new contract, Fernando de La Macorra intervened mainly as mediator and sponsor of local life with personal ties to most of the members of the local community. A former trade union leader remembers:

> Look, I tell you, in San Rafael, there was a very protective mentality. It was like the factory was your mother…They gave us everything. Don Fernando would arrive and his word was law…If you had a personal problem, you would ask for a talk with him, explain your problem and he would have the solution. (Interview, 2 October 1999)

On his retirement in 1968, he was praised by the municipal authorities as 'a great contributor to the welfare of the municipality' and by the trade union as a 'model general director'. Another former union leader's remarks illustrate his closeness to the community:

> Don Fernando helped the people a great deal. He used to live with the people. He used to go to the fiestas with the people. Yes, he knew people's needs and for that reason the people miss him and we love him for real. (Interview, 10 January 2000)

Under the reassuring presence of the general manager, these golden years were an era of sustained economic growth, increasing national ownership and model contractual labour relations. Firm–community relations were based on a pattern of paternalism carried out within a stable national corporativist structure. The head of the company played the role of bene-factor and mediator in interpersonal relations within the framework of the corporativist system. San Rafael workers during these years had the best of two worlds: the protection of paternalism inside the factory-local commu-nity sphere while simultaneously having the protection of labour rights enforced by the state. Retrospectively, however, Fernando de La Macorra's retirement in 1968 appears to represent an important point of transition in San Rafael's history. As problems accumulated, it became more obvious that the factory was living beyond its means. This configuration of relationships was 'unreformable' in the short run and unsustainable in the long run.

A rigid and eroding configuration of relations (1970–91)

In the 1970s, life in the San Rafael community was determined by the pace of daily work, annual negotiations and celebrations. However, the world was changing around the factory enclave, internationally and nationally. At the international level, a trend towards market concentration shaped the new dynamics of the world's paper industry. Several small- and medium-sized companies, predominantly active in national markets, were acquired by or merged with a few pulp and paper conglomerates based in countries well-endowed with natural resources – especially Scandinavia, the US and Australia (Arango Miranda, 1997, p. 64). At the national level, the Mexican miracle (1940–70) showed some signs of exhaustion. Built on a corporativist political system and an inwardly oriented import substitution economic strategy (see Chapter 10), the Mexican model of 'conservative moderniza-tion' that had brought 30 years of unprecedented economic growth showed increasing signs of fatigue in the 1970s. Paradoxically, despite decades of industrialization, the Mexican economy still relied on oil for 75 per cent of its exports – a problem inherent in Mexico's industrial structure. As a whole, industry depended heavily on government subsidies and protection; it had a very limited capacity for technology and innovative development; and it produced relatively high-cost products through inflexible and outdated production methods (Haber, 1989, p. 46). The gradual devaluation of the Mexican peso against the US dollar reflected these difficulties and further exacerbated the problems facing Mexican companies. In 1970, the US dollar was worth 12 pesos; in 1977, 22.69; and in 1982, after a major devaluation, 1405 pesos.

In the 1970s, the San Rafael Company revealed its Janus faced character – the apparent strengths of an everlasting industrial powerhouse with increasing internal and external vulnerabilities. San Rafael continued to employ around 2700 workers. It was the principal benefactor of the village and an unchallenged regional employer. It produced around 10 per cent of the paper consumed in Mexico and offered a wide array of quality papers distributed by retailers. In 1973, President Luis Echeverria praised the company as 'a model and the mother of all Mexican pulp and paper companies' and even considered nationalizing it. However, its eroding market position and bleak financial situation seriously threatened its future. San Rafael's production had not grown at the same pace as the Mexican market. For instance, Atenquique, one of its competitors, increased its production from 30 000 tonnes a year to 120 000 by the end of the 1970s, the average growth of the paper sector. San Rafael, on the other hand, only increased its production twofold. Also in the 1940–70 period, 35 new companies entered the Mexican pulp and paper market; new products were launched, such as tissue and new cardboards. It became increasingly obvious that most of the value was created with these new products, which in turn relied on the internal capacity of firms to be innovative in their operations and product lines (Celorio, 1998).

Equipped with old machinery, hampered by an old and expensive labour contract, San Rafael was limited in its ability to react to these changes. The gradual deterioration of its finances exacerbated this inertia. It had become a Mexican-owned company; but it turned out to be a poor investment, since returns were much lower than the industry average. The company's debt had also increased during this high-growth period. In 1970, the Nacional Financiera, its main creditor and a State financial institution, finally bought the financially bankrupt company. Eleven years later, in 1981, San Rafael was purchased by Crisoba, a subsidiary of Scott Paper and one of its main competitors. These changes in ownership and control equally hampered the company's capacity for restructuring, as it seems that the managers and leaders appointed by the Nacional and later by Crisoba displayed a limited commitment to the ailing and brittle company. The general managers that the Nacional Financiera appointed were changed frequently. A worker recalls:

> They did not know the pulp and paper industry. They were bankers appointed by the banks. Almost every year, there was a new general manager. (Interview, 10 January 2000)

In the Crisoba years after 1981, a difference in product strategy between the two companies further limited San Rafael. While Crisoba, as a Scott company, focused on tissue papers, San Rafael specialized in quality papers for writing and Crisoba Scott pursued a product strategy that was detrimental to San Rafael and restricted reinvestment in the plant and equipment. It seems that the task of restructuring San Rafael was a daunting one for the new owners both in terms of modernizing equipment and reforming rigid labour relations.

The 1970s were a crossroads for management. In the turmoil of change, management limited its investments in the plant and there were frequent changes in positions. As a result, workers reduced their commitments to their work roles in the plant. Morale eroded. There was an increase in acts of sabotage, strikes and absenteeism, all of which were covered up by colleagues and the trade union. A former worker says:

> This is when the decline started. There are many things that contributed. First, we the workers were lazy... managers used to take machinery out. They said it was old and they would build their own little plant around here... management was never concerned about the future and they believed that the factory would be forever. (Interview, 13 January 2000)

Reduced managerial and labour commitments further eroded trade union–management relations. Interpersonal trust and commitment, probably the prevailing characteristic of the relationships before 1970, gradually deteriorated. A former trade union leader recalls:

> In the 1980s, the management always gave us red numbers. We did not believe them, partially because we did not trust them. Also because none of us knew about accounting and finance, we did not know for sure whether numbers were really red. Every year they were telling us that the factory was losing money... We did not trust them any more. (Interview, 9 January 2000)

In sum, this third configuration of firm–labour relations was marked by rigid patterns of interaction between management and the trade unions. These patterns became rituals at the annual bargaining roundtables, regardless of the economic and market performance of the company. While the external position of the company was eroding, the rigidities of its internal relations made it difficult, if not impossible to reform. This inability to reform the structure led both the managers and the workers to become disengaged from the company. There was a high turnover rate among managers who, in contrast to the previous administrators, were oriented primarily by returns on investments. The workers, beset by low morale, also became disengaged from the company and rates of absenteeism and acts of sabotage soared.

In June 1991, management announced the closing of the factory. The official reasons included:

> ... lack of investments, extreme obsolescence of the machinery and of the equipment, the disposal of polluting emissions into rivers and the atmosphere and innumerable problems of various nature ... All these problems have become so persistent that our company is in a poor competitive situation ... For these reasons, the board of directors has decided to close the plant on June 9, 1991. All collective labour relations are terminated at this date. (Barreto Flores, 1998, p. 52)

In September 1991 the company opened again with about one-fourth of the personnel and a new social contract based on federal labour laws. The 'old' labour contract based on the 1936 contract was cancelled and the company discontinued its sponsorship of community activities. A polluting cellulose plant was closed and the San Rafael-Crisoba plant stopped using local pulpwood. A wall was erected, physically and symbolically separating the factory from the village. In 1995 Kimberly-Clark merged worldwide with Scott Paper. The San Rafael plant then became part of Kimberly Clark de México, the leading pulp and paper producer in the country. As of 2003, the San Rafael plant had around 400 workers.

San Rafael's location as a point of exchange between the capital city and the mountains, once an advantage in the early industrial era, has become a liability, as pressures from the urban area threaten the local balance. Uncontrolled urban sprawl from the Mexico City metropolis disrupts the sense of local identity. Two other trends threaten gradually to transform San Rafael into a bedroom community. First, the local economic situation now offers very few employment opportunities; about half the local workforce commutes daily to the metropolitan area (Noyola Rocha, 1999). Second, many dwellers from the metropolitan area are settling in Tlalmanalco, as land there is more affordable than in densely populated urban areas (UAM, 2000). As a result, the population of Tlalmanalco has grown from 29 000 in 1980 to 43 000 in 2000. Population forecasts based on current trends predict a population of 80 810 in 2010 and 151 705 in 2020 (UAM, 2000, p. 88).

For most San Rafael residents, the company is gone. The enclave is increasingly becoming part of the metropolitan area and locals feel a sense of powerlessness in the face of these new threats.

Conclusions and discussion

The experience of the San Rafael pulp and paper company illustrates the meeting of two opposite worlds: a formerly modern, capital-intensive firm and a traditional, rural community. In this chapter we have considered how labour relations and company–community relationships have emerged and evolved – literally built the infrastructure of the village, becoming the 'mother of the Mexican pulp and paper industry'.

Although the factory, by it sheer size, largely dominated the local social, economic and political life for over one century, management–labour and company–community relations continued to evolve during that period. In the beginning, the factory took on some features of the traditional hacienda configuration, based on paternalistic master–servant relations (1893–1936). The owning family assumed the main functions of the traditional *hacendado*; workers' rights were limited. Management improved the life of the workers as a part of its generous, though necessarily voluntary initiatives.

The integration of this paternalistic approach into Mexico's corporativist state and labour institutions was the main feature of the second (1936–70) and third (1970–91) periods. This integration allowed the institutionalization of workers' rights and the establishment of regular labour–management negotiations. This configuration of relations served as a counterweight to the preponderant influence of management, and it worked well as long as the economy maintained its steady expansion within national boundaries. After 1970, however, it failed both to deal with key internal problems and to resist external changes.

The history of the San Rafael Company documents two dilemmas proposed by Bird (Chapter 1). The first concerns the creation of a productive workforce. Interestingly enough, in its first years, San Rafael used the master–servant template of labour relations, inherited from the hacienda, to establish itself as an employer (Selznick, 1969). In its first 4 decades, the pulp and paper mill took over certain key features of the hacienda system, particularly an authoritarian (if benevolent) form of management over workers who, while lacking any basic employment or economic security, retained a mixed 'farmer-worker' identity. One important difference between the San Rafael company and the old hacienda system was the inclusion of a newly imported group of skilled workers and managers: technicians and managers who, though 'pampered' by the owners, nevertheless enjoyed cordial interpersonal relations with the workers among whom they were introduced.However, these relations of paternalistic protection and mutual loyalty, and the difficulty of changing them when the times changed, were probably the likely major causes of the relatively low levels of innovation and adaptability. It seems that in San Rafael, management was a highly exclusive affair, with little or no input from workers, who were restricted to operations. San Rafael was a system with limited mobility between workers and management groups. Few workers were able to access management positions. The absence of upward mobility within the plant was an additional reason for technical stagnation.

The second dilemma documented by the San Rafael company concerns the relations between firm and community. The firm created the village of

San Rafael, which became an urban/industrial enclave in the rural regional landscape. In the pre-revolutionary period (1893–1910), the firm prioritized housing for engineers and technicians, while providing only precarious employment and living conditions for workers. In the 1920s, the company's investments in fringe benefits, social welfare and aesthetic urban design schemes were intended strategically to avoid enforcement of labour rights gained by workers in the 1917 constitution. In the post–1936 period, workers and the community seemed to enjoy the best of both worlds. On the one hand, union affiliation with the national CTM, a key player in the national corporatist system, ensured collective rights and institutionalized protection. On the other hand, the continuing La Macorra family presence, in the person of Don Fernando, supplied a traditional authority figure to arbitrate workers' own personal or family-related issues – an old-style *pater familias*, yet one whose arbitrary power was now limited by national laws and collective agreements. Neither of these accommodations addressed the long-term future of the paper company; still, workers believed that their trade union and the goodwill of the general manager would protect them from technological and market changes.

In the 1970s and 1980s this 'best of both worlds' configuration of relations became a liability. The San Rafael firm had created a ritualized configuration of relations with its workers and trade union that were static and non-adaptive: they had never tackled the issue of the future of the system as a whole. Overshadowing all other economic and institutional players, the San Rafael Company had created an over-dependent and over-embedded community. Locals knew or sensed that the company was in trouble – that its problems were compounding with every year that went by. But their ritualized labour negotiations prevented them from generating creative solutions for the structural impasse in which the company was stuck – let alone anticipate a post-San Rafael era. As a result, this local community has not been able to recuperate from the 1991 closing and seems to be ill prepared to face the current challenges the region is going through.

A visitor to San Rafael today cannot fail to note the strong presence of nostalgia in the village for the 'good old days of paternalism'. However, the current disarray, powerlessness and the gradual disintegration of the San Rafael-Tlalmanalco community suggests that this paternalism actually represented a mixed blessing. Paternalism brought material wealth and dependency; however, the rigidities it created impeded the emergence of interdependent relations and limited learning. The San Rafael Company shaped the urban, social, economic landscape of the village San Rafael. However, the dependent relations this very system created led to a community which does not seem well prepared to effectively address the present and future social, environmental and economic challenges related to increasing urbanization threats from the Metropolitan area of Mexico City.

Notes

My research for this chapter is based on qualitative methods. My sources include interviews conducted between July 1999 and January 2000 with employees active at the functional, executive and corporate levels of the San Rafael Company; they also include ex-workers and the inhabitants of San Rafael. All interviews were conducted in Spanish, tape-recorded, transcribed and coded. Municipal archives and writings on various issues relating to the San Rafael factory and the village were also consulted and analysed.

1. Founded in 1933 and led by Fidel Velazquez until his death in 1997, the CTM was the dominant confederation of Mexican Trade Unions and the labour pillar of the Partido Revolucionario Institucional (PRI), which dominated the national political system.

2. This acquisition was mentioned to me by Indalecio Celorio (then in his 88th year) who was referred to me by the director of the Mexican pulp and paper association as being 'the most knowledgeable person on the history of the pulp and paper industry in Mexico'. Neither the San Rafael archives, nor the Stock Exchange archives, nor the National Archives yielded any information about who these new owners were – nor who the existing investors were at the time of the acquisition. The existence of gaps such as these, even in modern records, is one of the limitations a historian must face when attempting to do research in Mexico.

References

Annual Report (1923), Compania de la fabricas de Papel San Rafael y Anexas, (Mexico City, DF).

Arango Miranda, A. (1997) *Industria y espacio en San Rafael, México: Formacion, desarollo y desenclave*, licentiate thesis in Geography, UNAM (Mexico, DF).

Barreto Flores, S. (1998) *El movimiento campesino en la región Itzaccihuatl-Popocatepetl y la explotacion forestal por la fabrica de papel San Rafael (1986– 1992)*, dissertation, Faculty of Political and Social Sciences, UNAM (México, DF).

Celorio, I. (1997) *Historia del papel corrugado en México* (Mexico: privately printed).

Espejel, L. (1994) 'San Rafael, una enclave' in A. Tortolero (ed.), *Entre lagos y volcanes: Chalco Amecameca, pasado y presente* (Toluca: el Colegio Mexiquense) pp. 481–520.

Garcia Luna, M. (1998) *Los origenes de la industria en el Estado de México (1830–1930)* (Toluca: Gobierno del Estado de México).

Haber, S. (1989) *Industrialization and Underdevelopment* (Austin, TX: University of Texas Press).

Huerta Gonzalez, R. (1994) 'Identidad y clase obrera: los papeleros de San Rafael, 1918–1936' in A. Tortolero (ed.), *Entre lagos y volcanes: Chalco Amecameca, pasado y presente* (Toluca: el Colegio Mexiquense) pp. 451–80.

Lenz, A. (1990) *Historia del papel en México y cosas relacionadas* (México, DF: Editorial Porrua).

Noyola Rocha, J. (1999) *Monografia municipal de Tlalamanalco* (Toluca: Instituto Mexiquense de Cultura).

San Rafael (1931) Compania de las Fabricas de papel de San Rafael y Anexas, *Congreso Mundial de la prensa* (Mexico, DF)

Selznick, P. (1969) *Law, society, and industrial justice* (New York: Russell Sage Foundation).

SUTIPRM (1936) Sindicato Unico de trabajadores de la industria papelera de la R. M., *Pliego de peticiones a la compania de las fabricas de papel de San Rafael y anexas, S.A.* (México, DF).

UAM (2000) Universidad Autónoma Metropolitana, *Atlas Municipal de los recursos naturales del Municipio de Tlalmanalco* (Mexico: UAM).

12

Green Mountain Coffee Roasters: Supplier Relations and Community Development

Anders Riel Müller

Introduction

Green Mountain Coffee Roasters (GMCR) in Vermont has in recent years gained widespread recognition for the integration of profitability with environmental and social responsibility. Rapid growth in the 1990s gave the company the sixteenth rank on the Forbes list of best small businesses in 2001 and CEO Bob Stiller was named 'Entrepreneur of the Year' (Kroll, 2001). Green Mountain Coffee Roasters' efforts in the area of socially and environmentally responsible supplier relations were also recently recognized by *Business Ethics* magazine, which ranked GMCR eighth on their list of top '100 Best Corporate Citizens of 2003', making it the highest-ranking newcomer to the list (*Business Ethics*, 2003). The company furthermore received top ranking in 'Service to Non-US Stakeholders' for its efforts in coffee growing regions (*Businesswire*, 2003). Much of this recognition has been based on the company's adoption of organic and Fair Trade certified coffee into their product line.

In this chapter I am concerned with how GMCR's social and environmental commitments have been translated in the different social contexts of two coffee cooperatives in Mexico, Cooperativa La Trinidad (La Trinidad) and La Unión Regional de Pequeños Productores de Café de Huatusco (UR Huatusco). This study is structured as follows. First I clarify the causes of the recent crisis in world coffee markets – a crisis in which wholesale prices for coffee beans have dropped precipitously. I argue that the causes for the crisis are linked to the attempt of coffee roasters and importers to maintain or increase profit margins at the expense of coffee farmers. In the second part I focus on GMCR and its motivation for implementing socially and environmentally responsible purchasing practices and how these practices have been integrated into its supplier relations. Next I examine how GMCR has responded to the needs of the two coffee cooperatives in Southern Mexico as part of its contractual relations with these producers. Finally I discuss the ambiguities and challenges that GMCR faces in its efforts to be a socially and environmentally responsible business partner.

Coffee, trade and development

Coffee provides a good subject for investigating the economic and social ramifications of international trade and international supplier relations. Coffee is one of the most preferred beverages in North America and Europe. People in these areas consume 75 per cent of the coffee produced in the world. All coffee is produced in the tropical zones of Asia, Africa and Latin America. For much of the period following Second World War coffee was the second most important trade commodity in the world, fuelling emerging economies such as Brazil, Colombia, Kenya and Tanzania. It remains a major income source for many countries.

An estimated 20 million people are involved in the production of coffee. But the golden days of coffee are over. Coffee producers are facing a major economic crisis due to rapidly declining coffee prices. Trade liberalization and surplus production have driven down prices of the green coffee bean,[1] causing economic hardship and social disruption. Rural livelihoods are threatened in Latin America, sub-Saharan Africa and South-East Asia.

In August 2001 Nestor Osorio, the Executive Director of the International Coffee Organization (ICO),[2] called attention to the increasingly skewed distribution of profits of which farmers are receiving a diminishing share. While coffee-producing countries have experienced a decline in the value of coffee exports from a total worth of US$12 billion in the early 1990s to US$5.5 billion in 2001, retail sales have exploded from a total value of US$30 billion to US$70 billion over the same period (Osorio, 2001). The 15 million small-scale farmers who grow 75 per cent of the world's coffee and the many landless farm workers have suffered in particular. Families can no longer send their children to school or afford healthcare. Some families have been forced to abandon their lands and seek economic opportunities in urban areas. In Mexico, the farmers, not unlike the profits, are heading north: the coffee crisis has led thousands to risk their lives crossing the US border in the attempt to find employment.

The situation has not always been so. Up to 1989 economic returns to producing countries were ensured through an international price stabilization scheme known as the International Coffee Agreement (ICA). By assigning production quotas to each producing country, prices remained relatively stable in most of the post-war period. The ICA regulated the world market for almost 4 decades, but in 1989 it collapsed due to increased pressure from consuming countries in Europe and North America and also some producing countries who were unsatisfied with their assigned quotas (EFTA, 2001; Ponte, 2001). As a result, prices declined steadily in the following 5-year period as producing countries tried to capture and consolidate their share of the new unregulated market by increasing production. In the summer of 2002 coffee prices reached an all-time historical low (OXFAM, 2002; Ponte, 2002a; ICO, 2003).

The liberalization of international and national trade left many farmers unprotected against heavy price speculation on the New York and London commodity exchanges, where most of the world's coffee is traded. Commodity traders thousands of kilometres away now determined their livelihoods. These traders have little other interest than maximizing their own profits, even if such speculation causes human and social devastation. But the government policies of many of the producing countries are also to blame. By encouraging intensive output-oriented farming methods, they have contributed to the worldwide increase in the production of coffee; as a result, supply is now growing at twice the speed of demand. Since coffee is a perennial crop[3] that thrives primarily in mountainous regions where not many other crops can be produced, farmers often have few alternatives to coffee growing. They are at the mercy of a free market, which seems to have little to offer them.[4]

Meanwhile roasters and distributors have benefited from trade liberalization. When international coffee prices hit a 100-year low in 2001, Nestlé, the world's leading coffee company controlling 13 per cent of the world market, posted record profits in its beverage division, where coffee constitutes 37 per cent of total sales (Nestlé, 2001). Sara Lee, another leading multinational food conglomerate, posted a 17 per cent profit within its beverage division, which deals primarily in coffee. Starbucks, the world's leading specialty coffee retailer, posted record high earnings in 2001, acknowledging that low world market prices and increasing retail sales prices were the main contributing factors (Starbucks, 2001). Such profit margins are uncommon in an otherwise very competitive global beverage industry. Coffee is indeed a profitable business to a few. So is it really possible to talk about a coffee crisis?

Do ethical standards and guidelines benefit small-scale farmers?

The obvious inequities in the liberalized coffee supply chain have mobilized concerned NGO's and consumers to demand increased socially responsible business practices from roasters and retailers. Some companies have collaborated in the establishment of alternative trade structures in which small-scale farmers receive a higher price for their coffee; others oppose such initiatives that hinder the mechanisms of the free market. Growing concerns about the social, economic and environmental impact embedded in drinking a cup of coffee has evolved into small but still significant niche products such as organic and Fair Trade coffee (Giovanucci, 2001). Being able to sell under these 'socially and environmentally ethical' labels[5] can mean considerably better prices for coffee farmers as well as improved access to information on production, processing, marketing and services. Both proprietary and third-party standards address a variety of social and environmental concerns such as worker's rights, environmental protection and quality control. Unfortunately many of them have been developed with little or no consultation with producers themselves. For example, in many cases organic practices demand little or no adjustment of already established cultivation techniques. Many small-scale farmers do not use chemical fertilizers or herbicides. But the costs associated with organic certification often prohibit small-scale farmers from being recognized as organic producers. Further, these standards, while helping to increase economic returns for coffee producers and improving the quality of coffee, may also become rigid and static, imposing additional economic, technical or educational requirements on small-scale coffee growers (Ponte, 2002b). On the other hand, one should not underestimate the positive impacts that some of these certification initiatives have had on small farming communities. The Fair Trade label system, which ensures above-market prices for producer cooperatives, has benefited many communities, especially in Latin America (Giovanucci, 2001; Waridel, 2001; Watkins and Fowler, 2002).

Business relationships and long-term commitments

While third-party certification and labelling initiatives have been adopted by some coffee companies and while they provide important guidelines and lessons, it is ultimately in the day-to-day business relationships between the coffee company and the farmer that we should look for the answers for how coffee companies can act more responsibly towards coffee farmers and their communities. One such initiative has been taken by a small group of coffee roasters and importers in the US. They see their sourcing policies as the basis for social and environmental responsibility. Their approach provides the basis for an extended analytic framework by which social and environmental concerns can and should be included in business relationships between coffee growers, processors and marketing firms.

The initiative in point is called 'relationship coffee'. While using very few standards and guidelines, the partners involved in producing 'relationship coffee' are committed to promoting long-term, mutually beneficial business relationships based on trust, transparency and a commitment to meet the needs of the business partner. The 'relationship' model also incorporates social and environmental concerns. Indeed these concerns are at the heart of the business relationship. As in any close relationship, attention to and understanding of the partner's needs are required. David Griswold, the relationship model's father and foremost promoter (he is also president of the Specialty Coffee Association of America, a nationwide association of high-end coffee roasters and retailers), devised the model as a result of his travels through Latin America in search of high-quality coffee for his import business. Griswold's company, Sustainable Harvest, which promotes the 'relationship coffee' business, has managed to establish long-term business relationships between US companies and coffee growers throughout Latin America. The benefits are numerous for both parties. Coffee companies are ensured of consistent quality and on-time deliveries while farmers are ensured a stable income-flow and a price that better reflects the true cost of production (Griswold, 2000; Jordan, 2003).

As with any enduring, supportive social relationship, reciprocity, trust and connectedness are important; but the business relationship between a small-scale coffee farmer in Guatemala and a multimillion-dollar business in the US can hardly be seen as an equal partnership. While the farmer in most cases is economically dependent on the income from such a relationship, the company is less likely to be as dependent on the farmer. It is therefore important that the company be committed to help producers in as many ways as possible. While the farmer commits to quality improvements and on-time delivery, the business should commit to improving the livelihoods of the coffee-producing households or communities. In the following section I attempt to shed some light on the dynamics of these relationships through the experience of Green Mountain Coffee Roasters with two different coffee-growing cooperatives in Mexico.

Green Mountain Coffee Roasters: Social and environmental responsibility

Green Mountain Coffee Roasters (GMCR) was established in 1981 when founder, CEO and President Bob Stiller bought a small café in Waitsfield, Vermont. Twenty years later, the company has become one of the most important and best-known companies in the North American specialty coffee industry, with sales of approximately US$100 million in the 2002 fiscal year when it shipped more than 13 million pounds of roasted coffee to markets in North America (GMCR, 2002). Incorporating social and environmental concerns in its purchasing policies has been a part of its business practice since the mid-1990s, when GMCR's proprietary stewardship programme was launched. The programme rewarded suppliers with higher prices and longer-term contracts if they met certain social and environmental requirements. GMCR was also one of the first for-profit companies to promote Fair Trade certified coffee in which it is now a market leader. GMCR's 'Fair Trade organic' coffee[6] sales currently make up 12–15 per cent of the company's total sales (GMCR, 2002).

GMCR's commitment to social responsibility has become its trademark and is a prized value in its organizational culture. Its operating practices include fostering a healthy relationship with all constituencies, employees and business partners as well as local communities. It also includes support of policies that protect the natural environment. For example, the company donates paid work-hours to employees who wish to do volunteer work on local environmental or social projects. GMCR also supports small local companies selling organic products and handicrafts. It also monitors and evaluates the overall impact the company has on the natural environment, and evaluates the energy consumption of all its operations around the world, including business travel and roasting processes.

Stakeholder responsibility is regarded as an asset that pays in the long run. GMCR's Chief Executive Officer has clearly stated that the company is not merely a 'good Samaritan'. It expects financial returns on its efforts. It makes business sense to provide stable, secure and sustainable livelihoods to coffee farmers in order to sustain the production of high-quality coffee among its suppliers (Kroll, 2001).

The company consistently tries to increase farm-direct purchases. These now make up 40 per cent of total coffee purchases. This farm-direct policy is closely related to the earlier-mentioned 'relationship coffee' model, and David Griswold has played an instrumental role in many of GMCR's supply relations. Farm-direct relations are established between GMCR and producers, which may be either large coffee *fincas* (plantations) or producer groups (cooperatives). The farm-direct model eliminates traders and other middlemen who are otherwise important logistic links between producer and roaster-importer. But these links are also additional profit seeking nodes in the marketing chain. While producers commit to deliver a certain amount of high quality coffee, GMCR pays producers above market prices and gives purchasing guarantees for a fixed period of time. By maintaining long-term relationships and close dialogue with producers, both parties get the opportunity to address their needs and develop long-term plans. For GMCR the relationship helps them secure coffee that meets specific taste and quality requirements, deliverable in adequate amounts. For the coffee farmer the relationship can help secure both social and economic needs not obtainable through conventional trade. GMCR has helped finance a range of different social and economic projects in coffee-producing communities. Some projects have a direct focus on the coffee process itself, while others are of a more social character. GMCR has supported projects such as business and community buildings for a cooperative in Indonesia, concrete drying patios to a cooperative in Guatemala and a processing facility and mini hydroelectric plant in Peru, to mention only a few (GMCR, 2003). The company is also involved with coffee growing communities through its financial support to non-governmental organizations such as Coffee Kids, Grounds for Health, Central American Drought Relief, and Ecological Enterprise Ventures. All these organizations run social or environmental projects in the communities of GMCR suppliers. Partnerships have also been formed with the US Agency for International Development (USAID). Each year the company also donates money to suppliers through solicitations. If GMCR feel the proposed project will be of mutual benefit, directly or indirectly, funding or a financial contribution will be provided. The idea behind solicitation rounds is to make sure that projects are actually formulated, developed and valued by the producers while directly or indirectly furthering GMCR's interests. These projects are not necessarily coffee-related. They can be used to support environmental or social projects that producers see as especially needy.[7]

Another important aspect of the business relationship is to develop a mutual understanding between the company, its employees and producers. To achieve this, GMCR arranges trips to coffee-producing areas for employees, while also inviting coffee producers to visit their facilities in Vermont. These trips allow employees and farmers to meet and exchange professional as well as personal experiences. The initiative helps employees and farmers to gain better knowledge of the many processes involved in coffee production and how their individual work shapes the lives of other people involved in the same production processes. Some of these trips have also opened up new business opportunities through contacts with potential suppliers.[8]

Social responsibility in practice: GMCR supply relations in Mexico

The following case studies look closer at the business relationship between GMCR and two Mexican coffee cooperatives, Cooperativa La Trinidad (La Trinidad) and Union Regional de Pequeños Productores de Café de Huatusco (UR Huatusco). The two cases depict two different socio-economic and organizational contexts to which GMCR has had to adjust in carrying out its social and environmental commitments. They also illustrate the sensitive nature of these commitments. Coffee growers may welcome financial and technical assistance; but they are also wary of outside interference in local affairs. This suspicious attitude towards outside interference is in both cases closely related to a long history of insensitive autocratic government interventions, abusive local landed elites and the fact that many coffee growers belong to indigenous peoples (Barry, 1995). Most coffee growers in Mexico today remain poor, with scarce land holdings and marginal incomes.

In 1982 the centralized Mexican government adopted a loan package from the IMF/World Bank to pay off Mexico's massive debt. As part of the deal, the government agreed to liberalize its economic and political sectors, including the elimination of many government services and subsidies to the agricultural sector. Coffee producers in Southern Mexico saw in these new economic and political liberties an opportunity to organize themselves into community-based producer cooperatives and collectively target direct export to companies in the US and Europe (Carruthers, 1996; Wise and Water, 2001; Boersma, 2002). To many cooperatives, the most important issue was to keep their distance from the ruling Partiolo Revolucionario Institucionál (PRI) party and government agencies. The national coffee board, known as INMECAFÉ, was particularly loathed and notorious for rampant corruption. While many farmers lost subsidies and other government services due to economic liberalization, farmers also enjoyed the newly won political freedoms (Barry, 1995; Porter, 2002).

Mexican coffee cooperatives have positioned themselves solidly in relation to the emerging Organic and Fair Trade markets. These niche markets actually originated in Mexico. The first Organic coffee in Mexico was produced in 1968; the Fair Trade label emerged in 1989 through collaboration between the UCIRI cooperative in Oaxaca State and a Dutch non-government organization (NGO). Mexico today is the largest supplier of organic and Fair

Trade certified coffee. Quality and the geographic proximity to the US, the single largest coffee market, have been major contributing factors to this success. This would not have occurred without the emergence of a very active rural civil society, which through collective action, managed to take advantage of Mexico's political and economic liberalization. Producer cooperatives have become an important economic and social institution in the many small coffee-producing communities spread throughout the rugged mountains of Southern Mexico.

Two such cooperatives have achieved success by connecting directly to GMCR, to whom they now sell the majority of their coffee. Formal trade relations in both case studies comply with the rules and regulations of TransFair's Fair Trade standards, including giving producers access to credit, paying Fair Trade prices and binding long-term contracts. But in addition, GMCR is continually assisting coffee-producing communities in their efforts to reduce social, technical or economic factors that can impede the suppliers' ability to meet quantitative and qualitative requirements. Technical impediments include obsolete equipment or lack knowledge about quality control. Socio-economic factors include the farmers' ability to feed their families, pay for children's education and access to medical care. Understanding that not only productive capacities (labour, technology and skills) determine the coffee growers' ability to produce quality coffee represents the first step towards more socially responsible business practices. The second and even more important step is to conduct business operations in ways that communities and producers perceive as valuable, without being intrusive on local norms and values. It is also of importance to recognize that the relationship is unbalanced from the outset; the cooperatives are far more economically dependent on GMCR than vice-versa. This imbalance in economic dependence can and certainly has in many cases been used to the advantage of foreign businesses at the expense of local workers and communities. Thus the main questions to be answered in the following two case studies are: What does GMCR do to assist these coffee communities? Do its policies add value to these communities? Finally, is the company conducting its operations in ways that are responsive to the particular needs of the community while respecting local autonomy?

Case study 1: Cooperativa la Trinidad, Oaxaca

Cooperativa la Trinidad [La Trinidad] operates in three separate communities, all of which are located in the rugged mountains of the Sierra Madre del Sur in the southern state of Oaxaca – one of the poorest states in Mexico, with a very large indigenous population. Most members of La Trinidad are poor. They all belong to the Zapotec indigenous group. Electricity and running water did not arrive in these communities until the mid-1980s, and literacy levels among adults are very low. Many of them do not speak Spanish. All villagers are farmers with land size ranging from 0.5 to 10 hectares per family; the majority of the inhabitants have only 2 to 3 hectares of mountainous land on which they grow primarily coffee, as it is one of the few cash crops that can be grown in this mountainous area. Some families grow corn for their own consumption and most families have other income generating activities, but coffee remains the mainstay of the local economy. Growing coffee means hard manual labour in this area. Picking, de-pulping, washing and drying the coffee beans are all done manually by family members. The 60 kilogram coffee bags are transported from fields to warehouse either on the backs of the farmers themselves or on mules.

Compared to Mexico's larger cooperatives, La Trinidad is very small, representing approximately 250 households or around 2000 people. The cooperative itself was formed in 1998 by a group of discontented administrative employees and members from a larger cooperative named UCI. La Trinidad was founded by UCI dissidents who alleged that Fair Trade price premiums[9] had been spent by the directors of UCI to support a presidential candidate in the state elections. Thus the major motivation behind the formation of La Trinidad was that organic and Fair Trade premiums were to be distributed directly to the communities and farmers according to each person's and community's production. This was done in order to encourage more local initiative and socio-economic development. Finding appropriate and suitable buyers in the North American market was also of major importance. Business contacts of the former trade manager from UCI and one of the founding members of the new cooperative put La Trinidad in contact with David Griswold and his company, which in the first years of operation became the sole distributor of the cooperative's coffee. With Sustainable Harvest as the mediator, La Trinidad and GMCR established trade relations under Fair Trade terms. This agreement ensured that prices paid to growers would be almost double the price of conventional coffee. Additional price premiums would be paid to farmers having an organic certification.[10] At present, GMCR purchases practically all the coffee that La Trinidad produces and it has agreed to continue to do so in the future.[11] The economic well-being of La Trinidad members is therefore dependent upon GMCR's long-term commitment to the cooperative. What GMCR receives in return is a steady supply of Fair Trade and organically certified coffee that fits the company business portfolio in terms of taste and quality.

Considering the cooperative's short history, its economic success compared to many older cooperatives is remarkable. While most other Fair Trade certified cooperatives sell only a fraction of their coffee under Fair Trade terms, nearly all La Trinidad coffee production is sold at Fair Trade prices to GMCR. La Trinidad farmers have not only protected themselves against the international coffee crisis, which has put many Mexican coffee producers out of business in recent years, but they have also managed to initiate a number of social projects and material improvements related to both coffee production and to their communities in general. It is up to each community how they wish to use their share of the Fair Trade and organic premiums;

the community usually distributes part of the premium to each member while allocating the rest to a community fund. Members in each community then decide democratically to what uses this fund will be put. In one community where two-thirds of all cooperative members live, members have used price premiums to purchase a truck that is used to transport coffee to the processing plant 5 hours away. The truck is also used to deliver a variety of supplies to the community. The same community has also constructed a warehouse, an office building and an office supply outlet that has the community's only photocopier. In the two other communities where membership is smaller, the cooperative has opened food supply stores to the benefit of the entire community. These services in turn, further enhance the economic viability of the cooperative by providing extra incomes.

While social and environmental responsibilities as well as trade principles are formally embedded in the Fair Trade and organic certification systems, establishing high levels of mutual trust and commitment with La Trinidad has been the most impressive feature of GMCR. In the past these communities had experienced highly exploitative relationships with external institutions. This had been especially the case with government agencies and even cooperatives. These experiences had left many farmers deeply suspicious of outside intervention.

An important reason for rapid implementation of major projects is that most financial support and projects have been channelled through FomCafé, a local NGO. It has been in charge of the actual project implementation of most community projects for the cooperative. FomCafé is formally an independent NGO, but was established as the 'social arm' when La Trinidad was founded. La Trinidad is somewhat unique among cooperatives in the area in that most of its operations are performed by small independent organizations and not by the cooperative itself. This structure was a deliberate attempt to allow each community to focus on improving on-farm coffee processing and community organizing. All other activities were 'outsourced' to affiliated but formally independent organizations and business. As La Trinidad's social and technical arm, FomCafé is in charge of technical training programmes relating to organic practices and quality control, as well as a range of social empowerment and economic diversification projects.[12] FomCafé is also the most important link in communicating non-business-related issues from La Trinidad to GMCR. FomCafé is funded primarily by the coop, and GMCR has often made financial contributions, but GMCR itself has no direct involvement in the implementation phase of these projects. In leaving the direct involvement and implementation to FomCafé, GMCR not only supports the development of local organizational capacities but it is also allows for project implementations that are unusually unique in their cultural and socio-economic characteristics.

Not all funding comes directly from the company. Other funds are channelled to the communities via US-based NGOs such as Coffee Kids, Grounds

For Health and Ecological Enterprise Ventures (EEV). Most of these organizations then provide financial support to FomCafé or to the cooperative. Only Grounds for Health is actually operating in the region.

Table 12.1 gives an overview of current and previous activities in La Trinidad funded by GMCR, GMCR-sponsored organizations or through the Fair Trade premiums paid by GMCR. Activities are divided in to three categories. *Production-related services* are services that directly assist farmers and the cooperative in improving quality, output and logistics. *Welfare services* are those projects that focus on the specific infrastructure needs of the communities. *Product and income diversification services* are intended to broaden the productive and income-generating range of activities in the communities. Some improvements financed by Fair Trade, such as the truck, warehouse and food stores, are not included as these have already been mentioned earlier.

The sugar and honey projects were initiated by one community group through their allocation of the Fair Trade premiums. While the sugar project is in its infant stage, the honey project has been started in cooperation with

Table 12.1 GMCR-funded Projects in La Trinidad

Project	Project description	Funder	Implementation
Production-related services			
Hablamos de café	Improve on-farm quality control	GMCR	FomCafé
On-farm washbasins and patios	Improve washing and drying processes	GMCR	FomCafé
Coffee tree nursery	Help farmers replace old coffee trees	Fair Trade	FomCafé
Operating credit	Assist cooperative financing	EEV	EEV
Welfare Services			
Cervical cancer screening	Improve women's health	Grounds for health	Grounds for health
Product and income diversification			
Vegetable garden project	Improve diet, Women's empowerment	Coffee Kids	FomCafé
Mushroom project	Micro-business, Women's empowerment	Coffee Kids	FomCafé
Microsavings programme	Microbusiness, Women's empowerment	Coffee Kids	FomCafé
Sugar production	Income diversification and Empowerment	Fair Trade	La Trinidad
Honey production	Income diversification	Fair Trade	La Trinidad

a Mexican cosmetics company that produces organic soaps and skin care products. These projects are based within the community itself with no external assistance. The objective of the projects is to broaden the income base of the community while gaining administrative and organizational capacities. The long-term economic security guaranteed by GMCR has also enabled the cooperative to have longer-term visions.

Challenges facing GMCR in its relationship with La Trinidad

While results have been impressive, GMCR will also have to face some challenges regarding its future involvement. These challenges are directly linked to the long-term economic and organizational viability of the cooperative. Economic dependency, democratic participation and capacity building are of special concern.

The three communities that make up La Trinidad are now almost entirely economically dependent on GMCR purchases. This raises the question of whether such a heavy dependence on one company is economically sustainable over the long term, as shifts in market conditions could lead to reduced demand. Under the current circumstances La Trinidad's destiny is intimately linked to GMCR's business strategy and retail market performance. It is thus arguably in the interest of the cooperative to reduce its economic dependence on GMCR, in order to insure the long-term livelihoods of its members. To decrease its dependence, La Trinidad could search for other buyers and thereby diversify its sales into other marketable products; GMCR could actively help La Trinidad find new customers in ways that would not threaten its own strategic position. This could be done by finding another buyer for the European market, for example, where GMCR has no business interest.

For individual households, economic uncertainty and poverty remain a widespread problem. Fair Trade prices increased household income significantly; but many still cannot afford some basic services such as education beyond the sixth grade for their children. Land scarcity is a major factor contributing to the low income levels. An average household with 2 hectares of coffee earns an annual income of less than US$2000 from coffee production. As a result, many families seek off-season employment away from home, often leaving children to find for themselves in the village for weeks at a time. In other cases children who accompany their parents miss significant times at school. For these and related reasons there is a compelling need to expand and diversify the income base in the communities of La Trinidad.

This, of course, poses the question of the extent to which GMCR can be expected to actively help establish alternative economic opportunities for the cooperative's members. How would this fit with GMCR's interests in improving coffee quality? Could GMCR assist the cooperative in finding other coffee companies who would be willing to buy from La Trinidad or would this be detrimental to GMCR's own interests? Broadening the cooperative's customer base and thereby reducing its risks would be, in the long term, in the interest of La Trinidad as a cooperative; but for individual households, diversifying the income base seems to be a more immediate and practical solution. So if sharing the coffee supply with other companies does not serve GMCR's interests, the company could actively encourage and assist product and income diversification. They could, for example, support La Trinidad members in developing *local* markets for other products that members could produce. Such assistance could give these communities a significant economic boost that could lift many families out of poverty.

The second issue, which seems even more pressing for the successful development of the cooperative and hence the communities, is the development and dissemination of managerial and administrative skills among cooperative members. The absence of these skills is probably one of the most acute challenges for the cooperative. This has led to a situation where only two elected representatives are in charge of practically all of the cooperative's activities. Since more than half of the members are illiterate and 30 per cent do not speak Spanish, training and education are crucial not only for strengthening administrative competence, but also to strengthen the democratic component so vital to a cooperative organization. While the decentralized structure of the cooperative assures that each community can autonomously decide how it wishes to spend their allocated funds, there is a need to improve the democratic component in *all* phases of cooperative operations. To accomplish this there needs to be greater competence and greater inclusiveness in the administration of the cooperative.

There are some hopeful signs. For example, the leader of the smallest of the three communities was highly committed to developing members' administrative capacities. He did this by instituting inclusive decision-making processes in dealing with the problem of diversification. As a result several small diversifications programs in honey and sugar production have been started. This community leader was especially committed to leaving decision-making to community members while playing a more consultative role. This has created a high level of active participation as well as a strong identification with the cooperative.

The situation was somewhat different in the largest community. This community has a higher level of material development. These physical improvements, however, have come with only minimal participation of the inhabitants in the decision-making processes Participation, of course, is crucial for the cooperative's long-term viability. The elected community leader is an adept negotiator and businessman and has played a central role in the cooperative's success; but his leadership style is in many ways autocratic. He unofficially manages and administers all activities in the community despite the existence of councils and work groups for each project. Not only is this leadership style detrimental to the furthering of local administrative capacities, but it has also created distrust between the leader and members who are suspicious of his way of administering the cooperative's finances. While we saw no indication of fraud (we were allowed access to all financial transactions), the *suspicion* of possible fraud created distrust towards the leader among some members. It was evident when interviewing members in this community that social cohesion and identification with the cooperative were lacking. Many would state that convenience – improved transport of the coffee beans – and improved prices were the primary reasons for their membership in the cooperative. Meanwhile, old family feuds between the leader's family and other local families added to the loosely organized and very fragile nature of the cooperative.

These problems may appear to be beyond the concern of GMCR if cultural sensitivity and respect for the local traditions are to be maintained. The leadership style, however, can be detrimental not only to the survival of the cooperative and community development but also to GMCR operations. Since cooperatives are voluntary organizations, members can easily sell their coffee elsewhere, thereby reducing coffee supplies available to GMCR. It is therefore in the interest of GMCR to establish a well-functioning socially cohesive cooperative organization. Intra-organizational trust and commitment seems as important to both GMCR and the cooperative as the inter-organizational trust and commitment that GMCR has been building up through all its support during the years. The leader, however, was democratically elected – though mostly because of the absence of other serious contenders – and represents an expression of ancient Zapotec community governing structures. GMCR may not wish to interfere with these traditions. While direct intervention seems to be an undesirable and certainly also unwanted solution, GMCR could offer funding for training and education of members in administrative and managerial skills even though such an offer would still depend upon the agreement of the cooperative and its leader. Support for such a project could come directly from GMCR or through one of the many partner organizations that deal with the cooperative. Such a programme need not be costly, but it would help develop the organizational and developmental capacities of the cooperative.

This case illustrates the dilemmas that GMCR faces in trying to be a socially responsible business. It is not entirely clear what it means to act responsibly in this situation. Standardized ethical guidelines appear inadequate. 'Doing good', while respecting local customs, traditions and autonomy, is not an easy task.

Case study 2: UR Huatusco, Veracruz

La Unión Regional de Pequeños Productores de Café de Huatusco [UR Huatusco] is a move to a different world. The town of Huatusco, which includes approximately 100 000 inhabitants in the hills surrounding the town itself, is located in the oil-rich state of Veracruz on the Gulf coast of Mexico. The population is mixed indigenous and European, with a strong

Italian presence. The region of Huatusco is composed of gentle sloped hills and a temperate tropical climate. It is more fertile and slightly more diverse in its agriculture in contrast to the region of Oaxaca where La Trinidad operates. The history of Huatusco is closely related to coffee, which has been a dominant and profitable crop for a century. However, declining coffee prices have been disastrous to the region.

When entering the town of Huatusco one sees little immediate evidence of economic hardship: the two-mile-long main street is dotted with restaurants, coffee shops and fashion boutiques. In the past decade, however, 25 per cent of the population has left Huatusco to seek employment and income elsewhere. The local economy is no longer based on coffee but primarily on remittances from family members who live and work in the US (UR Huatusco, 2002).

In contrast to the experience of most indigenous coffee farmers in Chiapas and Oaxaca, coffee was for a long time a profitable business; it fuelled economic progress and material welfare even for small-scale farmers. Farmers with only a few acres of land could afford to send their children to school, build houses and buy cars. But the elimination of federal subsidies and the liberalization of the global coffee market put an end to prosperity. The Huatusco region was hit especially hard: many farmers, encouraged by the Instituto Mexicano del Café (INMECAFE), the federal Mexican coffee marketing board, had invested heavily in modernizing their coffee production; when prices began declining in the late 1980s, a major part of these investments was lost. Unemployment, bankruptcies and migration increased dramatically.[13]

UR Huatusco was founded in the early 1980s in order to strengthen the bargaining power of local small-scale farmers in their negotiations with INMECAFE. This government agency controlled all coffee related activities such as processing, subsidies and credit. When Mexico's coffee sector was liberalized in 1989, INMECAFE was dismantled and UR Huatusco, at that time primarily a credit union, negotiated the purchase of two former federal coffee processing facilities. In 1991 it took over not only operation but also ownership of the two processing facilities and became officially recognized as a cooperative. Membership grew fast and has now reached more than 2000 members in 49 communities. The cooperative buys coffee from an additional 3000 farmers on regular basis and has been active in promoting better conditions for small-scale coffee farmers in the region. It has transmitted coffee producer grievances to the attention of federal and state governments; it has also supported the construction of schools and health clinics in member communities. In less than 10 years UR Huatusco has become an important economic and social institution in the region.

Business relations with GMCR were established in the mid-1990s through David Griswold and Sustainable Harvest. Since then trade relations have expanded and UR Huatusco is now GMCR's largest single supplier. The company buys 20 per cent of the cooperative's total production, making it

UR Huatusco's single largest customer. Approximately 50 per cent of GMCR purchases are traded at Fair Trade premiums while the remaining half is traded at quality premium prices, somewhat lower than Fair Trade but significantly higher than the official market price.

The cooperative, like the rest of the region, has struggled because of low world market prices. In an attempt to financially assist members who were in danger of losing their land because of debts, the cooperative has taken loans from private banks and credit institutions to pay off farmers' debts. However the persistently unfavourable environment in the world coffee market has made lending institutions cautious, and thus they are only willing to provide short-term high interest loans. This has led to severe cash flow problems for the cooperative and has affected its ability to pay farmers for their coffee. In 2001–02, the cooperative was close to financial ruin. Fortunately, GMCR and EEV provided the cooperative with low interest loans, which allowed the cooperative to continue operations into 2003.

Another consequence of the uncertainty of world markets has been an increased effort of the cooperative at targeting its marketing strategy on more lucrative niche markets. Fair Trade certification was obtained and the entrance into this market has been quite successful. In 2001–02, 15 per cent of all coffee was sold at Fair Trade prices and this was expected to rise to 20 per cent in 2002–03. While GMCR is by far the largest Fair Trade customer, contracts from European companies are also significant.

The cooperative is also attempting to tap into the lucrative organic coffee market and it actively encourages members to convert to organic cultivation practices. But convincing farmers is a slow process. Only a small number have actually obtained organic certification, while other farmers are going through the transition period. The cooperative's target is to have 50 per cent of the members certified by 2006. The major challenge has been to convince farmers to see the financial benefits of conversion as the 3–6 year transition period normally results in significantly lower yields. During this transition period liquidity problems continue to be a major concern for most farmers. Many organic farmers however, report comparable or higher financial returns than they experienced prior to the transition mostly due to a significant reduction in production costs.

GMCR remains an important customer and cooperative representatives noted that without GMCR's financial assistance and purchases they would have been forced to shut down operations in 2001. GMCR offered direct loans and credits as well funding through EEV. UR Huatusco has also received financial support for other projects such as modernizing machinery, purchasing waste, reducing technology and establishing an information-sharing network among farmers. The latter project involves training farmers from each community to improve communication between the cooperative and members on issues regarding cultivation practices and cooperative activities.

Investigating the relationship between GMCR and UR Huatusco reveals significant differences from the experiences at La Trinidad. UR Huatusco is larger; it is well established and has a more formalized governing and management structure that includes elected representatives and a professional administration. The social and ideological cohesion is also strong, with the 99-year-old founder, Professor Manual Sedas Rincón, serving as its charismatic leader. Manuel Sedas Rincón has devoted his life to the struggle of coffee pickers and small farmers in the Huatusco region. Inspired by the revolutionary hero Emiliano Zapata, he formed the first organized resistance to the exploitation of farm workers in Huatusco back in the 1920s. Over the years he has become a recognized national figure through his involvement in the mobilization of small farmers against the government.

The Huatusco region has significantly better access to a number of public institutions including a hospital and a university. Education levels are also somewhat higher than in La Trinidad even though illiteracy rates remain higher than the national average. Many of the upper-level administrative employees have engineering degrees. Finally, it should be noted that UR Huatusco is not as dependent on GMCR as La Trinidad; the larger cooperative trades with additional coffee companies from Europe and North America.

UR Huatusco is nonetheless committed to meeting GMCR requirements. The cooperative appreciates GMCR's business practices. Representatives and management praised the company for being an exemplary business partner. GMCR's company logo is painted on machines in the cooperative's main processing facility in order to remind members and employees that the company had helped finance the new machinery and that strict quality control is important. Appreciation of GMCR as a customer goes beyond the fact that it pays above market prices. It has helped the cooperative to achieve higher operating efficiency, quality control and other production-related improvements, including worker safety.

At the time of this case study, a group of GMCR employees were visiting the cooperative in order to get to know the people and the area and to exchange knowledge and ideas. One example of this exchange was the visit by GMCR's operations manager to the processing facilities. While he was there he interviewed workers about safety and quality control. In collaboration with workers and management, he helped improve security in the plant, which had lagged far behind Mexican minimum standards. Such visits are all part of GMCR's effort to develop a better understanding of local needs and also important for GMCR since it helps ensure a continuing supply of high-quality coffee.

Challenges facing GMCR in UR Huatusco

There is no doubt that UR Huatusco has benefited from its business with GMCR. The cooperative would most likely have gone bankrupt without the purchases and financial aid provided by GMCR. But these benefits were more difficult to observe at the household level. Most members still face the imminent threat of losing their farms if prices do not increase within 1 or 2 years. Producers are struggling to survive on what the land can produce and much of the income from coffee is either reinvested in the farm or is used to pay off outstanding debts. This forces most families to find other sources of revenue. Several farmers indicated that if prices were not to improve within the next year they would have to sell their land and move. The cooperative itself also continues to struggle financially and it has been forced to close many social projects. It is also less able to offer financial support to individual farmers and this has had a negative impact on member support. Is it possible that GMCR could assist the farmers and the cooperative in overcoming this economic crisis?

GMCR could possibly play a more proactive role in promoting organic cultivation practices, either through direct support for the program or by demanding greater amounts of organic certified coffee. This would not only enable farmers and the cooperative to receive higher prices for their coffee but also help diversify production through organic practices. It could help farmers get out of the vicious debt cycle that is a result of using expensive chemical inputs. Soil conditions might also be improved. This is an area where extensive monocultural farm practices have taken their toll. Soil exhaustion and soil erosion have reduced yields on most farms. The adoption of organic practices could help diminish this problem. Finally, GMCR might offer more support in developing other money-earning projects. Greater economic diversification could offer some protection against the vagaries of the coffee market.

Efforts by the cooperative to implement such programs have been few because of its limited financial resources. External financial assistance seems to be critical for the cooperative to remain an organization for economic and social progress in the Huatusco region. The few diversification projects operating in the region are most often federal or state sponsored projects, many of which are based on unofficial political commitments. It is evident that GMCR has contributed to the cooperative in a number of ways that have actually compensated for the loss of state-sponsored subsidies. Nonetheless, although GMCR cannot single-handedly secure the future for the cooperative and its members, there remain a number of ways in which GMCR could play a more active role in securing the livelihoods of the thousands of households who work in the coffee fields.

Conclusions

The two case studies illustrate how Green Mountain Coffee Roasters of Vermont is practising social responsibility in its relations with two suppliers in Mexico. While organic and Fair Trade standards are present in both cases, this study reveals that complying with marketing standards of Fair Trade and organically grown coffee does not necessarily ensure the welfare of the coffee producers. What is required is an ongoing effort to assist producers in achieving increased economic security through economic diversification and socio-economic development through a strengthening of the organizational aspects of the cooperatives.

Fair business practices and financial assistance for social projects can contribute to this objective. The communities' problems cannot be solved by simply adhering to an abstract set of standards and requirements; rather their solutions require a higher degree of in-depth understanding, in order to meet the specific needs and wants of these communities. Such an approach requires an ongoing social relationship that is based on reciprocity, trust, mutual commitment and gradual improvements. GMCR has taken steps in this direction. One consequence of its actions is the creation of highly devoted suppliers. In return, the company's overall business performance has been strengthened.

The two cases also demonstrate that involvement in local affairs can be complicated. Balancing the need for change against respect for local autonomy often creates a high degree of ambiguity as to what course of action to take. Should GMCR interfere with intra-organizational situations that appear to be unjust? Respecting local development often requires the company to allow producers to make their own decisions. But as the case in La Trinidad shows, unresolved internal problems and conflicts can reduce the ability of the cooperative to make decisions and, indeed, these problems can threaten the long-term viability and stability of the cooperative. While direct intervention most likely would be perceived as undesirable by the local communities, there might be other, indirect measures available to GMCR. These might include funding for training and education in administrative and organizational skills. In the case of La Trinidad especially, this could help expand the democratic component of the cooperative and enable members to play a more active role in the day-to-day operations of the cooperative.

GMCR has shown that economic success and social responsibility are compatible. Its involvement in and commitment to the well-being of these coffee-growing cooperatives contribute somewhat towards these communities' ability to raise themselves out of poverty and to develop more socially rewarding lives. With the withdrawal of the state from many social and economic activities, GMCR has come to play an important role in the socio-economic development process of these communities. It can only be hoped that GMCR will continue its operations in dialogue with the cooperatives and help improve local opportunities and capacities, economically and socially.

Acknowledgements

Empirical research for this article was performed during January and February of 2003 in Mexico. The author would like to thank Green

Mountain Coffee Roasters, FomCafé and all the members of Cooperativa la Trinidad and La Unión Regional de Pequeños Productores de Café de Huatusco for their cooperation.

Notes

1. Coffee is usually traded on the international market in the form of 'green' (unroasted) beans. After the ripe coffee cherries (typically containing two beans) are picked, the beans are removed from the fruit pulp, cleaned and dried. The surrounding parchment layer and 'silver skin' are then removed, leaving the green beans ready for export.
2. Established under the auspices of the UN in 1963, the International Coffee Organization is the main intergovernmental organization for coffee. The ICO has administered six International Coffee Agreements (ICAs). Its membership includes nearly every coffee exporting country on earth and the majority of importing countries, with the notable exception of the US, the world's largest coffee consumer. ICO documents including a very extensive fund of information are available on the Internet at www.ico.org.
3. It takes 3–5 years from the time a coffee bush is planted to the first harvest. A coffee bush remains productive for 30–80 years, depending on habitat and variety. New hybrid varieties usually give higher yields but they also have the shortest lifespan.
4. It is important to distinguish between national and international trade liberalization. While international trade liberalization has caused severe price deterioration, national liberalization has in some cases helped farmers capture a higher share of total income. Bureaucracy and corruption have been widespread on national marketing boards in many coffee-producing countries. The gain from national liberalization, however, has by far been offset by the decline in world market prices. For a further discussion about this subject see Talbot (1997), Ponte (2001), OXFAM (2002).
5. Some of the most common labels are Fair Trade certification (TransFair, Max Havelaar, The Fair Trade Foundation, etc.) and Organic certification (QAI, CERTIMEX). Other lesser-known certification systems and standards include Rainforest Alliance's Sustainable Agriculture Certification System (Eco-OK) and the Smithsonian Institution 'Bird Friendly' label.
6. Green Mountain Coffee Roasters follows a double certification policy in which they aim to receive both organic and Fair Trade certification for a particular product. Coffee blends are Fair Trade certified by Transfers and certified organic by Quality Assurance International (QAI). Green Mountain Coffee Roasters now have more than 20 double certified coffee blends.
7. John Winter, Director of Social Responsibility, Green Mountain Coffee Roasters, (personal communication, 26 October 2002).
8. Rick Peyser, Director of Public Relations, Green Mountain Coffee Roasters (personal communication, 26 October 2002).
9. 'Fair Trade premiums' are here understood as the being amount of money that the cooperative receives above market prices.
10. Organic certification remains an ongoing process in the cooperative since certification is given on a per-farm basis. For new members, obtaining organic certification usually takes 2 years.
11. Peyser, personal communication.

12. José Luis Zarrate, Director of FomCafé (personal communication, 28 December 2002).
13. In the 1970s coffee farmers were encouraged by INMECAFE to plant high-yield coffee trees requiring chemical fertilizers, pesticides and herbicides. These inputs remained subsidized for about 15 years, until Mexico liberalized the coffee sector. When the subsidies were removed, many farmers could no longer afford the inputs, resulting in rapidly declining harvests and soil depletion.

References

Barry, T. (1995) *Zapata's Revenge: Free Trade and the Farm Crisis in Mexico* (Boston: South End Press).

Boersma, F. V. (2002) *Poverty Alleviation through Participation in Fair Trade Coffee Networks: The Case of UCIRI, Oaxaca, Mexico* (Fort Collins: Colorado State University).

Business Ethics (2003) '100 Best Companies of 2003', 31 March.

Businesswire (2003) 'Green Mountain Coffee Roasters Ranked #8 on Business Ethics Magazine's List of 100 Best Corporate Citizens', 31 March.

Carruthers, D. V. (1996) 'Indigenous Ecology and the Politics of Linkage in Mexican Social Movements', CERLAC Working Paper Series, Number 5 (Toronto: York University). http://www.coffeekids.org/profiles/microcredit/huatusco.htm, accessed 20 December.

EFTA (2001) European Fair Trade Association, *Fair Trade Yearbook 2001* (Brussels: European Fair Trade Association).

Giovanucci, D. (2001) *Sustainable Coffee Survey of the North American Specialty Coffee Industry* (Long Beach, CA: Specialty Coffee Association of America).

GMCR (2002) Green Mountain Coffee Roasters, *Annual Report 2002* (Waterbury, VT: Green Mountain Coffee Roasters).

GMCR (2003) Green Mountain Coffee Roasters, 'Helping in Coffee Communities', *Green Mountain Coffee Roasters* [website] (updated 20 December). http://www.green-mountaincoffee.com/social_environmental/scripts/coffee_communities.asp, accessed 20 December 2003.

Griswold, D. (2000) 'Relationship Coffees', *Badgett's Coffee eJournal*, vol. 1(29), http://www.badgettcoffee.com/issue29.htm.

ICO (2003) International Coffee Organization, 'Frequently Asked Questions on Membership', *International Coffee Organization* [website] (updated 20 December) http://www.ico.org/frameset/icoset.htm, accessed 20 December.

Jordan, P. (2003) 'Fair Trade, Sustainable Coffees Tantalize Roasters', *Reuters News Service*, 10 October.

Kroll, L. (2001) 'Entrepreneur of the Year: Java Man', *Forbes Magazine*, 29 October.

Nestlé (2001) Nestlé Corporation, 'Products and Brands', Nestlé Management Report 2001 (Vevey: Nestlé).

Osorio, Nestor. (2001) 'The Coffee Crisis: A Threat to Sustainable Development' (London: International Coffee Organization).

OXFAM (2002) Oxford Committee for Famine Relief, 'Mugged – Poverty in Your Cup' (London: OXFAM).

Ponte, S. (2001) 'Coffee Markets in East Africa: Local Responses to Global Challenges or Global Responses to Local Challenges', CDR Working Papers 01.5 (Copenhagen: Centre for Development Research).

Ponte, S. (2002a) 'The "Latte Revolution?" Regulation, Markets and Consumption in the Global Coffee Chain', *World Development*, vol. 30(7), pp. 1099–122.

Ponte, S. (2002b) 'Standards,Trade and Equity: Lessons from the Specialty Coffee Industry', CDR Working Papers (Copenhagen: Centre for Development Research).

Porter, R. M. (2002) *The Coffee Farmers Revolt in Southern Mexico in the 1980s and 1990s* (Lewiston, NY: Edwin Millen Press).

Starbucks (2001) Starbucks Corporation, *Annual Report 2001* (Seattle: Starbucks Corporation).

Talbot, J. M. (1997) 'Where Does Your Coffee Dollar Go? The Division of Income and Surplus Along the Coffee Commodity Chain', *Studies in Comparative International Development*, vol. 32(1), pp. 56–91.

UR Huatusco (2002) Unión Regional de Pequeños Productores de Café de Huatusco, 'Diagnostico' (Huatusco, Veracruz: Unión Regional de Pequeños Productores de Café de Huatusco).

Waridel, L. (2001) *Coffee With Pleasure: Just Java and World Trade*(Montreal: Black Rose Books).

Watkins, K. and Fowler, P. (2002) *Rigged Rules and Double Standards: Trade, Globalisation, and the Fight Against Poverty* (London: OXFAM).

Wise, T. and Water, E. (2001) 'Community Control in a Global Economy: Lessons from Mexico's Economic Integration Process', Global Development and Environment Institute, Working Paper No. 01–03 (Boston: Tufts University).

13

Managing Security Problems through Community Relations: A Comparative Study of Petroleum Companies in Colombia

Titus Fossgard-Moser and Frederick Bird

Introduction

Many multinational enterprises (MNEs) currently operate in areas or countries characterized by varying degrees of ongoing social unrest and civil conflict. In southern Mexico, Sierra Leone, Angola, Congo, Sudan, Zimbabwe, Nigeria, South Africa, the Philippines and Indonesia (among others), social discord and civil violence assume diverse and overlapping expressions: overt civil wars, guerrilla insurgencies, irregular acts of sabotage, kidnappings, commandeering of mines or minerals and/or random acts of violence (Global Witness, 2000; Smillie *et al.*, 2000; Renner, 2002). MNEs may be directly attacked or their personnel may be endangered. They may be threatened with violence if they fail to cooperate with either official or unofficial militia[1]. In other settings, they may find themselves working with community groups or local partners that have direct or indirect links with groups encouraging these acts of violence. Businesses operating in these areas face security problems that are frequently more extensive and more pressing than in areas with greater civil accord.

What options do businesses have for managing these security concerns to protect their employees and their investments? They can ask for additional protection from the police and armed services; they can hire their own security guards and build secure barriers around their operations; they can also contract out for these services. Alternatively, they may decide that security risks are so great that it makes sense temporarily or permanently to withdraw their investments, or at least cease active operations within specific endangered areas (Wade, 2000). A number of advantages and disadvantages are associated with each of these alternatives. It is clearly irresponsible to put employees and property at great risk without carefully considering alternatives.

At the same time, MNEs may unwittingly contract for security services from people who seem reliable but have unannounced links with illegal paramilitary movements. Some businesses have hired security guards who have over-reacted, injured and maimed legitimate protestors, ignored the civil liberties of local residents and thereby undermined relations with local communities. Divestment may be a viable option in some settings. In South Africa during the 1980s and early 1990s, many businesses treated divestment as the preferred alternative, not only out of concern for security issues but also in protest against the apartheid policies of the South African government (Sethi and Williams, 2001). In contrast, MNEs have withdrawn from countries like Sierra Leone primarily for security reasons (Smillie *et al.*, 2000).

In this chapter we examine how one small international petroleum company, an overseas independent, which we will call 'Interpet', successfully dealt with these kinds of security problems in Colombia from the late 1980s to the present. It did so not by hiring securing guards and not by divesting, but rather through commitment to an ongoing community relations programme. We will briefly contrast Interpet's strategy with that of a much larger international firm – an MNE, which we will call 'Largeco', operating in the same region. We will explore to what extent the successful policies of 'Interpet' in Colombia might be pursued by other firms in other settings.

The situation in Colombia

Since independence from Spain in the early nineteenth century, Colombia has made steady but not spectacular economic progress. The rate of economic growth between 1945 and 1995 was 5 per cent per year. Despite a semblance of stability in recent decades, with the election of a series of Liberal or Conservative governments, Columbia has a long history of political violence and unrest, which continue to this day. Colombia is currently the world's second-largest producer of both coffee and cut flowers. By 2000 it had a population of 41 million and the third-largest economy in South America – diverse, vibrant and for the most part domestically oriented (Reid, 2001).

From independence in 1824 until just after the end of Second World War, Colombia enjoyed periods of social peace interrupted occasionally by periods of intense violence. Its war of independence against Spain continued for more than a dozen years, and did not really end until Venezuela and Ecuador declared their independence from Colombia in 1830. An intense period of social strife, known as *la Guerra de los Mil Días* (the War of a Thousand Days), broke out between 1899 and 1902, resulting in more than 100 000 deaths (Bergquist *et al.*, 1992; Bushnell, 1992). There were smaller outbreaks of civil violence in the 1920s and 1930s. Colombia's comparative social peace disappeared completely in 1948 when a populist Liberal leader was assassinated in the capital, Bogotá. During the next eighteen years, in a period referred to as *La Violencia*, between 100 000 and 200 000 Colombians were killed. Left-wing guerrilla movements arose at that time and have continued ever since. The central government has remained weak, despite various attempts made to reform the political system (a new constitution was ratified in 1991). The guerrilla movements, claiming to seek greater social justice for the poor, have historically attracted supporters in a number of rural areas throughout the country; they have also recruited followers among disaffected urban youth. They also have the support of a number of left-leaning Catholics who, using the language of Liberation Theology, have variously sympathized with the guerrillas' attacks on economic injustices and their efforts to provide a better life for the very poor (CELAM, 1968). Currently the guerrillas are organized into two principal groups: The Revolutionary Armed Forces of Colombia (FARC) and The National Liberation Army (ELN). Both groups have grown more powerful during the 1990s, even though they seem at the same time to have lost much of their original ideological vision. Simultaneously there has been a marked growth in the number of people joining right-wing paramilitary forces. These are organized through the United Self-Defense Forces of Colombia (AUC). In an attempt to resolve the conflict, the Colombian government has at times arranged truces with the guerrilla movements and created several specific demilitarized zones. In spite of intense social conflict and civil unrest, the overall economy grew steadily up until the mid 1990s. Poverty rates declined from 70 per cent in 1970 to 27 per cent in 1995.

Colombia's periods of violence and civil strife preceded by many years the more recent growth of the cocaine and petroleum industries. A number of factors have contributed to the ongoing violent civil conflict. Disputes over land claims, however, have been central. Late-nineteenth-century legislation allowing individuals to lay claims to sections of land they farmed did not lead to the distribution of property among thousands of small holders, as intended, but rather to the consolidation of title in a comparatively small number of landlords. Many would-be homesteaders who had set out to colonize Colombia's lowland regions became farm labourers instead. Subsequently the courts and the various governments have sought, with mixed results, to help these groups regain possession of the lands they had once claimed as their own. Violence increased after 1948, as groups sought to re-claim or protect their lands through use of armed force. Their efforts were met by both public and private violence. These conflicts were especially fierce in the coffee-growing and cattle-raising areas, and in the former were promoted in part by agents directly involved in coffee production: the state managers, who administered the large plantations for absentee landlords, and the local coffee merchants, who bought coffee beans from smaller producers and sold them to big coffee businesses (Bergquist, Penaranda and Sanchez, 1992).

Social and economic conditions have worsened since the mid-1990s. The economy has slumped. The number of impoverished persons has increased by 3 million. The overall level of civil violence has increased over the past decade and half. The current murder rate is one of the highest in the world: 40 000 people were killed in the 1990s (Feroro, 2002). The rate of kidnapping is also higher. There were 3707 kidnaps in 2000, or almost 10 per day. There are over 2 million internally displaced people and over 1 million Colombians have left the country since 1996. The unemployment rate has climbed to 20 per cent (Reid, 2001).

Over the past two decades, as Colombia became a major site for growing and manufacturing cocaine, the US government sought the Colombian government's cooperation in dealing with the cocaine problem by eliminating the sources. But while the American strategy seemed to work in Bolivia and Peru, where coca crops were destroyed by spraying, the areas used to grow cocaine in Colombia correspondingly expanded. The sources were not eliminated; they just moved. Today, indeed, as the US now focuses its attention on reducing coca production in Colombia, there is evidence of increased production in Peru and Bolivia. So far, efforts to eliminate the crops have been largely unsuccessful and Regional governmental officials have protested against the spraying. The marketing of cocaine has provided a source of income for both the guerrillas and the paramilitary forces. Rebel groups earned more than $2 billion from the cocaine business between 1991 and 1998 (Wade, 2000).

The marked expansion of the oil industry during the 1990s has also been connected with increased violence. Rebel groups have used kidnappings and extortion to fund their operations and undertaken repeated attacks on oil pipelines. In 1992 the Colombian government initially responded to this situation by imposing a tax of US$1 per barrel tax on all oil extracted, in order to pay for increased military protection for pipelines and refineries (Williams, 1997). To guard its refinery at Barrancabermeja, the government stationed two battalions in the city of 283 000, plus a 70-man special forces squadron (Reid, 2001). Most of the large oil companies have hired their own security guards, either contracting with private companies or working out special arrangements with the Colombian army. In some cases these private security forces number more than 1000 (Dudley and Murillo, 1998). In the meantime rebel groups have increased their attacks. They have especially targeted major pipelines, such as those running from north-eastern oil fields both to the refinery and to Caribbean ports. Colombia's second most important pipeline, the *Caño Limon* pipeline, was attacked 170 times in 2001. In hopes of addressing some of the unresolved land claims/disputes that may fuel such acts of sabotage, Ecopetrol, the nationally owned petroleum company, has transferred title to large tracts of land to indigenous groups in one of its areas of operation. The rebel groups have responded by saying these arrangements are inadequate. In the meantime oil production has continued to grow; oil now exceeds coffee as Colombia's largest source of export earnings (Dudley and Murillo, 1998).

Contrasting strategies of two international petroleum companies

Within this context the remainder of this chapter will examine the approaches adopted by two international oil companies to the security aspects of their operations. Both companies operated in the remote eastern region of Colombia, an area characterized by grassy plains and foothills. Prior to the discovery of oil, cattle raising and agriculture were the major economic activities. About 30 per cent of the population were members of indigenous groups. Much of the land was organized into large estates held by wealthy landowners and worked by largely landless and impoverished peasants. Subsequent to the discovery of oil, the region has also experienced a significantly increased presence of guerrilla and paramilitary groups seeking to benefit from the oil bonanza. In Colombia only 12 per cent of all government royalties, which typically represent 85 per cent of the value of the oil produced, are returned to the region of production.

The large multinational petroleum company, Largeco, addressed its security needs through the use of private security advisors working in collaboration with the Colombian army. With most of its oil reserves located within six concentrated areas and two large production stations in the same vicinity, it was possible to ensure its security by constructing protective barriers manned by the army around the company's operations. For the most part this strategy worked. Largeco suffered few overt attacks and limited damage to its operations, though a number of its employees and contractors were kidnapped and released only after the payment of ransoms. Its pipelines also remained vulnerable and suffered from several attacks. Notwithstanding Largeco's capacity to satisfactorily manage its security needs in this way, the overall security strategy served to isolate the company from local stakeholders and communities. The latter were aggrieved that the MNE seemed more concerned for its own security than for that of the broader community. This was not helped by the physical separation created by the company's approach.

The operations of the overseas independent oil company, Interpet, were geographically much more dispersed. Although its total oil production was not nearly as large as Laregco's, Interpet had 51 drilling sites, 16 production stations and over 450 kilometres of pipeline spread over a much more extensive area. Interpet could simply not afford to address its security needs in the same way as Largeco. It would have had to hire a much larger security force to cover its more widespread operations. It was forced by circumstances to explore alternatives. Beginning in the mid-1980s, the company undertook a series of initiatives that intermixed security measures with good community relations and social performance.

Following a series of protests by local community members and a growing security threat, Interpet began by hiring a local Colombian, Hector Lopez[2] to handle public affairs, security issues and community relations. Lopez had served in the armed forces, largely in areas marked by guerrilla insurgency. His military background served him well in formulating a strategy to address Interpet's security needs. In particular, his prior experience had taught him that in situations where a high security risk existed, one of the most effective security mechanisms, particularly against guerrilla threats, was to develop a close relationship with the local community. Lopez therefore began by consulting a range of local stakeholders, including community members, community-based organizations, local government representatives and religious leaders. He encouraged these people to voice their opinions on the impact of Interpet's operations, discuss their more general development needs and explore collaborative ways that Interpet could help address some of these concerns.

Local communities viewed the petroleum industry primarily in negative terms. Exploration and drilling brought immediate and dramatic environmental change in remote areas, with the construction of roads (many of which literally ended nowhere and, in time, became unusable), followed by quantities of heavy equipment. Oil companies caused pollution; they flared gases. They brought in expatriates to work their drilling operations, strangers who seemed to enjoy creature comforts and have money to spend far beyond the dreams of locals; yet little of this money went into the local economy, apart from a modest increase in local government revenues. At the same time, rents and food prices rose with the influx of people migrating to the area in search of work with the petroleum companies and their suppliers. Yet for many migrants there was only temporary work; few could expect long-term opportunities. Migration, inflation, irregular employment all produced a rash of social problems: abusive hunting, cattle rustling, prostitution and violence.

Lopez decided that Interpet needed to find ways of gaining the trust and support of local communities by generating local benefits such that people would feel that the company's operations were doing more good than harm. It was important to work closely with local communities from the beginning. One of Interpet's first initiatives was to change its arrangements for maintaining access roads to the drilling and work sites. Interpet had previously contracted with an engineering firm from Bogotá to build and maintain 500 kilometres of access roads. Under this arrangement the work had often begun late and was of uneven quality. Quarrels had arisen with local people who wanted to use the road, and on several occasions locals had blocked roads to impede the passage of the heavy equipment that degraded road surface conditions. When the bulldozers, graders and other road building machines supplied by the government fell into disrepair, they were not fixed because the government did not have a budget for maintenance. The engineering firm itself charged high rates.

To address these problems, Lopez looked into the possibility of turning the road maintenance contract over to local communities. He persuaded the regional and municipal governments to merge their several budgets devoted to road maintenance and to combine this with portions of Interpet's social investment budget as part of an overall account devoted to roadwork. He then arranged to turn these funds over to a local community-based organization, which was in turn assigned responsibility for maintaining roads in the vicinity. Interpet agreed to pay the upkeep costs for the state-owned road maintenance equipment. Local people obtained regular jobs for roadwork. Local communities also helped provide materials, food and accommodation for workers.

As a result of these arrangements, maintenance of the roads improved, costs were lowered by 50 per cent, construction of new roads was augmented and jobs were created for local workers. Conflicts between the company and community were markedly reduced. All involved felt grateful.

To further generate local benefits, Interpet undertook a number of initiatives to involve local people directly in various aspects of its operations. It started a programme to train and recruit local operators to work at its 16 different production stations. Despite initial difficulties due to the lack of locally relevant skills, after 5 years nearly all the Interpet production stations had at least one person working there directly from one of the local communities. In another area the company instituted a programme under which people in the local community were directly responsible for monitoring the performance of contractors hired by Interpet. In another case a local indigenous group was trained to assist in various aspects of an environmental impact assessment for a new development. In each case, the initiatives generated not only local economic benefits but also provided local people with a better understanding and confidence in Interpet's operations and associated impacts.

Lopez undertook a further project closely connected with Interpet's own operations. Interpet had been flaring the excess gas that was a by-product of their oil production. Lopez proposed that the petroleum company build pipelines to transport this gas to nearby communities, where it would be used to generate electrical power. Interpet first built a pipeline to a local town of 50 000; later the company obtained government support to build pipelines to several additional (but slightly smaller) towns. As a result of this initiative, Interpet reduced the taxes it had to pay for flaring gas and it helped local communities gain additional power, with less pollution, at much lower costs.

Lopez undertook a similar project adjacent to the territory of an indigenous tribe, an area where both rebel insurgents and paramilitary groups were active. In this case he persuaded the government to build a 42-kilometre power line to transport electricity, which Interpet would contribute. The company built a natural gas-powered generator with excess capacity at one of its production sites, and then transported the excess power to a group of seven remote villages not accessible by road. The villages received the power at cost. The supply of gas for the generator is expected to last 15 years. The power lines in this case were relatively safe from attacks by the guerrilla factions, neither of which desired to be seen as aggressors against their own people.

In addition to activities directly related to Interpet's operations, Lopez promoted a number of initiatives related more broadly to improving the quality of life in the region. One of these concerned primary education for children within the area of Interpet's operations. There were 11 different schools, each with one teacher and approximately 20 students at five different levels of learning. One or more teachers were usually absent about 30 to 40 per cent of the time due to sickness, meetings and other problems. Financing for the schools was irregular and seemed to depend upon the influence of local politicians. Lopez felt that there might be ways Interpet could help to address the local school problem. He proposed a scheme for merging the 11 scattered schools over time into a single regional school managed by the parents, with dormitory spaces provided for the teachers. Two schools would join the scheme each year. After several years, additional grades beyond the fifth level would be added. As the school expanded, Lopez expected that it would acquire computers, a cafeteria, a medical clinic, sports facilities and other improvements. Recognizing the challenges that many children would face in getting to school, Lopez also developed an innovative transportation scheme. Five trucks were purchased and converted into school buses suitable to the region's rough terrain; these vehicles would be used to transport children to and from school at the beginning and the end of school days. Drivers were to be chosen by local communities. At other times, the buses would be made available to local communities for errands, helping farmers to bring products to market and other purposes. Lopez was able to persuade the provincial government to pay 40 per cent of the cost of building the new school, while the municipality and the oil company each contributed 30 per cent.

As a result of these initiatives, the new school was built near the main Interpet production site. Local transportation costs were lowered. Educational opportunities were expanded and improved. The sense of community between the dispersed towns and villages in the area was markedly strengthened. Interpet was viewed as making an ongoing, long-term commitment to the well-being of the local community.

In still another case, without contributing money or resources, Lopez was able to use his influence and connections to help change a community's image. In a migrant settlement that had sprung up near one of Interpet's production stations, people had problems securing basic social services from the local government, which perceived the settlement as a haven for prostitutes, drug dealers and guerrillas. To bolster the settlement's self-respect as a community, Lopez arranged for several highly regarded figures in the Catholic Church of Colombia to hold a concelebratory mass in the settlement.

The impact of this event, with its public show of support by religious leaders, was considerable: subsequently, the local government agreed to provide the requested social and administrative services, and the settlement community's image was raised significantly.

Interpet also involved itself in the local community in a number of less dramatic ways. It sponsored and provided meeting space for a women's association. It allowed the telecommunications facilities at its operations to be used in emergencies and frequently helped evacuate ill or injured people from the region. It encouraged a local cooperative. It maintained active contact with local mayors. It helped to create a local environmental group to foster and actively monitor ecologically sound practices within the company itself.

Lessons learned

Interpet was perceived by the local community as a firm that was generally interested in ensuring that not only the company and the national government benefited from its operations but also the local communities that were most directly impacted. As the result of its initiatives, the company became much more involved locally, at little cost, through a series of collaborative activities, which were highly valued by people living in the area. Interpet came to be perceived not as an international business seeking its own advantage, but as a company linked to the local community through a series of initiatives involving local people in the operation and management of their facilities – a major partner in providing better roads, better elementary education and more energy to Colombians living near its production sites. Perhaps even more importantly, Interpet was seen as a business enterprise that listened to the concerns of local residents and sought ways to work with them to realize mutually beneficial objectives.[3]

Ever since 1985, Interpet has managed its security in Colombia very successfully, without recourse to extra guards or police. There have been no guerrilla attacks on pipelines or drills, no attacks on contractors and no kidnappings. Three minor attacks on power stations have occurred; but these caused very little damage and there were no casualties.

What stands out most strongly in Interpet's example is its willingness to work collaboratively – allowing the local community in some sense to set its own agenda. Did Interpet simply make a virtue of necessity? Certainly it had very few alternatives; it was too vulnerable and its operations were too widely dispersed to address its security needs from a defensive position, as larger firms might do. Instead of focusing directly on the guerrilla problem, the company had to find ways of operating that would make it an integral part of the local community. Perhaps because the person charged with responsibility for security was also responsible for public affairs and community relations, Interpet was able to develop a series of initiatives addressing all three concerns at once.

Acknowledgement

This research was made possible in part by a research grant from the Social Sciences and Humanities Research Council of Canada. The basic field research was undertaken by Titus Fossgard-Moser in preparation for his doctoral dissertation at Cambridge University (1998).

Notes

1. To cite an interesting and ambiguous example: When a European multinational firm began work on a pipeline in a South American country, the local police informed the company that it was operating in territory controlled by protection gangs, who would damage personal or corporate property unless they were paid off. The police then agreed to protect the company if *they* received payment for their services.
2. 'Hector Lopez' is a pseudonym.
3. For a discussion of comparable social involvement roles played by other firms, see Wasserstrom and Reider (1998) and Williams (1997).

References

Bergquist, C., Penaranda, R. and Sanchez, G. (eds) (1992) *Violence in Colombia: The Contemporary Crisis in Historical Perspective* (Wilmington, DE: Scholarly Resource Inc.).

Bushnell, D. (1992) 'Politics and Violence in Nineteenth Century Columbia' in Bergquist *et al.*, (eds), *Violence in Colombia: The Contemporary Crisis in Historical Perspective* (Wilmington, DE: Scholarly Resource Inc.)

CELAM (1968) Consejo Episcopa Latinamericano (Latin American Bishops Conference) 'Medellin Documents: Justice, Peace, Family and Demography, Poverty of the Church', in Gremillion, J. (ed.), *The Gospel of Peace and Justice: Catholic Social Teaching Since Pope John* (Maryknoll, NY: Orbis Books) pp. 445–76.

Dudley, S. and Murillo, M. (1998) 'Oil in Time of Trouble', *NACLA Report on the Americas,* March/April 1998, pp. 42–4.

Feroro Juan. (2000) 'Burdened Colombians Back Tax to Fight Rebels', *New York Times* September 8, 2002, p. 6.

Fossgard-Moser, T. (1998) 'Transnational Corporations and Sustainable Development: The Case of Colombian and Peruvian Petroleum Industries', PhD dissertation, Cambridge University.

Global Witness (2000) 'A Crude Awakening: The Role of Oil and Banking in Angola's Civil War and the Plunder of Assets' (London: Global Witness Limited).

Reid, M. (2001) 'Colombia: Drugs, War and Democracy', *The Economist*, 21 April.

Renner, M. (2002) *The Anatomy of Resource Wars*, World Watch Paper 162 (World Watch Institute).

Renner, M. (2002) *The Anatomy of Resource Wars*, World Watch Paper 162 World Watch Institute.

Sethi, S. P. and Williams, O. F. (2001) *Economic Imperatives and Ethical Values in Global Businesses: The South African Experience and International Codes Today* (University of Notre Dame Press).

Smillie, I., Gberie, L. and Hazleton, R. (2000) 'The Heart of the Matter: Sierra Leone, Diamonds and Human Security' in B. Taylor (ed.), *Insights Series* (Ottawa/Addis Ababa: Partnership Africa Canada).

Wade, J. (2000) 'Violence, Crime Continue to Cast Shadow over Future Oil Investment in Colombia', *Oil and Gas Journal*, 17 January, pp. 32–7.

Wasserstrom, R. and Reider, S. (1998) 'Petroleum Companies Crossing New Threshold in Community Relations', *Oil and Gas Journal*, 14 December, pp. 24–7.

Williams, P. (1997) 'Oil, Guns and Money', *Oil and Gas Investor*, September 1997, pp. 48–54.

Index